The market or the public d<

The market or the public domain? Global governance and the asymmetery of power examines the powerful idea of the return, reconstitution and redeployment of the public domain in a post-Seattle and post-Washington consensus world order. Increasingly as the future prospects of market fundamentalism are troubled, the zero inflation, global free trade beliefs of what has been called the Washington consensus face a doubting chorus of professional experts and highly articulate critics from a civil society about the policy processes that occur outside the reach of the present nation state.

In the past two decades, countries have focused on broadening and guaranteeing market access and as the pendulum has begun to swing away from the market, the issue of re-investing in the public domain becomes a priority. The authors of this volume believe that devising new institutions of governance for a globalizing world requires fundamental change nationally and internationally. They argue that new public spaces, places and services are required to strengthen democracy and create sanctuaries in society where the market mechanism cannot reach. The public domain is an incipient concept that enables states to reduce the intrusiveness of markets and at the same time develop a strong national performance to reduce the inequality and social exclusion in an increasingly volatile global economy.

This highly innovative and pioneering volume boasts an impressive list of contributors, including Amitav Acharya, Harry Arthurs, Richard Devetak, Kyle Grayson, Richard Higgott, Robin Hodess, Inge Kaul, Georg Kell, David Marquand, Sol Picciotto, Simon Reich, Marcia Rioux, Alasdair Roberts, John Ruggie, Keith Stewart, Geoffrey Underhill and Ezra Zubrow. This defining volume will strongly appeal to advanced students, academics and policy makers involved in the field of global governance and international political economy.

Daniel Drache is Director of the Robarts Centre for Canadian Studies and Professor of Political Economy at York University, Canada. He is the editor of *Public Success, Private Failure: Market Limits to Health Care Reform* with Terry Sullivan (Routledge 1998) and *States Against Markets: The Limits of Competitiveness* with Robert Boyer (Routledge 1996).

Innis centenary series: governance and change in the global era
Series Editor: Daniel Drache

Harold Innis, one of Canada's most distinguished economists described the Canadian experience as no one else ever has. His visionary works in economic geography, political economy, and communications theory have endured for over fifty years and have had tremendous influence on scholarship, the media and the business community.

The volumes in the Innis Centenary Series illustrate and expand Innis's legacy. Each volume is written and edited by distinguished members of the fields Innis touched. Each addresses provocative and challenging issues that have profound implications not only for Canada but for the new world order, including the impact of globalization on governance, international developments, and the environment; the nature of the market of the future; the effect of new communications technology on economic restructuring; and the role of the individual in effecting positive social change.

The complete series will provide a unique guide to many of the major challenges we face at the beginning of the twenty-first century.

Innis Centenary Series is supported by the Robarts Centre for Canadian Studies and York University. Proposals for future volumes in the series are actively encouraged and most welcome. Please address all enquiries to the editor, by email drache@yorku.ca or by fax 1.416.736.5739.

Other titles in the series include:
States Against Markets
Edited by Robert Boyer and Daniel Drache

Political Ecology
Edited by David Bell, Lessa Fawcett, Roger Keil and Peter Penz

Health Reform
Edited by Daniel Drache and Terry Sullivan

Democracy, Citizenship and the Global City
Edited by Engin F. Isin

The Market or the Public Domain?
Global governance and the asymmetry of power
Edited by Daniel Drache

The market or the public domain?

Global governance and the asymmetry of power

Edited by Daniel Drache

London and New York

First published 2001
by Routledge
11 New Fetter Lane, London EC4P 4EE

Simultaneously published in the USA and Canada
by Routledge
29 West 35th Street, New York, NY 10001

Routledge is an imprint of the Taylor & Francis Group

Typeset in Goudy by Taylor and Francis Books Ltd
Printed and bound in Great Britain by MPG Books Ltd, Bodmin, Cornwall

British Library Cataloguing in Publication Data
A catalogue record for this book is available from the British Library

Library of Congress Cataloging in Publication Data
The market or the public domain? Global governance and the asymmetry
of power / edited by Daniel Drache.
p .cm (Innis centenary series) Includes bibliographical references and
index. 1. Commercial policy, 2. Democracy, 3. Industrial policy, 4.
Capitalism, 5. Free trade, 6. International trade, 7.Commercial law, 8.
International law, 9.World Trade Organization. I. Title. II. Series
HF1411 .D693 2001
338.9 - dc21

ISBN 0–415–25469–8 (hbk)
ISBN 0–415–25470–1 (pbk)

Contents

PART 1
REINVENTING THE PUBLIC DOMAIN

Section 1
Revisiting the fundamentals in a post-Washington consensus era

PART 3
THE RETURN OF THE PUBLIC

Section 5
New sites of policy contest

Contributors

Amitav Acharya is a Professor of Political Science at York University and a Visiting Professor at the Institute of Defence and Strategic Studies, Nanyang Technological University, Singapore. He is an expert in South Asian security issues and has published extensively on South-East Asian policies and politics.

Harry Arthurs is University Professor of Law and Political Science at York University. He has published widely on global labour standards and the role of legal ordering as a norm-setter at a time of globalization.

Richard Devetak was a Visiting Researcher at the Centre for the Study of Globalization and Regionalization at the University of Warwick but teaches at the Monash University, School of Political and Social Inquiry, Australia.

Daniel Drache is the Director of the Robarts Centre for Canadian Studies and Professor of Political Economy at York University, Canada. He has written widely on globalization, trade blocs and the limits of markets.

Kyle Grayson is a doctorate candidate in International and Security Studies at York University, with a special interest in issues around organized crime, human security and the public domain.

Richard Higgott is the Director of the Centre for the Study of Globalization and Regionalization at the University of Warwick. He is a major contributor to international political economy specializing in Asia and global governance.

Robin Hodess is Project Manager for Transparency International in Berlin and formerly a Research Fellow at the Carnegie Council on Ethics and International Affairs. She has extensive experience in building links between social movements and private international funding agencies.

Inge Kaul is the Director of the United Nations Development Program's Office of Development Studies and has published most recently on the human development agenda and global public goods.

George Kell is an economist in the Executive Office of the Secretary-General of the United Nations.

David Marquand is Principal of Mansfield College, Oxford University and is an eminent political theorist of contemporary liberalism, citizenship and social democratic thought.

Sol Picciotto holds the Chair in Law at the University of Lancaster and has published extensively on all aspects of international financial regulation and global governance.

Simon Reich is the Research Director of the Royal Institute for International Affairs, Chatham House, London. He is on leave from the University of Pittsburgh, Graduate School of Public and International Affairs, where he has written extensively on the impact of globalization on public policy-making.

Marcia Rioux is an authority on human disability and formerly the Director of the Roeher Institute in Toronto, a leading Canadian research centre on disability. She is an associate of the Robarts Centre for Canadian Studies, a consultant to many international organizations and chair of the School of Health Policy and Management, York University.

Alasdair Roberts taught at Queen's University Kingston, School of Public Studies and has now been appointed to the Maxwell School of Citizenship and Public Affairs, Syracuse University, and is the Director, Campbell Public Affairs Institute, there. He is a specialist in new information economics and public policy issues.

John Ruggie is on leave as the Burgess Professor of Political Science and International Affairs at Columbia University and is currently serving on the Executive Staff of the United Nations Secretary-General Kofi Annan, as policy adviser and expert. His research and essays on international institutionalization have made him one of the most original and insightful theorists in international political economy.

Keith Stewart recently received his doctorate from the York University Political Science Programme in environmental politics. He is now the Smog and Climate Change Coordinator for the Toronto Environmental Alliance, a non-profit, non-governmental environmental organization.

Geoffrey Underhill is the Chair of International Governance at the University of Amsterdam, The Netherlands. He is an international specialist on global finance and banking practices having published widely in both areas.

Ezra Zubrow is a Professor of Anthropology at the State University of New York at Buffalo and an Honorary Fellow at the Department of Archeology, Cambridge University.

Acknowledgements

This volume grew out of a seminar entitled 'Governing the Public Domain Beyond the Era of the Washington Consensus?: Redrawing the Line Between the State and the Market', organized by Daniel Drache, Director of the Robarts Centre for Canadian Studies, York University and Richard Higgott, Director of the Centre for Regionalization and Globalization, University of Warwick. It was supported by York University, Social Science Research Council of Canada, the Centre for the Study of Globalization and Regionalization, at the University of Warwick and the Social Sciences Research Council, UK.

As part of a collective effort edited volumes are very difficult to produce at a high level. They require a great deal of cooperation, patience and support from all the contributors. As well, they require that all contributors keep an eye on deadlines and deliver what they promised. On all accounts, the contributors have been exemplary and generous to a fault. Many of the papers from that conference are now part of this volume but others have been commissioned particularly for it.

Richard Higgott co-shared responsibilities for the organization of the original conference and his involvement in the project has made a significant difference to it and the final publication. Harry Arthurs and Marcia Rioux have functioned as an informal sounding board for the public domain project and for this I am grateful. Martin Rhodes and Philippe Schmitter asked some tough doubting kinds of questions that demanded clear answers. Alain Supiot made useful suggestions about the provision of public goods in the European Union. Others who have been early supporters of the public domain project include Michael Adams, Daniel Latouche, Mike McCracken, Geoffrey Underhill, Arthur Donner, Stephen Clarkson, Robert Lawrie and David Bell. Hélio Janny Teixeira and Hélio Zylberstajn introduced me to the private world of São Paulo public space. José Augusto Guilhon and S.K. Goyal have helped clarify the importance of the public domain in developing countries.

A special thanks is due to Dayna Barr for the compelling cover design. Special thanks is also due to Laura Taman who oversaw the many different drafts and revisions of the manuscript and provided important editorial input throughout. She had the key role of managing this large and complex manuscript and did so flawlessly.

Robert Langham and Heidi Bagtazo were eager supporters of this volume from the beginning and have smoothed its editorial passage.

I would also like to thank former York Vice President, Michael Stevenson for his support of the original conference and for his encouragement to publish this volume. Finally, I would like to acknowledge York President, Lorna Marsden and Vice President for Research and Innovation, Stan Shapson, for their continued support for the work and activities of the Robarts Centre for Canadian Studies.

This book is dedicated to Robert Cox, Susan Strange (1923–98) and Jim Rosenau, three very different kindred spirits, good friends but also best critics, whose pioneering and against-the-grain innovative writing, over the past thirty years or more, has helped make us (hopefully) better practitioners of international political economy.

Daniel Drache
30 November 2000

Introduction: The fundamentals of our time

Values and goals that are inescapably public

Daniel Drache

This volume is about 'after the triumph', a short-hand for a much larger and more powerful idea, namely, the return, reconstitution and redeployment of the public domain in a post-Seattle and post-Washington consensus world order (Williamson 1990, 1999). The emergence of the global economy with its predilection for market fundamentals, tough zero-inflation bench-marking, an unstoppable political dynamic of one worldism and silence on the need for an expansive notion of the public sphere is unquestionably the watershed event of our times. The meta-narrative of globalization has no rivals as the last grand political discourse of the twentieth century and if we understand anything about the endless capacity of the globalization narrative to reinvent itself in a new guise when conditions demand it, today is one of those defining moments. A new kind of state is emerging with its own particular institutions, practices and innovative forms (Held 1995; Castells 1996). Yet after the battle in Seattle, the future prospects of 'market fundamentalism' are increasingly troubled. A turning point has been reached in the debate over the rising costs and elusive benefits of globalization (Millennium 2000).

The once solid fundamentals now face a doubting chorus composed of professional experts and loud and insistent highly articulate critics from civil society about the policy processes that occur outside the present reach of the nation-state. As times have changed, the policy capitals of the world have adopted a new rhetoric of poverty reduction, equity and strengthening the role of the state in economic management. The distancing from the old consensus is quite stark and unmistakable (Birdsall and de la Torre 2000). Take just one measure. John Williamson, the economist who first coined the term the Washington consensus, is no longer an unqualified partisan supporter of its efficiency pro-market advocacy. He joins the distinguished company of other leading economists, such as Joseph Stiglitz, John Helliwell, Paul Krugman, Sylvia Ostry and Dani Rodrik, who have publicly expressed strongly dissenting views about its rigid policy prescription and one-worldism (Naim 2000).

This public soul-searching has given the tough structural adjustment goals of the Washington consensus a human face and spawned a moderate vision of reformism among policy insiders. The new policy objectives include: poverty-reduction, improving equity and building socially inclusive societies, heading the list. Adding the hot-button words civil society, capacity building, transparency, institution building and safety nets make a fundamental difference at the level of public discourse but the basic problem still remains unaddressed. So far, there is still little recognition of the negative correlation between social cohesion and the purist goals of neo-liberalism. The proponents of the new consensus continue to rely on many, if not all, of the old policy instruments of efficiency and structural reform. What is still not grasped as a policy axiomatic is that these efficiency dedicated policy instruments are not compatible with the new equity outcomes espoused by Washington consensus reformers and until goals and outcomes are linked in a radically different way, the rules and norms which underpin the present order will not provide any new hope for global governance.

Governance and the normative aspects of institutions

The authors in this volume start from quite a different assumption, namely, that they have an obligation to contribute, at the very least, to devising new institutions of governance for a globalizing world. Globalization, in its primary sense, refers to networks of interdependence linking vast continental distances by means of all kinds of institutions. As the short twentieth century has come to an end, what sort of governance depends on the design of the front-line institutions that effect governance? In Higgott's powerful description, 'the global market place of the 1980s and the first six to seven years of the 1990s were largely an "ethics free zone"' (see his chapter in this volume). Trade liberalization, financial deregulation and asset privatization increased the tempo of the globalization of the world economy and free enterprise. Everywhere, the market culture appeared to have triumphed. As the need to redraw the line between the state and the market has gained legitimacy, through a series of events in the world of international politics, the mood of resistance to globalization has visibly stiffened and sharply escalated. Among other factors, it has been spurred on by the highly visible social deficit caused by unfettered global market forces and civil society's growing scepticism that the existing global order can survive without major reform (Halliday 2000).

The basic problem is that there is no provision at the global level for elementary social justice, the provision of social goods globally and other non-income objectives. Hence, poverty alleviation remains a distant goal rather than a highly compelling world movement that has the power and influence to reshape the agenda of global governance. So far, global economic management is very far from its principal goals and has not been able to integrate the economic imperative of development with the explicitly ethical commitment to a socially inclusive global economy. At its best, public policy aims at the minimization of public bads, largely a reactive process, individualist but not collective (Higgott and Phillips 2000). Despite all the soul-searching and the work of individual scholars, positive problem-solving through collective action is largely at a standstill, a distant goal rather than an emerging trend-line. Asian, Latin American and first world economies play only a marginal role in the provision of global public goods ranging from the environment to sustainable labour, health and human rights standards.

Importantly the disconnect between the international institutions governing the global economy in Washington, New York and Geneva and the understanding of the crisis that until recently has been unbridgeable has visibly begun to ease (Cox 1999). Intellectual thinking about the 'big picture' has undergone a dramatic transformation after the Seattle, Washington and Prague protests and many experts, as well as NGOs are beginning to conceptualize the global 'reconnect'. Globalization used to be seen as driven predominantly by the neo-liberal economic agenda but scholars, practitioners and non-state actors have become overtly more normative in their approach (Rodrik 1997). The fundamental question today is not, what do corporations want, but what do citizens demand and expect from the new international order. The new emphasis is on bar-raising standards of all kinds that include the well-known examples of the environment, human rights and health and labour standards but also financial ones such as closing off-shore tax shelters, a recent initiative of the Group of Seven industrialized countries (Picciotto and Mayne 1999; OECD 2001).

Importantly, at the level of policy-making where previously opposition voices could be safely ignored, civil society actors have now gained a welcomed but unaccustomed degree of credibility in world forums. The result is that the utopian pursuit of the universal seamless market has lost much of its legitimacy and a good deal of its drive. In its place is something quite new, the prospect of an international order with a 'polity' that needs to be governed. If the Washington consensus embodied the belief of 'governance without politics', the post-Washington consensus world is about building institutions, international as much as national, by political means (Millennium 2000).

It used to be accepted as though it were a self-evident truth that the most important regulatory and economic management policy processes now occur beyond the territorial boundaries of the nation-state. The fact is that this notion has been increasingly challenged because the nation-state has not crumbled as the seat of public authority but governance requires much more effort, ingenuity, focus, leadership and co-ordination than ever (Drache 2000). As a discipline, the theory of international political economy has not always been helpful in providing a way out of the economism that permeated so much policy-thinking. In the 1980s and 1990s, international political economy surprisingly lost sight of the domestic–international divide and instead focused on a system that was seemingly fixed and unchangeable, rather than fluid and soft at the centre (Boyer and Drache 1996). This disjunction between the economic side of globalization and its social impact has gradually broken down. The financial crises dominating policy-making throughout the 1980s and 1990s have provided the impetus that without equity there can be no stability and without equity kinds of measures and institutions, financial instability of the kind experienced in Mexico, Russia and Asia will become recurrent and chronic.

Rebundling identity and territory: enter the public domain

If there are to be clear sites of national authority and a stable international community, the re-emergence of the public domain, in which consensus, co-operation and public discourse figure predominately, has a compelling, if neglected, role to play as one of the co-ordinates that will rebundle 'identity and territory' in Ruggie's evocative words. With material and institutional dimensions that are large and complex with overlapping aspects, the public domain should not be used interchangeably with the public sector, with which it is often confused. Nor should it be limited to the provision of public goods, a staple of modern economic liberalism. In the primary sense of the term, the public domain is about the resources carved out from the market that empower and transform both the state and non-state actors.

David Marquand's definition is the most innovative to grasp the power, ambiguity and paradox of the public domain as a necessary condition of greater global justice and effective public policy. The public domain is an area of social life, with its own rules, norms and practices, cutting across the state and market and other public private agencies. Its values are those of citizenship, services and the notion of the public interest and it has long furnished civil society with the much needed resources to function effectively by creating sanctuaries where the price mechanism does not operate. The public domain was 'ring-fenced from the pressures of the market place, in which citizenship rights rather than market power governed the allocation of social goods' (Marquand 1997: 5). In Victorian Britain, the emergence of the public domain, in many policy areas including social policy, housing and autonomous public spaces, became a fact of national life that joined the other institutions of liberal democracy.

State policy was carved out from the 'adjacent private and market domains at different times that enabled society to erect barriers against the inevitable market incursions into it'. The state was to be facilitator and partner rather than the engineer of democratic citizenship and the public domain was part of defining 'the mutual obligation of common purpose' (Marquand 1997: 40). For other countries, as the reader will discover, this robust public sphere emerged from similar conditions and social needs when global and local markets threatened communities and the social order. It was one of the great achievements of the last hundred years. The active performance of citizenship required a strong public realm composed of different elements outside of the direct control of the state. Social rights had to be recognized and citizenship learned. But aside from the gains there were losses as the public realm was taken over by powerful state interests. Much later the public domain became a site of bureaucratic empire-building and heavy-handed overload. Self-centred corporatism and bureaucratic centralization of the welfare state in many jurisdictions robbed the public domain of its original vitality and democratic impulse. At a time when this older and larger notion of the public is no longer bounded by the welfare state to the degree that it once was, it is important to understand the public domain's genesis, appearance and prospects in an era of global markets (Walzer 1989; Sen 1999; Marquand 1997).

This publication is meant to start to clarify the concept of the public domain in an open and self-consciously critical manner. The reader needs to be warned in advance that there is no single definition that all contributors to this volume agree on. Rather, there is a consensus that the line between the market and the state is moving in sharply contrasting directions and that there is a large public domain to be mapped and strengthened. This strategic opening, conceptually as well as for policy purposes, provides a unique opportunity to revisit state–market relations at a time of unprecedented flux and change (Rosenau 1997a, 1997b).

The definitional quandary is only half the story

It is at the conceptual level where clarity is in short supply. Simply put, the public domain is a crucial idea to explain how society is motivated to reach out, at a time of intense globalization, to delimit property rights and rein in markets, even though it appears that markets are triumphant and dangerously pervasive. Then every society will take needed measures to reinforce its public domain, either in a conscious way or in piecemeal fashion, to reclaim all or part of it where it detects the need to defend public space from powerful market actors and renew the public interest.

Market intrusiveness occurs when private actors appropriate the public interest, and its collective goods that are shared in common, for private gain. Market intrusiveness is also about unregulated market forces and their capacity to redefine the line between the state and the market, by moving it towards the market-end of the spectrum. Market forces can also be said to interfere with the normal functioning of civil society when corporate merger and takeover activity becomes an end in itself, one so alarmingly predatory that it puts social stability at risk, weakening the redistributive bite of public authority (see Marquand's chapter). There is no shortage of contemporary examples of the new-found power these frequently 'stateless corporations' exert to enhance the rights of business at any price. Many experts believe that they now overpower the regulatory authority of states. Take just one measure, Infosys of the Bombay Stock Exchange. Its assets are larger than Pakistan's GDP and the share value of the Bombay Stock Exchange is larger than the foreign currency earnings of India in 1999.

While none of these figures tell us very much about 'the private use of public interest', they are worrying and psychologically damaging for the public everywhere because they give credence to the idea that the battle for an autonomous and vigorous notion of the public is in full retreat (Schultze 1977). Global free trade, as embodied in the WTO, is able to regulate domestic regulation in a way that no one could have predicted ten years ago. Health, labour standards and culture are directly and indirectly subject to the WTO's trade codes. The result is that domestic policy sovereignty is no longer insulated from international disciplines (Ostry 2000). Property rights have been entrenched in the WTO's commitments. Markets are back and the state is now seen, in the corridors of power and in the halls of academe, as a major facilitator of private interest.

Governments everywhere continue to privatize, deregulate and out-source the business of government to business. Whatever the strengths of market-organized economies, the policy goals of the Washington consensus have resulted in deep tensions within each of the existing strategies of contrasting market economies.

The public at bay in contrasting economies

Anglo-Saxon economies, with their commitment to trade openness, corporate control exercised by shareholder's capital, limited forms of regulation and lower rates of taxation seem least anchored to their public sphere. To an unprece-dented degree, markets and economic elites are increasingly arrayed against the old public order with its stable institutions and consensus-building commit-ments. The once-deemed indispensable employment-hiring and layoff practices of the labour market are now regarded as too rigid and costly. Social policy, born in an age of the democratization of wealth, is attacked on the grounds that it is too generous to maintain any longer. Many other state policies, designed to protect people from the swings of the global economy, are stigmatized as anti-quated barriers to the free movement of goods and services.

The world-wide movement of economic liberalization and falling trade barriers invokes an age of diminished expectations and a powerful restatement of classic liberalism (Brittan 1988). With the resurgence of liberalism, as the standard for all countries, Western society is marked by a threshold event, 'the revolt of the elites and the end of the democratization of wealth' (Lasch 1994). Elites no longer want to pay for services that they can provide for themselves. It is this ideology, with the psychological imperative of the elites' need to convince themselves, that the new global pressures require drastic new prac-tices on the part of governments and corporations, which is redrawing the boundaries between public and private within states everywhere. In Sylvia Ostry's words, 'the power of the nation state is eroding, from above by global-ization and from below by devolution' (Ostry 1998). For scholars of the Left persuasion, the global corporation is at once the principal agent, architect, villain and major beneficiary of the new world order. It is the sole dedicated actor that is in a position to benefit directly from the dramatic changes that are occurring.

In Anglo-Saxon economies with the least amount of regulation and consensus, state disinvestment in health, education and social policy has led to a contraction of the public sphere in recent times. Without these collective goods, is this model likely to underperform in the future? With such a single-minded preoccupation with competitiveness and the new lowering of social standards, this model is likely to wreck havoc on the social and economic poli-cies of other countries tied to it by trade and investment flows. With relatively weak institutions to constrain market forces, will this model be able to survive the competitive devaluation or the trade wars that might be triggered by a major market plunge in stock values? With such limited notions of governance, can the strategic rationality of the Anglo-American elites, dependent on unprecedented rising stock values, enable such a system to survive the 'great correction' when it occurs?

Social market economies organized around corporatist principles with high wage labour markets, such as Germany, France and Italy, remain a bench-mark for many but these highly regulated economies are also vulnerable to rent-seeking opportunistic behaviour. They continue to maintain a high standard of living, an excellent quality of public goods, high wages, high taxes and less wage dispersion but are also marked by inequality and the growth of exclusion (Ferrera *et al.* 2000). In contrast to US policy reforms, corporate tax rates have fallen very little in the rich EU countries since the 1990s. Among the poorer members, corporate tax rates have risen contrary to the impression that lower tax rates are the key to competitiveness (Krugman and Baldwin 2000). They also operate with high labour costs and strongly regulated labour markets and these central institutional arrangements are increasingly under pressure to modernize and adopt the US model of labour market best-practice (OECD 1994). If their large and complex public sphere were principally the product of the Keynesian-Beveridge welfare state, it would only be a matter of time before this model collapsed. What makes it so resilient, despite pressures from within and without, to the introduction of far-reaching structural reforms?

Social market Europe and its powerful regulatory levers

Unlike Anglo-American societies, the European Union has powerful regulatory levers in its institutional framework but so far has not been able to develop a more realistic view of the crisis of work and employment and workplace prac-tices (Supiot *et al.* 1999). Existing labour relations have been undercut by the new skill levels required by modern production methods, the acceleration of the pace of technology, women's entry into the labour market and the highly competitive conditions in many product markets. These contradictory trends have challenged the existing model of work relations and have increased the economic insecurity among many sectors of the workforce. This insecurity has also created a very large group of youth and others who have been marginalized by both the worlds of work as well as society. To address these and other pressing concerns, the social market economies of Europe need to broaden their social security laws, extend them to the non-standard and casual workforce, as well as accept trends to non-standard working times and the re-regulation of working time. The search for a new occupational status has important implica-tions for the way power is distributed and requires quite a different institutional response from the Commission and member-states.

The constitutionalization of employment rights at the European level, as recently advocated by the Supiot Report in 1999, demonstrates that its institu-tional structures have a capacity to change and adapt so that the EU is in a position to forge a consensus, one that promotes work mobility and new equality provisions between men and women. Beyond strengthening labour rights at the EU level, respect for national diversity remains a fundamental part of a distinctly EU approach that takes account of national differences. So far, it has not been able to agree on a common regulatory approach but it has adopted a highly pragmatic approach to social dumping and damaging fiscal competition. It wants to create a better balance between social policy and economic policy without, as the French Minister responsible for European integration frankly admitted, any more power being devolved to Brussels. 'People do not have much appetite for fresh transfers of sovereignty' (*Financial Times*, 21 November 2000).

Even so, the social market countries are better placed than Anglo-American jurisdictions to rethink, in a systematic way, the links between labour market reform, the reform of the welfare state and a heightened role for the public in addressing social exclusion and inequality. High profile studies have been commissioned on the first two issues and a final report on inclusion and exclusion is expected in 2001. These documents will have an important effect on public debate and have provided a 'big picture' framework to resist market-favouring kinds of reforms. Up until now, the high tax, high skill, high wage economy of core member states, including France, Germany, Italy, Belgium, Netherlands and Sweden, have provided the resources and the political will to maintain a significant level of public goods and services but there is no guarantee that this level of commitment will continue into the future. Must the EU also change as it faces long-term joblessness and domestic demand for immediate tax reform? Or does it have the political consensus and the social will to maintain its commitment to redistribution and an enlarged and vigorous role for the public and new public goods in the post-Thatcher period?

Developing countries' social deficit

In developing economies faced with massive population growth, chronic joblessness, and mounting social exclusion, the older political economy concept of the public domain issues has intuitive appeal. These countries have seen their standard of living fall and today face many structural obstacles in terms of their development. Even if the public sphere is embattled in many jurisdictions, rethinking developmental strategy remains a priority. New institutions are needed with policy capacity to address the social deficit of global free trade.

In the post-Washington consensus era, it is not enough to have the bare liberal minimum of a stable currency, rule of law, state transparency and enforceable commercial contracts. Many developing countries are struggling to find a way out of the debt crisis. External debts have been driven to record highs by real interest rate hikes that now exceed the growth rate of the economy. Real per capita income has fallen and, compared to the 1950s and 1960s, a time of catch up, poverty rates and family incomes have worsened (ECLAC, 1998). Levels of rural poverty have barely improved despite increases in social spending in parts of the region, including Mexico, Brazil and parts of Central America. The poorest sectors of rural Latin America have not benefited. Rural poverty remains largely a structural problem unaffected by broader economic cycles. Those living throughout rural Latin America are denied access to basic services such as drinkable water, education and health care. Funds are not available for providing such public goods when public spending on non-market necessities is declining.

Countries in Latin America and elsewhere are trapped trying to stabilize the ratio of their debt to GDP that has caused further cuts to government spending. The nub of the problem is that borrowing on international markets cannot give developing countries sufficient command over the real resources needed to rebuild public services, revitalize their badly deteriorating infrastructures and provide other collective goods, without producing an unsustainable hike in their debt burdens. According to the rules of the restraint policies of the Washington consensus, growth rates are inadequate to convince financial lenders to bring down interest rates or to attract new foreign direct investment inflows in sufficient quantity.

Interest rates are now so high in many parts of the world that the only way to convince investors that a developing country can meet its obligations is for it to obtain a better investment grade rating (Martin Wolf, *Financial Times*, 22 November 2000). So far very few have succeeded in breaking the interest rate barrier. Increased investment, rather than leading to faster growth has led to a reliance on the preeminence of market forces to maintain a low-inflation economy and to the further privatization of state enterprises, particularly in banking, telecommunications and energy areas. Many developing countries have big surpluses on the primary account that have been achieved by cutting programme and infrastructure spending in order to make their industries more competitive. This too has required them to lower nominal labour costs through traditional and non-traditional wage restraint measures. This is tough medicine and the squeeze on wages has seen real family and individual incomes fall precipitously in Argentina, Chile, Brazil and Mexico. Throughout the region, the leading economies remain desperate for increased levels of foreign capital inflows but short of devaluation their economic performance is too weak to generate the much needed capital to pay for health, educational and social welfare assistance (Silber 2000).

If the liberation of market forces has not resulted in sustainable forms of economic growth for Latin America and other developing regions, what is the next model of structural adjustment? What new functions are needed and what new forums does the state require if it is to strengthen its fiscal capacity, limit the intrusiveness of markets and mobilize resources not taken on by the market (ECLAC 1998).

Sanctuaries outside the reach of markets

Here is where this older notion from political economy is crucial. It is a conceptual benchmark that enables the public and policy-makers alike to find a way out of this conceptual dilemma and policy predicament on the most basic of questions – what properly should be a public responsibility and what clearly should be privately provided? The public domain enables us to grasp what many in the public policy community have overlooked in recent times, namely, the processes and institutions that furnish society with its collective and social goods, public space and social inclusiveness. If, in a triumphant world market, it is a relatively straightforward proposition to clarify where private goods come from, the expansion of investment rights at all levels, then the infinitely more complex undertaking is to explain the processes and decisions that enable society to establish the goods and assets owned in common and not traded on the open market.

The traditional answer provided by the most rigorous economists is that public services, spaces and places are provided through public regulation and market failure (see chapters by Kaul and by Grayson). But social theorists, on the other hand, are equally adamant that the necessities of existence also come from citizens' efforts to enlarge the not-for-profit sector, from education through health, to parks and public places, these are goods that enhance the social bond rather than weaken it. In the potent words of Jacques Attali, the state and civil society require large state-constructed 'sanctuaries outside market logic', outside the reach of the price system.

As readers of this volume will quickly discover, social theorists have not formed any hard and fast consensus about the supply of social goods, despite an impressive array of evidence that there is a very large terrain between atomized civil society and state dominated public practice. What is not in dispute, however, is that government is supposed to be the agency of choice to promote collective goals and to renew public institutions. This issue of establishing the boundary between private interest and public purpose is an immensely important one. Particularly at a time of unprecedented interdependence, when national borders seem less meaningful than ever, every society has need of common resources, places, spaces and services – the sanctuaries and protected social space of the public interest. It is at this vital point that the public domain enters the picture. One of the most telling and richly endowed examples is the modern world city with its complex defining characteristics (Kasinitz 1995).

Public domain and the great world cities

Many capital cities have long had highly visible and very prominent public domains. Some are primarily *commercial domains* comprised of service sector tourism, the financial sector, public and private museums, art galleries and other meeting places, which are largely organized and maintained by the private sector for profit. New York and Los Angeles are prototypical cities in this respect, a mix of public cultural sites and spaces and private interest with the private predominant (Zukin 1995). Look at a map of Manhattan. It is only in the USA that there are so many private institutions functioning as public museums, art galleries, opera houses and music halls etc. They are not public institutions because they are private creations, owned and managed for profit

leaks in the system and its accountability is problematic for community-based groups.

It is not difficult to see the origins of this ingenious form of the quasi-public. São Paolo is a city that outgrew itself and has seen its population explode from one million in the 1950s to over ten million today. Two million inhabit favelas; another six hundred thousand live in slums and another nine thousand on the streets or in shelters. In a fundamental sense, São Paolo is a city of failed publics unable to provide basic housing and adequate levels of security for its inhabitants. Yet it is replete with the public space provided from the private worlds of community associations, the church, samba and sports clubs and community centres. Some of the most important and influential are financed from private donors. These publics are not 'for all' but only 'for some' and this cosmopolitan multicultural city has had to rely on the 'good side' of the private to create these mixed worlds of the private publics.

A striking example is the Hebraica Club established by the Jewish community to swim, dance, exercise, play cards, debate and discuss. With its Olympic-sized swimming pools its thirty thousand members have created a powerful and highly visible civic engagement of responsibility for the Jewish community. Unlike its Canadian equivalent in Toronto, membership is not open to non-Jews, at least up until now, in any significant numbers. Other communities have similar kinds of civic-recreational centres. Sesci Pompeii is another innovative example of the non-profit but private sector creating collective goods financed by a payroll tax. In its former existence, Pompeii was an old turn-of-the-century textile factory that at one time must have employed close to ten thousand employees. Today it is a unique kind of community centre that houses day care, meeting rooms, local activities of all kinds, an art gallery, music hall and other kinds of similar facilities for São Paulians. Samba clubs and soccer teams have also given São Paulians their strong sense of community and local identity.

São Paulo's solution to the public–private dilemma may be the mirror of the future in many developing countries where private encroachment on public life grows ever more pronounced and becomes the rule and not the exception. Without badly needed public goods, such as full educational opportunity and adequate health services, the poor cannot improve their lives. Nowhere in the southern hemisphere has macro-economic growth targets of 5 and 6 per cent been sufficient to bridge the distance between the elites and the socially excluded. Only an adequate supply of collective goods can make a fundamental difference to the quality of life for the mass of low-income families. What São Paolo shares with other world cities is that it has the need for social connectors, like community meeting places to strengthen the social movement side of society, redistributive collective goods such as Sesci Pompeii to provide educational, social and other services that the state cannot deliver to its vast and overcrowded ill-housed metropolis. Finally, public goods of a traditional kind, such as public housing and security, both of which are in critical short supply, are essential to São Paolo's democratic future.

If we use the city as a proxy for the public domain, we can see clearly its fundamental characteristics. In recent times, the capital city has been historically connected with the use of public space to promote commercial well-being, redistributive policies, such as public housing and social welfare during times of intense industrialization and the growth of public activities that define civic identity in its full complexity. Beyond the city the public domain has another and even more compelling presence.

The under-valued fourth pillar

In a post-Thatcherite age, the public sphere remains at high risk because markets have overshot their boundaries and continue to underperform in many regions of the world. They have failed to deliver a cleaner environment, eradicate poverty and provide for a range of social services to low-income people. Globally, the Washington consensus decades have been catastrophic for many Latin American countries, such as Brazil, a one-time show case for consensus policies. There, for more than a decade, open markets have supported very weak economic growth while generating short and weak economic cycles. This has caused excessive reliance on foreign resources and increased vulnerability to foreign shocks.

The adjustment policies advocated by the World Bank have pushed Brazil back to a 1930s balance of payment problem, with an escalating balance of payments crisis. The social costs of these policies have been pronounced, with Brazil facing some of the highest levels of unemployment, growth in precarious employment and social exclusion in the last fifty years, taxes have risen and incomes have fallen (Mattoso 2000).

The need for a strong and resilient public domain alerts us to the fact that social goods of all kinds, from human security to sustainable environmental practices, can and do override entrenched private property rights in specific instances. The imperative associated with these collective necessities furnished by the public domain is also compelling because its message is both direct and democratic – that the environment, labour standards, the organization of a better life, redistributive goals – all need the collective 'we'. As well, it speaks to the concern that the goods and services owned in common belongs to us – the people – and not to them. Since they are ours, they should be returned to the public. This is the fundamental idea behind the modern notion of the public domain. It is about the sustainability of the public interest and the social bond, in the generic sense of the term.

For theorists who are also looking for a more substantial answer, the public domain can be thought of as the fourth element that abuts on civil society, which is itself the legal creation of the state. It is a reaction to markets exceeding their boundaries and the need for society to provide for both basic and complex needs. But it is quite different from civil society, its close neighbour and cousin. Civil society is defined by the complex relations between non-market and non-state actors, *à la* Putnam's liberal definition of individual civic engagements of local commitment (Putnam 1993). Civil society emerges from the social relations which are separate from the state and which underlie democratic institutions. By contrast, the public domain is about the collective goods carved out from the state or from the market and, as in many contemporary settings, significantly and increasingly is from both.

New governance issues and the global marketplace

If the issue of governance has taken us in new directions and created the possibility of new political forms at the local, as well as the supra-national level, the old notion of the state-centred public is being challenged and refashioned. If an important part of 'the public' is increasingly identified with being 'outside state authority and hierarchy', these developments suggest yet another notion of the public domain linked to new forms of governance. Thus, we require new analytical and theoretical ways to re-link the macro public domain with its crucial micro aspects. This linkage must directly involve citizens where they live, work and assemble in public places, outside the state but in public settings, where the private and public worlds meet in intense enterprises of all kinds. Rodrik asks the crucial question, why do more open economies have bigger governments with public services that buffer individuals from the volatility of markets? The contributors to this volume pose the strategic corollary, why do societies with larger public domains have less social fragmentation, exclusion and inequality?

The redistributive impulse making public space and social policy a palpable reality has very different institutional impulses in all jurisdictions. Europe with its fundamental dichotomy between the public and private has kept a very large part of its public sphere intact, compared to the Anglo-American model. Supiot insists that *'la culture juridique dominante continue de dresser un mur entre le privé et le public'*, not in an absolute way but in a powerful one nonetheless (Supiot 2000: 13). The EU has given the market much smaller scope to grow in new directions. It has provided for more non-negotiable goods and mixed goods. No European country, including the UK, has been prepared to spend important political capital on flattening national diversity. They have been highly cautious about making themselves over-dependent on the neo-liberal principles of privatization, de-regulation and down-sizing the state.

De-regulation is a no-go zone, as the recent report on the future of social policy insists, because the EU values social policy goals and programmes that enhance solidarity and equity. The absence of any consensus to promote narrow-gauge harmonization of the public domain reflects a deeper set of concerns. For instance, Germany and Britain are not willing to give up their national veto on social security to aid the freedom of movement of workers. Germany and France for constitutional reasons cannot accept a single EU policy with respect to asylum and immigration policies. France opposes a common EU trade policy on services and intellectual property because it regards culture as a 'non-tradable commodity' and wants to safeguard it from Anglo-American attempts to treat it otherwise. France prefers its own voice in international trade negotiations and is not prepared to leave trade negotiations to Brussels. Britain, Luxembourg, Ireland and Sweden want to keep a grip on tax policy including moves to prevent tax fraud and updating the existing tax rules.

Unlike in the 'purer' Anglo-American model, pro-integration forces in the EU cannot move forward easily even though all members are for more co-ordination provided that the principle of diversity is respected. Few countries are willing to give up their national veto that would involve sacrificing sovereignty over highly sensitive areas of public interest (Council of the European Union; 2000 *Financial Times*, 22 November 2000). Significantly, the Charter of Fundamental Rights of the European Union has taken a first step towards the provisional entrenchment of many aspects of an emergent European public domain with a strong market-limiting dimension including citizenship rights, freedom of thought, conscience and religion (Chap. II. art. 10), freedom of expression and information (Chap. II, art. 11), freedom of assembly and association (Chap. II, art. 12). Chapter IV protects solidarity as a part of social citizenship including workers' right to information (art. 27), protection against unjustified dismissal (art. 30), social security and social assistance (art. 34) and access to public services (art. 36). Markets cannot easily intrude and carve out larger space for the EU's private domain actors. Of course, what is in the constitution will not hold powerful market forces at bay without other legislative initiatives. So far the EU has the political will to maintain its institutional barriers protecting its public domain sanctuaries from the privatizing demands of powerful market actors (draft Charter of Fundamental Rights of the European Union, Convent. 50, September 2000).

In other jurisdictions similar kinds of institutional protection guarantee the general public an adequate level of public service, a *de facto* non-tariff barrier made by governments in the past. Canada, a highly open economy with a strong *laissez-faire* economic culture has embedded in its Constitution a provision that ensures that every province can provide a reasonable level of public services.[1] So even though federal and provincial governments have cut spending, important programme spending cannot be altered. Equalization payments fall into this category and operate both as a minimal floor and redistributive mechanism with a clawback provision, should a province raise money on its own, the transfer payment is reduced. Ottawa is obligated to give funds to the poorer provinces so that they have the same capacity to spend on a bundle of public goods and services as wealthier ones. In 1999, Ottawa transferred close to $10 billion to six out of the nine provinces. The idea of providing a floor for public services limits rent seeking, in all of its many novel financial forms, as the new public norm. If Ottawa were to end this spending the poorer jurisdictions would have to double their tax rates just to maintain spending levels with the same debt burden as they have now

(Kneebone and McKenzie 1999). This demonstrates just how vital these transfers are for keeping the poorer provinces on the same fiscal footing as the haves.

In sharp contrast to the US, Ottawa is a big spender on public and social goods. Even after a decade of economic integration with the US, a full 70 per cent of the budget in the 1990s was directed to programme spending: old age security and guaranteed annual income, $21 billion; employment insurance, $13 billion; Canada Health and Social Transfers, $14 billion; public investment in infrastructure $23 billion and employment insurance, $8 billion. These small differences in the end have a fundamental impact on restricting the private use of public interest. Even so, Canadian governments continue to underestimate their own powers in the face of these new circumstances and perpetuate the belief that Canada is moving towards the less state-less tax model US style, when the evidence points to divergence and not convergence in terms of publicness (Drache and Monahan 2000). In the US, federal programmes are targeted to meet criteria for policing, education, food stamps and medicare. Washington has no formal responsibility, as in Canada, to build a level playing field in the critical sphere of public services. In Canada, Ottawa is required to provide public services to a fixed standard.

The perception in elite policy-making circles is that the public sphere is everywhere in decline and this erosion of capacity militates against a more robust view of collective action. How wrong this idea is that so long as the notion of the public is troubled and undervalued, even in social market economies governance debates remain off in one corner without any real impact on the normative challenges facing the changing nature of the public domain and the social bond. If territory and social policy are to be rebundled and the redistribution of wealth and resources addressed globally, how will any of this be realized without the powerful presence of new institutions and different kinds of political practices? So far this debate commands little atten-tion in the larger policy community.

A final word

Small and large public spaces, in their infinite variety, are very much the order of the times. While the public domain, in the final analysis, rests on building sanctuaries, sanctuaries are themselves a product of public finance. Communities that control their tax base are always able to construct a large and vital public, with its non-market services and protection of the public interest, that critical ingredient so necessary for the mutual obligation of common purpose. A robust public sphere emerges from the adjacent private and market domains that society inevitably erects against private incursions into it.

At a time when all are interrelated in one global marketplace, policy-makers and their advisers cannot be absolutely certain about the future conditions and prospects for global order. When the circulation of capital and the trade of goods is largely conducted beyond the reach of any one state, no one can predict accurately whether there will be a worldwide recovery, whether economic integration will provide a sufficient number of jobs, whether trade blocs will improve the welfare of their member states or whether the World Trade Organization has the capacity to provide the institutional basis for a secure international order. Given these uncertainties, there is a powerful intellectual case for states to look again at the intrusiveness of markets against growing global disorder. The question that cannot be avoided any longer is, should global free trade fail, faced with the rising demands for social protection, then what? Is the public domain ready to make a come back?

Increasingly, market intrusion has appropriated many parts of the public domain and as Harry Arthurs has so powerfully demonstrated, closed off the 'commons' as in times past. Few countries have ever opted for a hermetically sealed economy but those who embrace the world market so unreservedly may also discover, too late, that they are falling behind. The old ideology that their industries will be punished and their voters will face a drop in their standard of living if they step out of line does not carry the same ring of truth that it once did, in this post-Seattle world. It is evident to all that the global emperor and the regulatory institutions of the world economy have far fewer clothes than ever. The need for bar-raising standards from human rights to labour and environmental standards are at the centre of the debate. The globe's trade and financial institutions need to be reformed to make them accountable, democratic and transparent.

As the globalization debate enters a new critical phase, policy elites should listen to the advice of Joseph Stiglitz, former chief economist at the World Bank, given in a recent address. The bottom line, he warned, is that stability at any cost is simply the wrong target (Stiglitz 1998). If he is right, the political market for social protection, jobs and a higher standard of living, promises to be a more potent force than the most arduous tenants imposed by the dynamics of a *laissez-faire* globally directed free trade regime.

If this volume has a single unambiguous message to convey, it is that in the new international political economy nothing should be taken for granted or written off as politically or economically naive and impossible for a very specific reason. The twentieth century has been brutally successful in destroying broad-based ideological movements that seek to impose a single vision on people and governments everywhere. Triumphant liberalism may also share the common fate of all the other visionary movements: painful and costly failure. Far from being a universal programme for all, sovereignty and territoriality are likely to collide with the spirit of the new internationalism and, in these circumstances, the world's trading system will become the arena for bitterly fought trade wars amongst G7 bloc members and the emergent economies of the developing world. At the edge of the envelope where change inevitably occurs, more than ever, appearances are deceiving. Sounder fundamentals are said to usher in new state practices and broader change in policy-making. In the prescient words of a local back street wall scrawler, 'Explain it, don't complain, get re-connected. It's all we've got'.

Inge Kaul's reflection on the global public is an extremely important examination of the public provision of collective goods. As she underscores, there are many reasons why people, individually or collectively, prefer a public good to its private equivalent, the key is to strike the right balance. The current international financial architecture as well as trade and environmental regime display an almost chronic insensitivity to publicness, both in terms of decision-making and also with respect to the distribution of benefits.

The global economy has become a place for the increased consumption of global public goods but the Washington consensus has reduced the role of publicness to a bare minimum. There is a dual problem here. One is to expand and enhance the public so public goods are possible. The other is to identify which public goods should be provided so that there is a just distribution of the benefits from a well-functioning global trade order. At present, the global economy would prosper from new arrangements to enhance much needed increased cooperation across borders.

Kaul highlights future global public goods, including banking regulation, recognition of property rights, investment laws, human rights, clean air, protection of the ozone layer and control of infectious diseases. She argues that these public goods not only require international cooperation, but that they also constitute a new order of global public goods. In this new era of public policy-making, the public has to play a more active role in shaping the public domain and its constitutive elements.

Yet, the tool kit of policy-makers has not been refurbished and conceptually these kinds of public goods are still not high on the agenda of international authority. Her chapter concludes with a powerful analytical argument on the need to expand the definition of global public goods and reform the international trade regime.

For Geoffrey Underhill, the public domain is synonymous with the common will, public interest, public good and national interest – 'busybodies' through the ages that have tried to tell us, as individuals, what is good for us. Often over-zealous authorities have rigidly tried to determine the preferences of individuals. The social engineering, so evident in the way markets define consumer choice, rarely is effective in defining the more basic notion – the public good. Social scientists and philosophers need to tread carefully in their attempts to show how public goods emerge from private interests.

Using Adam Smith as a spring-board, Underhill demonstrates how the father of liberal political economy explained the relationship between 'the selfish pursuit of individual interest and the wider interests of the [publik], as a whole'. Preventing the merchant classes from grabbing hold of the public agenda, so as both to widen the market and narrow competition, has always been an uphill struggle, particularly in times of global free trade like our own.

Underhill focuses on how the past three decades have redefined the public interest, as well as the objectives of state policies with its corresponding impact on the way the public good is conceptualized. The nub of the problem is that financial institutions, often along with governments, have proven incapable of restraint when faced with bull markets for risky financial products. Even when democracy has shifted the regulatory goal posts in a positive fashion and expected political authority to be an effective regulator, frequently the provision of public goods has been inadequate and so markets continually function in less than optimal fashion.

Underhill contends that global governance requires a strong normative dimension because defining the public domain and the nature of public interest, entails defining what kind of society we want. Underhill provides a much needed corrective when he highlights the fact that the current discussion of the global monetary and financial system continues to ignore these basic questions and assumes that the public good is a given.

He also raises another fundamental question, whether the international monetary and financial system should be part of the public domain or whether the public good would be better served if it was thought of as a private market responsibility. His answer is that the regulation and supervision of the practices of national firms depend on defining the public good in this vital policy area. Unfortunately, a great deal of economic literature regards government as an unnecessary intrusion onto market processes and that the model of governance is based on a bare minimum of state intervention.

By contrast, Underhill makes a compelling case that states and markets are integrated ensembles and good governance requires very different kinds of global policies than presently exist. The task of global governance is to have a compelling and vital sense of the public interest, one that will reflect the important differences in policy mix and normative preferences of contrasting economics. For him and others, the most fruitful solution lies in strengthening the accountability of monetary and financial governance. The task will be greatly facilitated when it is understood that even global markets are not the exclusive terrain of private agents but belong firmly in the public sphere.

The Asian crisis of 1997–9 has produced a backlash against globalization, even among countries that are counted as its most ardent champions. Regional autonomy and self-reliance are much in evidence throughout Asia, Africa and Latin America, as developing countries' elites attempt to make the regions more competitive in the global economy. Amitav Acharya's chapter examines the revival of regionalism, in MERCOSUR and ASEAN, and provides a study in contrasts in the way regional institutions are prepared to expand their public domains.

His innovative thesis is that the growth of the public domain depends critically on a region's attitude towards human rights and democracy, and on their ability to accommodate new social forces. Further, he boldly argues that in recent times, too much attention has been placed on the central role of civil society actors while the importance of state-led regional institutions, to adapt to new circumstances calling for a more democratic approach to managing the public domain, has been badly understated.

Acharya's chapter provides an important corrective to the idea that the new regionalisms of the last decade are only about broadening market access. In fact, his detailed account shows that the sub-regionalisms in Latin America and Asia Pacific, with their concerns about regional public goods, are challenging the hegemonic dominance of neo-liberalism in the realm of ideas and institutional entrepreneurship. Second generation reforms have a clearly visible social agenda to them, including improvements in education, health care and social security, as well as restoring public confidence in such key areas as the administration of justice, personal security and financial supervision.

The need to develop adequate social safety nets has become an important part of the agenda, not only for national governments, but also for ASEAN itself. It remains to be seen whether soft regionalism can be transformed into a more durable and effective arrangement. One of the primary conclusions of Acharya's study is that regional and trans-national networks have the capacity to challenge neo-liberalism and regionalism.

Part 3 is appropriately called 'The Return of the Public, New Sites of Policy Contest'. As global markets increasingly face a crisis of legitimacy, the challenge for the international community is to devise a different kind of institutional equilibrium. Calls for a new Bretton Woods or a new economic architecture reflect this quest but until now they have shown little sign of significant progress. Certainly there has been no evidence of a breakthrough, as yet. One of the reasons for this is that transnational corporations are not prepared to be at the table with non-governmental organizations, nor to accept corporate responsibility for the growing social deficit that is associated with the drive for open markets and smaller governments.

An attempt to bridge this need is found in the core set of principles elaborated by John Ruggie and Georg Kell. They propose a Global Compact that challenges transnational companies to be good corporate citizens by embracing nine core principles derived from a decade of United Nations summitry, as well as the Universal Declaration of Human Rights. In recent times, UN summitry has been an important source of new ideas, principles and practices that have raised expectations for reforming global governance beyond its current minimalist arrangements.

Significantly, the Global Compact is not designed as a code of conduct, rather it is designed to be a frame of reference, a kind of bench-mark of best practice, in order to bring corporate policies more in line with universally shared values. Becoming 'better and best' corporate citizens, among other things, requires that these global economic giants accept responsibility for their policies and practices, which until now they have refused to do. It is somewhat ironic that the Global Compact tries to enlist the business community in an advocacy role on behalf of the United Nations and it is far from clear that this controversial decision will significantly strengthen the UN's authority and resources.

Critics charge that it could increase the governance gap and be a source of tension. Tentative supporters have pointed out that getting business to the table is but the first step towards addressing environmental, labour and human rights concerns. Historians remind us that there would have been no post-war consensus unless business, as well as labour, had accepted, in Ruggie's most memorable term, embedded liberalism that restricted property rights. The heightened tensions between transnational corporations and NGO actors carries with it considerable risk because the available institutional mechanisms to define and enforce global rules are weak and the demands for change from NGOs insistent. Seen in this light, the Global Compact is an important but modest initiative to strengthen the role of the UN where the external pressure is the greatest.

Sol Picciotto's paper focuses on the way the new global sphere is constituted. The transformation of political practices leads him directly to address the democratization of international regulation, a dimension not found in Ruggie's and Kell's examination of best practice global governance. For Picciotto, the question of democracy is at the heart of the debates about the nature of multi-layered governance, which increasingly characterizes the global public sphere.

In recent times, the public sphere has been subject to much functional fragmentation often involving a weakened public. Central governments have often been by-passed in many areas – from tax regulation, environmental protection to international criminal law enforcement. Picciotto is undoubtably correct when he says the democratization of global governance is not a matter of creating a global version of an already outdated 'national model of government'. Rather, he believes that democratic legitimacy needs to be enhanced by ensuring that public power is responsive to human rights principles.

The introduction of human rights principles, or what he calls, obligations on state to respect human values, would be an important counter-weight to the neo-liberal dynamic of unleashing the forces of economic self-interest. In calling for new concepts and forms of democratic accountability, Picciotto advocates active citizenship through democratic participation, principles and practices. The four principles of direct, democratic deliberation are transparency, accountability, responsibility and empowerment.

International organizations have had very little experience with developing mechanisms of direct accountability to the people affected by their activities. Even when corporations come under pressure to be responsive to the needs and demands of communities and the wider society, they have not abandoned their traditional focus on the bottom line. But in recent times, as shown by Shell's experiences over the Brent Spar oil platform, the impact of its oil fields on local communities in Eastern Nigeria, and those of bio-technology industries, in relation to genetically modified organisms, NGOs, with relatively few resources, have been able to establish 'a wilderness of single instances' to damage investor confidence in a number of cases. Often NGOs, through dint of hard work and a great deal of luck, have been able to force governments, corporations and international organizations to accept their obligations and responsibilities.

Picciotto makes a compelling case that, as civil society actors have become more effective in redefining and policing the line between accountability, transparency, openness and empowerment, the issue of governance has moved from the edge of the envelope to the centre of world public opinion. There are now many public forums and arenas where the concerns of the many are increasingly on a collision course with the interests of the few. Ironically, allowing markets to operate 'freely' and with supposedly neutral roles continues to attract, not only media attention, but it has re-awakened the public's commitment to developing mechanisms of direct accountability. All this has highlighted the inadequacy of the political processes for regulating the new global economy. For Picciotto, the next critical step is to find more effective means to democratize the global public sphere.

The constant pressure to adopt a model of smaller government and free trade has created deep asymmetries between the global economy and the nation state. The signature of our times is the weakening of the social bond in an era of globalization. As the social bond has become increasingly frayed, societies everywhere find it more and more difficult to address the complex needs of social justice.

For many of the past fifty years, the social bond was nurtured by the distributive capacity of society and modern state practice. As international institutions increasingly influence the redistribution of wealth and resources on a global scale, Sylvia Ostry raises the very tough question, 'does anyone seriously think we are going to launch a drive to a single global market with such a minimalist global governance structure?' If five years ago no one was asking this question, many are today. This is why the chapter by Richard Higgott and Richard Devetak is indispensable for addressing normative questions about governance.

The prospects for a robust synthesis of a liberal theory of globalization with a normative political theory of global governance are not reassuring. There is no accepted consensus about the form of the social bond needed to compensate communities and nations who have seen their standard of living and well-being decline, as a result of the rules and principles of the Washington consensus. Significantly, there has been a rise in popular sovereignty, unquestionably a backlash against the policy agendas motivated by the cruder drive for commercial gain at any cost.

Higgott and Devetak remind us that the failure of economic liberalism, in our time, is due to the fact that free markets along with failing to provide for compensatory domestic welfare are, in their words, 'a potent cocktail in the hands of the dispossessed'. Add to this, the other failure that even where liberalization has enhanced aggregate welfare, it has not solved any of the attendant political problems that arise from a weakened social bond. At the present time, non-state actors hold public authority and international organizations to account more than ever. This is evidence of the need to reinforce and expand public institutions wherever they are.

This iteration of the public domain is confirmation that civil society has need to create, in Jacques Attali's powerful idea, sanctuaries. In the past, non-market sanctuaries were places where the price system was not able to pursue its legitimate profit motives. In the current period, these sanctuaries are often a mix of the global and the local, and are indispensable to reconstructing a new social bond, one that is not bounded by older notions of territory and identity.

Elite driven globalization is under challenge everywhere and as Higgott and Devetak underline in their chapter, there is a conscious attempt to universalize the NGO experience. It is too early to say whether it will be successful in the institutional management of global forces, but so far, the rationalist economic logic of global free trade has not been able to provide an effective deterrent nor to answer the charges of its critics. Economic liberalism has not allowed for the more effective provision of public goods and has not been able to strike a balance between the normative and the ethical. So far, the neo-liberal ortho-doxy has failed to understand the importance of the social bond and a resilient public domain to the development of a renewed commitment to social justice.

Notes

1   The 1982 Canadian Charter of Rights and Freedoms protects the public and the well-being of Canadians in Section III, 2 (b) reducing disparity in opportunities; and (c) providing essential public services of reasonable quality to all Canadians.

Bibliography

Barnet, Richard and Cavanagh, John (1994) *Global Dreams, Imperial Corporations and the New World Order*, New York: Simon and Schuster.

Birdsall, Nancy and de la Torre, Augusto (2000) 'Economic Reform in Unequal Latin American Societies', *Carnegie Endowment for International Peace* (June): 1–40.

Boyer, Robert and Drache, Daniel (eds) (1996) *States Against Markets: The Limits of Globalization*, London/New York: Routledge.

Brittan, Samuel (1988) *A Restatement of Economic Liberalism*, Atlantic Highlands, NJ: Humanities Press International.

Cable, Vincent (1995) 'The Diminished Nation-State: A Study in the Loss of Economic Power', *Daedelus*, 124 (2): 23–53.

Castells, Manuel (1996) *The Rise of the Network Society*, Cambridge, MA: Blackwell.

Charter of Fundamental Rights of the European Union (2000) Covent 50, September fundamental rights

Council of the European Union (2000) website http://ue.eu.int/en/summ.htm (accessed 11 April 2001).

Cox, Robert (1999) 'Civil Society at the Turn of the Millennium: Prospects for an Alternative World Order', *Review of International Studies*, 25, 1: 3–28.

Dahrendorf, Ralf (1995) 'A Precarious Balance: Economic Opportunity, Civil Society and Political Liberty', *The Responsive Community* (Summer).

Drache, Daniel (2000) 'In Search of North America: Do Borders Matter? Wuz Up?', Robarts Centre for Canadian Studies, York University, www.robarts.yorku.ca (accessed 11 April 2001).

Drache, Daniel and Monahan, Patrick (eds) (2000) *Canada Watch: Special Double Issue on Canada–US Relations in the New Millennium*, vol. 8, no. 4–5, Toronto: Centre for Law and Public Policy/Robarts Centre for Canadian Studies.

Ferrera, Maurizio, Hemerijck, Anton and Rhodes, Martin (2000) *The Future of Social Europe. Recasting Work and Welfare in the New Economy. Report for the Portuguese Presidency of the European Union*, Brussels: EU.

Giddens, Anthony (1998) *The Third Way: The Renewal of Social Democracy*, London: Polity Press.

Gray, John (1998) *False Dawn The Delusions of Global Capitalism*, London: Granata.

Greider, William (1997) *One World, Ready or Not The Manic Logic of Global Capitalism*, New York: Simon and Schuster.

Group of Lisbon (1995) *Limits to Competition*, Cambridge, MA: The MIT Press.

Hajer, Maarten (1993) 'Rotterdam: Redesigning the Public Domain', in Franco Bianchini and Michael Parkinson (eds), *Cultural Policy and Urban Re-Generation: the West European Experience*, New York: St Martin's Press.

Halliday, Fred (2000) 'Global Governance: Prospects and Problems', *Citizenship Studies*, 4, 1: 19–33.

Held, David (1995) *Democracy and the Global Order From the Modern State to Cosmopolitan Governance*, Stanford, CA: Stanford University Press.

Helliwell, John (2000) *Globalization: Myths, Facts and Consequences, Benefactors Lecture 2000 C.D. Howe Institute*, Toronto: C.D. Howe Institute.

Higgott, Richard and Phillips, Nicola (2000) 'After Triumphalism: The Limits of Liberalization in Asia and Latin America', *Review of International Studies* 26 (4).

Innis, Harold (1995) *Staples, Markets, and Cultural Change: The Centennial Edition of the Selected Essays of Harold A. Innis*, Daniel Drache (ed.) Montreal: McGill-Queen's University Press.

Garreau, Joel (1991) *Edge City: Life on the New Frontier*, New York: Doubleday.

Institute for Economic and Social Planning for Latin American and Caribbean (1998) *Reflections on Development and the Responsibility of the State*, Santiago, Chile: UN/ECLAC.

Jacobs, Jane (1984) *Cities and the Wealth of Nations*, New York: Random House.

Kasinitz, Philip (ed.) (1995) *Metropolis: Centre and Symbol of Our Time*, New York: New York University Press.

Keohane, Robert O. and Nye, Joseph (2000) 'Globalization: What's New? What's Not? (And So What?)', *Foreign Policy* (Spring): 104–19.

Kneebone, Ronald and McKenzie, Kenneth (1999) *Past (In)Discretions Canadian Federal and Provincial Policy*, Toronto: University of Toronto Press.

Korten, David (1995) *When Corporations Rule the World*, West Hartford, CT: Kumarian Press.

Krugman, Paul (1994) *Peddling Prosperity Economic Sense and Nonsense in the Age of Diminished Expectations*, New York: Norton.

Krugman, Paul and Baldwin, Richard (2000) 'Agglomeration, Integration and Tax Harmonization', Centre for Economic Research, Discussion Paper DP2630.

Lasch, Christopher (1994) 'The Revolt of the Elites', *Harper's Magazine*: 39–49.

Marquand, David (1997) *The New Reckoning? Capitalism, Citizens and States*, London: Polity Press.

Mattoso, Jorge (2000) 'Globalization, Deregulation and Labour: A Challenge for Work and Social Citizenship in Brazil', Wagenet Conference on Work and Social Citizenship in a Global Economy, Madison Wisconsin, November.

Millennium: Journal of International Studies (2000) 'Special Issue on the "Battle in Seattle"', *Millennium* 29 (1): 105–14.

Naim, Moises (2000) 'Washington Consensus or Washington Confusion', *Foreign Policy*, Spring: 87–101.

OECD (1994) *The OECD Jobs Study*, Paris: OECD.

34 *Daniel Drache*

—— (2001), Harmful Tax Practices, http://www.oecd.org/daf/fa/harm_tax/harmtax.htm, (accessed 20/04/01).

Ostry, Sylvia (1998) *Globalization and the Nation-State: Erosion From Above*, Timlin Lecture, Regina: University of Saskatchewan.

—— (2000) 'Making Sense of it All: A Post-Mortem on the Meaning of Seattle', in Roger B. Porter and Pierre Sauvé (eds), *Seattle, WTO and the Future of the Multilateral Trading System*, Boston, MA: John F. Kennedy School of Government, Centre for Business and Government Harvard University.

Picciotto, Sol and Mayne, Ruth (ed.) (1999) *Regulating International Business Beyond Liberalization*, London: Macmillan.

Putnam, Robert (1993) 'The Prosperous Community Social Capital and Public Life', *The American Prospect*, 13 (Spring).

Reich, Robert (1991) *The Work of Nations*, New York: Knopf.

Rodrik, Dani (1997) *Has Globalization Gone Too Far?*, Washington, DC: Institute for International Economics.

Rosenau, James (1997a) *Along the Domestic-Foreign Frontier Exploring Governance in a Turbulent World*, Cambridge: Cambridge University Press.

—— (1997b) 'The Dynamics of Globalization: Toward An Operational Formulation', Paper given at the International Studies Association, San Diego, 1997.

Ruggie, John (1993) 'Territoriality and Beyond: Problematizing Modernity in International Relations', *International Organization*, 47, 1, Winter: 157.

Schultze, Charles L. (1977) *The Public Use of Private Interest*, Washington, DC: Brookings Institution.

Sen, Amartya (1999) *Development as Freedom*, New York: Knopf.

Silber, Simão Silber (2000) *Globalização e Tendâncias da Economia Braslieira*, Univeridade de São Paulo FIA-USP.

Stiglitz, Joseph E. (1998) *More Instruments and Broader Goals: Moving Toward the Post-Washington Consensus*, Helsinki: The United Nations University, World Institute for Developmental Economics.

Supiot, Alain, Ed. (2000) *Servir l'intérêt général. Droit de travail et function publique*, Paris: Puf.

Supiot, Alain *et al.* (1999) *Au-Dela de l'Emploi*, Paris: Flammarion.

Walzer, Michael (1989) *Spheres of Justice: A Defence of Pluralism and Equality*, Oxford: Blackwell.

Williamson, John (ed.) (1990) *The Political Economy of Policy Reform*, Washington, DC: Institute for International Economics.

—— (1999) 'What Should the Bank Think About the Washington Consensus?', prepared as a background to the World Bank's World Development Report 2000, World Bank, July 1999, Institute for International Economics www.iie.com/TESTIMONY/Bankwc.htm (accessed 03.05.01).

Zukin, Sharon (1995) *The Cultures of Cities*, Cambridge, MA: Blackwell.

Section 1

Revisiting the fundamentals in a post-Washington consensus era

1 The return of the public domain after the triumph of markets

Revisiting the most basic of fundamentals

Daniel Drache[1]

In the public domain belonging to the public as a whole, *esp.* not subject to copyright.

In public, 1 in a place or state open to public view or access; openly. Formerly also, in a published form, in print. § 2 Organized society, *the* body politic; a nation, a State: the interest of welfare of the community. **b** *Sociol.* A collective group regarded as sharing a common cultural, social, or political interest but who as individuals do not necessarily come into contact with one another.

General Public = People collectively; *the* members of the community. Treated as *sing.* or *pl.*

(*The New Shorter Oxford English Dictionary*)

Rethinking governance

It appears that not only the state, as an organizing entity, but the public domain – the non-tradable social goods sector that exists in every society – is ready to make a come-back (Albert 1993). The current crisis of neo-liberalism has put on the agenda the need to move beyond the Washington consensus and its belief in the frictionless operation of markets. What needs specification and development is the modern notion of the public as an instrument of governance. Even if governments in the past have been reluctant to share decision-making with the public, at the present time government needs to find ways to empower citizens in order to improve public services, reduce public bads and introduce new regulatory instruments to act as a counterweight to global instability.

It is now apparent that in a post-Seattle world the new message from international organizations, such as the World Bank, is that public authority needs a more realistic view of governance, one not premised on simplistic ideas about the power of markets. International organizations are calling on governments everywhere to revisit the fundamentals of neo-liberalism and to rethink the 'public interest'. What public authority is being told is that it needs to relearn how to promote collective goals and revitalize public institutions (World Bank 1997; OECD 1994).

In theory, modern states have long recognized the social-binding importance of maintaining strong public domains. However for many experts, the public domain is not seen in these terms and is confused with the drive to reduce, in stark ways, the public sector. Specifically, they accept the requirement to curtail public expenditure, limit the perceived increase of government regulation of the economy and look to enhance the performance of the economy by a dramatically smaller, competitive-minded state presence (Schultze 1977). In recent times, it is this view of public policy that has prevailed. Notionally states have paid lip-service to the US bench-mark style of governance but in practice have been much more selective in their support of the goals and principle framework of the Washington consensus. Today few are persuaded that residual Keynesianism is the main obstacle inhibiting markets from efficient operation (Wolf, *Financial Times*, 5 April and 17 March 1999).

As the social bond is more frayed than ever (Devetak and Higgott 1999), this too has transformed the public sphere in unexpected ways. The unanticipated defeat of the Multilateral Agreement on Investment is another confirmation that civil society is alarmed by the social impacts of global free trade and is pressuring global institutions for greater accountability and transparency. In such circumstances, there is a larger role for organizations and institutions to mediate state policy and raw market power. Nor is it by chance that deeper integration and higher spending continue to be directly linked (Rodrik 1997).

What is now apparent is that governments have overstated the constraints of macro-policy, while frequently understating the size of their fiscal surpluses. Throughout the industrial world public authority is awash in large surpluses. For example, it is estimated that a middle power such as Canada will have over $70 billion dollars of surplus revenue to spend in the next five years once contingency funds have been set aside for a downturn. The US and much of the EU are in a similar situation and are making plans to expand the role of the state in the economy. All of this new-found activity suggests that the day of the sovereign state is far from over. Countries continue to govern their national economies despite important ideological and normative differences. Thus, the structure of their economies continues to be nationally contained notwithstanding an unparalleled degree of interconnectedness. This too needs to be given precision and theoretical clarity. In this borderless world, national institutions and arrangements remain as critical for good governance as deceptively simple supply and demand signals.

The question that merits examination is the very notion of the public domain as an incipient concept with its overlapping and multiple dimensions (see Figure 1.1). In the public mind at the neighbourhood level, the public domain is synonymous with the public park, the skating rink, the local library, music halls, art galleries, bus and subway routes and the local post office. Beyond the local community exist other and more important sets of interdependencies. The most important are the public spheres, which are the sites of political life, democratic values, institutions and debate, as well as the provider of public services that form a broad notion of citizenship entitlement with the

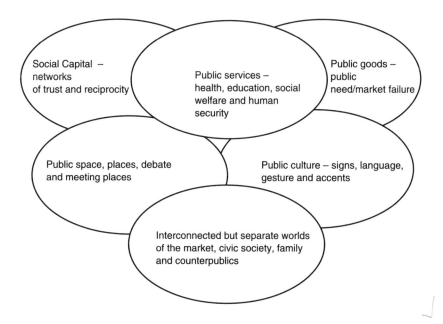

Figure 1.1 The overlapping and multiple boundaries of the public domain
Source: Drache 1999

corresponding legal, political and social rights. The assets that are shared and used in common cover a diverse group of subjects, including the environment, information, health, and education. It also includes civic engagements of responsibility, none of these are simple commodities to be bought and sold. In the new world order, conventional measures of government intervention often fail to capture the complexities of mixed economies and, particularly, ignore the contribution of this 'wider public domain' in maintaining political stability and economic growth in the face of significantly expanded markets and declining regulatory measures (Albert 1993).

Political economists have as yet to find a way out of this impasse despite an impressive array of evidence that there is a *very large terrain between atomized civil society and state dominated public practice.* Public authority also needs to adopt a more realistic view of governance, one that is not premised on simplistic ideas about the power of markets. At a time of unprecedented interdependence, governments have to promote collective goals and revitalize public institutions.

The existence of this public domain, in which consensus, cooperation and public discourse figure predominantly, has both material and institutional dimensions that are large and complex with overlapping aspects. At a time when this older and larger notion of the public is no longer bounded by the welfare state to the degree that it once was, it is important to understand its genesis, appearance and prospects in an era of global markets.

The basic issues are, what are the public domain's chief characteristics after the apparent triumph of markets? Why has it re-emerged at a time of globalization? What is its genealogy in the literature of political science, economics and urban sociology? Why does its expansion and reinforcement matter? And finally, what are its prospects as a strategy of public policy in a post-Washington consensus era (see Table 1.1)?

The argument in brief

This chapter begins with the case that there has been a surprising growth of public space, even at a time of global free trade and the emergence of a markedly smaller state. It then proceeds to locate the public domain between the state, market and civil society. It demonstrates that the critical issue for our times is not state-lessness – defined in its most extreme form as the end of the nation-state and the irreversible diminishment of national authority – but 'state-ness' finding the appropriate model, strategy and resources for maintaining public authority in contrasting market economies. The chapter also offers some critical thoughts on two other equally challenging issues: the defining characteristics of strong domains versus the inhibiting features of weak domains and the new demands for an expanded public domain in both developed and developing countries. Contrary to elite received wisdom (that well-placed public authority has to intervene to create public goods to preserve the virtues of the free market in the face of market failure), the emergence, enhancement and embedded quality of public domain issues is driven primarily by the need to limit the excessive rent-seeking behaviour of powerful market actors.

Still, as we will discover, there is much that needs clarification and empirical verification regarding the critical relationship between the public domain, state practices and markets. For instances, in re-examining 'state-ness' – what are the key elements of the modern state that enhance productivity, competitiveness and social cohesion, so that they are reinforcing rather than achieved at the expense of one or another? The story remains a compelling one for a principal reason. More than ever, contemporary public life is an entanglement of public interest and private markets. For governments who are looking at new policy ideas and principles to better grasp the contradictory dynamics of markets and to find ways to strengthen the international order, the strategic notion of the public domain requires, above all, clarification and greater precision as a benchmark of public life.

The return of the public domain: an older valued concept of policy-making

Despite the triumph of markets, there is nothing inevitable in the return of the public domain. If a revitalized notion of the public domain seems not on the radar screen of the public, the more pressing problem is that there is no clear consensus any longer of what the public is or consists of. At one time there was broad agreement when one said 'this concerns the people as a whole', 'done or existing openly', 'provided by or concerning local or central government', as in public money; public records; public expenditures or 'involved in the affairs of the community, especially in government' but no longer. Increasingly, the public is a permanent entanglement of bureaucratic and private interest, as in 'becoming a public company'. The regulatory role of public authority is much diminished with respect to health, education, finance, trade and culture. All of this seems so obvious that it barely is worth mentioning, but it is, because it highlights the all too evident predicament of our times that the very notion of the public is troubled, in crisis without any resolution in sight.

For instance, public opinion polls reveal a growing distrust of government in many jurisdictions, which only adds further fuel to the fire that the public suffers from a crisis of confidence. More importantly, our most prized idea of the public is suffering a gender-based legitimacy crisis. The term itself is troubling. 'Public' comes from the Latin *publicus*, itself derivative from *'pubes'*, the male adult. The public was never 'for all', as political theorists have intoned through the ages but only for some and, historically, has long been exclusive of women. The public was an exclusionary sphere, largely for male political actors and elites, with a gender based set of issues and practices.

So at a time when the public is at an all time low esteem, what is the public domain? Is there a case for reviving a concept? Do we need it at all? Political theorists have long recognized the importance of the public as a constitutive part of public policy-making. However, I do not intend to use public domain as a term of art to be defined mainly by reference to authoritative texts. Rather it needs to be thought of as an incipient but evolving concept which requires constant redefinition. It is important to stress that the 'public domain' is not a synonym for 'state', though sometimes the state is, in fact, the most obvious means of advancing public purposes. Instead it is meant to underline the fact that by whatever means they are achieved, many purposes, values and social goals – are inescapably *public*.

Conceptually consider it as follows. The public domain is the fourth element that abuts on civil society. It is the legal creation of the state when markets exceed their existing boundaries and it provides society with basic and complex needs. Its pedigree is long, having its roots in modern economic, political, social and legal thought (see Table 1.1). If one were to try to envision where the public domain is in relationship to the rest of the social order, we can see its place quite clearly. It is one of the centres of decision-making that allows society to organize itself, plan for consumption and support a mix between non-negotiable goods, mixed goods and negotiable goods. From it emanates the set of processes essential to a stable social order and a cohesive society.

If the state, market and civil society remain the great institutional markers of modernity, the public domain is at the intersection between civil society - largely norm-based, decentralized and hierarchically flat, the market - subject to the constraints and opportunities of the universal price mechanism, private

property rights and corporate profit-taking and the modern administrative state
- dependent on its full-bodied bureaucracy, large-scale financial resources and
vast legal powers. It is a large irregular space covering a range of activity and
organizations that belong to the public, as a whole, having flexible borders,
expanding and contracting in size, driven most by need rather than by any fixed
notion of rights.

What we now identify as the generic idea of the public domain evolved by
fits and starts, particularly in response to the primacy of markets and the spread
of democracy. The very idea of it emerged in antiquity from the health and
hygienic needs of early cities, the growth of democracy, the erection of public
buildings and the emergence of bureaucracy, military and the courts (Mumford
1986). Its boundaries have always been inseparable from the spread of
commerce and the growth, first of cities and then nations, but always linked
with political freedom. In Mumford's own words,

> the genuine improvement took place in the internal organization of cities
> throughout history since the introduction of drains, piped drinking water and
> water closets into the cities and palaces of Sumer, Crete and Rome. Cities
> needed an infrastructure, roads, harbours, ports and administration to collect
> revenues, maintain order and organize pageants and spectacles for the masses.
>
> (ibid.)

For political theorists, it speaks of the ethic of public responsibility – community networks of trust and social solidarity are some of the distinguishing
features that have been attributed to it. The public domain is about assets that
are shared, and hence, there is also a strong redistributive imperative defining
the boundary between the state and the market. These collective assets, outside
the reach of private property and the market price mechanism, have been part
of the standard tool kit of modern economics and political science. There are
many theories and explanations of why societies need collective goods (Olson
1982; Prebisch 1971; Kaul *et al.* 1999; Giddens 1998). Mainstream economics
identifies the public domain merely with the consumption of public goods
(Stiglitz 1988; Buchanan 1975). What makes this concept of public goods
limited is that it undervalues the intricacies needed for the creation and
consumption of such complex goods by all citizens and stakeholders. Since
these 'social goods' belong to all members of society, in theory, their benefits are
to be shared by all irrespective of private need. If this is so – and it is – public
goods cannot be explained by the efficiency conditions of Pareto optimality.
Society's collective goods are not the product of market failure, as many neo-
classical theorists posit, but of social need. The presumption is that markets and
firms can handle most, if not all, of society's other goals such as a fair distribution of income, a stable macro-economy and national security. In point of fact,
public goods are as likely to be a response to efficiency, equity, stability and
security needs as to reduced transaction costs. If this is so, public goods are ready
to make a comeback.

Economists are only now beginning to rethink this fundamental issue. For instance, Eden and Hampson make a compelling case that public goods are part of governance structures and that society needs to organize and manage their interdependency faced with uncompetitive firm behaviour and general allocative failures (Eden and Hampson 1997). While many economists do believe that these kinds of equity/governance issues are part of economics, public distributional questions need their own theoretical reiteration. It is for this crucial reason that we must realize that the notion of the public domain derives from an older view of the market economy, one premised on the idea that markets are not all encompassing and that civil society involves a critical non-market sector; part private and part public. In civil society not all goods and services may be bought and sold (Perroux 1950). Some assets, by their nature, cannot be transferred from one owner to another. These include intangible social, collective and political goods deemed to be non-negotiable and non-transferable, such as public freedoms, human rights, government transparency and public accountability (Perroux 1962). In the public domain, citizens not only enjoy collectively these non-commodifiable goods but also attribute utility to the social well-being these goods provide and contribute to their value.

For political economists, the concept of public goods demands an equally powerful explanation. The rapid growth in public goods for infrastructure, and later education and health, in all countries, is due principally to the growth of complex public needs rather than the exigencies of market failure. The market failure test that predominates in neo-classical economic literature remains problematic (Schultze 1977). The theoretical apparatus for identifying situations of market failure for 'correction and regulation' is too elaborate, ahistorical and frequently, too narrowly technical to be reliable for policy-purposes. By contrast, the new institutionalists, such as North and Romer, with a focus on endogenous growth, demonstrate that public goods are socially constructed and the standard public distinction does not allow one to determine which goods are publicly provided (Cornes and Sandler 1994). Outside of the industrial world, the state is not the instrument of last resort but is a primary mover, in developing countries and social market ones as well (Schonfield 1964; Prebisch 1971; Crouch and Streeck 1997). The fact is that state-provided services are most frequently a response to the need to curb the socially destructive rent-seeking behaviour of private actors (Coase 1960). The state is required to use its unique powers to organize the provision of social goods and resolve problems of collective action that private property regimes, with their short-term interests cannot address.

At its core, the public domain is defined as the collective assets and goods which are held in common and cannot be bought or sold on the open market. It is the large and complex 'terrain left between private holdings' (Kuntsler 1996), not limited to public services of a broad variety – health, education and workplace representation – but also including public spaces and places. These shared assets belong to the public and are open and accessible. In organized society,

The constitutive elements of the public domain
- social goods that benefit everyone and cannot be considered like private property belonging to the individual. The public domain is a by-product of social and state activity (Strange 1996)
- the social capacity of government to be an effective manager of market failure and the social distortions flowing from enlarged markets, as well as to provide public goods to limit the rent-seeking practices of corporations (Rodrik 1997)
- the non-market sector – public goods that cannot be bought and sold and that are under-provided and undervalued by the market – public freedoms, human rights, government transparency and public accountability (Polanyi 1957)
- the sizeable not-for-profit sector that acts as a buffer against global competitive pressures and gives voice to social movements and the policy-making processes within the territorial state (Drache and Sullivan 1999). The sphere that extends and enhances the democratic engagement of public discourse by including a wide range of actors from civil society
- the public sector including: budgetary transactions and programme expenditures, public enterprise, public regulation and state provided services such as health, education, social welfare and pensions (Albert 1993)
- networks of engagement and embedded social space that facilitate cooperation and coordination of the '*civitas*', particularly in the interface between the mega-city and the global economy (Lefebvre 1996)
- the inter-generational responsibility for the protection and conservation of the planet's 'common property' environment including ground water, fisheries, the atmosphere and the oceans (Sandler 1997). Governance of the global/local commons requires public goods that allow all countries to reduce risk and the moral hazard of efficiency failures.

one can speak of the welfare of the community, the body politic of the nation and state. What people share in common, they also use in common. This communal sharing of cultural, social, or political interests – even when individuals do not necessarily come into close contact with one another – differentiates the public domain from the state, the market and civil society. Its unique location makes it a privileged site, where the price mechanism of the market and the regulatory power of the state constantly clashes and vies for dominance. Its borders are not fixed but move in response to the interplay of state and market forces. In this complex process, it is possible to see that the public domain may be strengthened, weakened or transformed depending on the outcomes reached between the social actors and that the strength, vitality and organizational capacity of civil society are directly related to the resources it can access from 'the assets shared in common'. In an era of globalization, this 'terrain' is large and likely to become larger, as public needs, nationally and internationally, require states to address non-market areas of public life.

Table 1.1 A simplified genealogy of the 'assets and collective goods shared in common'

Infrastructure/ Local services	Ports/harbours, administration and customs in Crete, Rome and Greece (Bairoch)	Rights to the city, freedom and security (Pirenne) Town/city (Marx)	Industrial goods, use versus exchange value (Lefebvre) Modern city – product of the Industrial Revolution (1860s) – the metropolis emerged	City as a landscape of power (Mumford, Lefebvre, Jacobs, Sennett, Davis, Zukin, Sassen)
Public goods (neo-classical economics)	Wealth of Nations (Smith)	Draining of the meadow (Hume)	Collective goods, market failure (Wicksell)	Public bads/ public goods (Hayek, Samuelson, Bhagwati, Olsen Buchanan) New Institutionalism (North) Endogenous growth (Romer)
Public sphere	Public/ private domain defined (Hobbes)	Separation of the king's personal wealth for public moneys (Habermas) Rule of law and legality (Kant)	Liberal democracy and franchisement for men (J.S. Mill)	Public sphere is men acting together and where freedom can appear, civic virtue (Arendt) Public sphere is negotiated collective engagement – unstable, indeterminate, and open (Habermas) Public sphere is challenged by identity politics for excluding counterpublics (Fraser, Benhabib)
Non-market assets (Marxist and non-Marxist thinkers)		Tragedy of the commons (E. D. Thompson)	Limit of markets – labour, money, culture (Polanyi)	Development, structural change and society (Perroux, Prebisch, Albert, Hirschman) Regulation school (Boyer) Brundtland Report – governing the commons (Daley and Cobb, Ostrom et al.)

The return of the public: some empirical evidence

For governments who are looking at new policy ideas and principles to better grasp the contradictory dynamics of markets and to find ways to strengthen the international order, the strategic notion of the public domain is not to be confused with the Keynesian welfare state that boldly appropriated the public domain as a governance instrument. During the four decades following the Great Depression, governments had little difficulty demonstrating their capacity to regulate markets, promote growth and keep social inequality within strict limits. At present, markets are taking their revenge. Financial institutions decide which state policies are acceptable and which are not (Boyer and Drache 1996).

It is no accident that new global players have made efficiency the universal belief of all major corporations and most leading industrial powers. In this view, capital has to be free to move across national boundaries if the world economy is to recover its past *élan* (OECD 1998). Firms have to learn to reorganize their production to take advantage of the new opportunities. People are expected to adapt and accept new employment conditions, to accommodate a world where business is no longer bound by national borders. With all these dramatic changes to the social fabric of nations, governments have used market-like incentives, such as taxes, transfer arrangements, as well as fiscal policy to convert 'public goals into private interests' (Schultze 1977).

It is understandable why, for many experts, the public domain, a site of public culture and services, is confused with the drive to reduce, in stark ways, the public sector, as has occurred in the US. The difficulty is that from a traditional public finance perspective, the public sector has always been interpreted in a variety of ways including, budgetary transactions, public enterprise, public regulation and similar kinds of concerns (Musgrave and Musgrave 1984). It is possible to measure the size of the public sector by conventional measures, such as share of national income, share of transfer payments to individuals, and public share of GNP. These quantitative measures are all narrowly related to improving total output, employment and price stability. Within a globalized economy, it was expected that such advantages would be further enhanced by a dramatically smaller state presence.

Yet, significantly and contrary to what was predicted, in the post-Cold War era, as corporations and capital have become more mobile internationally, most governments have not evacuated the public sphere anywhere close to the degree expected. They are not approaching US spending levels nor adopting the American model of 'less state – less taxes'. Further, many developing and advanced states are confronting a range of intractable distributional issues, the social consequences of globalization and joblessness (World Bank 1997). The state may be in retreat but it is not fading away as once believed. Public sector activities are actually becoming more significant in many economies.

Government spending, as a percentage of GDP, has grown and has kept on growing even in those countries where government spending is not large. The trend is towards bigger government, not statelessness, and this trend has been almost universal (*The Economist*, 20 September 1997). When one examines where governments are spending in industrial countries as a group, public spending only fell in one category – that of public investment – from an average of 3 per cent of GDP to 2 per cent. By contrast, transfers to persons rose consistently; transfers to business increased as well and spending on interest and debt doubled. What these numbers tell us is that in all jurisdictions, public services are a primary site of public culture. Income support benefits to the unemployed, the disabled, single parents and the elderly are the most important causes for state expansion. Services such as education, health and social transfers, as well as defence and law and order remain the work of government. By contrast, deficit and debt payment represent less than 5 per cent of GDP in all government spending, even though accelerated deficit reduction has boosted this figure in many jurisdictions.

Despite this, across the OECD industrialized world, state spending is up and divergence from the US model has become the rule in almost all jurisdictions. In highly integrated settings, government spending practices have also diverged from the US example. Even within the Anglo-Saxon model, characterized by large, institutionally protected private sectors, spending patterns follow this norm. Initially the Canadian case seemed to conform with the pressures for 'deep integration' with US state practices. When NAFTA was signed in 1994, Ottawa imposed the deepest cuts of any G7 country in the 1990s, cutting spending from 51 per cent to 42 per cent of GDP. By contrast, when Washington tightened its belt, it cut its spending hardly at all, from 34.5 per cent to 31 per cent. No wonder Canadians have found this difficult to swallow. Even so, it is clear that Canadian spending on social programmes has not converged with US levels. Spending cutbacks have reduced the effectiveness of Canada's social security net, already weakened by Ottawa's rigid application of monetarist principles (Fortin 1996) but it is still more advanced than anything in the US. Canada's commitment to a redistributive model of federalism remains the defining difference between the two countries. Even in this highly integrated setting, Canada remains on a separate, unequal but parallel path. Significantly, public policy has not followed the market either to the degree anticipated.

Contrary to what many predicted, the fact is that the smaller Canadian state is not converging to the US model even though Canadian social cohesion is under pressure to do so (Drache 2000). Rather, it is a smaller version of what it was in the golden age of Keynesianism. Canada is a high spender compared to the US but a low-end welfare state compared to the social market economies of Europe. Even with deep integration, Canada's public domain is smaller than it once was, but it is still larger and better resourced than its US counterpart. Total government taxes and other revenues in Canada reached about 43 per cent of GDP, while the US figure has remained at the 30 per cent mark since the early 1970s. In a recent budget, the Minister of Finance chose to strengthen the non-market side of the economy and rejected corporate Canada's agenda of cutting taxes in order to cut spending! Fifty two per cent of the fiscal surplus supported new programme spending to reinforce social cohesion in health care; 38 per cent went to debt reduction; and only 10 per cent to reducing income taxes.

The fact is that Canada is not an isolated example. First-wave theorists of globalization were wrong in claiming that the new global order was supposed to bring convergence and uniformity across nations. Increasingly, it is evident that there is no coherent policy response to the deepening integration pressures from the global economy. 'Shallow integration' (referring to more conventional kinds of trade barriers, such as tariffs) and 'deep integration' (investment-led globalization leading to global production networks and highly integrated regional economies) have forced countries to revisit the fundamentals (Ostry 1998). This turn of events has taken many public experts by surprise. It was often assumed – wrongly as it has turned out – that interdependence would severely limit national room for macro policy and that liberalized trade flows would overtake government control of the economy. The idea was a pure Lockean fantasy – a vision of economic liberalism in which 'government has no other end but the preservation of property'. How far from the truth it is. Empirically the evidence indicates that social spending is not incompatible with trade and investment flows.

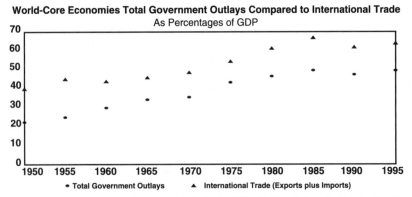

Figure 1.2 World-core economies total government outlays compared to international trade (as percentage of GDP)

Source: UN National Accounts Statistics 1952, 1959, 1973, 1985, 1996 and Analytic Databank OECD

Exports versus government outlays

Figures 1.2 and 1.3 trace total government outlays for the world's 'core economies' (fourteen countries including the social market countries of Austria, France, Germany, Italy and Sweden; all the G7 countries as well as major European states) and changes in international trade between 1950 and 1996.[2] They set out to test whether increased openness has outpaced government involvement in the economy. Part of the exercise included determining whether there was a strong inverse relationship between total government outlays, as a percentage of GDP and international trade as a percentage of GDP. In short, the point of the exercise was to test the hollowing out of the state thesis that many policy experts allege is occurring. Capital investment flows were not included.

Even the broad measure that compared general government expenditures with the dramatic increase in trade reveals that there is no foundation, empirically, to the notion that such an increase incontrovertibly equals less state involvement in the economy. Investment-led globalization has caused governments everywhere to shift priorities and revisit the fundamentals, mainly in terms of zero-inflation and zero-deficit targets but the idea that there is a single hegemon – capitalism – is wrong. There is no single model of a market economy. If this is to be a world, in the words of IMF Managing Director, Michel Camdessus, that 'will rely primarily on the private sector to mobilize resources for investment and growth' the triumphant vision of private space has not succeeded in checking public spending (*IMF Survey*, 8 March 1999).

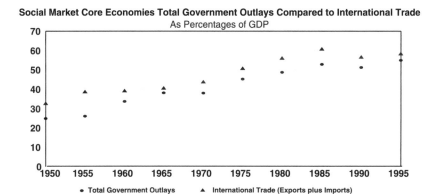

Figure 1.3 Social market core economies total government outlays compared to international trade (as percentages of GDP)

Source: UN National Accounts Statistics 1952, 1959, 1973, 1985, 1996 and Analytic Databank OECD

In the aggregate, government outlays of the most powerful countries have not declined as predicted, averaging 50 per cent of GDP in 1995. Only in 1990 was there a significant decline when the global crisis brought national growth to a standstill. Government spending in the aggregate recovered by 1995 when markets were supposed to be triumphant and the state in full retreat. Strikingly, the G7 countries much closer to a *laissez-faire* model of state–market relations were big spenders too. Where, as a group, they parted company with other advanced countries is that they were less dependent on the new international agenda of deeper integration as measured by their dependency on imports and exports. In this complex world of state–market relations, the social market economies Austria, France, Germany, Italy and Sweden – have not experienced any contradiction between their commitment to trade liberalization and their long-standing domestic institutions. These states continue to finance their social market institutions, at the same time as individually they have increased the volume of exports and imports.[3] The Netherlands and Belgium have the most open economies in the world and their government spending has increased as they remain committed to their social programmes.

After twenty years of triumphant market policies, the Anglo-Saxon, one-model for all–faster economic growth and lower unemployment – lacks many enviable features. It has lost a relatively equal distribution of income, has poorer quality of public goods and its average standard of living has declined for many, particularly low-income earners. The worst charge that can be made against the German model is that its growth is feeble and its economy creates too few jobs, but even then it may not be losing the race. It prefers slower growth with strong social institutions to prevent market failure. Recent studies challenge the view that the Anglo-Saxon model is always superior in terms of job creation. In the EU, the UK, has the widest wage dispersion of any country but the high-wage economies of Sweden and Denmark have a better success at net job creation (Employment in Europe 1998, EU, L/2985). So even slower growth is not a definitive measure of the quality and long-term viability of one economic model over another.

A larger but smarter state?

Market driven globalization has paradoxically created a larger state and also the need for a smarter one with more institutional capacity. So when one looks closely at the increased government expenditures, where is the money going? Debt interest repayment is the first reason that governments are spending more. The second is that social security spending has increased almost everywhere. In the case of Sweden, social spending rose modestly from 22 per cent to 25 per cent and this contrasts sharply with the UK, where spending shrunk by 3 per cent over this period. Contrary to popular perception US spending actually rose from almost 20 per cent to 23 per cent of total government outlays. Sometimes governments are cutting back their individual contributions to certain programmes, such as unemployment insurance, as in the case of Canada, but in other areas they continue to maintain their programmes.

The OECD has examined whether private expenditures on health and pension benefits are replacing the welfare state as the guardian of public need. In Sweden, the birthplace of the welfare state, ten years ago barely 0.1 per cent of GDP was spent on private welfare schemes; now it is 2 per cent – hardly the overwhelming triumph of markets. The two areas where governments have wielded the axe and downsized the public sector are first – in final consumption – principally public sector workers and services and second, gross fixed capital investment, that is, investment in infrastructures of all kinds that countries have relied on to make markets efficient and industries competitive.

The big picture story is that most of the variance among OECD countries is explained by one factor, namely social transfers to the working age population, which represents on average 7.25 per cent of GDP, more than double what they were in 1960. This factor accounts for almost three-quarters of the variation in government spending, according to the authors of this comprehensive study (MacFarlan and Oxley 1996). Their key finding is that most of the increase is explained by spending on insurance programmes, rather than social insurance. Furthermore it seems to be policy and administrative dimensions that are forcing governments to maintain their Keynesian engagement to transfer and other revenue replacing schemes. Unemployment insurance, disability, sickness, maternity, occupational injury, social assistance, housing and family benefits are where the money has been spent.

The system differences between social market, Anglo-Saxon and developing countries are large and, in fact, larger than indicated by even these state spending patterns or other conventional economic indicators. Experience demonstrates that markets have to be supported by extensive public interventions of a complex variety. Markets left on their own cannot deliver optimal results, except for standard kinds of commodities and then only under certain conditions. It is not easy to correct for the so-called externalities that enable firms to produce goods without paying the full costs.[4]

Society needs public institutions with the capacity to ensure that private actors disclose the needed information for corrective action. Without strong regulatory enforcement there is little evidence that new competitive conditions are likely to correct this market deficiency (Boyer 1999). Finding the vital ingredients for a sustainable social order requires a different kind of engagement at the state level. So far no amount of economic theorizing can adequately explain why, with markets rarely in equilibrium or responding only to simple supply and demand signals, the non-market, non-tradable side of society takes on a more important role. A large and vital part of the social order has been able to resist the conquest of markets. In modern times, the public domain has diverse impulses.

Table 1.2 Structure of general government outlays by type of outlays for twelve selected countries: comparing 1980 to 1996 as a percentage total of outlays in each year

Country	Final consumption		Social security		Debt interest		Investments		Other transfers and subsidies	
	1980	1996	1980	1996	1980	1996	1980	1996	1980	1996
Austria	36	36.3	20.1	22.3	5.3	8.7	8.8	5.4	27.8	27.3
Belgium	30	26.9	32.8	35.3	10.2	15.7	7	2.2	20	19.9
Canada	47.4	40.5	13.3	17.2	13.5	20.5	6.6	4.8	19.2	17
Denmark	46.9	40.5	29.2	34.5	6.9	10.7	6.1	3.2	10.9	11.4
France	38.6	34.5	33.3	33.2	3.1	7.2	6.9	5.5	18.1	19.7
Germany	41.3	39.7	24.2	28.3	3.8	7.3	7	4.4	23.6	20.3
Italy	34.3	30.2	32.5	35.5	12.4	20.3	7.3	4.1	13.5	9.8
Japan	30.6	26.8	24.5	33.1	9.8	10.4	19.1	18.4	16	11.4
Holland	29	26.5	34.6	35.5	6.5	10.5	5.9	5.1	24.1	22.4
Sweden	47	40.1	22.2	25.5	6.6	11	6.9	4.1	17.3	19.3
United Kingdom	48.1	47.8	14.2	13.7	10.5	7.3	5.5	4.1	21.8	27.1
United States	51	46	19.8	23	9.4	13.7	5.6	0	14.2	17.3

Source: Analytic Databank OECD

Definitions:

Final consumption expenditure: current (excluding capital expenditure) government operating outlays, net of sales of goods and services and of fixed capital formation for own account; of which compensation of employees encompasses payments of wages and salaries, and contributions paid in respect of social security, pension, income maintenance and similar schemes.

Social security: benefits paid to individuals under social security schemes, usually out of a special fund.

Debt interest: interest payments made on the debt including net purchases of land, rent, and royalties.

Investments: gross fixed capital formation plus increase in stocks.

Other transfers and subsidies: other current transfers (payments in the absence of economic exchange), intangible assets, and net capital transfers plus current government transfers or grants to private or public enterprises, mainly to offset operating losses.

Public services/market opportunities

For many, the public domain is often identified narrowly with state-provided services, but for good reason. The welfare state reform changed forever our perception of what is public and what is private. The Keynesian–Beveridge revolution redrew the boundary line between the public and private, dramatically because the focus was on narrowing the orbit of markets. From another perspective, its notion of the public was very traditional (Drache and Sullivan 1999). It maintained the dichotomy between private and public interests. Private refers to the property rights of the market and domestic personal and intimate matters. By contrast, 'the public' denotes state services accessible to everyone; the institutionalization of shared common social concerns and, most importantly, the public interest or common good. The revolutionary ideal of Keynesianism was that the public sphere would establish relations of solidarity through redistribution and a large role for the state in the economy and it aimed to create a unified public realm primarily around the delivery of services. For this, the state had to grow and have the resources at its command to deliver universal health care, full employment and a range of other social policies and safety nets.

The prototypical 'big state' of the Keynesian era established new institutional arrangements, conventions and practices that the full employment obligation, universal social policy and managed labour market regulatory practices entailed. The towering presence of the Keynesian welfare state also included protecting civic space – urban planning, rent control, commercial redevelopment, local rights issues and citizens' rights (Mumford 1961, 1986). Public authority everywhere invested in a strong municipal public sector – health, education, culture, social services, public and co-op housing delivered at the city level. In the process, the state became the arbiter of the rules under which markets could flourish and the Keynesian public sphere became a privileged site where civil society was able to scrutinize the exercise of its power and authority (Devetak and Higgott 1999).

Still, compared to its immediate predecessor the Washington consensus has failed at a more basic level.[5] It drove a large policy wedge between the public and the private and promised much in terms of economic benefits with few political costs. Its most important claim is that countries which open their borders, regardless of the cost and consequences, will derive a high standard of living, due to cheaper goods, stronger industries and more jobs. In theory all of this results in strong efficiency gains from better economic performance of industry and economy. Countries will automatically move up-market and produce more sophisticated products that require skilled labour, which in turn commands higher wages. Consumers will benefit because goods will be cheaper and hence disposable income will go further and effective demand will strengthen. The reality for many countries has not been these dynamic gains from trade but the asymmetrical benefits from participating in the world economy. Frequently, the costs of import penetration outweigh the benefits from the increase in exports; more jobs are lost than gained and factory closings multiply outweighing new factory openings. For many countries, investment and technology flows from the modernization of the economy and industry do not occur or occur too weakly. Instead of a dynamic comparative advantage, global free trade frequently results in the reinforcement of the existing trade specialization in primary products or low value-added exports. So, far from moving up-market in terms of value-added goods and services, the free trade effects are very different from the theory's promise. In many developing and even first world economies, the stress on competitiveness and market access has resulted in the deepening of the existing division of labour, which often is low value-added of a traditional kind. What can be said with an absolute degree of certainty is that global free trade has proven to be a poor substitute for national strategies.

So the pivotal belief has proven more often wrong than right. The incentives of free market price signals have not promoted the virtuous cycle of individual, self-seeking behaviour that neo-classical economies had predicted. The reason is that markets are not fully competitive nor is information costless. The price mechanism does not reflect the true value to society of all the uses of its resources (Carter *et al.* 1997). Levels of externally generated flexibility that are too high destroy trust between the social partners and undermines public authority if it remains a passive spectator. Rhodes is right when he notes that cost competitiveness and maintaining 'credibility with financial markets requires preventing wage drift and inflationary pressures'. In Europe, this has focused the attention of governments mainly on national wage bargains and incomes policy, as occurred in Spain and other jurisdictions. These kinds of measures 'bind the bargaining partners in the public domain more closely together than ever' (Rhodes 2000). Once flexible and consensual solutions to employment and competitiveness become a paramount objective, it reinforces the functional aspects of the idea that efficient public services are an important institutional condition of competitiveness.

The policy implication of the above is that cutting back the welfare state or labour market deregulation is unnecessary to remain competitive in the new era. So the welfare state is being transformed not dismantled from a European perspective, the contrast with the Anglo-American experience is stark. The deficit reduction targets followed by Canada, Australia, New Zealand and the US have led to an under-investment in health, education and infrastructural spending and has precipitated a supply-side crisis in public and collective goods. This crisis of confidence is far from being resolved in the industrialized world and in the developing countries the return to a pre-Keynesian past of social disparity in access to income, wealth, power and public goods has reached new heights. Structural reforms have increased the influence of creditors, shareholders and international financial institutions to the detriment of workers, governments and communities (Mattoso 2000).

While orthodox neo-classical economic theory predicted that deregulation would lead to a stronger and more efficient role for government, the opposite has occurred. Global flows of goods and services have not resulted in the much-anticipated convergence in the wealth of nations or the responsibility of government as a front-line provider of public services and goods. The harshest criticism has come from the United Nations' *Trade and Development Report* (1999). In part it reads: 'Unbridled competition, particularly among unequals, has never, by itself, delivered faster growth and shared prosperity, even in today's developed countries, and it has at times been destructive. There is no reason to expect a different outcome in a globalizing world.'

It is during a period of unprecedented globalization that the state always has a unique role in the provision of public services, particularly those critical for promoting social and economic development. The modern welfare state was born, in the first great wave of globalization, at the turn of the twentieth century. As Marquand notes in this volume, the great achievement of modern state craft has been to carve out from the private and market domain a public domain and 'to erect strong barriers against inevitable excursions into it'. Still today, Europe remains the 'Third Way' maintaining an elaborate, if often, fragile compromise between the state and the market where the economy is becoming much less central to ideological conflict and party politics (Ferrera *et al.* 2000).

Critically, a new public space and an even larger private world are emerging as jobs and work culture adapt to the new competitive circumstances. So is the explosion of private wealth, epitomized by the chaotic activity on the trading floor of the stock exchange, itself the most public of places, regulated by the state and driven by the passions of untrammelled individual self-interest. Most commentators focus only on these transnational actors and their demand for investment entitlements but equally important are questions about the reconstitution of citizenship, globalization and relations with civic society. Sassen makes the powerful case that there is increasing conflict and friction between the public and private as global cities become strategic sites for disempowered actors enabling them to gain voice and power in their own right (Sassen 1998). If she is right, this diversity of locally configured arrangements will continue to frame public policy debate in critical ways. The most important is the formulation of new rights and entitlements. These directly affect a large number of policy areas, namely taxation, wage levels, social spending and skill levels, but also the public-mindedness of those in a position involving responsibility to the public to act in the best interests of the community.

Public space/private worlds

For many, the public domain is synonymous with public space, a set of real places, a code of public conduct with concrete forms and places. It is the terrain left between private holdings and the connective tissue of social agreements that bind people together (Kuntsler 1996). Specifically, urban space belongs to particular groups of people – universities for the young; piazzas for 'male' citizens; ethnically homogeneous neighbourhoods – Toronto's Chinatown, Kensington market. All public space requires a large degree of public subsidization to be maintained and to pay the wages of police, gardeners and maintenance personnel of all kinds. Without this service infrastructure public space deteriorates (Walzer 1986; Zukin 1995; Mumford 1986). In Lefebve's terms, public space has to strike and maintain a proper balance between its use value for citizens and its exchange or commercial value for business. This is also why public space is never solely public but is always a mix between public and private use, the world of formal need and informal custom, spaces used by elites and those appropriated for popular and democratic action. These are also its unique set of characteristics and mentalities that protects the urban public core against the destructiveness of ruthless commercialism.

In recent times, strong public domains have been a powerful instrument against globally anchored forces in order to preserve ethnic, working-class and counter-cultural neighbourhoods. Cultural and commercial life will always exist side by side. Elites with their vast resources always have the greatest possibility to mould public culture. In cities, the shape of public culture is largely effected through the building and development of the city's public spaces in stone, concrete, steel and glass. As well, public culture is linked, through the architectural design of buildings, in many different ways to social identity and the social control of space (Zukin 1995). Capital cities of the world, possibly more than any other part of the political order, will always act as the accelerator of globalization, defending openness, diversity and cosmopolitan values. But these same urban settings are also the most resistant to it (Jacobs 1984). They are the sites of dominant corporate culture, as well as a 'multiplicity of other cultures and identities', each with their own claims on competing publics. The perennial question asked by the inhabitants of the urban centres of the world is whether there will only be a larger role for enterprise in their metropolis or whether the right to the city requires a vigorous expansion of the general public and public spaces.

In this contest to appropriate public space for private need, the modern city inevitably becomes a site of policy contest and confrontation. It has to choose between mega-shopping centres and malls in the suburbs or more freeways – the exit option – or full-scale urban renewal of the commercial and city centre – the voice and identity option. In terms of infrastructure, modern cities can favour industrial zones and parks, as well as satellite business districts outside the city centre linked to airports and auto-routes. Or like many European cities today, they can define their future through the public, by building inter-urban transportation systems between high-density urban areas, such as the TGV and regional airports located close to the urban centre. New information technologies pose other hard choices: to build science and technology parks, silicon valley look-alike high-tech industries and other kinds of industrial districts dominated by the giants of the information age or expand universities situated in the downtown core with the possibility of supporting private sector activities as well as poly-technical centres and redbrick universities situated in the larger metropolitan area with the same potential.

Municipal and sub-national state centres of decision-making have to determine their priorities too. They can contract out public maintenance provision, such as garbage and other vital services; impose user fees and tougher welfare rules that mean fewer recipients and lower benefits to low income families, as well as impose additional personal and property taxes. In this vision, the city becomes the dominant site of a powerful commuter culture dependent on the freeway and the private car with the suburbs weakly linked to downtown. It will be an urban environment with few social services or public housing. Cities can be dominated culturally by theme parks and amusement centres, *à la* Disney or Wonderland, or support cultural centres, such as museums, art galleries, sports facilities, dance-halls, theatre, radio, tv and film production. Alternatively, major local, state/province and national sites of public authorities can cooperate and strengthen public culture so that the social bond is strengthened at the municipal and city levels. Public transport would be extensive, cheap, accessible and safe and the large public domain would be financed by taxes to pay for public housing, education and social welfare programmes.

Everywhere the public has to decide between these diverse kinds of activities and enterprises (Walzer 1986). Who occupies public space has to be agreed upon through negotiations over physical security, cultural identity and urban communities. Hence the city, particularly at a time of global capital flows and the movement of peoples, has always been the flashpoint for anxiety, conflict and counter-movements, as the running battles in Seattle and Quebec against the WTO and other organizations vividly demonstrate (Zukin 1995).

In Lefebvre's theoretical world, public culture, like the city, is a system of signs and language embedded in urban life in concrete ways. It is the vital component of both the city and its core – 'the means for planned organization and consumption', which forms the place to exchange goods, information and ideas and to meet others (Lefebvre 1996: 81). Public space is protected because it is not subject to the price mechanism and hence, its use value for all represents a level of collective engagement and is part of the ideology of society as image and reality.

The growing multiplicity of connections, communication and information exchange plays a major role in organizing social activities through the public. It is the connective tissue of society *par excellence* through utterance of what happens in the street, strip malls, shopping centres and parks; through language that is expressed in gestures, clothing and the use of words, accents and idiomatic language by the inhabitants; through writing, particularly graffiti, about the city on the walls and other public places; and through signs, significant ensembles or super-objects of the city itself drawn from daily life (e.g. the safe city, the civic-minded citizen, hometown sports team, etc. symbolizing the city as place for living and collective endeavours) (ibid.: 115–16).

The manifold meanings of the public have particular importance both nationally and for the great capital cities. In the singular, it is always synonymous with the primacy of public life in all its complexity. Public space is one of the essential sites of political community, defined as the common activity of urban/national life in all its different facets – commerce, the family and work - connected by the shared experience that these communities construct and establish. Political community is also held together by the substantive idea of the common good. Common goods and services, shared values and democratic commitments resulting from city and national planning, local resources and the provision of public goods and services by local and national authorities are part of this. The public sphere also has its own defining characteristics. It is the idea of communal space for shared activity with common values and commitments. At a time of globalization the city is the prototype of social interaction in which commercial need is forced to accommodate the democratic life of the city. It requires the co-existence of the public and private realm and this interdependence masks the separate spheres of private need and public interest.

At the extreme, the post-modern 'edge/anti-city' is indeed a privileged site of consumerism, localism and statelessness. Decentralized, located near the inter-state freeway, organized around the ubiquitous shopping mall and motor

---

The resiliency of urban space at a time of globalization: Toronto's core public domain like that in many other capital cities remains a mixture of the public and private including

•   meeting places – churches, synagogues and community centres – often sharing the same locale

•   hospitals, schools, universities and colleges

•   marketplaces and districts to meet, buy and sell – Yonge and Bloor, The Danforth, Bathurst and Eglinton, St Clair Ave West, Spadina, Yonge and Eglinton

•   hangout malls like the Eaton Centre, Sheridan, Don Mills, Yorkdale

•   public squares and meeting places – Nathan Phillips Square, Harbourfront, Ontario Place, Mel Lastman Square, Queen's Park

•   bicycle paths, parks, jogging trails, ravines, places to sail and row along the lakefront, skating rinks and swimming pools, places to lawn bowl and have a match of petanque, picnic places and zoos

•   local parks in local neighbourhoods

•   flea markets, cinemas everywhere, art galleries and museums both private and public

•   police stations, firehalls and the post office etc.

•   public toilets and baths, municipal libraries, public housing, street-cleaning, snow-ploughing, community homes, drop-in centres of all varieties, non-profit day-care, creches, senior citizen apartments and co-op residences

•   parking lots, underground pedestrian walk-throughs, bus, train and plane stations and airports terminals, public transportation – subway, bus and streetcars

•   neighbourhood restaurants, cafes, pubs, local coffee and donut shops

•   sport teams and playgrounds

•   music, film and drama festivals and events

freeway, the edge city is the product of unregulated market forces and un-planning. There is no public space to act or initiate any new beginnings. Rather the anti-city has become a high security environment for the middle class because the US underclass has been 'enclosed' in the old inner cities. The 'official city' is a site of both diversity and contestation, as well as order and conformity.

In major cities, urban consciousness is marked by the fissures of class, race and exclusion but also strong popular identification with local and national communities through music, sports teams and local heroes. The strong sense of 'place' is the glue of urban reform movements everywhere to protect the city from outside forces. This is also, finally, why the cosmopolitan city is a mix of public and private engagements – a contested terrain of the civic. It is a place of pageants, spectacles, freedom and soli-darity that threatens the intimacy, privacy and established globalizing order. For many, the anonymity of the city is a protective skin with a weak sense of collective engagements of responsibility. For others, counter-cultural soli-daristic movements engender a powerful sense of civic and civil engagement against established authority.

Public discourse/a strong or weak public

In political theory, the public sphere is the site of debate, political life and public discourse. In Arendtian terms, it is the sphere of action as opposed to work or labour and is a privileged area 'where men act together in concert and where freedom can appear'. It is the quality site of life, not simply a way to have better roads and sidewalks (Benhabib 1990). For Arendt, public common space is essential to republican or civic virtue but is limited to dialogue, action, discussion, debate and argument, while issues of primary importance, such as labour and technology are relegated to the 'private' realm. Arendt's idealized notion corresponds then to a morally homogeneous but politically elite community whose action is relevant most often to the indi-vidual or small groups. Thus, the public sphere is largely removed from authoritative decision-making and is often only a testing ground of public opinion (Fraser 1999). Like Kant, her emphasis was on the need for a just and stable order and hence, the normative dimension and the emphasis on the rule of law and legality. The contrast between Arendt's notion of the public sphere and Habermas' is marked. He theorized public space in terms of the socialist-democratic discursive model of late capitalist society (1989). Unlike Arendt, the public sphere is not seen as a neutral meeting place for debate and discussion. For him, its principal virtue is that public life is seen as a series of collective engagements that are negotiated and change as the balance of social forces shift from the elites to the democratic end of empowerment. The merit of Habermas' public sphere is its radical indeterminacy and openness that conforms most to contemporary life that is being reshaped by the demands of the pro-democracy, anti-globalization social movement actors for accountability, transparency and openness nationally, no less internationally, in the practices of the World Bank and WTO.

Fukuyama defines civil society as the 'realm of spontaneously created social structures, separate from the state, that underlie democratic institutions. "Culture" is defined as phenomena such as family structure, religion, moral values, ethnic consciousness, "civic-ness" and particularlistic historical traditions' (Fukuyama 1995). As such, his expanded notion of the public sphere includes the private interests and needs that Arendt excluded in presupposing a sharp separation of civil society and the state.

These transnational networks of competing moral values, environmental conciousness, civicness have not reulted in over-arching agreement about the public realm and the common good. In part this is because there is no single coherent left-right political agenda in the way there once was. The political spectrum used to be organized around left and right poles. On income distribution, the left wanted a lot and the right as little as politically feasible; on the role of the state versus private ownership, the left believed in a large role for government and the right advocated a large and expanding role for private ownership. With respect to labour protection, the left advocated strong labour enhancing measures and entitlements, while the right wanted only minimal standards and practices. In terms of property rights, the left always gave a limited reading where the right advocated a strong belief in property rights. Finally the intellectual left has always championed restricting markets in favour of strong regulatory controls, while the academic right believed in the maximum room for markets to flourish with the state as an instrument of last resort (Cable 1995).

So what has changed? In many forums, identity politics now cuts across this once fixed and rock-solid political, undercutting any sharp left/right divide of times past. Identity politics is organized around a different set of issues and concerns. The most important are the group versus the individual with respect to gender, race and ethnicity. Identity politics is about minorities seeking self-determination against established majorities, as in Quebec, Scotland and Spain. In a global context, identity politics has redefined cultural policy along with the rights of people to restrict the movement of global capital and halt the intrusiveness of trade agreements, regionally and globally. Much of modern identity politics are defined by the continuing conflict and repeated clashes between religion and secularism. At the political level, its strongest expression occurs in federal states where devolution, rather than new initiatives for centralization, is now the order of the day.

Without the familiar left/right political markers, it is more difficult, than at any time in the past, to have a viable notion of the public good. We are at one of those infrequent cross-roads where there is a strong articulated desire for both larger and stronger national governments, as well as states that are smaller fiscally and more accountable. So far, there is no social consensus on how to reconcile these opposing tendencies; only the beginning of one. John Ruggie, one of the most original scholars on state practice and international power, reminds us that the rise of the modern nation-state required wholesale change in the mental equipment that people drew upon in imagining a different political community of an expanded public realm and lived experience (Ruggie 1993: 157). To flourish in a globalized world, nation-states have to learn to adapt to a different fundament entirely – a planet where the spatial dimension of political sovereignty and state power are more important than ever, but under radically different conditions from the immediate past. Here the common condition sought by global free trade is the contentious idea of people enlarging their freedom through investment rights and by living in a world that is self-created, not state-dominated. Even if the state is not about to fade away, powerful public and private entities are intent on changing our fundamental preoccupation with territoriality, identity and publicness.

Social capital – collective networks of trust and reciprocity

In the post-national state of the 1990s, social capital is increasingly considered to be a 'new' public good. However, the collective engagement of responsibility has long been part of Western democratic values. Many of these non-traded goods are non-transferable public freedoms, rights and public accountability (Perroux 1962; Albert 1993). Social capital, including collective engagements of solidarity, trust and legitimacy, epitomizes the commitment of the collective need to enhance social cohesion. Rights of the citizen, delimiting trade agreements and divergent social practices, at a time of increased social polarization, are part of the social process globalizing the *civitas*. Devolution of decision-making, the delivery of services at the city level and new information flows at a time of spatial and class polarization, all depend on networks, *à la* Putnam to promote trust. Putnam defines social capital as 'referring to features of social organization, such as networks, norms, and trust, that facilitates coordination and cooperation for mutual benefit' (Putnam 1993: 35–6). Individual engagements of responsibility reflect the depoliticization and breakdown in social cohesion that has progressed furthest in the US.

By contrast, collective engagements of responsibility, such as bonds of social solidarity, have been important in influencing public opinion to oppose government cutbacks. They have also served as a brake on the state's attempts to dismantle redistributive welfare arrangements. Social capital can be understood as political freedom, the right of association and the right to security. It has always been strongly connected with the emerging challenge to political authority and extending voice to the voiceless, increasing individual choice, creating agency at the margin and extending knowledge and contact for the powerless. What then does this complex notion convey theoretically about the increasing tension between markets, territory and identity?

The delusion of global capitalism is, in the words of John Gray, that 'encumbered markets are the norm in every society, whereas free markets are a product of artifice, design and political coercion'. The free market is not, as New Right thinkers have imagined or claimed, a gift of social evolution. It is an end-product of social engineering and unyielding political will. It was feasible in nineteenth-century England only because, and for so long as, 'functioning democratic institutions were lacking' (Gray 1998: 17). Still, there is much that needs clarification and empirical verification regarding the relationship between the public domain, state practices and markets. The design and make-up of public domains in contrasting market economies need to be empirically studied because public domain issues will continue to frame public policy debate in critical ways.

First, during a time of perceived declining sovereignty, the decline of civic capital has been a growing concern in many societies, a concern not readily addressed in economics-dominated public choice policy circles (Putnam 1993; Dahrendorf 1995). Yet, it is far from clear that civic capital has really diminished in market economies. Taking stock of what remains is a priority. In particular, auditing the 'residual' public space and domains in the north-south polarization of the globalizing world will require looking at the emergence of public domains in economically developing jurisdictions.

Second, at a time when governments are wrestling with the issue of the optimal size of the state, strategies of administrative reform have been used to bring about the commercialization of many government services in *laissez-faire* economies. Monetarism, in its many different forms, has been adopted as the policy fundamental for governments in surprisingly diverse political contexts (Williamson 1994). As well, many public enterprises have been put on a private sector footing or fully privatized. This has also occurred in European social market economies. In addition, there has been a considerable outsourcing of government functions. Much rhetoric prevails with regard to these controversial initiatives. Have these shifts gone too far (Hutton 1996)? To what extent have privatization and outsourcing reshaped the public domain, particularly in its consequences for social exclusion and undermining social cohesion?

Third, cutting back government services and state functions, by outsourcing, has made public authority dependent on external provision to a degree that needs close scrutiny. What have public policy officials learned about the functionality and dysfunctionality of fifteen years of privatization in the public realm? While the complete privatization of all the government's technical services is an extreme example of this tendency, it raises the larger issue of identifying the core functions of the state in contrasting market economies, including the *laissez-faire* Anglo-American model, the social market model and the model for developing countries. One hypothesis is that outsourcing can be construed as a form of de-skilling the public sector. If this is the case, does it presage the redesign of a smaller but smarter state with capabilities for learning and innovation? Or does it presage the emergence of the 'Kmart' state, with a narrow commercial orientation, ill-equipped to manage the complex needs of adjustment at a time of a highly volatile global economy (Drache 1996)?

The generic idea of the public domain has always been a powerful mainstream and alternative discourse that empowers individuals and groups. It is a narrative of potentiality and collective action because of the assets, experiences, places and concerns people share in common. The public domain is a key factor protecting and reinforcing social cohesion in the face of relentless market demands, which intrude on the world outside the market. In a primary sense, it always has a strong element of delimiting investment rights and ensuring that markets have a broad social purpose. As well, it highlights a view of public life and action that is not state-centred but is quite independent of it, even if the moving boundaries of the public domain are often dependent on the state for public services paid for out of public revenues. At a time when big government has appropriated the concept of the public for its own needs and agendas, the public domain represents a new grammar of policy conduct or what has been called 'tougher notions of public space'.

Public domains have long underpinned social and economic development and been a pivotal force for the state and no less for the market. Within a glob-alized world, public domain activities are becoming more significant in the core economic jurisdictions, as well as in many developing and advanced states that are having to confront globalization and a range of intractable distributional issues. International organizations, like the WTO, stress the need for trans-parency and rule of law, both of which require a strengthened civic order. For society to function smoothly, public authority in many contrasting jurisdictions will be increasingly under pressure to exercise its supervisory role 'when there are no other strong social values to compete with that of money and wealth' (Albert 1993: 104). If Albert's principal assumption is valid, public authority will be hesitant about transferring many of its prerogatives to the private sector. Indeed, there are many pressures forcing states to rethink the balance that society must strike with the market.

Society has always had need of well-constructed institutions where the rules and principles of contending interests can reconcile conflicting parties without giving any single group the power to make their views and interests always prevail over those of all others. Today there are many areas of public life where the need to limit the intrusion of markets is already on the public's agenda. The information revolution and associated problems of the public's right to know has raised the expectation that the information commons will be a sanctuary outside of the market. Product standards for food, environmental regulation and, potentially, labour standards are being pushed for by NGOs, nationally and globally. The public increasingly looks to government to exercise its fiduciary responsibilities and protect the environment from the needs of short-term wealth creation (see Table 1.3). Volatile financial markets, flexible and mobile manufacturing strategies, and 'social dumping' by corporations are requiring states to develop pro-active policy responses to manpower planning and labour market practices (OECD 1994).

In many domains the fundamental notion of the citizen has been transformed into a passive, consuming client of state services. This transformation distorts democratic expectations and obligations in serious ways. Increasingly, electorates are critical of their government's failure to reform its practices and address the costs of social exclusion (Hutton 1996; Dahrendorf 1995). The dysfunctional

Table 1.3 The emergence of the public domain at the global level: major environmental treaties and conventions

Treaty or convention	Date formulated*	Place	Number of signatories and ratifiers
Antarctic Treaty	1959	Washington, DC	39
Nuclear Test Ban in the Atmosphere, Outer Space and Under Water	1963	Moscow	120
Wetlands of International Importance	1971	Ramsar, Iran	84
Prohibition of Biological and Toxic Weapons	1972	London, Moscow, Washington, DC	122
Protection of World Cultural and Natural Heritage	1972	Paris	120
Prevention of Marine Pollution by Dumping	1972	London, Mexico, Moscow, Washington DC	73
International Trade in Endangered Species	1973	Washington, DC	111
Prevention of Pollution from Ships	1978	London	65
Transboundary Air Pollution (Europe)**	1979	Geneva	29
Conservation of Migratory Species	1979	Bonn	47
Conservation of Antarctic Marine Life	1980	Canberra	27
UN Law of the Sea	1982	Montego Bay, Jamaica	126
Vienna Convention Protecting the Ozone Layer	1985	Vienna	103
Early Notification of Nuclear Accident	1986	Vienna	80
Assistance for a Nuclear Accident	1986	Vienna	82
Montreal Protocol on the Ozone Layer***	1987	Montreal	96
Control of Transboundary Hazardous Waste	1989	Basel	58
Convention on Biological Diversity	1992	Nairobi	140
Convention of Climate Change	1993	New York	143

Source: Todd Sandler (1997).
Notes:
*The date formulated does not correspond to the date on which the treaty goes into effect.
**Four protocols putting limits on emission were subsequently formulated to curb sulphur and nitrogen oxide emissions. Tough limits on sulphur emissions have been incorporated in the 1994 Oslo Protocol to strengthen the Helsinki Protocol.
***Future protocols mandated the elimination of emissions by 2000.

behaviour of markets and the need to reinforce the role of intermediary institutions that limit the power of markets over people brings us full circle.

As an economic principle, the public domain emerges as a robust idea involving public goods problems, despite the fact they have fared poorly at the hands of the neo-classical framework. Public goods have always been a social necessity and socially constructed, but the precise relationship between non-negotiable goods, mixed goods and negotiable goods is inevitably complex, difficult to untangle and not well understood. Market failure is but one catalyst for action and explains little about public goods and the need for effective public goods structures (Cornes and Sandler 1994). Establishing practical forms of collectivism that are binding on private actors, rather than a pseudo-individualistic analysis of society, remains the principle challenge. This too explains why theoretical debate on the public domain is of signal importance. It corrects the mistaken idea that the public domain – the activities and assets that are held in common – is purely public.

Theoretically, it has always been apparent that this social–legal form of public space is an entanglement of public and private interest, that is, neither wholly public nor entirely private. This is why the emergent notion of the public domain is so rich and challenging. At a time of unparalleled global free trade, public space is a valuable resource, that government and society can find ways to use, for the community as a whole. Deepening, broadening and preserving these inter-generational resources is the challenge for public policy-makers everywhere. In its many reiterations, the assets shared in common are created when the price mechanism of the market and the regulatory power of the state clash and compete. If properly understood, strong public domains enable local and national communities to take defensive measures against powerfully anchored global forces.

The public domain has not always existed in its present form. It was created in the nineteenth century as part of a larger political project that was to enhance the security of the elites and be a privileged site of the middle classes. With the passage of time it has been democratized and transformed in ways that few could have predicted. The pivotal question for today is what determines where the markers lie between the public and private? Historically, the public domain has always expanded and contracted as civil society and the market have each sought to appropriate the assets held in common for strikingly different ends. More than ever, the end of the Cold War raises these fundamental issues again – what is private and what is public? In the short term, this pivotal issue will continue to dominate public debate everywhere because all societies require a wide variety of social goods and protective measures to address their needs and the allocative failures of markets.

Today there is no agreement to replace the Washington consensus. Psychologically, elites world-wide remain convinced, despite much evidence to the contrary, that there is no alternative – the TINA mentality. Yet, as we have seen, there is not one, but a range of alternatives on offer. As policy-makers revisit the fundamentals of governance through the prism of the public domain, there are some grounds for optimism. The public domain is an older concept of political economy that supplies civil society with its vitality and much of its organizational capacity. Building state capacity, revitalizing public institutions, promoting collective goals and empowering citizens, all require an activist state model.

For this singular reason, the public sphere is, first and foremost, always a place for the collective sharing of achievement. It is also fundamentally about the individual's freedom to come and go, the right of association, the right to secu-rity and, more than anything else, political freedom as much as commercial freedom. Public space is designed, as Michael Walzer perceptively noted some years ago, for a hundred different transactions and hundreds of interactions without which public life, civic culture and everyday chitchat would not exist. Those who use it have acquired a sense of ownership and ready access to it. It has to be attractive enough to draw people out of their private worlds and self-indulgent life-styles. The policy challenge is to erect strong barriers against the market intrusiveness into the public domain. New bench-marking ideas are needed to redraw the line between the state and the market and restore the public's confidence in what is ours. There is much to be done, and time is short, to broaden the 'terrain left between private holdings'.

Notes

1   Special thanks to Kyle Grayson for his statistical research and for preparing the tables on government spending and the growth of exports. Harry Arthurs, Daniel Latouche, Richard Higgott, Mike McCracken and Inge Kaul gave useful feedback and criticism at different times during the writing of this draft. Evelyn Ruppert and Engin Isin helped conceptualize the urban dimension in particular. Cheryl Dobinson made an important difference with her editing skills. An earlier draft of this paper was prepared for an international conference organized by the Instituto de Ciencia Politica, Universidad de Chile y del Area de Estudios Norteamericanos, ILPES (Naciones Unidas Instituo Latino Americano y del Caribe de Planificacion Economia Y Social) and the Robarts Centre for Canadian Studies, York University, Toronto, Canada, 'Revisiting The Fundamentals of Economic Liberalism – The Return of the Public Domain in Era of Globalization – A Comparative Examination of Canada and Chile, 19–20 April 1999 in Santiago, Chile.

2   Measures used: *General Government Total Outlays*, made up of current disbursements (i.e., final consumption expenditure, debt interest payments, rents and royalties, subsidies and transfers paid) plus capital expenditure (i.e. gross fixed capital forma-tion, increases in stocks, net purchases of land and intangible assets, net capital transfers). Exports of goods and services (excluding financial transfers) + imports of goods and services (excluding financial transfers) = international trade. Note: all three were measured as a percentage of GDP in current prices

Definitions of categories: *Social Market countries* – Austria, France, Germany, Italy, Sweden. *G7 countries* – Canada, France, Germany, Italy, Japan, United Kingdom, United States. *European countries* – Austria, Belgium, Denmark, France, Germany, Italy, Netherlands, Sweden, United Kingdom. Sources: *United Nations National Accounts Statistics: Main Aggregates and Detailed Tables*, 1952, 1959, 1973, 1985, 1996 and *OECD Analytic Databank*.

3   Economists have statistical tests, such as a scattergram to discover just how strongly correlated trade and investment is to government spending. This is one way to

measure whether finance-centred globalization is building a world order on the ruins of the once-powerful national economies. The scattergram and Rsq measure demonstrate that international trade explains 88 per cent of the variance (i.e. changes) in government outlays for the G7 countries as a group (the group part is very important). This measure shows us that trade would seem to have stimulated outlays but that technically the Rsq measure does not fully demonstrate that relationship. What can be said is that there is a very strong relationship between increased trade openness and government spending.

4   Of course, there are major differences between national regimes and between high and low spenders. What seems to be the determinant are eligibility requirements. A full-scale welfare regime defines this broadly and a more narrowly conceived one makes the individual responsible for his economic well-being. In 1992, in The Netherlands, 12.7 per cent of trend GDP was spent on transfers to the working-age population; in sharp contrast the figure for Japan was 1.2 per cent. Even these figures have to be taken with a grain of salt because tax systems also have a strong redistributive effect on low-income and high-income earners.

5   The Washington consensus was seen to be comprehensive but it left open many critical areas of macro-management where countries could pursue their own policies. Areas of non-agreement included the stabilization of the business cycle, the proportion of the GDP spent by the public sector and social policy, the need to eliminate indexation and the usefulness of incomes policy and wage/price freezes. Not surprising public authority chose to interpret its broad objectives so dissimilarly.

Bibliography

Adema, Willem and Einerhand, Marcel (1998) 'Labour Market and Social Policy. Occasional Papers no. 32 The Growing Role of Private Social Benefits', *Directorate for Education, Employment and Social Affairs, OECD, DEELSA/ELSA/WD(98)*, 3: 1–55.

Albert, Michael (1993) *Capitalism vs Capitalism*, New York: Four Wall Eight Windows.

Arendt, Hannah (1958) *The Human Condition*, Chicago, IL: University of Chicago Press.

Bannock, Graham, Baxter, R.E. and Davis, Evan (1998) *Penguin Dictionary of Economics*, 6th edn, London: Penguin.

Benhabib, Seyla (1990) 'Hannah Arendt and the Redemptive Power of Narrative', *Social Research*, 57 (1): 167–96.

Benjamin, Roger W. (1980) *The Limits of Politics: Collective Goods and Political Change in Postindustrial Societies*, Chicago, IL: University of Chicago Press.

Bergsten, Fred (1996) 'Globalizing Free Trade', *Foreign Affairs*, 75, 3 (May/June): 105–20.

Boyer, Robert (1998) 'Etat, Marche et Developpement: Une Nouvelle Synthese Pour le XXI siecle?', *CEPREMAP, CNRS Paris*, 98 (Novembre).

Boyer, Robert and Drache, Daniel (ed.) (1996) *States Against Markets: The Limits of Globalization*, London: Routledge.

Breton, Albert (1995) *Competitive Governments: An Economic Theory of Politics and Public Finance*, New York: Cambridge University Press.

Buchanan, James M. (1975) *The Limits of Liberty: Between Anarchy and Leviathan*, Chicago, IL: The University of Chicago Press.

Cable, Vincent (1995) 'The Diminished Nation-State: A Study in the Loss of Economic Power', *Daedalus*, 124, 2: 23–53.

Calhoun, Craig, (ed.) (1993) *Habermas and the Public Sphere*, Cambridge, MA: The MIT Press.

Carter, Michael, Cason, Jeffery and Zimmerman, Frederic (ed.) (1997) *Development at a Crossroads: Uncertain Paths To Sustainability After the Neo-Liberal Revolution*, Madison WI: Global Studies Program, University of Wisconsin-Madison.

Clark, J. (1995) 'The State, Popular Participation, and the Voluntary Sector', *World Development*, 23 (April): 593–603.

Coase, Ronald H. (1960) 'The Problem of Social Cost', *Journal of Law and Economics*, 3: 1–44.

Colm, Gerhard (1956) 'Comments on Samuelson's Theory of Public Finance', *Review of Economics and Statistics*, 38 (4): 408–12.

Cornes, Richard and Sandler, Todd (1994) 'Are Public Goods Myths?', *Journal of Theoretical Politics*, 6, 3: 369–85.

Crouch, Colin and Streeck, Wolfgang (eds) (1997) *Political Economy of Modern Capitalism: Mapping Convergence and Diversity*, London: Sage.

Dahrendorf, Ralf (1995) 'A Precarious Balance: Economic Opportunity, Civil Society and Political Liberty', *The Responsive Community*, Summer: 13–38.

Dasgupta, Partha (1993) *An Inquiry into Well-Being and Destitution*, Oxford: Clarendon Press.

Denoyer, Jean Francois (1969) *L'Exploitation du domain public*, Paris: Librairie generale de droit et de jurisprudence.

Devetak, Richard and Higgott, Richard (1999) 'Justice Unbound? Globalization, States and the Transformation of the Social Bond', Centre for the Study of Globalisation and Regionalisation, Working Paper No. 29/99.

Drache, Daniel (1996) 'From Keynes to K-mart: Competitiveness in a Corporate Age', in Robert Boyer and Daniel Drache (eds) *States Against Markets: The Limits of Globalization*, London: Routledge.

—— (2000) 'In Search of North America. Do Borders Matter Any Longer? Wuz Up?', Robarts Centre for Canadian Studies, www.robarts.yorku.ca (accessed 11 April 2001).

Drache, Daniel and Sullivan, Terry (eds) (1999) *Health Reform: Public Success, Private Failure*, London: Routledge.

ECLAC (2000) *Social Panorma*, Santiago: United Nations.

Eden, Lorraine and Osler Hampson, Fen (1997) 'Clubs are Trump: The Formation of International Regimes in the Absence of a Hegemon', in J. Rogers Hollingsworth and Robert Boyer (eds) *Contemporary Capitalism: The Embeddedness of Institutions*, London: Cambridge University Press.

Employment in Europe (1998) Brussels: EU, L/2985.

Evans, Peter (1997) 'The Eclipse of the State? Reflections on Stateness in an Era of Globalization', *World Politics*, 50 (October): 62–87.

Ferrera, Maurizo, Hemerijck, Anton and Rhodes, Martin (2000) 'The Future of Social Europe: Recasting Work and Welfare in the New Economy', Report for the Portuguese Presidency of the European Union, Brussels.

Fortin, Pierre (1996) 'The Great Canadian Slump', *Canadian Journal of Economics*, XXIX (November): 761–88.

Fraser, Nancy (1999) *Justice Interruptus: Critical Reflections on the 'Post Socialist' Condition*, New York: Routledge.

Fukuyama, Francis (1995) 'The Primacy of Culture', *Journal of Democracy*, January.

Giddens, Anthony (1998) *The Third Way*, London: Polity Press.

Gray, John (1998) *False Dawn: The Delusions of Global Capitalism*, London: Granta.

Habermas, Jürgen (1989) *The Structural Transformation of the Public Sphere: An Inquiry into a Category of Bourgeois Society*, Cambridge, MA: The MIT Press.

Hanson, Albert Henry (1959) *Public Enterprise and Economic Development*, London: Routledge and Kegan Paul.

Hayek, F.A. (1949). *Individualism and Economic Order*, London: Routledge and Kegan Paul.

Hirschman, Albert (1977) *The Passions and the Interests Political Arguments for Capitalism before its Triumph*, Princeton, NJ: Princeton University Press.

—— (1982) 'Rival Interpretations of Market Society: Civilizing, Destructive, or Feeble?', *Journal of Economic Literature*, 20 (December): 1463–84.

Hodgson, Geoffrey M. (1998) 'The Approach of Institutional Economics', *Journal of Economic Literature*, 36 (March): 166–92.

Hutton, Will (ed.) (1996) *The Stakeholder Society: The Ideas that Shaped Post War Britain*, London: Fontana.

Jacobs, Jane (1984) *Cities and the Wealth of Nations*, New York: Random House.

Jenson, Jane (1998) 'Mapping Social Cohesion', CPRN Study No. F\03 Ottawa.

Kaul, Inge, Grunberg, Isabelle and Stern, Marc A. (eds) (1999) *Global Public Goods International Co-operation in the 21st Century*, New York: Oxford University Press.

Keane, John (1998) *Civil Society Old Images, New Visions*, London: Polity Press.

Krasinitz, Philip (ed.) (1995) *Metropolis: Centre and Symbol of Our Times*, New York: New York University Press.

Kuntsler, J.H. (1996) *Home From Nowhere*, New York: Simon Schuster.

Latin American and Caribbean Institute for Economic and Social Planning (ILPES) (1998) *Reflections on Development and the Responsibility of the State*, Santiago, Chile: UN/ECLAC.

Lefebvre, Henri (1996) *Writings on Cities*, Eleonore Kofman and Elizabeth Lebas, trans. and ed, London: Blackwell.

MacFarlan, Maitland and Oxley, Howard (1996) 'Social Transfers: Spending Patterns, Institutional Arrangements and Policy Responses', *OECD Economic Studies*, 27, 1996/II.

Marquand, David (1988) *The Unprincipled Society*, London: Jonathan Cape.

Mattoso, Jorge (2000) 'Globalization, Deregulation and Labour: A Challenge for Work and Social Citizenship in Brazil', *Work and Social Citizenship in a Global Economy*, Madison, WI, November.

Mumford, Lewis (1961) *The City in History Its Origins, Its Transformations, and Its Prospects*, New York: Harcourt Brace.

—— (1986) *The Lewis Mumford Reader*, Donald L. Miller (ed), New York: Pantheon.

Musgrave, Richard and Musgrave, Peggy B. (1984) *Public Finance in Theory and Practice*, 4th edn, New York: McGraw Hill.

OECD (1994) *The OECD Jobs Study*, Paris: OECD.

—— (1998) *Open Markets Matter: The Benefits of Trade and Investment Liberalization*, Paris: OECD.

Olson, Mancur (1982) *The Rise and Decline of Nations*, New Haven, CT: Yale University Press.

Ostry, Slyvia (1998) 'Globalization and the Nation-State: Erosion From Above', Timlin Lecture, University of Saskatchewan, Regina.

Perroux, Francois (1950) 'Economic Space: Theory and Applications', *Quarterly Journal of Economics*, 64, 1: 89–104.

—— (1962) *Le Capitalisme*, Paris: Que Sais-Je?.

Polanyi, Karl (1957) *The Great Transformation*, Boston, MA: Beacon Hill.

Prebisch, R. (1971) *Change and Development: Latin America's Great Task. Report to the Inter-American Development Bank*, New York: Praeger.

Putnam, Robert (1993) 'The Prosperous Community: Social Capital and Public Life', *The American Prospect*, 4, 13, Washington.

Rhodes, Martin (1999) 'Globalization and European Welfare: Is There a "Third Way" for the Public Domain?', *Governing the Public Domain Beyond the Era of the Washington Consensus?*, Redrawing the Line between the State and the Market, Robarts Centre for Canadian Studies, York University, Toronto, 4–6 November 1999.

Rodrik, Dani (1997) *Has Globalization Gone Too Far?*, Washington, DC: Institute for International Economics.

Rosecrance, Richard (1996) 'The Rise of the Virtual State', *Foreign Affairs*, 75, 4 (July/August): 45–61.

Ruggie, John (1993) 'Territoriality and Beyond: Problematizing Modernity in International Relations', *International Organization*, 47, 1, Winter.

Ruigrok, Winfried and Tulder, Rob van (1995) *The Logic of International Restructuring*, London/New York: Routledge.

Sandler, Todd (1997) *Global Challenges An Approach to Environmental, Political, and Economic Problems*, London: Cambridge University Press.

Samuelson, Paul A. (1954) 'The Pure Theory of Public Expenditure', *Review of Economics and Statistics*, 37 (4): 387–9.

Sassen, Saskia (1998) *Globalization and its Discontents*, New York: The New Press.

Schonfield, Andrew (1964) *Modern Capitalism*, London: Oxford University Press.

Schultze, Charles L. (1977) *The Public Use of Private Interest*, Washington, DC: Brookings Institution.

Sennett, Richard (1977) *The Fall of Public Man*, New York: Alfred A. Knopf.

Squires, Judith (1994) Ordering the City Public Spaces and Public Participation. *The Lesser Evil and the Greater Good: The Theory and Politics of Social Diversity*. Weeks, Jeffrey, Rivers Oram Press: 79–99.

Stiglitz, Joseph E. (1988) *The Economics of the Public Sector*, New York: W.W. Norton and Company.

—— (1991) 'Government, Financial Markets, and Economic Development', *NBER Working Paper*, 3669 (April).

Strange, Susan (1996) *The Retreat of the State: The Diffusion of Power in the World Economy*, Cambridge: Cambridge University Press.

United Nations (1999) *Trade and Development Report*, New York: United Nations.

United Nations, Department of Technical Co-operation for Development (1986) *Economic Performance of Public Enterprises: Major Issues and Strategies for Action*, New York: United Nations.

Villa, Dana R. (1992) 'Postmodernism and the Public Sphere', *American Political Science Review*, 86 (3): 712–21.

Walzer, Michael (1986) 'Pleasures and Costs of Urbanity', *Dissent*, fall; reprinted (1995) in Philip Krasinitz (ed), *Metropolis: Centre and Symbol of Our Times*, New York: New York University Press: pp. 320–30.

Weintraub, Jeff (1995) 'Varieties and Vissitudes of Public Space', in Philip Krasinitz (ed), *Metropolis: Centre and Symbol of Our Times*, New York: New York University Press, pp. 280–319.

Williamson, John (ed.) (1994) *The Political Economy of Policy Reform*, Washington, DC: Institute for International Economics.

—— (1999) 'What Should the Bank Think About the Washington Consensus?', prepared as a background to the World Bank's World Development Report 2000, World Bank, July 1999, Institute for International Economics, www.iie.com/testimony/bankwc.htm (accessed - 03.05.01)

World Bank (1997) *World Bank Development Report 1997: The State in a Changing World*, New York: Oxford University Press.

Zukin, Sharon (1995) *The Cultures of Cities*, Cambridge, MA: Blackwell.

2   Reinventing Gladstone?

The public conscience and the public domain

David Marquand

In an article in the *Nineteenth Century* in January 1887, not long after the defeat of the first Home Rule Bill, Gladstone looked back on the lessons of his long career. He drew comfort from,

> a silent but more extensive and practical acknowledgement of the great second commandment, of the duties of wealth to poverty, of strength to weakness, of knowledge to ignorance, in a word of man to man. And the sum of the matter seems to be that upon the whole, and in a degree, we who lived fifty, sixty, seventy years back, and are living now, have lived into a gentler time; that the public conscience has grown more tender, as indeed was very needful; and that, in matters of practice, at sight of evils formerly regarded with indifference or even connivance, it now not only winces but rebels.
>
> (Matthew 1995: 85)

In this essay I try to re-examine the growth of the public domain in the nineteenth and early twentieth centuries; to suggest possible explanations for its erosion in the final decades of the twentieth century; and to sketch out the rudiments of a public philosophy which might provide the intellectual and cultural underpinning for its renewal in the twenty-first. Gladstone's *Nineteenth Century* evocation of the 'great second commandment' provides an ideal starting point.

Great transformations

Fifty years ago, Karl Polanyi depicted what he famously described as the 'great transformation' of the nineteenth century as a kind of pendulum, that swung from the harsh *laissez-faire* capitalism of the start of the century to increasing public regulation later (Polanyi 1957). As he described it, the process was almost automatic. The self-regulating free market of the *laissez-faire* theorists of the early nineteenth century was a 'utopia'. It logically entailed the commodification of land and labour. This was an impossibility, since in reality land and labour are not commodities like any other. The 'utopia' was thus profoundly unnatural. It was not a spontaneous product of unfettered human instinct, as its apologists claimed. On the contrary, massive state interventions, pushed through by a ruthless and centralized bureaucracy, were needed to impose it on the old society and to uproot the old value-system that impeded it. The interventions did not succeed. They could not, because the utopia they were designed to institute was an impossibility. But that did not mean that they had no results at all. On the contrary, they produced a social and cultural disaster which eventually provoked a spontaneous reaction against the free-market utopia, as society began to protect itself from the dislocation it had brought in its train. This reaction, however, was instinctive, almost blind, and utterly unideological. Theories, doctrines, and even principles had no place in Polanyi's explanatory schema. Nor had political leadership or the mobilization of opinion. As he put it himself, 'The legislative spearhead of the counter-movement against a self-regulating market ... turned out to be spontaneous, undirected by opinion and actuated by a purely pragmatic spirit' (Polanyi 1957: 141).

Polanyi's description of the course of events in nineteenth-century Britain still carries conviction, but his notion that a mysterious entity called Society, with a capital 'S', spontaneously embarked on a process of self-protection, in which the beliefs of human agents played no part, now seems curiously thin and oversimplified. And this, I suggest, is where Gladstone comes into the argument. Like Polanyi, he was trying to account for a transformation: in his case for the marked growth of social 'benevolence' which he believed to have characterized his lifetime. But for him, belief was central to the whole process. There was nothing automatic about it. The social evils which had been connived at in his youth and early manhood were being tackled because real people in real places had come to believe that wealth had a duty to poverty and strength to weakness: because of a change in the 'public conscience'.

Neither Gladstone nor Polanyi used the term 'public domain', but I don't think it is fanciful to suggest that the transformations they discussed can both be subsumed under that heading: that Gladstone's growth in benevolence and Polanyi's counter-movement against early capitalism are best understood as aspects of the emergence of a distinct public domain, marked off from the private domain of friendship and kinship and also from the market domain of what Adam Smith called 'truck, barter and exchange' (Smith 1976: 17). To put the point in another way, the growth of the public domain pushed back the frontiers of the over-extended market domain. The social damage which the market imperialism of the early nineteenth century had brought in its train was corrected – or at least mitigated – because the public domain grew in this way.

Definitions

Here, some definitions are in order. The public domain, as I shall use the term, should not be confused with the public sector. In Britain, at any rate, the public sector grew fairly slowly until the end of the nineteenth century. Government expenditure as a proportion of GNP was lower in 1900 than it had been in 1831, and in absolute terms it did not grow very much until the decade of the 1890s (Greenleaf 1983: 33). Indeed, the public domain should not be seen as a 'sector' at all. It is best understood as an area of social life, with its own norms and decision rules, cutting across sectoral boundaries: as a set of activities, which can be (and historically have often been) carried out by private individuals or even private firms as well as by public agencies. Central to it are the values of citizenship, equity and service and the notion of a public interest, distinct from private interests. In it, citizenship rights trump both market power and kinship bonds. Professional pride in a job well done, a sense of civic duty, Gladstone's 'benevolence' or a mixture of all of them replace the hope of gain and the fear of loss as spurs to action. As the Dahrendorf Commission put it,

> The private world of love and friendship, and the market world of interest and incentive, are not the only dimensions of human life in society. There is a public domain with its own values. In the public domain people act neither out of the kindness of their hearts, nor in response to incentives, monetary or otherwise, but because they have a sense of serving the community.
>
> (1995: 39)

That, of course, is an ideal. It is not always realized in practice. But that does not mean that is in some way unreal or ineffective: the same applies to the norms of the market domain and the private domain. Though sellers sometimes collude to do down buyers, and parents sometimes abuse their children, no one could pretend that the market and private domains are in some sense normless. The important point is that the ideal is distinct and, so to speak, autonomous: that the norms governing behaviour in the public domain, and the principles that determine how its goods should be distributed and its personnel rewarded necessarily differ from the norms and principles of the market and private domains. In the private domain, loyalty to friends and family is a (perhaps *the*) supreme virtue. In the public domain, it is not. E.M. Forster's famous assertion that he would rather betray his country than his friends was shocking because he had applied the norms of the private domain to a domain where they do not belong. Favouritism and nepotism are shocking for the same reason. To introduce the values of the private domain into the public domain is, in a profound sense, to corrupt it. It is equally shocking, because equally corrupting, to introduce market norms into the public domain. That is why it is a crime to buy and sell votes or public offices or justice. In the market domain, goods and services are – quite properly – commodities to be bought and sold. The price mechanism allocates resources, including labour; in principle at least, free competition ensures that they are allocated efficiently. But votes, public offices and justice belong to the public domain. And because they belong to the public domain they must not be commodified.

At this point, re-enter the transformations discussed by Gladstone and

Polanyi. The notion of a public domain goes hand in hand with the notion of a public interest. A public domain can take shape only when it is generally believed that there is, or ought to be, a public interest, in principle distinguishable from private interests. In most of medieval and early-modern Europe there could be no public domain because the notion of a public interest did not exist. (It did, of course, exist in city-states like those of Renaissance Italy and the Hanseatic League, and their public domains were remarkably vibrant.) Mostly, however, there was only a private domain and a market domain – the utopia of Mrs Thatcher. The distinction between the sovereign as a human person and the sovereign as the embodiment of public power did not, and could not, exist. Apart from any other reasons, there was no language in which to make it. Public offices were bought and sold. What would now be called nepotism was a mark of loyalty to clan or dependants or neighbourhood and, as such, a virtue. The nearest approximation to the norms of the public domain were to be found in a partially meritocratic Church, whose services were, in principle, available on equal terms to all believers and whose priests were deliberately freed of family ties – though, in practice, there was plenty of nepotism even there.

The Victorian achievement

In Britain, the public domain proper started to emerge in the eighteenth century, but it was not firmly established until well into the nineteenth. The great achievement of Victorian Britain, however, was to carve out an unmistakable public domain from the adjacent private and market domains, and to erect strong barriers against their inevitable incursions into it. That was the inner meaning of the gradual destruction of the networks of clientelism and patronage, which reformers denounced as 'Old Corruption' and of the growth of public regulation which accompanied it. The Reform Acts, the Ballot Act, the Northcote-Trevleyan reforms in public administration, the abolition of the sale of commissions in the army, the creation of the Public Accounts Committee, the factory and public health acts, the Alkali Act and the municipalization of public utilities in the great northern cities were all milestones in this process. (Gladstone, it is worth remembering, thought seriously of making railway nationalization another milestone.) Gladstonian liberalism – an extraordinary amalgam of social and economic liberalism, held together by a stubborn belief that it was possible to mobilize opinion in the cause of a public interest transcending the private interests of those who were mobilized – was, in a very profound sense, both parent and child of the emerging public domain and of the value system associated with it. In part, this amalgam operated through the central state. The reform of the civil service, the abolition of the right to purchase commissions in the army, the factory acts and the Ballot Act – all, in different ways, crucial to the emergence of a public domain governed by non-market principles – were the products of government intervention. But private initiatives by professional associations, churches, chapels, friendly societies, individual philanthropists, cooperatives and trade unions were almost as important. So was the 'gas and water socialism' of vigorous local authorities dominated by 'benevolent' local elites.

In the high noon of the Keynesian welfare state, it was fatally easy to take all this for granted. The public domain of citizenship, equity and service had by then expanded even further and the market domain of buying and selling had shrunk correspondingly. As T.H. Marshall famously argued, political citizenship had been supplemented by social citizenship (Marshall 1950). Health care and insurance against sickness and unemployment had been de-commodified, at least partially; the state had undertaken to ensure that market forces would no longer be the sole determinants of the level of unemployment. These achievements seemed unassailable. Anthony Crosland, the leading theorist of the 'revisionist' social democracy of post-war Britain based his argument that further public ownership was no longer necessary on the assumption that the welfare state and full employment were here to stay and that the growth of the public domain in the preceding 100 years was irreversible (Crosland 1956). The processes through which the public domain had first emerged and then developed were of interest to historians, but all too often social scientists – and active politicians – viewed them through the prism of a bland, social-democratic whiggery which made them seem unsurprising and even inevitable, the products of historical necessity rather than of political and ideological struggle. Thus Marshall implied that the growth of social citizenship, the chief driver of the expansion of the public domain in the twentieth century, followed logically once equal civil and political rights had been achieved – forgetting that, the United States, which had been ahead of Britain in establishing political equality (at least for whites), was well behind in extending citizenship rights to the social sphere.

The second commandment and the professional ideal

Things look different today. One of the central features of the capitalist renaissance of our day is the erosion of the public domain. The neo-liberal upsurge of the 1980s was marked, above all, by a persistent, even relentless ideological onslaught on its legitimacy, accompanied by an equally persistent policy onslaught on the institutions and practices in which its values were embedded. Deregulation, privatization, so-called public–private partnerships and the creation of surrogate markets in what remained of the public sector narrowed the public domain and – even more damagingly – blurred the distinction between it and the market domain. Public functions of all kinds were farmed out to unaccountable appointed bodies, constituted by ministerial patronage, dominated by business interests and managed according to market principles. Intermediate institutions like the BBC, the universities, the schools and the health service were forced, as far as possible, into a market mould. So was the senior civil service, where the frontiers of the public domain had been most zealously guarded, and in which its values had been most thoroughly internalized. Meanwhile, the overlapping discourses of private-sector management and public-choice economics undermined the self-confidence of its defenders.

Against that background, the nineteenth-century emergence of the public domain seems, at one and the same time, more remarkable and more precarious than it did fifty years ago. Bland, social-democratic whiggery no longer provides an acceptable substitute for an explanation. To take one obvious example, there was nothing inevitable about the reforms, which vanquished 'Old Corruption'. Here too, the United States provides a telling contrast. American reformers who sought to vanquish their version of 'Old Corruption' were much less successful. The truth is that the values which sustain and are in turn sustained by the public domain – the values of professionalism, citizenship and service – are, historically speaking, rare breeds. In the public domain, to take only a couple of obvious examples, parents have to subordinate the interests of their children to a remote public interest; monetary rewards have to count for less than the sense that a job has been well done. In most cultures, at most times, such behaviour and the attitudes that sustain it would have seemed (and in many still seem) cold, hard, impersonal, even a little inhuman. The social benevolence engendered in the public domain is an austere, slightly distant benevolence. Its values run counter to the familial loyalties and patronage linkages characteristic of pre-modern societies. They imply a certain discipline, a certain self-restraint, which do not come naturally, and have to be learned and then internalized, sometimes painfully. Their installation in a real-world society requires a cultural revolution.

Revolutions are almost always the work of elites; and the cultural revolution that sowed the values of the public domain in the originally inhospitable soil of nineteenth-century Britain was no exception. It too was the work of elites, confident of their legitimacy and proud of their status. Some of them belonged to the so-called 'Labour aristocracy' which campaigned for parliamentary reform and ran the co-operative societies and friendly societies of late-Victorian England. But in Britain, at any rate, the growth of the public domain owed most to the ramifying elite that belonged to what Harold Perkin, their most authoritative historian, has called 'the forgotten middle class' (Perkin 1969) – to the self-consciously professional elite which became increasingly numerous as the nineteenth century wore on, and which adhered, or claimed to adhere, to a distinct professional ethic centred on the values of service, function, equity and efficiency (Perkin 1989).

The public domain, as it developed and grew in the nineteenth and twentieth centuries, was quintessentially the domain of these professionals. Professional pride, professional competence, professional duty, professional authority and, not least, predictable professional career paths were of the essence. Professionals were the chief advocates of its growth; they managed most of its institutions; they policed the frontier between it and the adjacent private and market domains. Above all, its values were their values. Gladstone's 'second commandment' laying down the duties of wealth to poverty and knowledge to ignorance was the epitome of the professional ideal as interpreted by its exponents. In depicting the post-war 'plateau of professional society', Harold Perkin also depicted the era in which the public domain reached its zenith.

This did not mean a utopia based entirely on merit, social efficiency and social justice. It meant, rather, a society which accepted in principle that ability and expertise were the only respectable justification for recruitment to positions of authority and responsibility and in which every citizen had the right to a minimum income in times of distress, to medical treatment during sickness, to decent housing in a healthy environment, and an education appropriate to his or her abilities.

The very fact that there was disagreement on how best successive governments should carry out their responsibilities and what precisely the ideal meant proves that the ideal was taken seriously. To that extent, the professional ideal was the organizing principle of post-war society (Perkin 1989: 405–6.).

The backlash of the patronized

The implications are more complex and – for actors in and defenders of the public domain – more disturbing than they may appear at first sight. If I am right the public domain is, or at least historically was, inescapably elitist. Apart from any other reasons, it was elitist because professions and the professional ethic are themselves inescapably elitist. Professionals can function only if they are trusted. The surgeon's skill, the scholar's learning, the judge's impartiality, the policeman's probity, the social worker's insight have to be taken on trust by those who consume the services they provide. Appraisal systems, league tables, performance indicators and all the fashionable *bric-à-brac* of modern management may provide safeguards against the abuse of trust, but they operate in general terms and after the event. At the crucial moment – discussing the pros and cons of an operation with a consultant; instructing a solicitor about a divorce settlement; telling a policeman about the circumstances of a break-in; listening to a tutor's comments on an essay – they pale into insignificance. At such moments, the client has no option but to trust the professional; to withdraw trust is to corrode the essential professional relationship and to degrade the service, which it is the professional's duty to provide. It follows that professionalism is symbiotically related to authority. For trust and authority go hand in hand. I trust professionals because, and insofar as, I accept the authority of the professionals' office and the authority of those who certified them as competent to exercise their professional functions. We pay professionals for their services because, in their own field, they know more than we do and because we therefore defer to them. No elite, no professions – and no public domain either.

All this points to an uncomfortable paradox. The public domain is quintessentially the domain of citizenship; and citizenship is in principle inclusive. But it is manned and policed by elites; and elites are inevitably exclusive. They can, of course, be open to talent, meritocratic in their promotion procedures, and equitable in their approach to non-members. But not everyone can belong to them: an elite to which everyone belonged would not be an elite at all. The elite that manned Britain's public domain in its great days was, in the main, public-spirited, high-minded even self-sacrificing. But they were still elites; they still excluded more people than they included; and their public spirit and high-mindedness went hand in hand with an incorrigible propensity to patronize those outside their ranks and a blithe inability to see that their impartiality and devotion to the public good might not seem self-evident to those adversely affected by their decisions. Judges, civil servants, surgeons, professors, generals, chief constables, public-service broadcasters knew best. They knew best because they had been trained to know best. That was what professional status meant. They saw no reason to explain themselves; and if anyone had suggested that they might have to explain themselves (on the whole no one did), they would have found the suggestion irresponsible and destructive.

In the still deeply class-divided but in retrospect extraordinarily deferential society of the early post-war years, their condescension did them no harm and may even have done them some good. Their authority was accepted, along with their claims to competence and impartiality. The 1960s and 1970s, however, saw a backlash against their pretensions, indeed against traditional authority as such. The public, in whose name the elite of the public domain claimed authority, became less and less willing to take that authority on trust. The result was what Samuel Beer memorably termed a 'new populism' (Beer 1982). The growth of alternative medicine, exposures of police malpractice, attacks on allegedly sexist judges, exposures of the private lives of the powerful, probing television interviews and even the campaign for a written constitution were all among its symptoms.

That is only the beginning of the story. The new populism was a mood, or rather a medley of moods, not an argument. In the late 1970s and 1980s, however, it was given extra edge by the economic liberalism of the New Right. It is not difficult to see why. The Achilles heel of the British version of the public domain was lack of accountability, or at any rate perceived lack of accountability. The neo-liberals offered a solution: accountability through Exit in place of what they saw as the deformed, inadequate and corruptible accountability of Voice. The sovereign consumer would replace the disillusioned citizen. Wherever possible, consumer sovereignty would be achieved through the market. Where that was not possible, surrogate markets would be used instead. The implications went wide. Economic liberalism can accommodate the notion of public goods, in the plural. But public goods, as economists define them, are not to be equated with the public interest in the singular. Public goods are goods, like clean air or defence or law and order, which have to be enjoyed by everyone if they are to be enjoyed by anyone. Even the most intransigent economic liberals concede that such goods cannot be provided by the competitive market, and accept that they therefore have to be provided by public authorities, if they are to be provided at all. But the public interest – and therefore the public domain – goes much wider than that. Health care and education are not, in the economist's sense of the term, public goods. The case for placing them in the public domain is not that they *cannot* be provided by the competitive market. They can be. It is that, if they are placed in the market domain, the public interest will suffer. And the whole notion of a public interest, which is more than the sum of private interests, runs against the grain of liberal economics, which knows only individuals and not collectivities.

By the same token, economic liberalism – or, to be more precise, the pre-Gladstonian version of economic liberalism espoused by the New Right of the final quarter of the last century – was almost bound to be at odds with the values and structures of professional life. In New Rightist eyes, the professions were, in essence, market-distorting cabals of rent-seekers, engaged in an elaborate conspiracy to force the price of their services above their true market value. Professional qualifications close off entry and inhibit competition; professional career ladders make it impossible to ensure that rewards reflect the market value of labour. By virtue of all this, moreover, the professions – or at any rate some professions – are the carriers of an anti-market ideology which, the New Right concluded, had to be rooted out if a properly functioning market order were to be re-established. The result was a kind of *Kulturkampf* between the New Right governments of the last eighteen years and a range of professional groups, extending from doctors, teachers, academics, broadcasters, social workers and civil servants to barristers and even policemen. Profession after profession had to fit its practices and its relationships with its clients into a market mould – not just because those practices and relationships conflicted with the precepts of economic liberalism, but because they embodied and transmitted an implicit public philosophy subversive of the assumptions on which economic-liberal precepts are based.

Towards a counter-attack?

That, broadly, speaking, is where we are now. By the mid 1990s, the New Right was running out of steam. Slowly and rather apprehensively, left or centre-left parties, mostly belonging to the social-democratic tradition, began to come in from the cold. They did so because the New Right had over-reached itself; more particularly because the New Right's assault on the public domain and its values had engendered a Polanyi-style reaction. Strangely, however, hopes that they might undo the damage, which their neo-liberal predecessors had done to the public domain – or even mount a significant challenge to the neo-liberal discourse, which had legitimized the neo-liberal onslaught upon it – turned out to be misplaced. Rhetorically there was some common ground between Tony Blair's Third Way and Gladstone's second commandment, but rhetoric was not matched by action. Where Gladstonian liberals sought to ring-fence the growing public domain of their day from the incursions of the market domain, the centre-left regimes of the 1990s and 2000s did very nearly the opposite. The gains made by the market domain in the preceding fifteen years were left untouched, and the public domain suffered further marketization – now in the name of accountability and transparency, rather than of economic liberalism *per se*.

The results are complex and hard to summarize. The vitality and extent of the public domain vary from society to society. It is weaker and narrower in the United States than in Europe, stronger and wider in most of continental western Europe than in the United Kingdom. These differences are the legacies of history – in some cases of quite long periods of history – and they are not likely to disappear. No conceivable constellation of political forces will 'Europeanize' the attenuated public domain of the United States or 'Americanize' the much stronger public domains of France, The Netherlands or the German Federal Republic. The really interesting question, however, is whether the societies which experienced a determined New Right attack on the public domain – notably, Britain and the United States – are likely to see a counter-attack. All that can be said with certainty is that nothing of the sort has been seen so far.

Yet the need for a counter-attack is hard to dispute. Wise economic liberals have always known that a properly functioning market order depends on non-market values. Trust is fundamental to it. But the market domain *consumes* trust; it does not produce it. Trust can, of course, be produced in the private domain. There is some evidence that the continuing strength of the private domain in East Asian cultures deserves some of the credit for the strong, but culturally specific trust relationships that underpin (or until recently underpinned) East Asian capitalism (Fukuyama 1995). But in twenty-first-century western cultures, the private domain has decayed along with the public. Family ties have become weaker, loyalties to kin and neighbourhood have become more attenuated, friendships have almost certainly become harder to sustain. In Robert Putnam's haunting phrase, the societies of the twenty-first century, at least in the Atlantic world, are societies where individuals 'bowl alone' (Putnam 2000).

It follows that, in the Atlantic world, at any rate, a vibrant public domain is almost certainly a precondition of a culture of mutual trust. It is also a precondition of genuinely democratic governance, as the radicals of nineteenth-century Britain understood. If the public domain is annexed to, or taken over by, the market domain, the primordial democratic promise of equal citizenship will be negated. Citizenship rights are, by definition, equal. Market rewards are, by definition, unequal. Unless the public domain of citizenship rights is ring-fenced from the market domain of buying and selling, the 'universal pander' of money, as Michael Walzer has termed it, will invade the former and undermine the egalitarianism which lies at its heart (Walzer 1983).

The obvious conclusion is that there is now an urgent need to re-invent the public domain and to erect new barriers against incursions from the market domain. As in nineteenth-century Britain, it will need a lot of creativity, imagination and flexibility to do this, and it will almost certainly take a long time. As in nineteenth-century Britain, success will depend on a mixture of state intervention, private initiative and action by local authorities, probably with the second two in the lead. The most urgent need of all, however, is to develop a public philosophy capable of answering the negations of the New Right and of mobilizing the public conscience in the way that Gladstone's growth of benevolence did in the last century. At the heart of such a philosophy would lie the simple propositions that a healthy public domain is fundamental to a civilized society; that belief in the possibility of a public interest is fundamental to the health of the public domain; and that in the public domain, goods must not be treated as commodities or surrogate commodities. Performance indicators designed to mimic the indicators of the market domain are not appropriate, and are likely to do more harm than good. The language of buyer and seller, producer and customer, does not belong in the public domain and nor do the relationships which that language implies. Doctors and nurses do not 'sell' medical services; students are not 'customers' of their teachers; policemen and policewomen do not 'produce' public order. The attempt to force these relationships into a market mould merely undermines the service ethic, which is the true guarantor of quality in the public domain, and in doing so impoverishes us all. By the same token, the search for competitiveness – in practice, for higher productivity, achieved by substituting capital for labour – which is proper to the market domain, has no place in the public domain.

So far, so social-democratic. In these respects, the obvious vehicle for a revitalized public domain is a re-born social democracy. But more is needed; and the 'more' is not so congruent with the social-democratic tradition, at least as manifested for most of the twentieth century. It is equally necessary to combat the forces behind the backlash described a moment ago. To acknowledge that the condescension of the elite that managed the public domain in earlier decades, and their concomitant failure to see that the ethic of public service was hollow without a supporting ethic of democratic accountability and transparency, helped to make the New Right's market imperialism possible. Though market methods of safeguarding consumer interests and preventing the abuse of power do not belong in the public domain, other methods must be found instead. If Exit is inappropriate, Voice must be made effective – and be seen to be effective. Attempts to force activities, which ought to belong in the public domain to find a substitute for accountability in the procedures of the market domain, have done more harm than good. But that does not imply a return to the public domain of old days. What it implies is that accountability should be sought through participation and openness, not through the price mechanism. Since participation will be more effective in small units than in big ones, this in turn implies the principles of subsidiarity and of pluralism. And there is no denying that this is a hard lesson for social democrats: 'subsidiarity' has traditionally been a Christian Democratic or liberal value rather than a social-democratic one. Reborn social democracy, in other words, cannot revitalize the public domain all by itself. It can do so only if it is willing to abandon the bureaucratic centralism and top-down statism, which were fundamental to it for most of the twentieth century. It needs to marry its tradition with the pluralistic decentralism characteristic of Anglophone social liberalism on the one hand and of continental Christian democracy on the other.

Moreover, a still harder question lurks in the background: how to discover a twenty-first century equivalent of the Gladstonian 'public conscience' which the nineteenth-century architects of the public domain mobilized and entrenched, and without which subsidiarity and the pluralism it implies may lead to further fragmentation. When Gladstone talked of a public conscience he presupposed a common culture, based on a common moral code, ultimately derived from the Judaeo-Christian tradition. The elite of his day had been shaped by religious traditions and by the practices that embodied them. So had their audiences. Manifestly, things are different today. The common culture that the Gladstonian liberals took for granted no longer exists. The moral code they and their audiences shared is in contention. Some even claim that it has unravelled. The hedonistic possessive individualism of the 1980s – one of the chief motors of the market imperialism which has helped to erode the public domain – is the most obvious result.

The trouble is that the solution is far from obvious. If possessive individualism is replaced by a kind of possessive pluralism, if the Hobbesian war of all against all is transposed from the level of the individual to the level of the collectivity, our last state may be worse than the first. A combination of pluralism with moral relativism and a chip-on-shoulder, tabloid-style anti-elitism might reproduce the culture wars of contemporary America on British soil. Plainly, trying forlornly to return to the past cannot avert these dangers. In the multi-ethnic society we now inhabit, a new common morality would have to be based on something wider and more inclusive than the Judaeo-Christian tradition. Almost by definition, no one knows exactly what that 'something' might be. But that is not a reason for despair. Gladstone's public conscience had other sources beside the Judaeo-Christian tradition. It also drew on a confused, inchoate, but nevertheless unmistakable republican or civic humanist tradition, going back by way of the Commonwealth of the English civil war and the city states of Renaissance Italy to ancient Rome and Athens (Pocock 1975). The central question for the politics of the twenty-first century is whether that tradition can be retrieved, in a way that will resonate in societies almost inconceivably different from the ones in which it first emerged. In the academy, a start has been made (Pettit 1997; Skinner 1999). It remains to be seen whether the results can be translated into a popular idiom.

Bibliography

Beer, Samuel H. (1982) *Britain Against Itself: The Political Contradictions of Collectivism*, New York: Norton.

Crossland, C.A.R. (1956) *The Future of Socialism*, London: Jonathon Cape.

Dahrendorf, Ralf et al. (1995) *Report on Wealth Creation and Social Cohesion in a Free Society (the Dahrendorf Report)*, London: Commission on Wealth Creation and Social Cohesion.

Fukuyama, Francis (1995) *Trust: The Social Virtues and the Creation of Prosperity*, New York: Free Press.

Greenleaf, W.H. (1983) *The British Political Tradition vol. 1: The Rise of Collectivism*, London: Methun.

Marshall, T.H. (1950) *Citizenship and Social Class and other Essays*, Cambridge: Cambridge University Press.

Matthew, H.C.G. (1995) *Gladstone 1875–1898*, Oxford: Clarendon Press.

Perkin, Harold (1969) *The Origins of Modern English Society 1780–1880*, London: Routledge.

—— (1989) *The Rise of Professional Society, England Since 1880*, London: Routledge.

Pettit, Philip (1997) *Republicanism: A Theory of Freedom and Government*, Oxford: Clarendon Press.

Pocock, J.G.A. (1975) *The Machiavellian Moment, Florentine Political Thought and the Atlantic Republican Tradition*, Princeton, NJ: Princeton University Press.

Polanyi, Karl (1957) *The Great Transformation: The Political and Economic Origins of Our Time*, Boston, MA: Beacon Press.

Putnam, Robert D. (2000) *Bowling Alone: The Collapse and Revival of American Community*, New York: Simon and Schuster.

Skinner, Quentin (1999) *Liberty Before Liberalism*, Cambridge: Cambridge University Press.

Smith, Adam (1976) *An Inquiry into the Nature and Causes of the Wealth of Nations*, Chicago, IL: University of Chicago Press.

Walzer, Michael (1983) *Spheres of Justice: A Defense of Pluralism and Equality*, New York: Basic Books.

3 The re-constitution of the public domain

Harry Arthurs

Introduction

The Washington consensus represented a tacit but powerful agreement among neo-liberal ideologues, academic and government economists, central bankers, global business and financial institutions, publicists and politicians across the political spectrum. It expressed a few simple and seemingly irresistible 'truths': that during the post-war period, the state had become too expensive to sustain and too intrusive to tolerate; that if markets were freed of regulatory constraints, they would generate wealth and prosperity both locally and globally; and that wealth and prosperity were necessary (and seemingly sufficient) conditions for democracy and social well-being. The Washington consensus, as might be expected, was quite unsympathetic to any such notion as 'the public domain'. Moreover, it seldom put 'governing' on its agenda, except when emphasizing the need to govern less (by reducing social programmes and market regulation), to govern tougher (by coercing the poor, workers, undocumented immigrants or practitioners of non-standard life-styles), to govern 'smarter' (through privatization) or to govern more 'accountably' (to corporate interests).

But, it seems, the Washington consensus may be undergoing a transformation. First, its logic is no longer seen as irresistible. Currencies and commodities, corporations and countries once touted as exemplars are in varying degrees of disgrace and disrepair. As a result, local business elites, transnational social movements, ordinary citizens, even some national governments, are having second thoughts about neo-liberalism. Second, even 'truebelievers' in liberalized trade, open markets and diminished state activism have had to acknowledge publicly that the Washington consensus has delivered the goods only selectively and partially; that some of its peripheral features have to be reconfigured, if only with a view to preserving its core ideas; and – critical for the present discussion – that markets work best in reciprocity with other systems of social ordering (Wolfensohn 1998; Soros 1998). The result has been increasing interest within the World Bank and among leading representatives of the world business community in 'global governance' and 'civil society', in 'transparency' and 'accountability', and especially in 'the rule of law' (World Bank 1997). And third, recent research has hinted that despite the Washington consensus, the state may not, after all, have been 'hollowed out'; that most advanced economies have maintained relatively high levels of state expenditure; and that the idea of sustaining and reinvigorating the 'public domain' still commands widespread support (Drache 2001).

This essay takes issue with none of these hypotheses; rather it proceeds from a willing suspension of disbelief. It assumes that reports of the transformation of the Washington consensus are not premature; that the project of making global capitalism more benign will proceed; and that the new politics and policies of the 'public domain' are indeed authentic successors to social democracy and social market capitalism, not merely a sweet-smelling version of neo-liberalism by any other name. If all these things are true – if we are indeed in a moment of paradigmatic transition; if in Drache's phrase, we are 'redrawing the line between the state and the market'; if we are seeking to reconcile the imperatives of wealth creation with the claims of social justice, environmental responsibility and genuine democratic accountability – then two tasks seem to demand urgent attention. First, we must understand more clearly what we mean by the 'public domain', and second, we must begin to think about its 'constitution' – the values, symbols, norms, practices and institutions which will translate the idea of the public domain into a new social and political reality. That is the ambition of this essay.

Defining the public domain: the role of law

Daniel Drache has proposed that the public domain comprises 'the things we have in common', things which – in contrast to private property – 'cannot be bought or sold on the open market' (Drache 2001). In Drache's metaphor, of course, the public domain is more than 'things': it is a world view concerning 'things' which are held in common or for a public purpose, as well as constituencies of interest embedded within that world view, and an historically contingent set of institutions and processes which constitute, embody and administer it. Moreover, it follows that the public domain exists alongside and in tension with private domains – things we do *not* hold in common, things which *can* be bought or sold on the open market. Private domains are also defined by a distinctive ideology or belief system – one which privileges private property; are constituted and legitimated by institutions; and are sustained by processes of expansion and exploitation. And finally – to persevere with Drache's metaphor – public and private domains are divided only by shifting, permeable and contested boundaries. We have therefore to pay special attention to boundary disputes.

Boundary disputes in the non-metaphoric sense are typically settled by recourse to law. So too with those around the public domain, which, after all, is a term with a lengthy legal pedigree. An account of law's historical encounters with the public domain may therefore shed some light on the significance of contemporary efforts to redraw its boundaries. The story, as I will tell it, is that determined, powerful 'modernizing' interests have always sought to carve private domains out of public; that they have used the discourse, processes and agencies of law not only to bring about these encroachments but to legitimate them; and that in doing so, they have sought to discredit and suppress social institutions and practices, which embody traditional values of 'commons' and vague ideals of 'community'. This pattern, I suggest, repeats itself in the medieval and early modern 'commons' which were suppressed by the parliamentary enclosure movement of eighteenth- and nineteenth-century England; in the metaphoric public domains of classical liberal democracy, which in the inter-war period rapidly succumbed to a succession of economic, moral and political crises; in the post-war social democracies and their capitalist *doppelgängers*, which experienced a sudden erosion of credibility and political support in the 1970s; in the present, millennial version of the public domain whose shortlist of 'things we have in common' – the marketplace and the modalities of exchange – turns out to have been too short for its own good; and in the endangered global commons-in-the-making: our cultural inheritance, natural environments, deep oceans and outer space. In each of these cases, law has been used to shrink the boundaries of the public domain, to justify encroachments by private interests, and to introduce new institutional structures and constitutional regimes, which 'normalize' the new boundary conditions. And at the same time, law has often been invoked to defend the public domain – usually as an unavailing, last ditch strategy whose limited success tells us as much about law as it does about public domains.

This recurring pattern of events forces us to consider the highly ambiguous relationship among state, law and public domains.

The public domain is not coterminous with the state. Sometimes the public domain has been identified with local or communal institutions operating at arm's length from the state; sometimes the state has acted as trustee and executor of public domain values; sometimes deep contradictions of state policy towards public domain values have existed within and among the legislative, executive and judicial branches of government; and most recently, under the Washington consensus, state policy has been indifferent, even hostile, to the public domain. Given this complex and varied connection between the two, it is at least clear that to argue for the resuscitation of the public domain is not necessarily to argue for a large and active state sector.

Nor should state and law be conflated. It is true that in popular and legal-professional circles, law is generally defined as a body of norms promulgated and enforced by the state. But social scientists have long observed that both public and private domains also produce their own distinctive norms – bodies of 'law', which the state may acknowledge and enforce, or on the other hand, refuse to recognize or even tolerate.[1] In its post-modern formulation, this theory of 'legal pluralism' holds that law need not originate with or be enforced by the state; that law is immanent in all social and economic relations; that the outcome of encounters between state and non-state legal systems are unpredictable; and that state law ought to be respectful of non-state normative systems which express the 'otherness' of those who inhabit the plethora of private and public domains which exist in any society or polity. Any discussion of the public domain thus implicates a controversy over competing visions of law, over law's relationship to the state and over just how law 'rules' – if and when it does (Griffiths 1986; Merry 1988; Teubner 1992).

An understanding of the relationship among state, law and the public domain has become particularly important because recent attempts to renovate the Washington consensus place significant emphasis on 'the rule of law'. In one sense, this is not surprising: the 'rule of law' was historically used both to suppress communal interests and to hobble intervention-minded governments. In fact, the principal theorist and popularizer of the rule of law – A.V. Dicey – was an avowed foe of 'collectivism' (Arthurs 1979). But, as it happens, neo-liberals are not the only ones to have discovered the potential of law in resolving boundary disputes between public and private domains. Supporters of the public domain – no less than its critics – tend to look to law as well, and to put their faith in juridical strategies, especially those built around constitutional guarantees of social rights (Drummond 1992; de Villiers 1994; Samuel 1997). Law, they imagine, is cheap, rational and fair; constitutional law is, in addition, definitive and, for all practical purposes, unchangeable. By contrast, they see social and political action as slow, costly, uncertain and ultimately unavailing. But, I will argue, these perceptions are based on a misapprehension of what law is and what law does. Especially in circumstances of neo-liberalism, globalization and post-modernity, legal strategies intended to preserve or extend the boundaries of the public domain are ill advised. Far better for advocates of the public domain, to proceed pragmatically and opportunistically; to gradually resuscitate politics; to mobilize the forces favouring social change; to use conventional juridical strategies only sparingly; and to put their faith in ambiguity and paradox.

A short history of the public domain through the lens of law

The account that follows sweeps rather presumptuously across time, space and legal cultures, thus inviting readers to challenge its internal coherence, comprehensiveness and relevance. However, treated as allusion rather than as technical analysis – as a cautionary tale, in other words – this history of the public domain as seen through the lens of law may help us to better understand the overarching political metaphor of the public domain more generally.

The public domain as public property

Since Roman times, the existence of *res publicae* – 'inherently public property' – has been acknowledged by law. Indeed, since the term is the root of our word 'republic', the existence of public property is arguably an indispensable feature of modern democratic states. At different times, however, and under different legal regimes, this notion of public property has taken different forms. In the most rigorous conception of the 'public domain', all land not privately owned –

unoccupied land as well as land used specifically for public works – was thought not only to be vested in the state but to be 'inalienable'; it could not be bought and sold; it would remain forever public and vested in the sovereign, even if devolved under feudal tenures or leased to private parties for finite periods of time. But this rigorous position has never had much resonance with practical governments or aspiring magnates. More often, the public domain was treated merely as an asset which could be disposed of for politically expedient purposes. Thus, land grants were used by Roman, feudal and Imperial governments to secure the loyalty of troublesome warlords, reward faithful servants or pacify demobilized soldiers, just as they were used by modern states to endow their universities, subsidize their railways or populate areas of contested sovereignty. Today, the notion of the public domain signals no more than the existence of a general use-right. Under modern Anglo-American property law, for example, the community is entitled to access to highways, to the banks, beds and fore-shore of navigable waters and, by extension, to public squares and parks – access which cannot be forestalled by neighbouring property owners (Butler 1982; Rose 1986). This, of course, is a significant entitlement, but it speaks to a more attenuated understanding of the public domain than the original, rigorous conception.

In this gradation of legal meanings, we see a rough approximation of those which lend ambiguity to the notion of the 'public domain' in the metaphoric and political sense in which we are using it in this volume. Is there an irreducible public domain of state functions, of entitlements to public goods, which no state can refuse to honour? This view was fashionable once. However, the decline of the state is viewed today with equanimity by post-modernists who can conceive of democratic 'governance' advancing even as the state becomes less legitimate and effective (Hirst 1997; Matláry 1995), and with enthusiasm by neo-liberals who eagerly contemplate the ultimate retirement of even the arthritic night-watchman state. Or is the public domain whatever vestigial traces of the state sector remain at a given historical moment? This has been the pragmatic position of most contemporary centre and centre-left governments, it being accepted that the historical trend is in the direction of a smaller public domain rather than a larger one. Or is the issue of state ownership or state provision of public goods actually irrelevant? Is it, instead, the question of 'use-rights' – the right to be included, to enjoy the fruits of civic participation – which ought to be the ultimate concern? If these can be provided by the market or by civil society, rather than by the state, no matter: what counts is that they are provided somehow. This may be the sense in which the public domain re-enters political discourse in this era of 'post Washington consensus' (Devetak and Higgott 2000; Drache 2001, this volume). However, while the 'use-rights' metaphor has obvious appeal to enlightened financiers and pragmatic governments, it is not quite enough to resolve the problem. Someone must ultimately address the problem of what to do when access to use-rights is obstructed and economic deprivation and social exclusion grow apace.

Given its variable meaning and generally diminishing power, some suggest that the idea of the public domain may have lost its salience in legal discourse (McLean 1999); others fear that its abandonment may lead to destruction of the natural environment, inconvenience or economic ruin for public users, and the loss of the 'civilizing and socializing' effects of public space and facilities (Rose 1986). As this volume shows, similar controversy surrounds the utility of the public domain as what Drache has called a 'heuristic' or 'hosting metaphor' (Drache 2000).

The 'commons': early modern England

The metaphor of the public domain often comes to us, in the Anglo-American tradition, through the oft-told 'tragedy of the commons'. The 'tragedy', as it is conventionally understood, is that late-surviving medieval patterns of property-holding represented an obstacle to prosperity and modernity. Lands were held by villagers in common; cattle were grazed and grains were reaped in common; natural resources such as wood, peat, minerals, fish and game were exploited in common. Thus, no individual property owner had the incentive, the means or even the right to introduce new technologies, which might produce higher yields or more profitable rents. Moreover, since the customs governing common use were often unwritten, highly idiosyncratic and sometimes indistinguishable from the daily use routines themselves, they effectively excluded strangers, discouraged investment, perpetuated backward mining or farming techniques, and in the end, denied these benighted, collectivist communities the moral and material rewards of integration into a mercantilist, then capitalist, progressive or modern economy. As a consequence – so the story runs – rising populations pressed ever more severely on a dwindling common resource base with the inevitable 'tragedy' of declining living standards. Only with the shift to clearly defined, legally enforceable, individual rights of private ownership was it possible to forestall this 'tragedy'. This is the version of 'the tragedy' favoured by Adam Smith and political economists of the late eighteenth century (Neeson 1993), as well as their latter-day disciples in that other dismal science, biology (Hardin 1968).

But there is another version of the tragedy of the commons. Edward Thompson, the brilliant English social historian, shows how the abolition of common use-rights deprived the common folk of rural England of the only property they knew; the only property that could sustain their way of life (Thompson 1975, 1991). He recounts how the 'commons' were diminished through encroachments and enclosures under laws forced through Parliament – before or after the fact – by private cliques of self-aggrandizing landowners, how judges criminalized all forms of resistance and subordinated the ancient 'natural' and customary law, which had defined common rights to modern concepts of unambiguous property ownership.[2]

Thompson's account of the demise of the commons in early modern England is but one of many. The same phenomenon was recorded again and again throughout the eighteenth century and on into the nineteenth, and right across the British Isles from the 'clearances' of the Scottish Highland peasantry to the dissolution of the 'Stannary Court' of the Cornish tin miners to the enclosure of urban commons in the insalubrious new industrial towns of England and Wales (Arthurs 1985). Again and again, in language whose echoes we can hear down to our own time, these accounts of the end of the 'old' public domain are closely associated – whether as cause or effect – with a crisis of economy, politics, law and society (Perrot 1990).

Yet the story is not entirely a pessimistic one. The communitarian traditions documented by Thompson were not entirely erased in the eighteenth century. They were resuscitated during the nineteenth century in various forms: by the introduction of allotment gardens for the working poor, by the emergent trade union, cooperative and workers' education movements of Victorian England, by a few utopian colonies in the Americas and, by 'gas and water' municipal socialists on both sides of the Atlantic. They even lingered on in the intellectual traditions and political rhetoric of early twentieth-century progressive and social democratic movements, especially in English-speaking countries (Rodgers 1998). In that sense, they made their contribution to the survival of the idea of the public domain.

The frontier

The 'tragedy of the commons', moreover, was not solely about the fate of eighteenth-century plebian Celts or Britons. It was in fact rehearsed many times during the waves of exploration, colonization and globalized trade, which began earlier, lasted later and spread much further afield. According to some European jurists of the seventeenth to the nineteenth centuries, if territory could be described – however inaccurately – as *terra nullius*, as belonging to no civilized state, it could be lawfully claimed by the first sovereign to stumble upon it and occupy it (Slattery 1991; Simpson 1993–94). As the aboriginal, itinerant peoples of America, Africa and Australia were to learn each in their turn, being the inhabitant of such a public domain was a distinct liability. To be sure, the doctrine of *terra nullius* had a corollary, at least in theory: if an indigenous monarch did claim the land, it was not available to European trade or colonization except by conquest, cession or treaty. But this corollary was at most an inconvenience; if some such claim were made, it could be easily swept aside. And usually was: the great movement across the western frontier lands of the Indian nations in the United States and Canada, and the subsequent settlement of the 'open range', shows that even if nature abhors a vacuum, aggressive railway entrepreneurs, ambitious land merchants and impoverished immigrants were quite willing to create one where none existed previously. Nor I suspect was the story much different in Siberia or Indonesia or India or Southern Africa or the Canadian Arctic.[3] Everywhere the European colonizers went, as soon as they were strong enough to do so, they brushed aside indigenous notions of common property and customary law or at most tolerated them to the extent that they could be fitted within the Procrustean bed of metropolitan law

(Harrell-Bond and Burman, 1979). In the interim, it should be noted, they often instituted their own justice systems and improvised property regimes to protect trading, grazing, mining and water rights (Ellickson 1991), which were absorbed into or displaced by more conventional systems of state law, which ultimately arrived with the army, the police, the railways and finance capital.

The ancient dream of a public domain does survive here and there in the Americas. Aboriginal peoples have contested attempts to displace them from their common lands from the earliest moments of colonization down to the present era of globalization. Even though five hundred years of exploitation and resistance have bound the colonized and the colonizers together in societies, which are probably indissoluble, some aboriginal peoples on the periphery of development bravely persist in their efforts to preserve the last vestiges of communal property against the aggressive assertions of individual and corporate ownership. Ironically, globalization – their worst enemy – may also be the best hope aboriginal peoples have of preserving their ancient public domains of land, water and spirit. It is increasingly difficult for global or domestic capital to exploit natural resources without becoming vulnerable to the scrutiny of the media, social movements and NGOs, without exposure to potential boycotts by consumers, without pressure from governments sensitive to charges that they are collaborating in the abuse of the environment and human rights. This utterly unexpected outcome of globalization has, in fact, given some aboriginal peoples a new strategy, if not yet a new strength (Merry 1996).

Of course, the picture differs from place to place. In the United States, armed aboriginal resistance essentially ended a century or more ago. Today, Native American communities still attempt – with modest success – to recapture their dignity and distinctiveness, and to replicate their now-lost public domain, through strategies of litigation, institution-building and commercial enterprise. In Canada, by contrast, First Nations have favoured constitutional strategies during recent decades, with much effort focused on proposals to establish a 'third level of government' for aboriginal peoples within the Canadian state, and to reinvent the traditions and institutions which governed their ancient public domains.[4] No one who is sceptical about law and constitutions will easily accept that such proposals will do much in themselves to alter high rates of infant mortality, poverty, unemployment and incarceration. But as an important symbolic first step towards a change in the material and psychic conditions of aboriginal peoples, perhaps indeed new arrangements for self-government are worth trying (Royal Commission on Aboriginal Peoples 1996).

The public domains of political liberalism: nineteenth- and twentieth-century Europe and America

By the nineteenth century, the legal public domain of England was not large. Land ownership and wealth were largely concentrated in the hands of a few favoured groups: the great landowners; the local gentry and clergy; and the new metropolitan class of manufacturers, bankers, merchants and railway lawyers.

What remained as a metaphoric 'public domain' was the prerogatives of British subjects and the right to participate in politics. But most people were excluded even from this public domain: most urban tradesmen, skilled workers and small property owners, almost all industrial and agricultural workers, and of course, all women. The history of the long nineteenth century – from 1789 to 1914 – was written around the efforts of these excluded groups to participate in the public domain (Hobsbawm 1987). They sought to make their own particular 'property' rights as workers or shopkeepers more secure and profitable, to be acknowledged as reputable and worthy members of the community, and to become political actors, first as individual citizens and subsequently as members of organized groups whose interests had to be accommodated in the fundamental structures of the polity, society and economy.

By no means was their progress inevitable, easy or complete. But gradually property laws and labour laws were changed; the political franchise was extended; the rudiments of the welfare state were established; the utter rigidity of the class system began to become brittle and break apart; and women ultimately won the right to hold property and vote. By, say, 1918, one could begin to describe the United Kingdom as something resembling a democracy, albeit one which was still imperfect and incomplete.

The chronology differed from continent to continent, from country to country, but in general the long nineteenth century was one of awakening democratic aspirations. Those aspirations were only imperfectly realized in many, arguably most, countries. They were often suppressed by reactionary forces, diverted into nationalist struggles, betrayed by corrupt, incompetent or sectarian governments. But by the inter-war period, in most countries in western Europe and the Americas, even in some European colonies, it was beginning to be accepted that democracy was 'normal', that ordinary men – and later women – had the right to participate in and ultimately control the public domain of politics. Even monarchies, dictatorships, oligarchies and imperial elites in these countries usually felt compelled to borrow the language of democracy, describing themselves as custodians of a 'sacred trust' to act according to the people's will or in the people's interests, as the 'true embodiment' of popular sentiment, as agents of a 'transition' to democracy, as 'defenders' of democracy against anarchic elements or foreign conspirators. Even in such perverse and obscene distortions of democracy, however, there was at least an implicit recognition that governments must govern if not with the consent of the governed, then at least on their behalf. In that sense, it could be said that we had arrived at a moment in history when it could no longer be questioned that politics was unquestionably a public domain – 'the things we have in common which cannot be bought or sold on the open market'.

But in this formulation of the public domain, there were many ironies. One is that who 'we' are – who are stakeholders in the common enterprise of the nation, who can participate in the public domain of politics – has been ceaselessly contested across fault lines of gender, class, religion, race and ethnicity, with devastating consequences for the actual practice of democracy. A second is that political power has indeed often been 'bought or sold on the open market' even – perhaps especially – in the country which regards itself as democratic tutor to the world. And a third is that debate over 'what we have in common' is precisely what contemporary politics is all about. Is the public domain to be defined by our common participation in public processes – to vote, to hold public office, to be free from arbitrary constraints? Or is it to be measured by our common access to public goods – to education, health, dignity and justice?

Social democracy: mid twentieth-century advanced economies

This emphasis on equitable access to public goods was at the heart of the transition in political discourse from nineteenth-century liberalism to twentieth-century social democracy. That transition had apparently become irreversible after the depression of the 1930s, World War II and the reconstruction that followed these catastrophes. 'We are all socialists now', people used to say. Of course, 'socialism' in this sense seldom involved plans to return all private property to the public domain whence it had been snatched over two hundred years of mercantilist and capitalist appropriation. Rather, in its social democratic incarnation, 'socialism' consisted of a series of meliorative strategies designed to give everyone access to the full benefits of citizenship in what remained, at core, capitalist societies with strongly entrenched notions of private property. In most advanced democracies, these benefits included such public goods and services as reasonable prospects for employment and decent working conditions, health services, social insurance, education, public safety, the administration of justice, the infrastructure of transportation and communications and at least a modicum of amenity and culture.

In some key areas, to be sure, the state did not so much supply public goods and services as try to ensure that markets operated fairly honestly and with reasonably benign consequences. Hence, states with varying degrees of enthusiasm and diligence regulated interest and exchange rates, the securities market and the labour market, consumer and workplace relations, the use of land and other natural resources, import and export markets, and some oligopolies and monopolies such as public utilities, broadcasting, air transport and financial institutions. The interventionist state, in other words, became the repository of common values, the engine of collective enterprise, the custodian of what we may call metaphorically 'the public domain'.

It must be said immediately that the state's custody of the public domain was in some ways less than successful. Some of the goods and services it provided were themselves the source of considerable problems – public housing and welfare being two cases in point; some of its regulatory interventions – in land and labour markets, for example – were either counter-productive or ineffectual; and the cost of the whole enterprise imposed burdens on taxpayers which they became increasingly unwilling to bear. But the activist state did not just falter of its own infirmities; it was driven back by two powerful forces: neo-liberalism and globalization. The first weakened our desire for public goods, the second the capacity of the state to deliver them. Thus, at the turn of the millennium, we seemed to be abandoning the public domain of social democracy and returning to an earlier version of the public domain, the liberal version, built on the ideal of individual enterprise and opportunity but transposed from a local or national to a global scale.

And a final problem for social democracy: in conditions of post-modernity, understanding the 'public domain' – even as a metaphor – has become increasingly difficult. After all, there is no more 'public' – only constructed identities, multiple meanings and contested histories. And there is no more 'domain' – no more common land with finite natural endowments, its boundaries and use-rights defined by immemorial custom – but a limitless, ever-changing, normatively indeterminate, enormously complex and sometimes 'virtual' reality. In other words, the class- and interest-based coalition which supported social democracy in most western countries has been dissolving; and the policy agenda which once united and disciplined that coalition not only seems unlikely to be re-established, but to be irrelevant or even undesirable – even to many social democrats (see Hirst 1997).

The marketplace as public domain: millennial neo-liberalism

At the end of the twentieth century, ironically, the public domain which seems to be attracting the most attention is the marketplace. This is rather odd since, in a conventional sense, the marketplace seems to be not part of the public domain but its antithesis. It is, after all, where one buys and sells those things which we own privately rather than in common. However, the idea of the marketplace as a public domain is not altogether oxymoronic. It has long been understood that the public domain provides a context for the private activities of buying and selling. Public infrastructure is still used to transport goods, services and information to market; public agencies still stabilize interest rates and exchange rates; public security forces still prevent theft and fraud; public labour laws still maintain a quiescent workforce. Moreover while the marketplace is certainly the venue for buying and selling private goods, many public goods which were formerly 'free' are traded there as well: personal security, justice, civic amenity, education, health care, pensions and social insurance, access to nature and natural resources. The changing character of the marketplace argues for treating it as a public domain, if only to underline the ongoing need to regulate trade in these sometime public goods, even though they are no longer provided by public authorities.[5]

However, the problem is not so much whether at any given moment in the history of a mixed economy public goods are provided entirely or primarily within the public domain, or whether they can be purchased or sold in private market transactions; rather it is whether neo-liberals will concede that the marketplace, in fact, retains any public character at all. Among true believers at least, neo-liberalism is inconsistent with the notion that successful market economies depend upon the continuing – and in some ways increasing – vitality of the state. For them, faith in the unlimited potential of the marketplace is almost total, and free markets and democracy are inextricably linked. At the domestic level, they insist, the liberalization of local labour, capital and consumer markets leads to the liberalization of local politics. Productivity is the key to prosperity; and productivity requires the dismantling of artificial constraints – tariffs which shelter inefficient local producers, social customs which marginalize potentially productive citizens, political corruption and coercion which result in a mis-allocation of resources, and restrictive work practices which create inefficiencies in the labour market. As constraints are removed, as productivity rises, so too does consumer demand: a virtuous circle. And – the neo-liberal argument continues – with diminished state control, with increased consumer sovereignty, with a free market in goods and services comes increasing pluralism in ideas, social behaviours and relations and political options. For neo-liberals, the public domain – paradoxically – is invigorated by the elixir of private enterprise.

These effects are enhanced, moreover, when markets become global rather than local. First, globalization by ensuring a more logical division of labour based on comparative advantage, force-feeds the gold goose of advanced capitalism, thereby ensuring a reliable supply of golden eggs for its citizens. Those golden eggs may include traditional 'public goods', whether supplied privately or by governments with increased tax revenues. Second, globalization encourages corporations from the advanced economies to become stakeholders in developing nations, thereby allowing them both to take advantage of local resources and to create expanding markets for their expanding productive capacities. Third, they point to the 'CNN effect': the scrutiny of global media discourages abuses by local authoritarian regimes and reinforces the efforts of local democratic forces. And finally, neo-liberals argue, all stakeholders in the global economy will ultimately come to accept that they are also stakeholders in a global system of mutually assured stability and security.

These are rather extraordinary claims: that the marketplace is itself a public domain; that it generates not only private prosperity for the few, but ultimately public goods for the many; that among these public goods are honest government, democracy and peace; and that by implication, the more pervasive are marketplace values, institutions and processes, the more of these 'public goods' they will create. However, these claims should be tested empirically, not just taken on faith; and I suggest that the empirical evidence, so far, does not support them very persuasively. Contrary to the optimistic predictions of neo-liberals, the public domain of the marketplace – like so many other public domains – seems to be plagued by extreme disparities of access, power and rewards. As noted earlier, these inconvenient facts – and their destabilizing social and political consequences – have produced something of a crisis of faith even among true believers. It is this crisis which may have brought us to the verge of a new era, the era of the post-Washington consensus.

The public domain of cyberspace and the information economy

As it happens, the 'public domain' has long been a term of art in one of the most dynamic of all marketplaces, the marketplace for intellectual property. In the law of patents, trademarks and copyrights, the public domain is a sort of Elysian fields, the ultimate resting place of intellectual property rights which were never claimed, have expired due to the effluxion of time or were abandoned by improvident owners (Litman 1990). Here – in principle available for everyone's benefit, profit or delight – are the books of Dickens, the music of Strauss, Edison's first light bulb and Bayer's still-useful, but now unprofitably generic, 'aspirin'.

That at least was the original notion of the public domain in the law of intellectual property: the original creator of novel ideas, processes, signs or symbols would be granted exclusive rents for the material expression of his or her genius for a limited period of time; thereafter, anyone could freely take and use the property. But this is no longer the case, except in the most abstract sense. Intellectual property is central to the global economy. Its creation, dissemination, exploitation and defence are the main strategies by which corporations position themselves in the marketplace. Individual inventors, now seldom found in their garrets, are likely ensconced in well-equipped, very expensive corporate and university laboratories, creators of intellectual property are likely to work for, or on a short leash from, large entertainment, publishing, advertising and software companies; and most important, intellectual property of any residual value is likely to be kept out of the public domain by clever defensive measures sanctioned by a world-wide system of laws which have been relentlessly revised over time to ensure that nothing of value escapes the grasp of its corporate owner for a very lengthy period. Much intellectual property – especially software, know-how and firm-specific manufacturing technologies – remains 'proprietary', kept secret by its owners, not time-limited and not destined to pass into the public domain. And in Jeremy Rifkin's poignant phrase 'the most intimate commons of all' – the human genome – 'is being enclosed and reduced to private property that can be bought and sold on the global market' (Rifkin 1998).[6]

This brings us to cyberspace, supposedly the newest and most intriguing of public domains, the great democratic *agora* where ordinary people are supposed to be free to exchange their goods and ideas (Tapscott 1997; Alexander and Pal 1998). Access to the infinite possibilities of cyberspace is essentially free and unconstrained: it requires only a modest investment in equipment; and it is essentially immune to regulation by governments or to any but nominal control by powerful commercial gatekeepers. There is some truth to these claims: one can find websites for the *Zapatistas* of Chiapas, for small English Inns, for betting, smut and hate propaganda, for cars and houses, for books and art, for governments, corporations and law firms, for celebrities and cranks and college students. But cyberspace is not quite as democratic or as accessible as all that (Gutstein 1999). As with all public domains, cyberspace is increasingly subject to preemptive claims. The Microsoft Explorer software used to gain access to the Internet has been marketed aggressively and perhaps predatorily, and is the subject of an anti-trust proceeding in the United States. While it is easy enough to launch a new 'dot.com' company, it is much harder to make one profitable. Significant start-up and running costs – advertising, promotion, back-room functions, security – seemingly create undue dependence on continued infusions of capital rather than cash flow. It may well turn out that only those with deep pockets will survive in the electronic marketplace. And Internet use is still largely concentrated in a small number of countries and constituencies; vast disparities of access result from wealth- and education-related inequalities as between north and south, and even within advanced economies.

The new public domains: the 'global commons'

Recently, however, we have been reintroduced to the public domain as a spatial concept. It has been proposed that parts of the world should be regarded as 'a global commons' – the term has historical resonance – to be protected from private ownership and despoliation (Rifkin 1991). Some of these new commons – the Antarctic and the Amazon – should be left undisturbed, inviolable sanctuaries for the preservation of their indigenous human populations, cultures, flora or fauna. Others – offshore fisheries, deep-sea mineral resources beyond territorial waters – should be held in trust for the general welfare of humanity, and specifically for the poor peoples of the world. Outer space and the unexplored planets should be regarded as a new public domain (World Commission on Environment and Development 1987), so that all peoples may share in the great drama of exploration and in whatever gains exploration might one day bring. Santos – a self-styled utopist – proposes that cultural and the natural environments should be viewed as the 'common inheritance of mankind', which will be protected by an emerging *jus humanitatus* which transcends national law (Santos 1995).

Perhaps. These are all attractive ideas, in their way. They express values which speak to our noblest instincts or offer unconventional long-term solutions to some of our most intractable problems. Nonetheless, it is hard to believe that merely labelling the ocean depths or the Amazon rainforest or outer space as 'public domains' will forestall a new 'tragedy of the commons', prevent the invocation of a new doctrine of *terra nullius* to dispossess aboriginals and other weak claimants, or deter a new rapacious appropriation of communal resources for private profit. At least there is not much in the history of public domains so far which ought to make us optimistic.

Public domains: from definition to prediction

What does this long, impressionistic and largely sad account of public domains tell us? From the late medieval to the early modern period, many people understood the public domain as a form of communal property, which supported a way of life which was largely defined and regulated by indigenous laws and institutions. Some residue remains of this old property-based conception of the public domain: it animates efforts to ensure community access to natural amenities, to preserve the natural environment from destruction, and to reinvigorate communities of aboriginal peoples on the periphery of advanced economies. But for most of us, as citizens of contemporary democratic states, the public domain has ceased to have corporeal significance. True, we have continued to be fascinated by 'new frontiers' – intellectual property domains such as genetic engineering, information technology and pop music and domains of physical property such as the ocean depths and outer space. Like the 'old frontiers' of nineteenth-century America, these new frontiers are viewed as empty expanses available for private appropriation, as soon as their communally minded aboriginal inhabitants can be subdued, and the necessary capital and technology mobilized to exploit them.

In the context of the debates which have given rise to this chapter and others in this volume, however, the public domain is treated as metaphoric rather than as physical space. It conjures up the many venues in which public values are debated, public decisions are taken, public resources are deployed and public policies are implemented. The public domain, in this sense, is a political domain. But it is more than political: polity, society and economy are inextricably linked, and attempts to partition them into separate realms of discourse and action have come to be regarded as impracticable if not illicit. Hence, for much of the past hundred years, social democracy – hybridized into variants of corporatist, social-market and paternalistic capitalism – represented the moral equivalent of older concepts of the public domain. Free and equitable access to 'public goods, participation in civic institutions and a progressive tax system, it was once assumed, were an effective strategy for sharing the notional 'commons' of wealth, opportunity and power.

However, in recent years, both the modalities of social democracy and the moral impulse behind them seem to be exhausted, even anachronistic. 'There is no such thing as society', said Mrs Thatcher; and most people seemed to agree. The public domain has had little resonance lately, except to the extent that it can be seen as a potential increment to the private domain. But this negative approach to the public domain may be running its course. Recent disasters and near-disasters have reminded us that the contraction of the public domain and the marketization of just about everything has the potential for some very negative consequences. We are being forced to recall that the unconstrained exploitation of nature and people for private profit may ultimately produce physical, social and financial catastrophes for investors in the core advanced economies no less than for workers in those at the periphery, for national elites no less than for international bankers and entrepreneurs. So, very tentatively, we are exploring how to reconstitute the public domain.

The (re)constitution of the new public domain

This exploration, one might expect, would lead to a revisiting of the social democratic agenda, an agenda with an expansive view of the public domain.

But this has not happened. Although social democratic governments have come to power in many western democracies, they have been at pains to identify themselves as 'new' incarnations of old parties, to dissociate themselves from their own histories, alliances and ideologies and, in general, to adhere to the policies of their neo-liberal opponents. If their advent to office were in fact evidence of renewed concern for the public domain, the relative passivity of these social democratic governments would itself have ignited political debate and triggered the formation of new political alignments. But again, this has not happened. People – especially in the advanced democracies – seem increasingly disillusioned with electoral politics and estranged from most other forms of civic participation (Putnam 1995, 1996).

What has happened instead is that new social movements have appeared in both the north and the south, outside the traditional sphere of political life. These movements have acted with considerable imagination and energy to take up particular causes: women, the environment, ethnic minorities, the homeless, local cultures, human rights (Keck and Sikkink 1998). In one sense, they have been quite successful. They have attracted sympathy and support not only from 'the usual suspects' – leftists and liberals, moral entrepreneurs and crusading journalists – but from thoughtful conservatives, responsible business people and significant elements in civil society. And they have managed to win a number of battles, albeit few wars. Their successes, we might say, confirm the impression that there is considerable support for the reconstitution of the public domain. On the other hand, their media campaigns, direct actions and consumer boycotts have seldom been taken up by conventional political formations, mobilized permanent coalitions of support or yielded long-term state policies. Essentially, these social movements have each reclaimed only a small corner of the public domain, for a limited purpose and for a limited period of time; collectively they have not coalesced around an articulate, comprehensive and plausible vision of the whole.

However, in some countries at least, the rise of social movements has been closely associated with another development: an increased interest in constitutionalism. As some of these movements have come to realize, because their support is ephemeral and their campaigns episodic, their victories are less secure than they would prefer. Gradually, it seems, new social movements are coming to the conclusion that their hard-won gains in the public domain will only survive if they can be lodged in new institutions of effective governance, enshrined in law and, if possible, constitutionally entrenched. One can understand how this idea should have gained purchase. Litigation is always cheaper and sometimes quicker than social action and less abrasive and divisive than political agitation. Moreover it is, arguably, more definitive. A constitutional decree serves as a 'silver bullet' which magically slays evil, intimidates backsliding governments and obviates the need continually to jog the memories of sympathizers with short attention spans.

And it is not only adherents of particular social movements who favour a strategy of constitutionalization as means of protecting the public domain.

Respected public figures, scholars and editorialists have long urged that funda-mental principles, which acknowledge humanity's collective responsibility for its common fate, ought to be entrenched as the constitutional norms of nation states and transnational legal regimes (Beatty 1995; Ackerman 1997). Such a strategy, presumably, would ensure that the public domain is not laid waste by the politics of opportunism, alienation or greed.

In fact, this new, 'constitutional' rights-based approach to the public domain seems to be gaining support. At the transnational level, inter-state agreements and improvised transnational structures exist to protect the rights of labour, forbid the use of nuclear weapons and enable the prosecution of crimes against humanity; we have adopted conventions on global warming, the preservation of endangered species, and the protection of cultural property; and we have even created the rudiments of investor rights in the global marketplace by treaties which define the modalities of fair trade, safe navigation and international financial settlements. At the national level, an unprecedented number of coun-tries are engaged in similar juridical strategies involving both adherence to existing international regimes and enactment of domestic laws and constitu-tions: charters of human rights and social and political freedoms; emancipatory legislation protecting workers, women, children and minorities; and state poli-cies and practices which are supposed to ensure respect for the environment and cultural patrimonies. Even at the level of the global economy, optimists are able to point to the proliferation of codes of good corporate practice as evidence that respect for the public domain is being internalized – constitutionalized – by those who have often been most dismissive of it.

This gives rise to a difficult question: should the architecture of a reinvigo-rated public domain, of a new and less tragedic 'commons', begin with the design of constitutional foundations on which can be constructed new institu-tions of effective governance?

To understand the significance of this question, one must appreciate its ironic implications. Constitutionalism, it transpires, is favoured not only by enthusiasts for a new public domain but by its opponents. Neo-liberals too are intrigued by the silver bullet. During the years of their ascendancy – from the advent to power of Prime Minister Thatcher and President Reagan down to the present – they tried in their own way to constitutionalize their particular vision of society and economy. Not for nothing has the WTO (and, briefly, the MAI) been called 'the constitution of the global economy'. Regional trade regimes, such as the EU and NAFTA, limit the capacity of affiliated states to regulate markets (Schneiderman 1996); to that extent, they reduce the range of social policies which can be supported in a given national context; and they thus ulti-mately function as a neo-liberal 'conditioning framework' or super-ego for national governments (Grinspun and Kreklewich 1994). Similarly, 'balanced-budget' and 'tax-reduction' provisions have been introduced into domestic legislation and constitutions, effectively precluding recourse to the Keynesian strategies which used to underpin social welfare programmes in many states (Philipps 1996). Other neo-liberal policies, which amended the conventions and institutions of social democracy are designed to permanently diminish the public domain: the abolition of corporatist structures for consultation and consensus building; the radical reduction of trade union power and the disestablishment of cooperative institutions; the disempowering of local governments and specialized state agencies; the break-up and sell-off of long-established state-owned utilities, services and enterprises; the effective end of constitutionally mandated affirmative action in education, employment and electoral arrangements; the introduction of significant user fees for health care, public housing and education; and the enhanced use of the criminal law to imprison (and, in the United States, to execute) large numbers of poor people and members of minority groups.

In all of these cases, constitutions, or some approximation or parody of constitutions, have been used to lengthen the list of things which can be 'bought or sold on the open market', to shorten the list of 'things we hold in common', even to redefine who 'we' are, so that fewer of us share whatever is left of the public domain.

This is, to repeat, a considerable irony: both those who want to restore or expand the public domain and those who wish to retrench or diminish it look to constitutionalism as a means of redrawing its boundaries. They see law not only as a short-term tactic used to advance and legitimize their respective viewpoints, but as a long-term strategy to constitutionalize their particular values and assumptions, so as to ensure that their partisan view of the public domain will persist despite the pendulum swings of democratic politics. Thus the juridical high ground, the realm of law and constitutionalism, is hotly contested.

But there is more irony yet. Adherents of both positions tend to overestimate the ability of legal and constitutional strategies and institutions either to achieve or to prevent the transformation of society, economy or polity. Law – especially constitutional law – can do much less than we think it can; its effects are variable and sometimes perverse; and political and social activism, for all their limitations, remain indispensable features of any effective strategy to alter the contours of the public domain.

The limits and uses of constitutionalism

Conventional legal theory postulates that constitutions define and organize the governments of sovereign states whose legislative, judicial and executive branches in turn produce, adjudicate and administer law. In this sense, laws and constitutions – again, as conventionally understood – have been closely identified with the idea of state sovereignty. This close identification makes the constitution an improbable vehicle for advancing the project of a reinvigorated public domain. States today may or may not be 'hollowed out', disempowered, obsolescent or irrelevant, as much of the literature claims; but no one would deny that in every sense – except the purely formal – the capacity of most states to exercise their sovereignty has diminished. Sovereignty was never absolute, of course; its exercise was always compromised by *realpolitik* of both domestic and international provenance. However, today the exercise of sovereignty is also constrained by new and powerful forces – by the globalization of trade and communications, by universalistic norms of legality and propriety, by the debilitating insights of post-modernity. To this extent, national constitutions are no longer normative bedrock, no longer the ultimate standard against which the legality of government action is likely to be tested. Even enshrining a particular view of the public domain in a constitutional instrument will not spare it the indignity of having to pass muster under the terms of some international treaty or convention or – more humiliating yet – of winning the good opinion of bond traders and currency dealers.

Oddly, in light of its dwindling efficacy, constitutionalism – a central organizing concept of liberal democracy – has become more ubiquitous in political discourse, in legal-professional practice, even in popular culture. During the past half-century, it seems, more constitutions have been written than perhaps at any time in history, as new states have come into being, and as old states have redefined themselves in the wake of war or civil strife. Many states without entrenched Bills of Rights have adopted them – or attorned to such regimes as the European Charter – and those with entrenched Bills have begun to use them more frequently. Nonetheless, despite the growing popularity of constitutional discourse, the successful practice of constitutional law and politics is very much in question. Claims made on behalf of the conventional 'command model' of constitutions – the constitution speaks; citizens and officials obey – are being contested by legal theory and often disproved by legal science (Rosenberg 1991). We know – those of us who have the luxury to be sceptical about them – that constitutions often engage the energies and serve the interests of political and legal elites, not of ordinary citizens; that they are sometimes used to deflect or defeat democratic initiatives; that they seldom translate into effective rules which shape actual societies and polities. We do not need to hone our scepticism on, say, the 1936 Stalin Constitution of the former Soviet Union, or the other travesties passed off by repressive and lawless regimes as 'constitutions'. We need consider only the well-documented gap between constitutional aspiration and achievement in our own democratic countries, and in other countries which hold themselves out as exemplars of 'the rule of law'. Why then would we imagine that constitutions and laws have the power to extend or contract the boundaries of the public domain, to entrench neo-liberalism or to inoculate us against it permanently?

But imagine we do. Constitutionalism and the 'rule of law' – core principles of western democratic theory – have been awarded the ultimate accolade: they have come to be regarded as indispensable conditions of a free market economy. The post-Communist reformers of eastern Europe, George Soros and the other midwives of that great transformation, the visionaries of the World Bank, even the flinty-eyed negotiators of the IMF all seem to agree that successful capitalism is unthinkable without a democratic constitution. Does this represent a principled commitment to human freedom in all its dimensions? a propagandistic discrediting by the triumphalist west of Communist and klepto-cratic regimes? a pragmatic calculation that democracy will reduce instability, and thereby create more favourable conditions for investment? No doubt all of the above, to some degree: but there is a further explanation for this sudden outburst of constitutionalism, this sudden infatuation with the rule of law. What appeals to many of its enthusiasts is that constitutionalism is in large measure about adjectival and institutional arrangements, not about substantive policy. The new constitutions and charters, for the most part, focus on individual rather than collective rights; they do not mandate state activism or a vibrant public sector; and of course, they cannot operate extraterritorially to reach foreign economic actors. This has led Santos to conclude that the paradigm, which informs the current wave of constitutionalism is 'an efficient weak state suited to complement the efficient regulation of social and economic life by markets and the private sector' (Santos 2000). In such a paradigm, there is little room for an expansive view of the public domain.

And finally, a constitution is supposed to be imprinted with a nation's DNA, the repository of its distinctive national experiences, symbols, myths and compromises, the origin and expression of its unique political culture and legal institutions. It ought therefore, in principle, to offer compelling evidence as to how that nation conceives of and governs its public domain. This may have been true of revolutionary America or France, of fascist Spain or Italy or of Trudeau's Canada or Blair's United Kingdom. But it is less and less true that constitutions are unique. There seems to be a global trade in constitutionalism, a brisk after-market in specific constitutional technologies: charters of political, civil, social (and sometimes economic) rights; forums mandated to adjust the balance between dominant and subordinate communities; arrangements to ease the transition from a former to a future regime; and supreme courts or constitu-tional tribunals with responsibility for making the whole thing work (Choudhry 1999).

This tendency towards the generic presents us with a difficulty. If national constitutions no longer embody and express what is special about each country, what can they tell us about the governance of its public domain? Possibly, that many important decisions concerning governance are no longer made by national governments; that if minimal governance is the maximum ambition of a government, almost any constitutional arrangements will serve; that globaliza-tion has led to a convergence of national governance agendas and political cultures; that the hegemonic power of ideas about constitutions emanating from the most powerful nations – like ideas about economics or culture or technology – has caused a temporary short-circuit of the imagination, which will revive when a new paradigm of governance appears. Whichever explanation is true, they all point in one direction: to the extent that effective protection of the public domain is associated with the project of national identity, constitutions no longer serve the purpose well.

This is not to say that constitutions, the laws enacted under them, or the institutions which they create have no relevance to our discussion. For one thing, all of these may offer us important insights into the world-view, the values, the power structures and the intellectual orientation of their authors. If the authors borrow, say, the model of French republicanism or German federalism, they presumably do so as an expression of respect for what they understand to be the political ethos of those countries. If they give disproportionate influence to specific populations or interest groups, they are either attempting to placate those groups by perpetuating existing power relations or to reassure them by introducing new protections. If they reproduce language from the UN Declaration of Human Rights, this signals a commitment to a particular kind of internationalist vision, or at least the desire to create the impression that one exists. In other words, all constitutional language, all constitutional conventions, have a political provenance, which in some way implicates particular understandings about the value and character of the public domain.

For another, constitutions acquire a kind of derivative or secondary significance. Constitutional language is typically vague and indeterminate. In principle, gaps in meaning are filled in over the years in various ways. Patterns of political behaviour may come to be accepted as constitutional customs or conventions; the parliamentary system of the United Kingdom is a case in point. Judicial interpretations, rendered in the context of constitutional litigation, speak to a particular view of law; the inflation of the interstate commerce and equal protection clauses of the US constitution is a good example (Rotunda and Nowak 1999). And intra- or inter-governmental protocols help federal systems to redistribute responsibility and resources; Canada provides an instance with its tradition of 'cooperative' or 'executive' federalism. But even so constitutional indeterminacy persists, as it must if constitutions are to adapt over time to changing circumstances and new understandings.

This inescapable feature of constitutions gives rise to a peculiar dynamic, at least in countries which take their constitutions seriously. The mere threat to invoke the constitution – to challenge government action in litigation, to make adherence to a convention the focus of political debate, to press for a formal declaration clarifying or modifying previous interpretations – may trigger a sequence of unpredictable outcomes. Formal litigation outcomes are always difficult to predict, of course, but practical outcomes are even more so. For example, governments may try to avoid litigation in order to avoid costs and delays or possibly adverse precedential effects; exogenous political events may make it inconvenient for governments to deal with charges that they have violated basic understandings about constitutional practice; or governments may be reluctant to discuss constitutional change for fear of opening a Pandora's box. In each case, the resulting reconfiguration or reaffirmation of constitutional norms owes little to legal text. It is not just the words of the constitution which shape future governmental action, then, but the precedential, practical, cultural and political consequences of controversy over those words. And further questions arise: who speaks for the government and shapes its response to constitutional controversy? How does this allocation of functions affect the internal dynamic of governance? Which groups or individuals can afford to use the constitution to attack the government? What public attitudes towards the state, the law and the courts does constitutional controversy engender? What does a high (or low) incidence of constitutional controversy tell us about the political culture of a country? Indeterminacy, even – especially! – on fundamental issues of constitutional normativity is what frustrates attempts to constitutionalize competing visions of the public domain (Arthurs 1999).

Conclusion

We are, it seems, moving beyond the Washington consensus, though how far beyond is as yet unclear. The new era is likely to be characterized by two important innovations: a somewhat more equitable distribution of social goods – a new emphasis on what we have called 'the public domain'; and the strengthening of civil society, institutions of governance, democratic values and the rule of law – a new emphasis on what I have referred to as 'constitutionalism'. However, the extent and the efficacy of these innovations is by no means assured.

First, these innovations reflect fundamentally different concerns and are supported by fundamentally different constituencies. On the one side, there are those who believe in strengthening the public domain and constitutionalism as ends in themselves, on the other those who believe that these constitute a prudent investment in the creation of a more stable and profitable business environment. Those who embrace the former perspective are unlikely to be satisfied with modest measures; those who embrace the latter will arrive much sooner at what they perceive to be the point of diminishing returns. Given these contradictions, it is easy to predict the next crisis of the post-Washington consensus era. The cost of resuscitating the public domain, the unpredictable behaviour of empowered communities and the interventionist tendencies of democratically elected governments is likely to collide with the desire of powerful economic actors for low taxes, open markets and acquiescent labour.

Second, both 'the public domain' and 'constitutionalism' are capacious, even contestable, terms. As we have seen, there have been many versions of the public domain, and many versions of constitutionalism. But of course, these do not exist in a vacuum; they are both shaped by the forces of political economy. In Drache's diagrams (Drache 2001), the public domain is consequential or residual space – space created by the dynamic tension between state and market forces, space which is not even coterminous with civil society, itself the site of contestation. Likewise constitutionalism. Its most salient features, as I have tried to show, are substantive ambiguity and procedural indeterminacy. Attempts to flesh out what we mean by 'public domain' and 'constitutionalism' are enormously valuable in exposing possibilities for the future of the global economy, national polities and local communities: but they should not be conflated with attempts to shape that future through economic interventions or political and social action.

Third, the public domain and constitutionalism, in all their versions, have to this point been closely associated with the nation-state. A transnational public domain and transnational constitutional processes have emerged only in Europe, and even there they are by no means comprehensive or secure. Indeed, the frailty of 'social Europe' and the persistence of the EU's 'democratic deficit' arguably represent the Achilles' heel of the whole European project. By contrast, the Washington consensus – even in its post-consensus incarnation – is essentially global in its concerns. Obviously nation-states were the architects of the Washington consensus, the agents of its enforcement, the authors of its revision, and the focus of resistance to it. Obviously too, the Washington consensus is more closely identified with the ideology and interests of some states than of others. But that much said, the whole point of the consensus is to encourage or require states to abstain from being state-like, which is to say to avoid asserting their individual sovereignties and national interests so as to obstruct or encumber their own integration into a global economy. At the very least, we are far closer to achieving something that might be called a global economy than we are to defining a global public domain or global institutions of democratic governance.

Fourth, as my cautionary tales of the public domain have demonstrated, the two innovations of the post-consensus era will not be easily reconciled. The public domain in its many different manifestations – as commons, as frontier, as political liberalism, as social democracy, as 'new frontier' – has more often than not found itself at odds with law. And when it has not, when its proponents have turned to constitutional strategies and institutions, they have often been sorely disappointed. In part, this historical record is a reflection of the intrinsic incapacity of law to achieve social transformation; in part, however, it is a reflection of the fact that constitutionalism – the rule of law – has often been used deliberately by the strong to deprive the weak of their rights and entitlements. Enthusiasm for attempts to revise the Washington consensus in order both to resuscitate the public domain and to reinforce democratic values should therefore not be allowed to obscure the difficulty in reconciling these two ends with each other.

Are these concerns and contradictions the predicate of a dismal syllogism in which the public domain past and the constitutionalist present are so fraught with disappointment and ambiguity that neither offers hope for the future? Not at all. But neither is sufficient in itself, nor are the two in combination. Again, I will draw on history for my metaphor. The historic public domain was a place where inchoate but well-understood rights were, in E.P. Thompson's phrase, 'imbricated' in the work-a-day activities of the common people, activities which gave those rights shape, effect and legitimacy. So too with our metaphoric public domain. It surely ought to be a place where ordinary citizens are more than observers, funders, passive beneficiaries or victims of legal manoeuvres; it ought to be a place where their activities – in politics, social action, workplace organization and community participation – stand at least some chance of shaping relations of power and processes of governance. In other words, the public domain will ultimately be reconstructed – if at all – from the ground up; and constitutionalism will – at best – legitimize and reinforce this grass-roots effort, not substitute for it.

Notes

1   Examples include the 'natural' law of early modern common use rights, the law merchant of eighteenth-century insurers and traders, the customary law of nineteenth- and twentieth-century colonies and pre- and post-colonial states, the traditions of religious communities, the trading rules of stock exchanges and the policy manuals of public bureaucracies.
2   The advent of state law and its destructive implications for communal life were well understood. As an eighteenth-century rhyme observed: 'The law doth punish man or woman/That steals the goose from off the common/But lets the greater felon loose/Who steals the common from the goose.' And see generally Hoskins and Stamp 1963.
3   For example, the 'Governor and Company of Adventurers trading into Hudson's Bay', was granted a Charter by the British Crown in 1670, together with the ownership of all adjacent lands 'not now possessed by … the subjects of any other Christian Prince or State'. The Hudson's Bay Company ultimately claimed 'ownership' of a quarter of the North American continent, which was ceded first to the British Crown, and ultimately to the new Canadian state, in the last quarter of the nineteenth century (Woodcock 1970).
4   In April, 1999, Nunavut in Canada's eastern Arctic, became a self-governing homeland with territorial status, for some 26,000 Inuit. Nunuvut Act, Stat. Canada 1993, c. 28.
5   An example: Ontario has created the first privately owned electronic toll road, Highway 407, on which payment is enforced by denying non-payers renewal of their drivers' licences. However, recent reports have revealed that computer failures have led to billing errors and that the private owners have failed to provide any means of challenging these errors. The government has in effect enforced these illicit charges by threatening drivers with loss of their licences (R. Mackie, 'Ontario Won't Seek Money for Erroneous Highway Bills', *The Globe and Mail*, 24 February 2000, p. A26; R. Mackie, '407 Toll Outcry Spurs Reforms', *The Globe and Mail*, 25 February 2000, p. A1.
6   A belated attempt was made by President Bill Clinton and Prime Minister Tony Blair to ensure that knowledge of the human genome does not become the subject of private property, but remains available for use by research institutes, universities and laboratories which are willing to forgo their right to patent products developed on the basis of knowledge of the genome (D. Henke, R. Evans and T. Radford, 'Blair and Clinton Push to Stop Gene Patents', *The Observer*, 19 September 1999; and see P. Quéau, 'Defining World Public Property: Who Owns Knowledge?', *Le Monde Diplomatique*, January 2000; J. Martinson, 'Gene Research at Risk: Private Firm Demands Exclusive Rights on Human Genetic Code', *Guardian Weekly*, 9–15 March 2000; M. Munro, 'The Human Genome Project', *The National Post*, 13 March 2000.

Bibliography

Ackerman, Bruce (1997) 'The Rise of World Constitutionalism', *Virginia Law Review*, 83: 771.
Alexander, Cynthia J. and Pal, Leslie A. (1998) *Digital Democracy: Policy and Politics in the Wired World*, Toronto: Oxford University Press.

Arthurs, Harry (1979) 'Rethinking Administrative Law: A Slightly Dicey Business', *Osgoode Hall Law Journal*, 17: 1.

—— (1985) '*Without the Law*': *Administrative Justice and Legal Pluralism in Nineteenth Century England*, Toronto: University of Toronto Press.

—— (1999) 'TINA x 2: Constitutionalizing Neo-conservatism and Regional Economic Integration', in Thomas Courchene (ed.) *Room to Manoeuvre? Globalization and Policy Convergence*, Kingston: Queens University Centre for Economic Policy.

Beatty, David M. (1995) *Constitutional Law in Theory and Practice*, Toronto: University of Toronto Press.

Butler, Lynda (1982) 'The Commons Concept: An Historical Concept with Modern Relevance', *William & Mary Law Review*, 23: 835.

Choudhry, Sujit (1999) 'Globalization in Search of Justification: Toward a Theory of Comparative Constitutional Interpretation', *Indiana Law Journal*, 74: 819.

de Villiers, Bertus (ed.) (1994) *Birth of a Constitution*, Kenwyn: Juta & Co., Ltd.

Devetak, Richard and Higgott, Richard (2001) 'Saving the social bond and recovering the public domain' (this volume).

Drache, Daniel (2001) 'The Return of the Public Domain after the Triumph of Markets: Revisiting the Most Basic of Fundamentals' (this volume).

Drummond, Alison (1992) *The Social Charter: Evolution of the Concept in Recent Constitutional Negotiations*, Toronto: Ontario Legislative Library, Legislative Research Service.

Ellickson, Robert C. (1991) *Order Without Law: How Neighbors Settle Disputes*, Cambridge, MA: Harvard University Press.

Grinspun, Ricardo and Kreklewich, Robert (1994) 'Consolidating Neo-Liberal Reforms: "Free Trade" as a Conditioning Framework', *Studies in Political Economy*, 43.

Griffiths, John (1986) 'What is Legal Pluralism?', *Journal of Legal Pluralism*, 24: 1.

Gutstein, Donald (1999) *E.con: How the Internet Undermines Democracy*, Toronto: Stoddart.

Harrell-Bond, Barbara and Burman, Sandra (eds) (1979) *The Imposition of Law*, New York: Academic Press.

Hardin, Garrett (1968) 'The Tragedy of the Commons', *Science*, 162: 1243.

Hirst, Paul (1997) *From Statism to Pluralism: Democracy, Civil Society, and Global Politics*, London: UCL Press.

Hobsbawm, Eric (1987) *The Age of Empire 1875–1914*, London: Guild Publishing, esp. chap. 4 'The Politics of Democracy'.

Hoskins, W.G. and Stamp, L. Dudley (1963) *The Common Lands of England & Wales*, London: Collins.

Keck, Margaret E. and Sikkink, Kathryn (1998) *Activists Beyond Borders: Advocacy Networks in International Politics*, Ithaca, NY: Cornell University Press.

Litman, Jessica (1990) 'The Public Domain', *Emory Law Journal*, 39: 965.

Matláry, Jaan Haaland (1995) 'The Decline of the State as the Source of Political Legitimation', in *Cooperation and Conflict*, London/Thousand Oaks/Delhi: Sage.

McLean, Janet (1999) 'Property as Power and Resistance', in J. McLean (ed.) *Property and the Constitution*, Oxford: Hart Publishing.

Merry, Sally (1988) 'Legal Pluralism', *Law and Society Review*, 22: 869.

—— (1996) 'Legal Pluralism and Transnational Culture', in R.A. Wilson (ed.) *Human Rights, Culture and Context: Anthropological Perspectives*, London: Pluto Press.

Neeson, Jeanette (1993) *Commoners: Common Right, Enclosure and Social Change in England 1700–1820*, Cambridge: Cambridge University Press.

Perrot, Michelle (ed.) (1990) *A History of Private Life: From the Fires of the Revolution to the Great War*, Cambridge/London: Belknap Press.

Philipps, Lisa (1996) 'The Rise of Balanced Budget Laws in Canada: Legislating Fiscal (Ir)responsibility', *Osgoode Hall Law Journal*, 34: 681.

Putnam, Robert D. (1995) 'Bowling Alone: America's Declining Social Capital', *Journal of Democracy*, 6, 1: 65.

—— (1996) 'The Strange Disappearance of Civic America', *American Prospect*, 24: 34.

Rifkin, Jeremy (1991) *Biosphere Politics: A New Consciousness for a New Century*, New York: Crown.

—— (1998) *The Biotech Century*, New York: Jeremy P. Tarcher/Putnam.

Rodgers, Daniel (1998) *Atlantic Crossings: Social Politics in a Progressive Age*, Cambridge/London: Belknap Press of Harvard University Press.

Rose, Carol (1986) 'The Comedy of the Commons: Custom, Commerce and Inherently Public Property', *University of Chicago Law Review*, 53: 711.

Rosenberg, Gerald (1991) *The Hollow Hope: Can Courts Bring About Social Change?*, Chicago, IL: University of Chicago Press.

Rotunda, Donald D. and Nowak, John E. (1999) *Treatise on Constitutional Law: Substance and Procedure*, 3rd edn, St. Paul: West Group. (See especially Interstate commerce power – volume 2; equal rights – volume 3.)

Royal Commission on Aboriginal Peoples (1996) *Report of the Royal Commission on Aboriginal Peoples: Looking Forward, Looking Back*, vol. 1, Ottawa: The Commission.

Samuel, Lenia (1997) *Fundamental Social Rights: Case Law of the European Social Charter*, Strasbourg: Council of Europe.

Santos, Boaventura de Sousa (1995) *Toward a New Common Sense: Law, Science and Politics in the Paradigmatic Transition*, New York/London: Routledge.

—— (2000) 'Law and Democracy: (Mis)trusting the Global Reform of Courts', in Jane Jenson and Boaventura de Sousa Santos (eds) *Globalizing Institutions: Case Studies in Regulation and Innovation*, London: Ashgate Publishing.

Schneiderman, David (1996) 'NAFTA's Takings Rule: American Constitutionalism Comes to Canada', *University of Toronto Law Journal*, 46: 499.

Simpson, Gerry (1993–94) '*Mabo*, International Law, *Terra Nullius* and the Stories of Settlement: An Unresolved Jurisprudence', *Melbourne Law Review*, 19: 195.

Slattery, Brian (1991) 'Aboriginal Sovereignty and Imperial Claims', *Osgoode Hall Law Journal*, 29: 681.

Soros, George (1998) *The Crisis of Global Capitalism*, New York: Public Affairs.

Tapscott, Don (1997) *Growing Up Digital: The Rise of the Net Generation*, New York: McGraw-Hill.

Teubner, Gunther (1992) 'The Two Faces of Janus: Rethinking Legal Pluralism', *Cardozo Law Review*, 13: 1443.

Thompson, Edward (1975) *Whigs and Hunters*, Harmondsworth: Penguin Books.

—— (1991) *Customs in Common*, New York: The New Press.

Wolfensohn, James (1998) 'The Other Crisis', address to the World Bank Group, 6 October 1998. www.worldbank.org/html/extdr/am98-en.htm (accessed 11 April 2001)

Woodcock, George (1970) *The Hudson's Bay Company*, New York: Crowell-Collier Press.

World Bank (1997) *World Bank Development Report 1997: The State in a Changing World*, New York: Oxford University Press.

World Commission on Environment and Development (1987) *Our Common Future: Report of the World Commission on Environment and Development*, Oxford: Oxford University Press.

Section 2

Moving the boundary between the market and the state

The political theory of the public domain

4 Policy domain or public domain at a time of globalization

Simon Reich

Introduction

'Globalization', we are repeatedly told, challenges the governance capacities of the State and weakens sovereignty over decision making.[1] Some conclude that globalization represents a natural progression towards a 'borderless' world,[2] signalling the end of the modern international state system as we know it. The capacity for governance has been truncated, with finance just providing a leading example of a broader trend.[3] In its place we are offered a view of a complex world of state and non-state actors who share governance functions and are bound by a series of social norms and institutional linkages that transcend national borders.[4]

For others, the concept is over-stated and its influences are exaggerated. Rather than a structural change in the nature of capitalism beyond the scope of any individual actors, it is a subterfuge to justify the abolition of the welfare state.[5] States may choose to delegate authority rather than simply having it taken from them.

Central to these two perspectives is the contrasting response to questions concerning the effect of globalization on the emergence of alternative governance or authority structures, especially in the non-governmental and the corporate world, that compete with states. Yet state and non-state authority clearly exists in a more contingent, interactive and dynamic manner. Governance has changed, becoming increasingly conditional in character – with varied resulting capacities for states to deal with newly emergent issues.

The idea of the public domain, in a sense, intrudes on this debate by implying that governance structures are shared through social networks. Invocation of the term begs some questions. Under what conditions and in which ways do states retain influence? Furthermore, how and under what conditions are state and non-state actors tied together? What are the dynamics and contingencies of governance structures under globalization? Most importantly, in this context, what 'happens' to the public domain as a mechanism of cohesion protecting civil society – and linking state, society and economy – here? Its protective capacities seem, in certain instances, to disappear. If so, how can we reconcile the apparent eclipse of the public domain in many countries in the midst of the 1998 financial crisis with the central role that it appears to occupy in the context of much of Drache's formative chapter? The answer lies in an exploration of the contours and limits of the public domain in the context of a critical factor; the influence of the policy domain.

Towards an answer

In his discussion, Daniel Drache posits the notion that the public domain lies:

> in relationship to the rest of the social order [as] one of the centres of deci-sion-making that allows society to organize itself, plan for consumption and support a mix between non-negotiable goods, mixed goods and negotiable goods. From it emanates the set of processes essential to a stable social order and a cohesive society.
>
> If the state, market and civil society remain the great institutional markers of modernity, the public domain is at the intersection between civil society (largely norm-based, decentralized and hierarchically flat), the market (subject to the constraints and opportunities of the universal price mechanism, private property rights and corporate profit-taking) and the modern administrative state (dependent on its full-bodied bureaucracy, large-scale financial resources and vast legal powers). It is a large irregular space covering a range of activity and organizations that belong to the public as a whole, having flexible borders, expanding and contracting in size, driven most by need rather than by any fixed notion of rights.
>
> (p. 41)

Comprised of a host of components including public goods, services, places, norms and networks, Drache thus identifies a concept that links state, society and market. To be useable, however, we need to ascertain how, and how effec-tively, it establishes such linkages.

This chapter seeks to contribute modestly to the debates generated in this volume and to the utility of the concept of the 'public domain' by offering one version of a contingent argument. Rather than expressing its application in such grand terms, it will be argued that the utility of the public domain is intrinsically related to the sphere of public policy where it is applied. This vari-able utility is a function of the character of the central actors and the degree of cohesion that they share. Some policy domains have fewer actors with more consistent agendas and less contentious issues or sources of conflict. More explicitly, it will be argued that the relevance of the public domain as a tool in the context of globalization is distinguished by policy sector, in other words, the utility of the public domain is highly contingent. How far it penetrates and affects the relationship between state, society and economy is heavily influ-enced by the policy domain in which it operates because each domain offers differing degrees of potential social cohesion between state and non-state actors.

The theoretical genesis of this approach lies in Theodore Lowi's seminal

World Politics article of 1964.[6] Applying the concept that 'policy dictates politics', Lowi states, '*these areas of policy or government activity constitute real arenas of power. Each arena tends to develop its own characteristic political structure, political process, elite and group relations*' (original italics). Lowi wrote of national governments in the context of democratic, pluralist polities. This chapter is written in the context of a globalized polity but retains the same type of proposition. 'What remains is to identify these arenas in this context, to formulate hypotheses about the attributes of each, and to test the scheme by how many empirical relationships it can anticipate and explain.'[7]

The policy domain is important in determining the expansive influence of the public domain in the context of globalization. There are four central policy domains of globalization – redistribution, regulation, democratization (and modernization), and liberalization and the respective central analytical problems and institutional actors in each area. Second, the contours of each policy domain suggest that there is a direct relationship between the form of policy domain and the influence of the public domain. In essence, the public domain plays its most central organizing role in the realm of redistributive policy and then is successively less prevalent in the domains of regulatory policy, democratization and is least influential in the realm of liberalization. This is because the social cohesion characteristic of the concept of the public domain becomes increasingly attenuated as one successively moves through the policy domains.

Social networks become attenuated as power shifts away from a national context oriented around the state towards larger geographic units that may enlarge networks but which correspondingly entail less cohesive cultural and social linkages. Expanding the physical and cultural realm of governance weakens the legitimacy and thus, the authority of government endemic in the concept of the public domain. I contend that the specific character of a policy domain helps define the physical contours of such social networks. Therefore the policy domain essentially defines the nature of politics and thus the relevance of the public domain as an organizing instrument of interaction.

In the remainder of this chapter, the policy domains of globalization and the central actors involved in each domain will be delineated. I then offer a speculative linkage in which an argument about how the effectiveness of the public domain as an instrument of action respectively weakens across policy domains.

Public policy and public domain

Globalization potentially represents a fundamental evolution relating to the governance structure linking market power and state authority in the global order. It offers the prospect of a shift from public to private regulation and from territorial to trans-territorial forms of authority – and thus, an epochal stage in the development of capitalism.

Criticism often focuses on an apparent paradox: if globalization is redefining the boundaries of state power in a way that makes its 'retreat' so apparent, why does the state play such a prominent role in discussions concerning the retrenchment of the welfare state?[8] Sceptics, furthermore, suggest that the state retains an authoritative role, but one transformed in the context of bargaining within supranational organizational structures.[9] What is generally contested is the relationship between public authorities, the market and representatives of civil society. In Drache's analysis it is the public domain that provides the 'conceptual glue' that links them together.

If the public sector is indeed retreating, then the study of globalization might concentrate primarily on the private or non-profit sectors rather than the public sector. But this is not the case in much scholarly or policy-oriented literature. The substantive realm of what we term 'globalization studies' may be best described as in intellectual disarray due to an inadequate differentiation of the relationship between states and supranational or inter-governmental actors, and various types of non-state actors.

Studying the relationship between public policy and public domain potentially offers a solution to this deficit. These policy domains emphasize the participation and roles of differing actors. Whether we thus define globalization in historical, economic, cultural or sociological terms, we must initially offer a typology of public policy that captures the central components of globalization – and with that both the major actors and the relationship between them.[10]

Policy domains in the context of globalization

In this section, we delineate the four major policy domains that operate in the context of globalization. The selection of these four domains raises four fundamental questions that generally are addressed in the context of politics. These are:

- What are the rules?
- How are the rules made?
- What body makes authoritative decisions?
- What are the consequences of these decisions in terms of 'winners and losers'?

These four questions, in effect, correspond to four policy domains in modern polities, those of regulation, democratization/modernization, liberalization and redistribution respectively. Globalization influences the answer to those four questions, often in dramatic fashion, as legitimacy and authority shifts from the national polity to alternative venues either down to the sub-national level, up to the supranational level, or out to civil society or the market. Furthermore, that certainly affects the influence of specific actors, the cohesiveness of social networks, and ultimately the capacity of the public domain to link state, society and economy within a national context.

The next step is to address these four questions in the context of globalization with greater specificity, although not in the order outlined above. The ordering has been changed to reflect the degree to which the social networks become increasing attenuated and less cohesive – and thus, the public domain less effective in sustaining the fabric of linkages between state, society and economy.

Who wins and loses? Redistribution

If globalization represents an historical epoch marked by the end of 'embedded liberalism', it results in a new set of 'winners' and 'losers'. While economic pressures may build, political will and policy competence offers the opportunity for meaningful levels of policy autonomy over redistributive issues. Political and social development is not structurally determined. The agency of actors, albeit path-dependent, is important in bringing about change. The seeds of structural constraint of the kind emanating from processes of globalization have their roots in the actions of agents – be they public or private, state, regional, international or individual.

For many who focus on the role of redistributive policy, globalization is not simply an unfettered economic phenomenon but also a politico-ideological one that acts as a rationalization for emerging trends in contemporary governance.[11] But the replacement of the Keynesian welfare state with the neo-liberal one, in many countries, is not the same thing as the end of the state itself. Rather, it is the end of a particular form of state familiar to the developed democracies.

Is the state weakening or just changing its role under globalization? To many, the state no longer fulfils the Keynesian function of defending domestic welfare from exogenous pressures. Rather, it is a 'transmission belt' in which neo-liberal policy passes from the 'global to the national' policy domain.[12] They see the state primarily as a receptor rather than seeing the state as able to 'author' and 'encode' modern capitalism,[13] and thus as an instrument of globalization.

But students of globalization who stress the 'terminal nature' of the state miss the historic and political constraints that drive states.[14] Indeed, they still largely determine the issue of 'who gets what' within national borders. While international advocacy networks proliferate, the relevant social networks in the context of redistribution generally remain domestic in most countries. With the exception of a few states in the most extreme poverty, states' budgets still largely account for most welfare expenditures, and states are still largely determinative of how those expenditures get distributed. Although we are genuflectively told that the total amount of resources that states have to allocate has dwindled, this is not necessarily true. While the Clinton Administration has shifted the welfare focus from national to sub-national authorities, total welfare expenditures remained intact for much of the 1990s.[15] Drache's cross-national figures on public service expenditures in his formative chapter are consistent with this contention, as are his more specific contentions about social transfers in OECD states (see chapter this volume).

Whether defined in broad terms as 'assets that are held in common and cannot be bought or sold on the open market', those shared and used in common, or those vaguely discussed as beyond the workings of the market, the public domain does centre foremost upon welfarism. In this realm, a domestic platform is a necessary condition for the functioning of the public domain. A national context and social cohesion are complementary conditions. A shift away from this context attenuates those cultural linkages that lie at the heart of the public domain. As geography enlarges beyond national borders and the locus of authority changes (away from the state), so does the cohesive elements of the public domain weaken.

Welfare is where the linkage is most prevalent in the locus of public services and private philanthropy. Yet, unlike Drache, I would argue that not all parts of the public domain involve collective usage or equal access. Domestic interests do compete in a zero-sum game for limited resources. External factors may condition the size of the pie, but not how it gets divided. Still, the public domain is most evident in the context of redistribution because it is here that the social cohesion between state services, philanthropic foundations and organizations, and non-profit organizations are at their strongest. While states may dominate the organization and delivery of such services, they generally share goals and an allocative burden with non-state actors rather than competing for resources.

The assertion that the changing locus of authority and enlarged geography undermines the cohesion of the public domain suggests that different policy domains reflect such variance. The following three policy domains discussed reflect weakening social cohesion as they entail a successively geographic enlargement and a change in the locus of authority to include an increasing number and type of actors beyond national borders.

What are the rules? Regulation

Regulation remains a central policy domain in the context of globalization despite the apparent 'retreat of the state'. Huge increases in trade, investment and financial flows have exposed and magnified the differences between national economies. Efforts to arbitrate differences across systems or to achieve convergence, however, have often shifted the focus of regulation in the context of globalization from the national to the supranational level of inter-governmental organizations (IGOs). Regional organizations, in particular, have become more important and proliferated because they provide shared rules of behaviour and reflect the fact that the largest percentage growth has primarily been in intra-regional trade and foreign direct investment rather than across regions. The world is not so much globalizing as it is regionalizing, both in terms of IGOs and economic flows. In part, this tendency is a response to the need of states to address collective action problems beyond the capacity of governments, whether in the form of – as examples – environmental degradation or drug interdiction.

The central proposition of those who study regulatory policy is that the purpose of an economy and polity remains highly contested, even as liberal democratic forms apparently spread in influence. This approach finds voice in Samuel Huntington's polemic on comparative civilizations.[16]

Rather than abandoning economic processes to the instability of markets, regulation re-emphasizes the role of the state in stressing rules of conduct as a means to avoid conflict and to arbitrate fissures in contrasting forms of capitalism. It signals a shift towards cooperation rather than harmony, with states generally using organizations (even bilateral agreements) as a cipher for their own policy goals.[17] This is reflected in one of three options – institutional competition (mutual recognition), 'harmonization' (in the sense of imposing standards), or managed trade – all involving recognition of the differences that are negotiated and eventually considered legitimate by all signatures to an agreement.[18] Such approaches reassert the importance of inter-governmental negotiation in the functioning of markets across boundaries. But the challenge posed to globalization by the form of boundary (systemic, regional or local) differs markedly. The development of multilateralism, regionalism or even bilateralism implies some usurpation of unilateral state authority in recognizing that states must bargain – often with other states – in addressing collective actions to problems. As they do so, the social networks at the heart of the public domain become increasingly attenuated as geographic reach expands and authority becomes diluted.

For many proponents of regulatory policy, capitalism requires a sustained international governance mechanism in which states continue to play a central role. While economic sovereignty may have eroded, states continue to negotiate and arbitrate the international rules of economic conduct and thus define the parameters of interaction.

Regionalism, perhaps unlike multilateralism, here represents a way of manoeuvring separate forms of capitalism through the maze of global integration – evidence being the fundamentally different degree and form of institutionalization evident in NAFTA, the EU and APEC. It is a way of preserving differences while compromising with the global economy if not an act of resistance to globalization.[19]

Alternatively, regionalism may be considered as complementary to the spread of globalization, a stepping stone in the process of enlargement.[20] Proponents of such views contend that, at the governmental level, regionalism has resulted in states introducing policies to enhance competition, innovation and investment.[21] Regionalization is thus a response to globalization. Accordingly, we should see a trend towards regionalization as an intermediate and mitigating stage in the dynamic relationship between states and the globalizing economy. It is one where states pool sovereignty with other states for the purposes of achieving gains that can otherwise not be realized.

States, for sure, are not the only actors in the process of organizing and administrating regulations. Lobbies representing both business and public-interest groups often attempt to energetically engage in the adjudicative process. They certainly may engage states in the decision-making process and thus create an image of collective governance. But their influence is reflective of the issue area to which they contribute. Social and environmental legislation may provide more opportunities for effective contributions than narrower economic regulation. Cohesive though policy may be, it is the interplay between states that is ultimately more significant. The relationship between states and representatives of the non-profit and private sectors becomes diluted – and with it the social fabric of the public domain.

What are the rules of governance? Modernization and democracy

Work in this realm, at its core, focuses on the hegemony of American values – either implicitly or explicitly, repackaging many of the notions articulated in the 'modernization' literature.[22] It re-states an expectation of convergence, via the assimilation of political institutions in form, through the process of the acceptance of liberal democrat and capitalist values.

In the modernization literature, failure to converge towards liberal democracy as a normative prescription risks a moral failure. As David Apter comments, in describing the theme of the *Politics of Modernization*, 'analysis begins with moral content ... political life ... can only be understood in moral terms'. Thus the:

> difference between scientific work in the social sciences and the natural sciences ... [is] ... a difference in moral point of view ... beyond science lies moral intuition. ... [and] ... the overriding purpose of this book is to bring together some general methods and their moral implications,

the eventual objective being the formation of 'representative government' (a concept of freedom and choice defined as morality) which Apter equates with liberal democracy.[23]

Contemporary work in this field looks remarkably familiar. The common core is the assertion of a positive relationship between democracy and development as domestic political institutions in differing countries increasingly assimilate each other. In tandem, the values of liberalism and free market capitalism professed by the earlier modernization theories, bear a notable resemblance to this popular stream of contemporary 'globalization theory' which is replete with the teleological sentiments found in much of the earlier modernization literature. Fukuyama's arguments about the triumph of liberalism echo Daniel Bell's arguments of nearly four decades earlier that modernity in America signalled the end of ideology.[24]

Here, those nationally based social networks are further attenuated by their expansion to include international non-governmental organizations (INGOs) that play an increasingly influential role as agenda-setters and monitors of the development of the electoral process. They tutor and sponsor domestic NGOs but in the process destabilize the public domain by creating an alternative political culture that clashes with a national one.

Although independent of American government tutelage, these NGOs often reflect comparable values to those found in the United States despite their occasional tendency to pointedly accuse the United States of human rights abuses. Thus, while influential, the goals of NGOs often lie in contrast to that of their governmental counterparts because NGOs are seen as agents of foreign values and a challenge to national sovereignty. Here, the cohesion that is a foundation for the concept of the public domain begins to fray at the edges. Efforts at institution-building throughout the world have led to the creation of a vacuum in values, as traditional ones have been eroded while new ones have not taken root, as the case of Russia so clearly illustrates.

What body makes authoritative decisions? Liberalization

The substantive elements of this policy domain involve the liberalization and deregulation of markets, privatization of assets, dismantling or outsourcing of state functions (particularly welfare ones), diffusion of technology, cross-national distribution of manufacturing production, promotion of foreign direct investment (FDI), and the integration of capital markets. In its narrowest formulation, the term refers to a world-wide spread of sales, production facilities and manufacturing processes. In combination these reconstitute the international division of labour. Here, geography, authority and functionality have become most diffuse as various external forces intrude on the domestic context. The result is the relative atomization of society and even the individual.

Liberalization's most extreme theoretical perspective posits the view that we are witnessing a decisive shift away from industrial capitalism to a post-industrial conception of economic relations. The economic phenomena identified earlier are important not just because they represent a unique *cluster* of activity but because they represent a new form of activity, depicting a striking revolution among the techno-industrial elite that ultimately renders the globe a single market.[25] This is a comprehensive and complex vision: of globally integrated production; of specialized but interdependent labour markets; of the rapid privatization of state assets; and of the inextricable linkage of technology across conventional national borders.

We thus reconceptualize not only the importance of traditional factor endowments – land, labour and capital – in the context of new 'knowledge-based industries', but we also reconceptualize a variety of social and economic relations. It is labelled 'the new economy',[26] and its assumptions are embedded in the programme that became popularly known as the 'Washington consensus' (as discussed extensively by Drache in this volume).

The expansion of international economic activity relative to state-based activity offers enthusiastic proponents the prospect for efficiency gains through specialization. Arguing that a 'rising tide lifts all ships', they focus on distributive issues and discount negative redistributive consequences offset by overall welfare gains. Markets are the central authoritative mechanisms, as corporations develop strategies designed to transcend borders and institutionalize themselves locally.[27]

Critics castigate the assertion of inevitability that lies behind the transference of authority to the market mechanism. They claim that states have been significant contributors through their own 'regulatory reforms', which some now fear have led to a growing ungovernability of global financial markets.

This approach decries the significance of states as actors, proclaiming the renewed importance of the market as an authoritative mechanism in the allocation of resources, it attaches increasing import to the role of both international financial institutions and corporations (generally multinational or transnational) as institutional actors. To developmental economists, institutions may simply be rules. But, more persuasively, it is the substitution of the dominant actors, rather than simply a different conception of institutions that is occurring. Proponents of globalization (descriptively and normatively) talk of states in retreat as if they are living, coherent, organic beings. They certainly talk of corporations as organic and often as coherent hierarchies (like states). These non-state actors enjoy autonomy from states, as with that of the IMF. Thus, under liberalization, the conflict between the state and non-state actors that comprise the public domain is most evident in the arena of liberalization. As a consequence, the linkages inherent in the concept of the public domain eviscerate. The centrality of the market mechanism extends the interaction of networks to include transnational firms, international financial institutions, intergovernmental and non-governmental organizations (international and domestic), as well as traditional states. Authority is operated through a non-personalized, non-bureaucratized market structure diluting the mediating role of culture. The consequence is a world in which any national social fabric is subject to external forces that can (at an extreme) destroy the cohesion of the public domain, symbolized at the national level by the shattering effects of ethnic wars across the world in the 1990s.

Globalization, policy and the public domain

In Drache's analysis, he describes the public domain as 'increasingly autonomous and multi-dimensional, nurtured by the assets held in common that cannot normally be bought or sold or readily controlled by state authority' (Drache p. 45). The public domain is supported by a foundation of 'dense social networks', invoking the recent debates on social capital generated by Robert Putnam's work in comparative politics.[28] In Drache's view, diverse local arrangements in the formulation of new rights and entitlements, along with the degree of public-mindedness of those in a position of responsibility will frame public policy decisions. Such efforts are designed to avoid the 'tragedy of the commons' kinds of problems (see Table 1.1, pg 45).

Yet while such a view of the public domain as an 'irregular space' belonging 'to the public as a whole, having flexible borders, expanding and contracting in size, driven most by need rather than by any fixed notion of rights' (p. 45) may have utility, it may also overlook a significant constraint. For the policy area may condition the relevance of the public domain in which it is applied because the degree of public cohesion may vary across policy domains. As previously suggested, geography, diluting state authority and the capacity for functionality influence the density of those social networks. Therefore, to the contrary, these factors frame the cohesion of networks.

Despite the greater proximity of space posited by those advocates of globalization who focus on digital technological development, global or regional culture is at an elemental stage of development. Functionally, social cohesion provides the supportive foundation for dense social networks and these networks often remain organized around the state apparatus in the context of redistributive issues. Thus, where states play an expansive role and have collaborative institutional linkages into society, the social networks Drache describes will be more effective in mitigating the effects of market structures. NGOs, for example, generally operate in conjunction with states (or in response to states) in the area of social welfare. They often have an organic relationship in generating social networks. The 'common good' may be organized and paid for by philanthropy, for example, but it is still generally state-sanctioned (e.g. through tax policy) and often involves some distribution of burdens in which nonprofits 'fill holes' left by the state. The rules of philanthropy are often set by the state as an act of commission and NGOs cognizant of the location of 'holes' in the provision of public service. Major industrialists looking for public approval endowed the extensive supply of public parks and endowed arts in Pittsburgh. But they were under the state's jurisdiction in the provision and location of such parks.

Such a process takes on a different slant in Europe where the tradition of philanthropy is far less developed. This combination of welfarism and the social norms emanating from civil society that undergird such programmes is reflected in the concept of the 'social market economy', as applied in Germany. There it combines a corporatist institutional and ideological structure with an extensive and comprehensive state apparatus.[29] Corporations in Germany, often express concern about social obligations, unlike their British counterparts.[30] But, whether linked to charitable groups or corporations, functionally, the effect is the same as in the United States; the notion of public space and social organization extends through public, private and quasi-public organizations (like political foundations) to create a cohesion between state, market and civil society that defies the simple logic of market structures.[31]

Moving through the four areas of public policy, most states play a decreasingly influential role. While they still get to largely determine the distribution of the allocative pie (if not its size), their influence becomes increasingly attenuated when one turns to regulation, democratization and liberalization respectively.

While states play a regulatory role, much of it gets negotiated through supranational organizations with both other states and non-state actors. While states thus remain central to the process, individual states have an attenuated influence as a web of networks diffuses their power. And if the notion of the public domain emphasizes social networks, then the cultural norms that facilitate the effectiveness of the public domain weaken as the actors reflect national propensities. Mexicans, when negotiating with their US counterparts for example, stress the importance of retaining sovereignty in their efforts at cooperation.[32] To Americans this is not an issue. One doesn't have to self-consciously consider this issue when one is the dominant partner in a bilateral negotiation. States might therefore remain central but, functionally they often abandon influence – in this case to other states if not the market.

Over a decade ago, both the regime and the epistemic community literatures attempted to argue that such networks carried explicit norms. Yet, the value of this broad research programme was overstated once one moved beyond issues in which members of the scientific community played a central role. In an admitted glib tone, weekend golf trips organized between bankers does not seem the stuff of shared norms, nor (more seriously) do regimes organized around a shared desire to reduce the transaction costs of information and enhance stability.[33] Shared values and networks emerge out of a shared culture and congruent occupation of space in generating a notion of the public domain, and not simply a cooperative functioning of interests.

Democratization, in practice, further extends this process as states come under increasing scrutiny from international organizations, other states and the active participation of NGOs in the spread in the 'norm of democracy'. While Anglo-American capitalism would like to consider its export of the liberal variant of democracy to be both a success and universally well received, much of what we see contradicts such assessments.

Alternatives to the liberal variant abound. Once such alternative is the persistence of theocracies such as the Taliban.[34] A second is the resistance to liberalism evident in the debate on Asian values over the course of the last decade. And a third is reflected in the subsequent failure of the IMF to impose such systems as part of the conditionality for loans. The persistence of such alternative forms of regimes comes despite the heated accusations of crony capitalism made by American commentators who compare the rulers of such regimes to historical figures such as Hitler and Stalin.[35]

Yet despite the limited acceptance of democracy as a norm, there are plentiful examples of NGOs and international organizations seeking to impose themselves on the domestic process of decision making – and thus injecting a discordant note within the political and cultural traditions of many countries. Mexico, for example, has been the location of a variety of attempts at intervention to support the cause of liberal democracy during the course of the last decade-and-a-half. NGOs, seeking to provide advice on democratic reform or acting as electoral observers, are often locally interpreted as a challenge to both the traditional political structure in Mexico and to Mexican sovereignty generally by the domestic elite.[36]

Paradoxically therefore, while democracy may be considered to be an element that provides glue to many of its proponents within the context of civil society, efforts to introduce it are often discordant to the acceptance or sustaining of a public domain. Whether resistance is due to concerns about sovereignty or the failure of democratic reform is part of a general demise of the fabric of economy, polity and civil society (as in many of the cases of post-Communist Europe),[37] attempts to institute a new set of democratic norms have, in effect, attenuated and weakened the power of the public domain.

It is no surprise that it is in the arena of liberalization that the utility of the public domain to link state, market and civil society faces its greatest challenge. The self-regulating market here becomes most evident.[38] Liberalization implies reduced constraints on market activity in the absence of stronger regulation. And in the current context of globalization it is generally assumed that these factors work in tandem; liberalization includes privatization, reduced barriers to trade and investment, and deregulation.[39] Whether through the exposure to direct market forces or the conditionality requirements of IMF programmes, conceptions of shared values and assets come under intense pressure, in many countries, in the context of growing market pressures. Whether in the mild form of German debates about who should pay the bills for the retrenchment of their (beloved) welfare state or the upsurge in ethnic conflict in Indonesia, the process of liberalization serves to unhinge the relationship between state and civil society as market forces take on enhanced significance.

In the context of reduced state control and a limited number of IGOs who institute policies designed to enhance liberalization (as well as transparency), it is therefore not surprising to find that the social cohesion central to the public domain becomes increasingly frayed. Functionally, governance effectively shifts and geographically it becomes attenuated as both speculators and foreign officials have a greater influence on the process of decision-making – as Drache's comments on the Washington consensus makes clear.

The result is often civil (often in the form of ethnic) conflict at home as scapegoats are sought. Thus the social cohesion between both the international and the domestic, and among domestic actors, begins to break down.

Conclusion

In this chapter, two notions have been conveyed. The first is the idea that social cohesion is central to the concept of the public domain. Dense social networks are both institutional and cultural in character. They involve elements of both trust and shared values. The failure to generate either thus frays, if not eviscerates, the character of the public domain.

The second notion is that the degree of social cohesion that exists varies by policy domain. Four major areas of policy predominate in the context of globalization. Each has its own characteristics and emphasizes different roles and degrees of influence for different actors. Each has a differing propensity to 'stretch' or to 'tear' the cultural or social networks that are intrinsic to the notion of the public domain as characterized by Drache.

Sharpening the concept and strengthening its utility, thus entails further delineation of the conditions under which it has value. Geography plays a major role, influencing the capacity for shared cultural values to influence policy. The area of policy plays a further role, because of its linkage to the physical venue where the rules get made, interpreted and implemented.

While this chapter is speculative in tone and certainly inconclusive in terms of findings, it points to a way in which the application of the public domain can be developed. Other research currently runs an analogous (if not parallel) course, examining the linkages between globalization, the policy domain and degrees of sovereignty. Perhaps the next stage of the argument laid out here is to examine comparatively – in a more sophisticated theoretical framework and in greater empirical depth – the forms of linkages that constitute the public domain across issue areas. Such an effort could evaluate the hypothesis that a systematic variance exists, allowing a better delineation of the contingent conditions under which the public domain most influences behaviour.

Notes

1 A paper of this nature does not provide the format for an extended discussion of the definition of globalization. Elsewhere, I have written extensively on this matter, focusing on the political, economic, historic and ideological components of any definition of globalization. For analyses of the meaning of globalization see Simon Reich, 'What is Globalization? Four Possible Answers', working paper, Helen Kellogg Institute for International Studies, University of Notre Dame, Fall 1998, and Richard Higgott and Simon Reich, 'Globalization and Sites of Conflict: Towards Definition and Taxonomy', Working Paper Number 1, Centre for the Study of Globalization and Regionalization, Warwick University, June 1998.

2 Kenichi Ohame, *The Borderless World* (New York: Fontana, 1990) and *The End of the Nation-State: The Rise of Regional Economies* (New York: The Free Press, 1995).

3 See, for example, Susan Strange, *Mad Money: When Markets Outgrow Governments* (Ann Arbor, MI: University of Michigan Press, 1999).

4 For a debate on this issue see Jessica Matthews (1997) 'Powershift', *Foreign Affairs*, 76, 1, January–February: 50–66; and Anne-Marie Slaughter, 'The Real New World Order' *Foreign Affairs*, September/October, 1997.

5 See, for example, Paul Hirst and Grahame Thompson, *Globalisation in Question* (Cambridge: Polity Press, 1995), p. 6.

6 Theodore J. Lowi (1964) 'American Business, Public Policy, Case Studies, and Political Theory', *World Politics*, XVI, 4: 677–715. See especially pp. 688–9.

7 Ibid.: 689–90.

8 See, for example, Paul E. Petersen, *The Price of Federalism* (Washington, DC: Brookings, 1995).

9 This could be construed as Luke's 'third face of power' if implicit influences determine choice in a manner consistent with the greater power's interests, see Steven Lukes, *Power: A Radical View* (New York: Macmillan, 1974).

10 For a discussion of the various definitions of globalization see Higgott and Reich, op cit.

11 Hirst and Thompson's *Globalisation in Question*, op cit., exemplifies contemporary literature in this genre.

12 See Robert Cox, 'Global Perestroika', in Ralph Miliband and Leo Panitch (eds), *New World Order? The Socialist Register* (London: The Merlin Press, 1992), pp. 26–43. But see also Stephen Gill (ed.), *Gramsci, Historical Materialism and International Relations* (Cambridge: Cambridge University Press, 1993).

13 See Leo Panitch, 'Globalization and the State', in Ralph Miliband and Leo Panitch (eds), *New World Order? The Socialist Register* (London: The Merlin Press, 1992) pp. 60–93.

14 For example in 1970, Susan Strange was justly critical of the determinist nature of much economistic analysis. Susan Strange, 'International Economics and International Relations: A Case of Mutual Neglect', *International Affairs*, 46 (3): 304–15. In more recent work, she has forgotten her own admonition of twenty-eight

years earlier. As she now says 'markets win, governments lose', see Susan Strange, *The Retreat of the State: The Diffusion of Power in the World Economy* Cambridge, New York: Cambridge University Press, 1996), p. 5.

15 On the United States see Paul E. Petersen, *The Price of Federalism* (Washington, DC: Brookings, 1995).

16 Samuel Huntington, *The Clash of Civilizations and the Remaking of World Order* (New York: Simon and Schuster, 1996).

17 Robert Keohane, *After Hegemony: Cooperation and Discord in the World Political Economy* (Princeton, NJ: Princeton University Press, 1984) p. 12.

18 Miles Kahler, 'Trade and Domestic Differences', in Berger, Suzanne and Dore, Ronald, *National Diversity and Global Capitalism* (Cornell: Cornell University Press, 1996), especially p. 300.

19 Hazel Johnson, *Dispelling the Myth of Globalization: A Case for Regionalization* (New York: Praeger, 1991).

20 Robert Z. Lawrence, *Regionalism, Multilateralism and Deeper Integration* (Washington, DC: Brookings, 1996, p. 20). The OECD contends that regionalism and globalization are mutually reinforcing phenomenon, see *Regional Integration and the Multilateral Trading System: Synergy and Divergence* (Paris: OECD, 1995), p. 14.

21 As such, one of the aims of regionalization is to enhance the overall credibility of members of a region *vis-à-vis* external actors, those that are important potential sources of FDI for example. This is the case in the regionalization of investment that affected the nature of manufacturing and trade patterns in East Asia (taken to mean both South and Northeast Asia) throughout the period prior to 1997, see Walter Hatch and Kuzo Yamamura, *Asia in Japan's Embrace: Building a Regional Production Alliance* (New York: Cambridge University Press, 1996).

22 For a discussion see Richard Higgott, *Political Development Theory* (London: Routledge, 1986).

23 Apter, David, *The Politics of Modernization* (Chicago, IL: University of Chicago Press, 1965), pp. xiii–xiv and pp .3, 10–12 and 450–8 *passim*.

24 See Fukuyama, Francis, *The End of History and the Last Man* (New York: Free Press, 1992); and Daniel Bell, *The End of Ideology: On the Exhaustion of Political Ideas* (Glencoe, IL: Free Press, 1960).

25 Carnoy, Martin, Castells, Manuel and Cohen, Steven, *The New Global Economy in the Informational Age: Reflections on our Changing World* (Pennsylvania: Penn State University Press, 1993), pp. 4–5, use the term in a generic sense to refer to investment, production, management, markets, labour, information, and technology now 'organized across national borders'. See also Manuel Castells, *The Informational City: Information Technology, Economic Restructuring and the Urban Regional Process* (Oxford: Blackwell, 1991).

26 For a full discussion see Stephen A. Herzenberg, John A. Alic and Howard Wial, *New Rules for a New Economy: Employment and Opportunity in Postindustrial America* (Ithaca, NY: Cornell University Press, 1998). See also Peter Drucker (1986) 'The Changed World Economy', *Foreign Affairs*: 768–91; 'Assembling the New Economy', *The Economist*, 13 September 13, 1997: 71–73; Paul Krugman (1997) 'How Fast Can the U.S. Economy Grow?', *Harvard Business Review*, July–August, 75, 4: 123–9; Kevin Stiroh (1999) 'Is There a New Economy?', *Challenge*, July–August, 42, 4: 82–4; Steven Weber (1997) 'The End of the Business Cycle?', *Foreign Affairs*, July/August, 76, 4: 65–82.

27 For a list of policy prescriptions see Drache, Table 1.1, p.45.

28 See Robert D. Putnam with Robert Leonardi and Raffaella Y. Nanett, *Making Democracy Work: Civic Traditions in Modern Italy* (Princeton, NJ: Princeton University Press, 1993).

29 For a discussion see Patricia Davis and Simon Reich, 'Norms, Ideology and Institutions: The (En)gendered Retrenchment of Modell Deutschland?', in Beverly

Crawford (ed.) *The Postwar Transformation of Germany: Democracy, Prosperity Nationhood* (Ann Arbor, MI: University of Michigan Press, 1999).

30 For a discussion of the varied links between states and corporations in Germany, Japan and the United States see Paul N. Doremus, William W. Keller, Louis W. Pauly and Simon Reich, *The Myth of the Global Corporation* (Princeton, NJ: Princeton University Press, 1998).

31 A simple but powerful example drawn from Europe concerns the use of bicycles in Amsterdam. It is notable how well their usage has become integrated into the physical geography of the city; how a series of norms has grown up around their presence; how an efficient secondary market has developed to provide for the replacement of stolen bikes, and how all this yields public goods in terms of dealing with congestion, pollution and improved health. Yet the geographic proximity of this system is geographically limited. I am indebted to Bettina Schmidbauer for pointing this rich example out to me.

32 For examples see, Jorge Chabat (1991) 'Mexico's Foreign Policy in 1990: Electoral Sovereignty and Integration with the United States', *Journal of Interamerican Studies and World Affairs*, Winter, 33, 4: 1 (26); Secretary of State Christopher Warren and Mexican Secretary of Foreign Relations Jose Angel Gurria (1995) 'U.S.–Mexico Relations: The Beginning of a New Partnership', US Department of State Dispatch, 22 May, 6, 21: 422 (3).

33 For a comprehensive example drawn from the regime literature see Stephen D. Krasner, *International Regimes* (Ithaca, NY: Cornell University Press, 1983). For a comparable example drawn from the epistemic community literature see the work of Peter Haas, notably his *Saving the Mediterranean: the Politics of International Environmental Cooperation* (New York: Columbia University Press, 1990). On the utility of information and stability to members of a regime see Keohane, op cit.

34 For a discussion of this point see Meredith Tax (1999) 'World Culture War', *The Nation*, 17 May, 268, 18: 24 (1).

35 See, for example, the comments of William Safire in (1998) 'Gravy Trains Don't Run on Time', *New York Times*, 19 January: A15. For a critical discussion of Asian values see Martin Lee (1998) 'Testing Asian Values', *New York Times*, 18 January: 17. With specific reference to the cultural foundations of resistant Japanese attitudes towards American-style reforms see Murray Sayle (1998) 'The Social Contradictions of Japanese Capitalism', *The Atlantic Monthly*, June.

36 See Dean Peerman (1994) 'Poll Watching in Chiapas', *The Christian Century*, 16 November, 111, 33: 1081 (7); Carlos A. Heredia (1994) 'NAFTA and Democratization in Mexico', *Journal of International Affairs*, Summer, 48, 1: 13–38.

37 See Juan Linz and Alfred Stephan, *Problems of Democratic Transition and Consolidation: Southern Europe, South America and Post-communist Europe* (Baltimore, MD: Johns Hopkins University Press, 1996).

38 For a historic perspective on this issue see Karl Polanyi, *The Great Transformation* (Boston, MA: Beacon Press, 1944).

39 For a discussion of this issue in the context of the reform of the British and Japanese financial system see Steven K. Vogel, *Freer Markets, More Rules: Regulatory Reform in Advanced Industrial Countries* (Ithaca, NY: Cornell University Press, 1996).

5　The contested competence of NGOs and business in public life

Robin Hodess

Introduction

On 15 October 1999, the Nobel Prize for Peace was awarded to the medical relief organization, Médecins sans Frontières (Doctors without Borders).[1] The award of what is perhaps the world's most prestigious peace prize to a non-governmental organization (NGO) was the second time in recent years that an NGO was acknowledged for its contribution to the ultimate of public goods: peace and security.[2] While the Nobel Peace Prize has acknowledged the work of the NGO community in the past,[3] these recent awards have generated a wealth of attention to the increasing role of NGOs and NGO issues in global public affairs. Given the Nobel award and many other signs, it is possible to conclude that today's public policy now involves new actors and new agendas, both of which bring renewed interest in the concept of the public domain.

This chapter addresses actors, or agents, and their particular contribution to the public domain. It focuses above all on new economic and political actors. Just as the awarding of the Nobel Peace Prize reflects the significance of non-state, private actors in public life, this chapter suggests a stronger role for these same actors in the public domain. The public domain, it argues, not only requires the capacity of human vision – whether generated by the public or private sector – in order to realize innovation and ideas in public policy, but it draws on a variety of agents, some of them relatively new and untested in their public roles.

This chapter begins by defining the public domain. It then argues that incorporating the position of actors or agents into the public domain concept is a critical step towards making it more useful to the exploration of present day public policy dilemmas. Actors force us to consider, not only, structures and interests but also norms, ideas and capacities, all of which include expertise, authority, and the ability to execute policy and practices. The major actors in the public domain, both state (public) and non-state (private) are reviewed, with the strengths and weaknesses of both assessed. The chapter focuses on selected 'new' private agents, whose actions and innovations in the public domain have arguably forced a recasting of responsibility and accountability in the public domain. Finally, the chapter suggests that elite and public expectations, particularly with regard to governance and the kinds of public policy solutions appropriate in the context of globalization, may have changed as a result of the increased involvement of new private, non-governmental actors in the public domain.

The public domain defined

In his chapter (this volume), Drache paints a complex picture of the term, 'public domain', drawing on literature in economics, political science and sociology and including such overlapping concepts as public goods, public services, public space, public discourse, public culture and social capital. Drache locates the public domain amidst the state, the market and civil society. Yet it is important to note that the vitality and quality of the public domain are influenced by the interplay and competition of both public and private interests, and not merely by the 'public' identities that Drache employs in his definition of the concept.

The public domain is most usefully conceived of as a space for public policy-making and public discourse by both private and public agents. Defined in this way, the public domain aligns most closely with two of Drache's selected components: public goods and public debate. These two components serve as catch-alls for the other areas Drache is interested in, by attending to policy areas and policy debates, respectively, in the public realm. Thus defined, the public domain is well-suited to examining agency, since it privileges the norms and values that shape policy and policy debate.

Public goods, which have a long history in the study of economics, include both pure (non-rivalrous in consumption and non-excludable, with peace the ultimate example) and impure (partly rivalrous and/or excludable, such as public investment in the preservation of art) varieties, and stand in contrast to private goods, characterized by markets, exchange and the price mechanism (Kaul *et al.* 1999: 4–5; see Kaul chapter, this volume for a more detailed discussion). The condition of public goods is determined by public policy choices. As such, they are a logical part of the public domain, reflecting and contributing to the societies in which they are developed. In addition, the policy providing for public goods is guided by rules and norms that promote standards and expectations in many of the 'non-market' areas of public life, such as education, health, pension and infrastructure.

Public discourse, or debate, is crucial to the vitality of the public domain concept. The ideal-type for public discourse is taken from Habermas' idea of the public sphere, 'the sphere of private people come together as a public; … [who engage] … in a debate over the general rules governing relations in the basically privatized but publicly relevant sphere of commodity exchange and social labor' (Habermas 1993: 27). Paraphrased, the public sphere (like the public domain) is a realm for the evolution of public ideas and opinions apart from but relevant to state authority, with implications for both the rule of law and the functioning of markets. The public sphere's provision of public discourse is significant, as it makes the competition of ideas by a variety of actors (both public and private) a vital public activity. Indeed, according to Habermas, critical public debate is a key element in dispensing with state domination and establishing the bourgeois (liberal) constitutional state.

Which public domain? Assessing levels of analysis

In this volume, Drache argues that states have not forfeited to markets in the battle over the public domain, but that the (state's position in the) public domain has re-emerged 'after the apparent triumph of markets', due in some way to the forces of globalization. It makes sense that globalization would have consequences for (state) policy and capacity in the public domain. However, this assessment leads us directly to a level of analysis problem. After all, is the primary concern the *global* public domain, with its (nascent and sometimes unrecognized) global public goods and global public discourse? Or is the public domain concept more relevant at other (regional, national, local) levels? Does the issue of the public domain represent the same *problematique* at each level?

It may be necessary to consider whether the impact of globalization is greatest at the nexus of state, market and civil society – the public domain – *beyond* the nation-state. If so, globalization would necessarily influence such global public domain issues as the nature of global governance, including global commons such as the environment, health and population crises, etc. It would do so via policy debates at established international institutions (the UN and other IGOs) or in new channels of global discourse, such as the Internet, policy networks, etc. Because of considerable policy and academic attention to global-ization, it is tempting to isolate change in the global public domain and ignore the impact of globalization at other levels of governance and polity (for an examination of new public goods see Grayson, this volume).

Moreover, it is difficult to generalize about the public domain across the heterogeneity of political systems, economies, and social/cultural traditions that exist at all levels of analysis. It may be too simplistic to consider the public domain – at whatever level – as a uniform entity across all areas of public policy. Instead, it is more likely that the public domain itself contains many models of actor involvement - in idea generation, policy negotiation, and action, and that some of these models change over time; recent work by Wolfgang Reinicke (1999) suggests that this is the case with what he calls 'global public policy networks'.

Bearing in mind these concerns, this chapter takes as its conceptual starting point two levels/sites of the public domain: the global public domain and the public domain of advanced industrialized states, and it considers the importance of actors therein. To a certain extent, agents at both of these levels reflect the considerable changes within the public domain that led Drache (this volume) to conclude that the effects of globalization have ushered in a rediscovery of the non-market dimensions of public policy. And while unexplored in this chapter, the public domain at other sites/levels may well reveal similar trends.

Old actors, new actors, more actors

Given a definition of the public domain that explicitly focuses on public policy and public sphere debate, the link to agency is logical. The aim to define, understand and evaluate the public domain needs to account for the beliefs, priorities and activities that characterize it. And those beliefs, priorities and activities stem from the actors who participate in the public domain. Therefore, a focus on agency, or actors, is analytically useful as it privileges normative concerns, which are central to the 'market-state' debates that influence public policy and dominate this volume. In addition, the analysis of actors adds a necessary complexity to our understanding of the public domain, since activity in the public domain is often characterized by the combination, or cooperation, of actors, their values, and their respective bases of knowledge, power and legitimacy.

Like other sites of politics and policy, the public domain is a constructed institution; one embedded in a system of values. The public domain may be changing as a result of the introduction of different values and goals by the actors who comprise it. This change suggests that new policy agendas and concerns may be moving from being exclusively those of 'market' or 'state', toward the 'hybrid' of today's public domain. Interestingly, actors in the public domain may be compared to agents in the private sector, where, according to stakeholder theory, corporate management takes into account various stakeholders (Donaldson and Preston 1995). The public domain is also comprised of various stakeholders, governmental and non-governmental, public and private, all of whom are engaged in the determination of public discourse and public policy.[4]

Old actors

The traditional or 'old' actor responsible for shaping the public debate and public policy in the public domain is government. In conceptualizing 'government', it is easy to assume many things: that government is *national* government; that government is the actor responsible for providing public goods, as a compensatory measure for markets failures and externalities; that government implies a link to territoriality and established social bonds (Devetak and Higgott 1999). Putting the level of analysis issue raised above aside, it is clear that these assumptions remain at least in part valid in the analysis of the public domain, and that government at any number of levels continues to have a critical function in the public domain.[5]

To clarify the continued importance of 'old' actors, it is worth restating why government has been central and successful in the public domain, both in setting terms of debate and exercising public policy. Democratically elected governments, of course, have a legitimate function as the representatives of public will and opinion. National (and local) government, therefore, reflect an electoral process, while regional and international governmental bodies constitute delegated, representational authorities also based on the electoral process, although at a greater distance from constituencies. With these clear lines of accountability comes the expectation that government develops and implements appropriate public policy, giving government actors a privileged and authoritative position as key public domain stakeholder. While this status may seem obvious, the very lack of similar legitimacy by other stakeholders puts them in marked contrast to government. The accountability of government in no way guarantees equity, justice, freedom, or any other sort of socially or culturally demanded outcomes; it does, however, underline government's position as an 'actor of last resort' in many public policy issues, indicating that moral hazard need not be a concern.

Given this status, why have states, as old actors, declined in stature and faced increased competition as the principle authorities in the public domain? Rosenau (1990) attributes this to a global crisis of authority, one related to a generalized crisis of legitimation (see below). Another factor is the force of globalization, which many scholars and practitioners claim has either weakened or at least altered the ability of nation-states to achieve their policy goals. As Slaughter (1997: 184) has argued, 'The state is not disappearing, it is disaggregating into its separate functionally distinct parts.' Technology and the declining relevance of geography and territory to the exercise of power – both related to the global imperative – also contribute to the reduced dominance of state authorities in developing public policy and responding to societal demands in the public sphere (Sassen 1999). In terms of international organizations, another 'old' actor group linked but not limited to national government representation, Weber (2000) argues that they too are less capable of responding to public needs in an era of globalization, with the Bretton Woods institutions in particular having outlived the conditions of their original mandates.

Whether the changes taking place among 'old' governmental actors are linked to issues that are internal (legitimacy, backlash) or external (globalization, technology), the resulting evolution of the public domain is not a purely zero-sum game for state authority. Rather, these changes in the public domain have resulted in a greater degree of power sharing among a larger pool of actors. Newer actors create potential tension with state actors, in that they often purport to redress weaknesses in the government sector. Private actors operating in public roles, whether market oriented (such as business) or drawn from civil society, such as NGOs, often represent solutions to 'old actor' incapacity and/or failure to provide voice for distinct segments of society.

New actors – business and NGOs

Business and NGOs are the two new actors critical in the analysis of the changing public domain. By evaluating the impact of business and NGOs on the public domain, it is possible to make a prognosis about 'new' norms in public debate and public policy-making.

Exercising market rules in the public sector: business actors

The first of these new actors is private sector actors: the business community. In the global and national public domain, business actors are those multinational corporations whose scope of operations and access to capital provide them the resources and, as some would argue, the obligation to extend beyond traditional profit-oriented, market-driven activities into socially oriented, publicly beneficial tasks.

The notion that business is engaged in public life, or that it should be, might seem non-contentious. Under societies that subscribe to market capitalism, the role and action of the private sector influences the very fabric of society and social relations. Nevertheless, the expansionist interpretation of business' role and purpose as a social or societal or even public domain actor is far from the pure capitalist model of business as purely rent-seeking and profit-maximizing – where 'the business of business is business'.

There are hundreds of examples today of corporate involvement beyond this classically defined role and outside the strictly defined marketplace, suggesting that some segments of the business community have established themselves as societally focused and socially aware actors (Zadek and Weiser forthcoming). In addition, numerous initiatives from the traditional public domain actors encourage business in this direction: for example, Kofi Annan's call for a global compact between the UN and the business community (see Ruggie and Kell, this volume).

In her work on *Building Competitiveness and Communities*, Jane Nelson (1998), of the Prince of Wales Business Leaders Forum in the UK, makes the case that there are three main areas for business to create value-added in society: in their core business activities (generating investment, income, jobs, products, business infrastructure, standards and best practices); in their engagement in policy and institutional development (interaction with other actors, creating an enabling environment, promoting ethics and good governance); and in their social investment and philanthropy (contributing to the wider community in a strategic fashion over time). While the first of these could loosely be considered business' traditional means of adding value, the latter two may be becoming more prevalent and to a certain extent, more in demand.

The call for greater business involvement in public life is in part a response to global economic integration and the notion that government and other 'old' actors can not design and execute public policy in an economic and financial vacuum, irrespective of trade and investment. At the same time, old actors can not always compete with the skills, breadth and wealth of the multinational corporation – and therefore may themselves encourage business to take on new, public domain interests. As a result, market realities now increasingly characterize strategies in the public domain. The relationship between the state and market actors is by no means merely purely adversarial, but the demands of governing the public domain in conditions of globalization blur the boundary that once defined their respective functions.

There are numerous examples of business taking an active, interventionist, and non-traditional role in public policy formation and execution. This activity has generally fallen into two categories, one reactive and the other proactive. In the case of reactive involvement, business has generally had to respond to a demand made by other actors in the public domain, such as the 1999 case of Monsanto backing down on its intent to produce and sell infertile crop plants. Calling this involvement 'reactive' is not to say that this action is of no consequence; to the contrary, change in business practices do have an impact on public policy issues. In the case of Monsanto, business practices will continue to influence the debates surrounding the ethics of GM food, the control and sale of seeds, etc. However, these reactive engagements in the public domain are not the result of values, goals, or behaviour on the part of business actors that reflect an original intention to engage in public policy or debates.

In contrast, some corporate action in the public domain has been the result of proactive intervention in issues of public concern and public policy. In such cases, a business actor has seized on a particular public domain issue and, in conjunction with others, steered change in policy and practices. Here, examples include: Merck's role in the eradication of River Blindness, a major public health concern in West and Central Africa;[6] the Apparel Industry Partnership[7] and its offshoot the Fair Labor Association,[8] which involve the commitment of major apparel manufacturers to ensure their products are produced under decent and humane labour conditions; the Ethical Trading Initiative in the UK, launched to address labour standards;[9] and the CEOs of Intellectual Property Committee who achieved a public policy standard for intellectual property, later embodied in the GATT's Trade Related Aspects of Intellectual Property (TRIPs) agreement (Sell 1999).[10]

Reactive involvement in the public domain probably continues to be the dominant approach of business to its public and societal role. And while cynics would argue that business involvement of any kind in the public domain is nothing more than an attempt by business actors to conduct good public relations and brand management, this assessment of motives misses the point and impact of such involvement. Rather, the significance of corporate social and public policy engagement is its influence on *expectations* regarding business behaviour. Simply put, when business actors show they can have an impact, particularly one desired (and possibly legitimated via its efficacy – see discussion below) across actor groups and society, they become part of the solution, and part of a more effective public domain.

Indeed, as was indicated above, the public domain stands to benefit from business actor attributes, such as innovation, efficiency, access to capital, and so on. Business actors operate with different incentives from state actors, even when they take on challenges of public policy. They are generally more solutions-oriented than participatory, however, which may explain the widespread dissatisfaction with the privatization of public services in recent decades. In addition, while the management capacity of the private sector is widely esteemed, it does not always translate into the ability to manage public policy and debate, which do not conform to the profit-principles applied to market goods and services. The popularity and fortunes of numerous political stars drawn from the private sector (with the American Ross Perot and the Italian Silvio Berlusconi to name but a few) attest to some of the difficulties of bridging the private–public divide.

As the expectations for corporate social involvement change, particularly for the largest and most visible global business actors, proactive involvement in the public domain may become the norm for a certain calibre of global private sector players. At the level of small and medium-sized enterprises, however, collective action problems will continue to inhibit substantial interest in taking on greater public domain roles.

Giving back? How philanthropic foundations participate in public policy and debate

One particular way that business has involved itself in the public domain in the proactive pattern is via the establishment of foundations. Foundations, which strictly speaking are philanthropic ventures, provide the means for business actors to articulate a clear and systematic programmatic agenda for engagement in the public domain. Foundations are legally independent of the corporations or individuals that endow them. Nevertheless, they reflect the sensibilities and aspirations of their founders, particularly if those endowing the foundation continue to play an active role in the executive board. Foundations have no particular responsibility to address the interests of elected officials, government agencies, civil society actors, or the public at large.[11] Arguably, foundations are the ultimate expression of the business world's involvement in the public domain. Nowadays, with corporations implored to think and act with more attention to social responsibility, the establishment of a foundation dedicated to social or societally relevant causes is one way business involvement in public life has been realized.

While many business actors have been increasingly involved in corporate social responsibility initiatives, only a select few have taken the steps of a Ted Turner in establishing the United Nations Foundation or a Bill Gates in setting up the Bill and Melissa Gates Foundation. Wealth is obviously the primary enabling factor in the ability of business actors to take on this kind of sustained commitment to financing projects in public life, the tax benefits of foundations notwithstanding. However, even a quick assessment shows the extent to which these foundations, born of corporate profits and dedicated to the goals of business actors taking on public challenges, do not have to follow established routes in democratic terms in order to influence public affairs. Via foundations, business interests go beyond considering the micro-level impact of their own policies on labour, human rights and the environment, to consider macro-level public policy issues – some far removed from the actual business sector or product of the owner (Ted Turner on population growth; Milken Family Foundation on medical research and education), some rather close (Milken Institute exploring economic growth and Gates addressing issues of the digital divide/technology gap).

Moreover, foundations seem to be part of a typically US philanthropic tradition. Since the US has the world's largest economy and its private sector is habitually referred to as the motor of globalization, there is no small irony in the 'redistributive', socio-political aims of philanthropic organizations. Cynics would argue that, like the ability to embrace corporate social responsibility, only the richest owners of the richest companies can afford to be philanthropic, and that, at heart, the philanthropist has interest only in avoiding the tax collector (and perhaps in attracting the historians). It may be true that it takes a wealthy society to produce a business actor who can afford to turn to the needs of the public domain, and that much of the world's wealth is concentrated in a small number of countries and societies, traditions of philanthropy and 'giving back' exist in most cultures and religions. This means that the increased role of private sector actors in the public domain is possible beyond the two prominent (global and advanced industrial) public domains examined here.

Philanthropy turned crusade? The case of the Soros foundations

One business actor turned philanthropist who has made a tremendous impact on many public domains is George Soros. By now, the personal story of Soros is fairly well known: Soros is the Hungarian-born, British-educated investor whose Quantum Fund made $1 billion on the ill fortune of the British pound sterling in 1992. Soros first set up a foundation, the Open Society Fund (the name Open Society is taken from the work of one of his intellectual heroes, Karl Popper) in New York in 1979. Soros foundations in Hungary and the then Soviet Union soon followed this. There are currently more than thirty Soros foundations operating world-wide, although the Open Society Institutes in New York and Budapest provide an umbrella function in terms of administration and focus across this enormous foundational network. Soros foundations spend approximately $500 million annually on their programmatic activities.

Soros' foundational activities have been concentrated in Central and Eastern Europe. More recently, programmes in other locations, such as Guatemala, Haiti, South Africa, and even now the United States, have also been the recipient of Soros funding. According to the Soros foundations website, these foundations:

> share the common mission of supporting the development of open society. To this end, they operate and support an array of initiatives concerned with arts and culture, children and youth, civil society development, economic reform, education, legal reform and public administration, media and communications, and health care.[12]

While his overarching commitment has been to enable the development of democracy, rule of law, civil society and respect for minorities in now formerly communist lands, the progressive or liberal (in a US sense) nature of Soros' activism has not gone unnoticed (Demko 1996; Morais 1997; Shawcross 1997;

O'Brien 1998). Indeed, Soros' largesse has made him a favourite media target in this regard: one *Forbes* article even characterized him as a friend of socialists and communists (Morais 1997). Despite these occasional polemics, Soros' political interests form a clear pattern: Soros foundations have supported such issues as the ban on landmines and the call for needle exchange programmes. In addition, the President of the Open Society Institute in New York, Aryeh Neier, is former Executive Director of Human Rights Watch and former National Director of the American Civil Liberties Union, both well-known progressive organizations.

Interestingly, one shift in the work of the Soros foundations seems to have put Soros and his public-policy projects into a more contentious role in the eyes of the West. As long as Soros' money supported greater freedoms in Central and Eastern Europe, there was relatively little ground or reason for West European or North American critique of his programmes. However, when Soros began to increase grantmaking to US projects after 1994, the foundation received a flurry of attention and criticism for being soft on crime and too lax on immigrant rights. Undeterred, Soros has himself continued to maintain a high profile for his profits and his projects. Indeed, after the world economic crises in 1997,[13] Soros embarked on a campaign to promote reform of world financial architecture, suggesting that short-term investors were a grave danger to global economic stability and advocating new international institutions, such as an International Credit Insurance Corporation and other supervisory and regulatory bodies (Soros 1998).

Despite the eyebrows Soros himself has raised over the years, the Soros foundations have provided tremendous resources to many public domains around the world; particularly those in societies engaged in the transformation from planned economies to democracy and free markets. The Soros Foundations Network has undoubtedly influenced the material conditions and resources available to numerous groups working on issues of human and minority rights in countries with less-established civil society traditions. Soros' money has flown abundantly into education projects as well: examples include the establishment of the Central European University, based in Budapest with a Warsaw campus, providing university training to a new generation of Central and Eastern Europeans, and the International Soros Science Education Program, supporting science education in the Russian Federation (and to a lesser extent in Ukraine and Georgia) by providing money, equipment and materials to educators and students. Soros gives generously to support activism of a progressive stripe in other fields, as well: criminal justice, immigration, landmines and economic development in South Africa. Soros sponsors the promotion of these and other issues via grants to documentary filmmakers. And while Soros the investor/philanthropist may be dismissed as odd or hypocritical from time to time, his book on *The Crisis of Global Capitalism* (1998) was a timely diatribe against the dangers of unfettered capitalism. It generated significant media attention and arguably contributed to policy debates then taking place on reform of global financial architecture.

In sum, Soros and his foundations are a good example of a business actor in its new role because of the systematic and clearly programmatic nature of his interventions in public affairs. His actions, however, point out the problems of unaccountability and lack of access that plague all business actors in the public domain. It is necessary to be clear about the consequences and even contradiction of asking business to become more engaged in public debate and public policy formation. Many voices now call on corporations to redistribute their wealth; in so doing; business will play an increasing role in the agenda setting for and execution of public policy initiatives. Given the traditional role of business as employers and wealth creators and, in the case of corporations, their fiduciary responsibility to shareholders, there are few definitive markers to guide business as they navigate the public domain. What are they required to do (in 'justice' terms? legally?), with what intended outcomes, and how can the impact be assessed? Some of these consequences of business engagement in public life have been overlooked in the zeal to promote business 'doing good'.

Non-governmental organizations: another new actor in the public domain

The second of the 'new actors' involved in public policy and public debate are non-governmental organizations, whose dramatic growth and more recent demand for a 'seat at the political table' have made considerable changes to the public domain landscape (Mathews 1997). Not only do non-governmental organizations influence the themes and focus in the public policy debate; they provide an alternative if contentious (in democratic theory terms) means of representing public interest in the sphere of public policy. There are innumerable instances of NGO influence on the public agenda, whether it be the role of Greenpeace *vis-à-vis* Shell in the case of Brent Spar, the presence and impact of NGOs in UN world summits in the past decade, or NGO activism at the WTO Seattle ministerial in 1999 and the World Bank/IMF meetings in spring 2000, not to mention the now Nobel-sanctioned work of Médecins sans Frontières.

As an agent of change in the public domain, NGOs have many functional similarities to the news media, perhaps more so than to other public domain actors, including business. First of all, NGOs have little formalized accountability: the degree to which they do what they promise in mission statements is vastly open to interpretation. (In contrast, corporations, striving to achieve financial gains for shareholders, must report a bottom line.) Like media, if NGOs stray from their stated mandate or prove themselves incompetent, they lose their credibility, the very element that gives them a critical niche in the sphere of public policy. For business, brand management matters, and does influence how business behaves in the public domain, but not every business has a brand that is a distinct public face. This limits accountability and credibility issues for business actors in some sectors, due to their (limited) public exposure.

Like media, NGOs can suffer from an 'establishment complex'. They often struggle to decide whether they should remain outsiders to the realm they wish to influence, refusing funding or even dialogue with establishment actors, in a sort of outsider fundamentalism? Or whether their cause is better served by gaining access to the table, by engaging with their opponents and creating potential partners, and by accepting financial support from establishment (foundation, corporate or government) coffers?[14] According to Medea Benjamin, co-founder of Global Exchange, an NGO whose mission is to fight human rights abuses and that has been especially involved in sweat-shop issues, this sort of 'establishment complex' has caused a number of major schisms within the NGO community.[15] Arguably, unlike most NGOs and some media organs, business *is* the establishment.

Finally, as with media, the power of NGOs is in part derived from their access to and dissemination of information. Keck and Sikkink (1998) make this last point succinctly, pointing out that advocacy networks, of which NGOs are a principle player, are themselves *communicative* structures. While business is also governed and measured by the power of ideas-as-information, these informational innovations by businesses are principally oriented toward profit making rather than intrinsic to business' role in any public domain function. Given this affinity between the function of NGOs and media in the public domain, there is perhaps little surprise at the receptiveness of media to NGO voices and causes, which may serve to the mutual benefit of both agents in achieving their public domain goals.

Distinct from (news) media 'neutrality', however, NGOs have clear advocacy aims. Typical goals include the promotion of improved human rights (civil, political, economic, social and cultural), adherence to rule of law, increased social and economic justice, and greater environmental sustainability. Unlike many government actors, NGOs are not bounded by territory (as are nation-states) or by formalized memberships and/or voting rules (as are international organizations). Keck and Sikkink (1998: 30) suggest that advocacy networks, which include NGOs, are motivated not by instrumental goals (such as business might be) or shared causal ideas (as epistemic communities might be), but by *shared principled ideas and values*. Quite simply, an NGOs' rationale for acting in the public domain is different from other actor groups. As NGOs gain in status and power, it is important to consider their normative make-up and their goals for public policy, as well as how these are conferred to the public domain.

Finding the way 'inside' public policy and debate: the case of Transparency International

A good example of an NGO that has taken on a significant role in recent years is Transparency International (TI). TI, headquartered in Berlin, Germany, was set up in 1993 to fight corruption, which it views as a principle cause of exploitation around the globe.[16] TI is the very model of a NGOs that seeks to cooperate with a broad spectrum of actors, especially business, other NGOs and governmental agencies. It does not explicitly pursue headlines or shock tactics to effect its goals, but prefers to build consensus via broad participation on issues of transparency. With more than seventy national chapters, TI believes that mobilizing for its work against corruption is probably most effective at the national level – where it can involve the appropriate agents to encourage reform of corrupt practices but allow them to adapt to specific national institutions and circumstances. It takes on regional and global initiatives on a more limited basis, as it deems appropriate, such as in its contribution to the OECD Convention against Bribery, which came into effect in February 1999.

TI first aimed to change the focus of debate – to open public discussion on corruption. It tackled the issue of bribery, revealing its presence in the economies of both developing *and* advanced industrial societies. TI later targeted international organizations, such as the World Bank, since it felt their involvement was essential to the success of the fight against corruption. TI has developed a number of tools that have helped to spread information about corrupt practices and to engage business in the anti-corruption process, such as the Corruption Perception Index and the TI Integrity Pact.[17]

In recent years, as the veil of ideology has been lifted from international politics and the global financial and economic agendas have increasingly taken on board the concerns of human development (and above all poverty alleviation), transparency and good governance have become buzzwords at the World Bank, UNDP and in governments the world over. Examples of this new governance-oriented agenda are abundant: from the World Bank's influential 1997 World Development Report, focusing on the changing role of the state and highlighting corruption issues, to the good governance focus brought in by the UNDP's new Administrator, Mark Malloch-Brown, in 1999.

Funding for Transparency International has followed aplenty, with foundations such as Ford, MacArthur, and many others, on the one hand, and governmental institutions, such as national development agencies and UN groups, on the other, providing almost $1 million each of TI's $2.7 million dollar budget in 1998. And while TI was set up by a number of former high-ranking World Bank executives, its establishment credentials were further reinforced early in 1999 when its Advisory Council Chairman, General Olusegun Obasanjo, was elected president of Nigeria, promising to re-establish democracy there. TI and its issues have arrived.

TI has gone a long way to placing an old problem, and a new, globalization-relevant issue – the fight against corruption – on global, regional, national and local agendas. It has brought with it a specific set of objectives regarding government accountability, together with a particular normative view that corruption damages integrity and distorts equitable economic processes. Both its goals and perspective now inform the public domain. In addition, the way TI has gone about its work, involving a wide range of relevant political, business, and societal actors, has set an example for cooperation and consensus building among diverse actors in the public policy sphere. While TI is but one NGO actor, its success is indicative of growing NGO status, agenda-setting power, informational control and expertise, all of which have consequences for shaping the public domain.

New actors, more actors – what does it mean?

New agents in the public domain have clear implications for public debate and policy-making, and therefore for the public domain and democracy. Processes including the legitimation of political action and political accountability, mentioned throughout the chapter, need to be re-evaluated in light of the rise of business and NGOs as public domain actors. Some evidence suggests that new agents bring with them new rules for democratic engagement and foster a great deal of change in the public domain.

First, political legitimacy as was discussed above, old actors (chiefly governments and government agencies) passed the test of 'democraticness', gaining legitimacy via the electoral process. New actors have a harder time justifying the legitimacy of their power and actions. However, it is worth considering whether the legitimacy 'bar' has itself begun to move. Stated differently: after decades of public backlash against 'politics as usual' and repeated claims of legitimation crises, it may be time to rethink the rules regarding political legitimacy.

James Rosenau (1990: 381) has suggested a new way of evaluating the legitimacy of political actors, writing:

> Where legitimacy once derived from habitual and traditional norms perpetuated by macro structures and processes, today the enlarged analytic skills and cathectic capacities of citizens increasingly enable them to ascribe legitimacy on the basis of performance activities that they perceive as appropriate.

According to Rosenau, ability and efficacy – *appropriate performance* – may be relevant to the attribution of legitimate power to old and new political actors. Cutler *et al.* (1999: 18) don't go as far as Rosenau, but they do argue that the growth of private authority (chiefly among corporate actors) can be explicitly undemocratic and yet, 'evoke a sense of legitimacy and achieve a high degree of acceptance through recognition by others of specific knowledge, expertise, and representational skills'. In other words, states may still be legitimate in electoral terms and therefore, 'rightful' actors in the public domain, but it may now be appropriate to explore new ways and means to ascribe legitimacy in order to reflect the complexity of politics in the public domain. As a result, and by new standards, new actors such as business and NGOs may be considered legitimate after all.

Next, accountability; the higher profile of the foundation-as-actor and the now insatiable growth of NGOs raise critical issues of access and responsibility, both of which are key components of accountability. Who controls the way they spend their money or how they prioritize their social objectives? Who manages the impact of their interventions? Here, it should be stressed that even if a business or an NGO support the most consensual of societal goals, such as peace and security, there is no formal, legal way (beyond the rule of law) to ensure that these 'good intentions' result in processes that can be influenced by state and society. A good example is Ted Turner's $1 billion commitment to the

United Nations Foundation, which is dedicated to promote the goals of the United Nations and its charter, but which of course is not accountable to the UN in its selection of issues, in its grant-making, or in its advocacy.[18] The lack of accountability of most business and NGO initiatives in the public domain may be problematic, but is tempered by the role that public censure can play in the public domain in question. However, it also points up the problems that lack of access (influence, information, etc.) can present in the case of both business and NGO activities.

Despite these areas of caution, the presence, involvement and growing status in the public domain of business actors, such as the Soros foundations and NGOs such as Transparency International, have resulted in a number of changes that could broadly be considered positive for the public domain and for its distinction from purely market-driven processes. The evolution of new actors and new modes of interaction between new and old actors have affected governance in the public domain in the 'post neo-liberal' era. Four changes stand out.

First, new actors have successfully thematized and prioritized new issues in the public domain. Public goods still include peace and security, health care and education, as they always have, but they also include human rights, protection of minorities, economic justice, fair trade and trading conditions, good governance, and more. The expansion of public domain issues owes much to the rise of new economic and political actors. TI's promotion of corruption is just such an example of new issues entering into the public domain as a result of the norms held by a new agent, an NGO. Other examples of NGO values and priorities making their mark on the public agenda are repeated activism of (mostly North American) NGOs opposed to globalization (namely, the WTO in Seattle, November 1999, 'A16' in Washington and Prague 2000) and the Jubilee 2000 movement, which has thematized debt-relief as the major priority of the international community.

Second, new actors may have unleashed new expectations at all levels of society, including public expectations of who will participate in and determine the balance of means and ends in the public domain. For instance, citizens have come to expect NGOs to have a say on child labour and to demand best practices and environmental sustainability from corporations. In other words, while many economic and political experts assumed that the neo-liberalism of the early 1990s validated market solutions for public policy puzzles, the emergence of new *public* agents (even business is wearing a public domain hat!) may reinvigorate expectations of what can and should be achieved in the public sphere, beyond mere market driven calculations. NGOs and businesses acting in and influencing the public domain have raised the expectations, of citizens and consumers' regarding the way public policy is pursued, in terms of process and goals.

Third, and closely related to the second change, there may be developing a new attribution of authority in the public domain. As legitimation becomes more and more *de facto* de-coupled from electoral processes (and based on other factors, such as performance), new actors may take on the responsibility and assume the accountability – both key elements of authority – previously assigned to the state with regard to public domain activities. This change has profound consequences for the problems of the democratic deficit that have plagued certain levels of governance. At a minimum it promotes news ways and opportunities for private, non-governmental actors to take on legitimized roles and thereby reinvigorate governance.

Finally, new actors mean new values for the public domain. If business inter-ests and NGOs are active in setting agendas, building capacity and cooperation, and carrying out public policy initiatives that shape the public domain, they do so in a fashion that is consistent with their 'core values' and principles. This means they participate in the construction of public domain values, whether at the global, regional, national, or local levels. As the discussion above showed, this contribution may tend towards creating support for the goals of social equity and economic justice, but these new values do not come with any guar-antees or any hard and fast definitions. No public authority can label them as definitively good or bad; rather it seems, public domains will necessarily now engage in a process of fleshing out what norms from what agents will adhere and make possible new rules for governing public life.

Conclusion

In order to give potency to the concept of the public domain, it is necessary to examine the normative input of economic and political actors. Both old and new actors now constitute the public domain, contributing to policy outcomes in terms of process and content. Indeed, it now seems necessary and desirable to widen the spectrum of actors in the policy arena, thereby making the public domain a product of more capacity building and consensus building across actor groups, this despite some of the attendant dangers for democracy. This is not to say that corporations or their foundational offshoots are now the panacea to solving public policy dilemmas or that NGOs can provide solutions to social injustice, nor does it suggest that government is devoid of innovation and ability to manage public domain concerns. But it does imply that new actors such as business and NGOs bring a wealth of new resources, ideas, methods, and so on, to the public-policy table.

There are downsides and risks to this new and changing public domain, however. Even if elevating the status of profit and market solutions in the public domain proves itself a temporary trend, societies have been exposed to new norms for public policy action. Some of these values may threaten to trans-form market economies into market societies – a fear very much on the minds of several European political leaders by the end of the 1990s. By turning to NGOs for answers and activism where the state fails, the values of political participation associated with representative democracy are undermined. Working together with state actors, business and NGO goals are moderated. It is possible that these myriad actors can achieve a societally acceptable balance in public policy, and can aspire to the social innovation (Mathews 1997) necessary for the political and economic challenges that now face the sphere of public policy. Ultimately, it is possible to be optimistic about the way the involvement of new public domain stakeholders reinvigorates democratic processes, if not along traditional electoral lines.

It is time to think and act creatively in the attribution of legitimacy and power, and to generate appropriate rules of the game to serve the broadest possible interests

Notes

1 Of course, there is a degree of irony in the fact that this preeminent prize for peace was originally funded by a wealthy industrialist, Dr Alfred Bernard Nobel, who made his fortune in the production of dynamite. For more on Nobel and the dichotomies of his work and legacy, see www.nobel.se (accessed 03.05.01).

2 In 1997, Jody Williams and the British-based International Campaign to Ban Landmines were awarded the Nobel Prize for Peace. Generally, Nobel Peace Prize recipients have been individuals, such as Theodore Roosevelt (1906), Woodrow Wilson (1919), Dag Hammarskjöld (1961), Martin Luther King, Jr (1964) and Mikhail Gorbachev (1990). However, they have also included a number of international organizations, these largely created and funded by national governments, such as the Institute of International Law (1904), International Committee of the Red Cross (1919 and 1944), Office of the United Nations High Commissioner for Refugees (1954), UNICEF (1965) and the ILO (1969).

3 It awarded Nobel prizes to the Friends Service Council – the Quakers (1947), Amnesty International (1977) and International Physicians for the Prevention of Nuclear War (1985).

4 In addition to the management sphere, the stakeholders approach also derives from the examination of policy networks, which has been tremendously useful in the analysis of public policy development in the European Union setting (Richardson 1996).

5 For the purposes of this discussion, 'state' and 'government' are used interchangeably. In other words, use of 'government' here refers generically to a publicly legitimated apparatus that governs, rather than any particular government of the day.

6 For more on this endeavour, see http://www.merck.com/philanthropy/9.htm (accessed 03.05.01).

7 For the US Department of Labor reports on this partnership, see http://www.dol.gov/dol/esa/public/nosweat/partnership/report.htm. For the members, see http://www.dol.gov/dol/esa/public/nosweat/partnership/members.htm.

8 See http://www.dol.gov/dol/esa/public/nosweat/partnership/aip.htm.

9 For more on this initiative, see http://www.ethicaltrade.org (accessed 18.05.01).

10 As Sell (1999: 172) has written: 'In effect, twelve corporations made public law for the world.'

11 For a very critical analysis of foundations' agendas – above all the excess of funding for progressive causes, see MacDonald (1996).

12 Taken from the foundation's 'about the network' website description, www.soros.org.

13 Soros was especially involved in the Russian crisis, taking on the role of an activist investor, which immediately raised conflict-of-interest concerns, see O'Brien (1998).

14 For the canonical work on normative press (media) theory, evaluating media's role in politics, see Siebert *et al.* (1956). Donohue *et al.* (1995) offer one interesting update.

15 Conversation with Medea Benjamin, June 1999.

16 According to TI, corruption 'undermines good government, fundamentally distorts public policy, leads to the misallocation of resources, harms the private sector and

private sector development and particularly hurts the poor', see Transparency
International (1998).
17 The Corruption Perception Index is a country index based on survey data that serves
as a tool for investors assessing risk and for economists assessing the impact of
corruption of economic growth, trade, and so on. By signing up for TI's Integrity
Pact, companies bidding for public procurement projects are compelled to refrain
from making bribes, and are threatened with sanctions if they engage in bribery.
18 As the United Nations Foundation website points out, the foundation promotes the
UN but also public outreach and education and the encouragement of private-public
partnerships in supporting UN activities. The website description of the foundation
also makes mention of Turner's own particular interest in encouraging philanthropy
to help create 'a better world', see www.unfoundation.org (accessed 04.03.01).

Bibliography

Adler, Emanuel and Barnett, Michael (eds) (1998) *Security Communities*, Cambridge:
Cambridge University Press.
Cutler, Claire, Haufler, Virginia and Porter, Tony (eds) (1999) *Private Authority and
International Affairs*, Albany, NY: State University of New York.
Demko, Paul (1996) 'Soros Goes West', *Chronicle of Philanthropy*, 5 September.
Devetak, Richard and Higgott, Richard (1999) 'Justice Unbound? Globalization, States,
and the Transformation of the Social Bond', *International Affairs*, 75, 3, July.
Donaldson, Thomas and Preston, L.E. (1995) 'The Stakeholder Theory of Corporation:
Concepts, Evidence, and Implications', *Academy of Management Review*, 20: 65–91.
Donohue, George, Tichenor, Phillip and Olien, Clarice (1995) 'A Guard Dog Perspec-
tive on the Role of Media', *Journal of Communication*, 45, 2: 115–32.
Drache, Daniel (1999) 'The Return of the Public Domain after the Triumph of Markets:
Revisiting the Most Basic of Fundamentals', paper prepared for the conference on
'Governing the Public Domain Beyond the Era of the Washington Consensus?:
Redrawing the Line Between the State and the Market', York University, 4–6
November.
Habermas, Jürgen (1993) *The Structural Transformation of the Public Sphere*, Cambridge,
MA: MIT Press.
Hall, Peter A. and Taylor, Rosemary C.R. (1996) 'Political Science and Three New
Institutionalisms', *Political Studies*, 154: 936–57.
Held, David (1997) 'Democracy and Globalization', Working Paper 97/5, Max-Planck-
Institut für Gesellschaftforschung, May 1997 (www.mpi-fg-koeln.mpg.de/publikation/
working_papers/ wp97–5/wp97–5.html), p. 3 (accessed 11 April 2001).
Kaul, Inge, Grunberg, Isabelle and Stern, Marc (eds) (1999) *Global Public Goods: Inter-
national Cooperation in the 21st Century*, New York: Oxford University Press.
Keck, Margaret E. and Sikkink, Kathryn (1998) *Activists Beyond Borders: Advocacy
Networks in International Politics*, Ithaca, NY: Cornell University Press.
Mac Donald, Heather (1996) 'The Billions of Dollars That Made Things Worse', *City
Journal*, Autumn.
Mathews, Jessica T. (1997) 'Power Shift', *Foreign Affairs*, 76, 1, January/February.
Morais, Richard (1997) 'Beware of Billionaires Bearing Gifts', *Forbes*, 7 April.
Nelson, Jane (1998) *Building Competitiveness and Communities: How World Class Compa-
nies are Creating Shareholder Value and Societal Value*, London: Prince of Wales
Business Leaders Forum.

O'Brien, Timothy (1998) 'George Soros Has Seen the Enemy: It Looks Like Him', *New York Times*, Sunday, 6 December.

Reinicke, Wolfgang H. (1999) 'The Other World Wide Web: Global Public Policy Networks', *Foreign Policy*, Winter 1999–2000: 44–57.

Rosenau, James N. (1990) *Turbulence in World Politics: a Theory of Change and Continuity*, Princeton, NJ: Princeton University Press.

—— (1992) 'Governance, Order and Change in World Politics', in J. Rosenau and E.-O. Czempiel (eds) *Governance without Government: Order and Change in World Politics*, Cambridge: Cambridge University Press.

Rosenau, J. and Czempiel, E.-O. (eds) (1992) *Governance without Government: Order and Change in World Politics*, Cambridge: Cambridge University Press.

Richardson, Jeremy (ed.) (1996) *European Union: Power and Policy-Making*, London: Routledge.

Sassen, Saskia (1999) 'Territory and Territoriality in the Global Economy', paper presented at the Carnegie Council on Ethics and International Affairs, 29 June.

Sell, Susan K. (1999) 'Multinational Corporations as Agents of Change: The Globalization of Intellectual Property Rights', in Claire Cutler, Virginia Haufler and Tony Porter (eds) *Private Authority and International Affairs*, Albany, NY: State University of New York.

Shawcross, William (1997) 'Turning Dollars into Change', in *Fortune*, 150, 9, 1 September.

Siebert, Fred, Peterson, Theodore and Schramm, Wilbur (1956) *Four Theories of the Press*, Urbana, IL: University of Illinois.

Slaughter, Anne-Marie (1997) 'The Real New World Order', *Foreign Affairs*, 76, 5, September/October: 183–97.

Soros, George (1998) *The Crisis of Global Capitalism: Open Society Endangered*, New York: Public Affairs.

Transparency International (1998) *Combating Corruption: Are Lasting Solutions Emerging?*, Annual Report, Berlin: Transparency International.

Weber, Steve (2000) 'International Organizations and the Pursuit of Justice in the World Economy', *Ethics and International Affairs*, vol. 14, New York: Carnegie Council on Ethics and International Affairs.

Wendt, Alexander (1987) 'The Agent-Structure Problem in International Relations Theory', *International Organization*, 41, 3, Summer.

—— (1992) 'Anarchy is What States Make of It: the Social Construction of Power Politics', *International Organization*, 46, 2.

Zadek, Simon and Weiser, John (forthcoming) 'Conversations with Disbelievers: Persuading Companies to Increase Corporate Involvement'.

6 Social disability and the public good

Marcia Rioux and Ezra Zubrow

Seattle and Prague have made evident the divisions that have arisen over the current and future course of globalization. The majority of the world's countries feel they are being treated unfairly in the global system by the rich nations. People outside the mainstream because of ethnicity, gender, religion and disability see themselves as the particular targets of disadvantage in economic globalization. And there are concerns over the failure of political leaders to address such critical issues as global poverty and a deteriorating environment. The widening gap and the imbalance between rich and poor that appears to be the legacy of economic globalization is considered by many to be both intolerable and unnecessary. Basic human rights such as food and nutrition, primary health care, drinking water, basic education, and shelter are not available to millions – including many in the high-income countries. The World Health Organization, in its most recent reports, has recognized the relationship between income disparities and health status. Their figures show significantly lower overall health status in countries with wider income discrepancies than in countries with more equalized income distribution.

Emerging post-national identities have shown little capacity to withstand inequality, injustice, exclusion and violence. As Eduardo Portella, of Brazil, said of culture in the context of globalization:

> To subordinate culture to criteria developed in the laboratories of the dominant ideology, which make a cult of the ups and downs of the stock market, the uncertainties of supply and demand, the snares of functionality and urgency, is to cut off its vital supply of social oxygen and to replace creative tension with the stress of the marketplace.
>
> (Portella 2000)

The influence of economic globalization on the subordination of social justice, equality, basic rights and human dignity to the narrow constraints of economics cannot be missed. This is usually attributed to the increasing interdependence of national economies within the world market, and the idea that this has constrained the abilities of national governments to follow the economic, and therefore social, policies of their choice. This interdependence is seen as arising from the increased volume of trade, foreign direct investment and cross-border financial flows. As social policy is bound by economic policy, this leads to budget constraint and privatization. As one commentator puts it 'governments are no longer total masters in their own countries and welfare developments are, to some extent, at the mercy of globalizing influences'.

A 'new orthodoxy' (Holden 1999) has emerged among policy-makers, that governments can only engage with the constraints imposed by the IMF, WTO, global capital and economic initiatives such as the Washington consensus. The constraint of social policy by economic policy, while hardly new, has been legitimated by globalization. As Moran and Wood have noted, 'Constructing external constraints ... allows particular national elites to present their policy preferences as the more or less unavoidable consequence of forces over which nationally organized institutions can have little or no control' (1996: 125–42).

There are other examples of constructions of external constraints that have allowed particular national elites to present their policy preferences as inevitable and necessary, - presenting of the state as powerless in the face of globalization. These provide ways to present, in political discourse the inequities and disadvantage faced within nations and across nations as unavoidable.

This chapter examines the way in which international norms and standards and democratic national governments have recognized well-being as a public good while simultaneously rationalizing its content and scope. Thus the state presents its role as the judicious balancing of competing interests of the monetarist policies, which demand deficit reduction, with the social justice interests - of equality, social well-being and the reduction of poverty.

Well-being and social justice as public goods

The ways in which a society provides for people who are more socially and economically dependent and more culturally marginalized throws into sharp focus the problems of the public domain as a political construct (Drache 2001). Concepts such as well-being and, more broadly, social justice help delineate the state's responsibility in ameliorating disadvantage, social isolation, income redistribution, inequality and ethnic homogenization.

The post-war framework for social justice and well-being recognized that international economic issues could not be treated in isolation from domestic social change. High unemployment and the lack of effective systems of support were widely perceived as socially, politically and economically unfeasible. They made clear the importance of social well-being as a public good. Security was a key element of the post-war framework, both as a realist concept (Grayson 2001)[1] and because the experiences of the Great Depression, the Second World War and the return of veterans brought uncertainty as to whether people could meet their basic needs on their own (Grayson2001).[2] Through the depression people faced hunger, homelessness, ill health and disability on a scale not seen before.

The framework for social well-being as a public good, therefore, grew out of the desire to find an alternative to the social and economic upheaval caused by the Great Depression of the 1930s and the inability of international leaders to achieve a lasting peace after the First World War.[3] These goals were articulated at Bretton Woods (1944) and in the Atlantic Charter of 1941. Both recognized that distributive policies and social justice were international public goods (Kapstein 1999). They focused on the role of the state in bringing about security, democracy and opportunity within the context of citizenship.

To the extent that these arrangements would lead to the fulfilment of social and economic goals, social well-being was achievable (Roeher 1992). World leaders linked economic growth, political stability and social justice, as, for example, in the United Nations Charter.

With the new framework for well-being came a renewed belief in the social, economic and political institutions of society. It made no difference whether they were social democratic or welfare statist states, such as Sweden and Norway, or liberal residual welfare states, such as Canada and Britain or corporatist welfare states, such as Germany, Austria, Italy and France. Because social well-being was in the public domain, it meant that decisions by government were not simply *ad hoc*, but were the outcome of rational deliberation and strong public administration. Among the most commonly agreed upon elements of the welfare state is that it embodies a public commitment to improve welfare by achieving a greater measure of social equality (Korpi 1983; Ruggie 1984). Mishra defines the welfare state as the 'institutionalization of government responsibility for maintaining national minimum standards' (Mishra 1984: 34). A key goal of the welfare state is to modify market forces so that the well-being of individuals and families is not subject exclusively to their market power, that is, it is the decommodification of labour (Esping-Anderson 1985).

Until the mid 1970s, arguably, there was a consensus that 'well-being', encompassing basic needs of physical security, civil and political rights and democratic processes, was a public good. In most countries, institutional structures were established that increased government involvement in the management of the economy and provided for the security of citizens.

But the political winds have changed in the past twenty years, and the result has been that national policies directed to achieving distributive justice are constrained by internal and external economic forces, globalization and a lack of political will.

Well-being as a reinvented public good

The notion of well-being[4] as a public good encompasses the recognition of unequal opportunities within the market economy and the need for the state to be proactive in addressing those inequalities (Kaul *et al.* 1999). It recognizes that the market and the state have to work together to optimize the prospects for well-being among the least advantaged members and the least advantaged communities by increasing their capacity and their opportunity.

T.H. Marshall observed, in 1950, that the core idea of the welfare state is social citizenship. This is the extension of civil and political rights to the sphere of social provision so that there is a general enrichment of life, a reduction in risk and uncertainty and a reduction of social inequality. While the granting of social rights, did not necessarily directly reduce inequality, by conferring a sense of status on individuals, through access to services, social citizenship does compete with and even replaces one's class status (Marshall and Bottomore 1992). This concept of social citizenship finds its moral foundation in liberal notions of justice (Rawls 1971) in which survival and autonomy are basic needs. There is an obligation on the state to assure that all citizens can meet these needs. Society is compelled, on moral grounds, to compensate those who the market fails and to care for the sick, the elderly, the unemployed and other dependent groups, even if it means sacrificing some economic efficiency to do so. Social goals such as the development of community or social citizenship supersede market-determined goals of efficiency.

Mohan Rao (1999: 7, 70) argues that, as in the case of peace, equity and justice cannot be obtained separately by individual consumers in the market place. There is a strong instrumental role for equity and justice – in helping to jointly provide other public goods, and in defining their prioritization. Thus, eliminating poverty benefits not just the poor, but also the rest of society. It strengthens peace and stability, global health and market efficiency – quite apart from its intrinsic value. Well-being is not predicated on market failure, inclusiveness or cooperative consumption. It is predicated on social justice. This leads to a shift in perspective from 'survival' to 'sustainability' and is impacted by factors other than market conditions including political, cultural, and historic values.

Resulting from both the ideological and economic crises in the 1970s, social expenditure increasingly came to be viewed as an excessive burden. A progressively more hegemonic view of the market led to a breakdown of the consensus about the positive role of government that had guided social policy development for the previous thirty years. Government and the mixed economy were viewed by neo-liberals as the fundamental problem and retrenchment as the effective solution.

It seems evident that the social benefits of the welfare state, which were articulated by the Allies at the end of Second World War have not led to social well-being or to social justice. Market values, as represented in the Washington consensus, intervened and it became clear that the articulation of social well-being as expressed in social welfare programmes, was insufficient and subject to ideological and economic forces. There remained a social deficit (Osberg 1990). Well-being, when limited to the securing of civil and political rights, basic needs for income, safety and support, and the exercise of political democracy, was not sufficient to ensure justice or to develop distributive policies. To ensure well-being as a public good requires that the challenges facing governments are managed in ways that satisfy the very diverse elements and interest groups in society. Among these elements are included the increasingly complex nature of governing and the need for policy coherence, the need for a foundation for fairness and the rising costs of social welfare (in the form of income support, education, unemployment insurance, and health and social services). Self-determination, democratization and equality provide the basis for a revised notion of social well-being as a public good in the current context.

Elements of social well-being

An expanded notion of social well-being would then have six elements (Roeher 1993). They are security, citizenship, democracy, self-determination, democratization, and equality. The first three are those that were identified in the post-war period. The latter three have strong elements of indivisibility and non-exclusiveness that are characteristic of public goods and fit within an understanding of public goods that encompass social justice and distributive justice. Rao argues that equity and distributional criteria must be at the core of our notion of public goods. At a minimum, notions of horizontal equity (the equal treatment of equals) and vertical equity (a progressive distribution of burdens) in financing are often invoked. At a minimum, they are necessary for the expanded definition.

Self-determination can be defined as the choice and pursuit of aspirations and the development of capabilities, which are made autonomously and free from coercion. It is usually exercised by individuals, communities and societies when their aims are articulated and implemented. Self-determination is important in this 'reinvented well-being', by allowing the individual to decide, on the basis of self-knowledge, self-management, and resource availability, how they want to lead their lives. In the realm of health, the World Health Organization recognizes the relationship between increased self-determination and control of one's environment, on the one hand, and health status on the other. It also increases human dignity and self-worth. In the case of the workplace, when workers are expected to make decisions about their education, training and the organization of their workplace tasks, job motivation increases. Under these conditions of self-determination there is a greater potential for innovation, increased productivity, and work satisfaction.

Democratization is the process of enabling the democratic participation of individuals and diverse groups, in a wide scope of decision-making processes that directly affect their lives. It is, in this way, a component of well-being. Democratization involves a constructive politics of recognition (Taylor 1992), equal participation of diverse interests in decision-making, and democratized decision-making in societal institutions. These requirements ensure the cooperative behaviour necessary for the provision of public goods (Rao 1999), as people will participate more willingly in a system that they perceive to be fair and equitable. Democratization is important because it requires the mutual recognition of others' aims and needs as a means to providing a counter balance to the abuse of power. Also, it provides a mechanism for social bonding and a basis for agreement on individual limits to self-determination.

Equality as an element of social well-being is defined as the absence of barriers to mutual respect and recognition between people 'who are equally free from political control, social pressure and economic deprivation' (Lukes 1980). Equality refers to equality of outcome rather than equality of treatment, thereby incorporating notions of equal enjoyment of well-being, institutional recognition of differences, and accommodation and support to ensure equal freedom to pursue aspirations.

The notion of 'well-being' as a public good affects the outcome of public policy in several ways. First, it creates a framework that leads to a redefinition of social conflict and institutionalizes diversity and democratic social bargaining as a basis for decision making. Second, not only does it institutionalize social diversity, it moves toward, the coordination and integration of economic, social, and environmental policies. It recognizes that sustainable economic growth and social development are integrated problems that cannot be addressed by sectoral solutions. Third, the framework provides a system of measures to index 'the social health' of a nation. This results in a change from policy fragmentation to policy coherence.

The privatization of social well-being

A strong case can be made for social well-being as a public good in as much as it has such characteristics as equity, shared communal benefits, indivisibility, non-rivalry, and non-excludability. Yet, governments have limited their investment of public funds directed towards its achievement. This disjunction between the political commitment and the economic investment suggests the off-loading of government responsibility to the private domain. Social well-being is increasingly market-driven and privatized. However, because there remains a political commitment to it as a public good, governments have had to rationalize their decisions to reduce their fiscal expenditure. The increasing governmental limitations on expenditures in this area have meant that the public's needs are being met selectively rather than universally. The coherence that social well-being as a reinvented public good offers is being circumscribed by political action rather than by market conditions – political action that rationalizes government disengagement from its own recognition of social justice and social well-being as public goods.

Deficit reduction, it has been argued by neo-liberal governments, represents a greater common good than the availability of social programmes. Individual self-sufficiency has triumphed, as a valued economic and cultural commodity. Consequently social well-being, as evidenced in health, culture, equality and equity, has shifted for a significant number of people from a public good to a private good. This shift can be seen in the restructuring of the welfare state, away from universal provision based on citizenship rights to provision based on social need. Thus, any prospect of entitlement has been removed. The expectation is an increasing reliance on private provision with a greater emphasis on self-reliance.

Social disability provides an example of the way in which governments have invoked scientific rationalism, economic determinism and philosophic traditions of utilitarianism to shift the responsibility from the public domain to the private domain. The boundary between the public and private domain shifts towards the private, as scientific rationalism and economic determinism comes into play. There are two rationals used to justify the boundary:

1   To set or establish a hierarchy of social or cultural goods, which enables one to take precedence over another, in terms of public expenditure, and to use that hierarchy to legitimize the place where the line is drawn between a public and a private good. This economic rationalization, based on a simple notion of utilitarianism, has provided a means to limit social expenditure (Sen 1999b, 1999a). Thus, the issue of subsidizing lives becomes, as Martha T. McCluskey puts it, an aspect of the ideology of efficiency. Welfare and health care are reduced under the rubric of utilitarianism.

2   To differentiate between people, based on such characteristics as social status, biology or culture and legitimize these criteria as a basis of providing for some and not for others. This limits the state responsibility for disadvantage and leaves it to the market to correct. Scientific rationalization makes it possible for politicians, economists, and policy analysts to use science to justify a particular set of political actions. From this perspective, it is the function of the science to assess the most crucial problems besetting society.

Social welfare as a limited public good

The question of how far the global economic relationship affects national welfare provisions is affected by the power relations behind the nationalist boundaries of welfare obligation and how the movements of capital, as well as labour, affect the potential for welfare provisions. The role of the state, in regulating and correcting inequality, may be either expansive or restrictive, arguably in response to international monetary pressures and to the importance placed on economic efficiency and effectiveness as state goals. Where increasing equality, rights entitlement, social well-being, and full employment are state social values, the role of the state in providing well-being is much clearer. But recent government redefinition of the boundary between public and private has resulted in greater private responsibility for inequities and increased dependence on the market to correct the imbalances.

Economic rationalization and utilitarianism

From about the end of the First World War to the 1960s, most Western governments established a social safety net that placed the responsibility for care of those who were most disadvantaged in the public domain. High unemployment and the lack of effective systems of support were widely perceived to be socially and economically unacceptable.

For those who could not participate in the labour market, the state made a growing commitment to provide for their security through a number of income programmes and social services. Key social security reports of the 1940s recommended a full employment economy as a matter of policy, and entitlements to income and social support in the event of illness, old age and unemployment. There were always, however, restrictions to the demand that the state had to bear. In order to limit an open-ended public responsibility for social justice, governments limited their redistributive policies based on an economic determinism grounded in utilitarian principles. A distinction between the worthy and the unworthy poor provided a means for distinguishing what was the individual and family responsibility and what was a public obligation for social justice and the actualization of social well-being.

The distinction between worthy and unworthy has been used to rationalize redistribution by placing a ceiling on the demand for excessive social spending on social justice. It provides an indicator of how people are differentiated and the way in which the differences are formulated to affect the public–private differentiation and the subsequent social policy. It is a public good to ensure that those who cannot work and gain a secure income to take care of themselves be provided for by the state, as a matter of social justice. Providing for individual misfortune, to which anyone might be subject, through such factors as age, accidental disability, or unavoidable unemployment is recognized as a public good. But fiscal limits to the obligations of state redistribution on this basis are justified, because the boundary of the public good is drawn such that the state does not have to provide for those who are able to work but are not working. That is, as a matter of economic efficiency, some people who do not have income security will have to fend for themselves. This 'monetarist approach' supposedly fosters growth by restraining demand in order to reduce consumption. The focus on markets and free trade is justified because of the belief that growth will eventually 'trickle down' to protect the environment and assure minimum standards of health and labour welfare.

In contrast, distributive justice and social well-being, as public goods, invoke an ethical principle of fairness, rather than utilitarianism. From this perspective, the rich, the wealthy capital investors or high-income earners can afford to give up more than the poor low-income earner. Utilitarianism, as applied to well-being, represents a break from benefit theory and allows greater taxation in the service of maximum social utility. In other words, it should 'improve the distribution of income and wealth arising from free competition' (Schoenblum 1995).

The upheaval

By legitimizing differences between people's misfortune through categories such as 'worthy' and 'unworthy', the demands placed on the public sphere are reduced. Only those who are 'worthy' will be provided for through the public sphere. As already noted, this legitimizes the reduction of public expenditure, but it also makes social well-being a selective public good. The goal of the English Poor Laws[5] and those modelled after them in many countries, established this tradition of a distinction between the worthy poor and the unworthy poor. Through the evolution of this distinction in the succeeding years, the state established some obligation to care for those considered worthy poor. These included people who were old, sick or disabled. The implications of this distinction have most often been analysed from the perspective of those considered unworthy. These are the 'able-bodied' and 'able-minded' men and women who were considered able to but who were unwilling to work. For those who fell into this category, the welfare state has been minimalist and residual, based on the 'less eligibility' principle. Without recognition of the structural factors which have led to unemployment, poverty, ill health and illiteracy, welfare state provision has entangled people and families in a web of meagre provision, disentitlement, discretionary benefits, contradictory eligibility rules, surveillance and targeted programmes. These have had the effect of entrenching and privatizing rather than ameliorating inequality and social isolation. As many of the poor are seen as 'unworthy' through the lens of the welfare state institutions, provision for this group has remained minimalist and residual. Obviously this reduced social cost and delimited what was in the public domain (see Figure 6.1).

From the perspective of the 'worthy' poor, a different set of obligations was established than for those who were 'unworthy'. These obligations could only be exercised by constructing legal and social differences that have served to legit-imize different treatment and obligations between the worthy and the unworthy.

The category of 'worthy' poor has become a double-edged sword for many disadvantaged, marginalized people. Under the legal and social regime of 'worthy poor', people with disabilities, the old and the infirm, become the object of

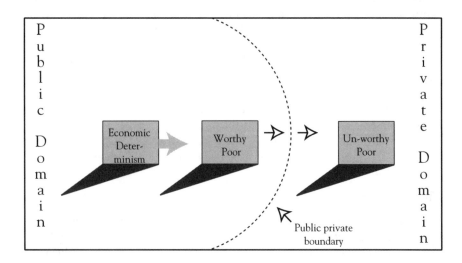

Figure 6.1 Economic determinism as a legitimizing mechanism for determining the public/ private boundary

charity, but at the cost of basic social citizenship. Considered incompetent to function in society, this being the entrance to becoming 'worthy', some public responsibility is assumed for the misfortune and for meeting those needs, where for the 'unworthy' the misfortune is private. The social programmes and policies for the 'worthy' then become part of the public domain.

In the immediate post-war period, the framework of obligations emphasizing security, citizenship and democracy entrenched the worthy/unworthy (public/private) distinction. These became the pillars of the framework for social well-being (and state obligation) and provided the basis for investment in building the institutional infrastructure for welfare provision. The notion of citizenship, as a broad set of social, economic and political entitlements, was being formulated in this period (Marshall and Bottomore 1992). However, the figure of the 'citizen', that remained entrenched, was that of the self-made, rational and independent individual exercising basic democratic and legal rights. A democratic state and society was to be constituted by such individuals securing for themselves and doing so largely on their own, the 'good life'. Because many people did not meet the tests imposed by such a concept of citizen (e.g. those with disabilities, old, etc.), they were to be taken care of through the 'security' pillar of welfare.

Governments established highly targeted and categorical programmes, with restricted eligibility requirements to ensure that people were seen to be different and treated differently as the condition for obtaining welfare provision. It is a matter of demonstrating the state's obligation to those in need (the public domain), while the burden on the state is minimized (enlarging the private domain). The result is to increase the private and decrease the public responsibility. Charity, pity and incapacity are within the public domain – simple need is not. The interrelationship of the public and private has varied from country to country and the entitlement to the social goods is variable.

Although there was, in some countries, a move towards greater recognition of a wider notion of social justice from the 1960s to the 1980s,[6] international global pressures resulted in a retrenchment.

Deficit reduction has become a greater good than social justice and social well-being in government priorities. So the balance is shifted to deficit reduction, and individual self-sufficiency is valued as an economic and social commodity. International pressure for deficit reduction has trumped social arguments and a history of welfare 'statism' in determining social policy and the public–private division of responsibility for disadvantage.

The promotion of selective poverty programmes, as opposed to integral, comprehensive and universal social policies, results from their being compatible with the permanence of basic neo-liberal economic policies and state withdrawal from its responsibilities as the main financier and organizer of social service. Given the scarcity of public resources, the argument continues, the way to achieve this objective is through carefully targeted poverty programmes that complement the satisfying of social needs through market and family mechanisms. The end result is the same as that stated by the neo-liberal doctrine: social welfare belongs primarily to the private domain – to markets, family and community – and only when it cannot be resolved in this way should the state intervene and guarantee social minimum using public resources (Laurell and Wences 1994).

Social disability and the public good within this framework

Scientific rationalism has provided a further state mechanism for recognizing social justice as a public good, by differentiating those whose well-being is a public responsibility from those whose well-being is not. It legitimizes the variable boundary between the public domain and the private, leaving it to the market to correct inequalities, and for the family and charities to provide when the inequities are not resolved. Katz (1986) documented an earlier example of what he termed 'scientific charity'. In the 1870s in the United States, in the public sector, policy was developed to abolish or reduce relief. In the private sector the result was the formation of charity organization, societies that attempted to rationalize and systematize philanthropy.

> Reformers wanted to do more than cut expenses and purge the able bodied from relief. To these familiar goals, they added a new element: a concerted drive to make relief primarily private. Alarmed by the disorder of American cities in the last third of the nineteenth century, frightened by the spectre of a militant, organized and undeferential working class, the charity organizers responded as harshly as employers and governments confronted with similar problems. The task charity organizers set themselves was to teach the poor that they had no rights. Afraid that relief was turning into a right, the new reformers put all their energy into transforming it back into charity.
>
> (Katz 1986: 58)

Disability benefits and entitlements provide an example of a case in which a particular status can be differentially interpreted as within either the public or private domain. This shows quite clearly how interpretations of political obligation are constructed as a means to justify where the boundary between public and private is drawn.

The scientific and social justification for political action related to disability can be traced to identifiable and shifting conceptual frameworks. These dissimilar formulations of disability underlie the kinds of policy and programmes that can be found in most nations of the world. This suggests that knowledge in this field is created internationally not nationally. While the models of disability have led to different social policy and social responsibility in different countries, there are identifiable commonalties in these spheres that emanate from the particular characteristics of the models themselves.

The following figure (Figure 6.2) provides a general view of the various understandings and formulations of disability.

There are four identifiable social and scientific formulations of disability reflected in the treatment of persons with disability in law, in policy, in

Social and Scientific Formulations of Disability	
Individual Pathology	
Bio-medical approach (consequence of biological characteristics)	Functional approach (consequence of functional abilities and capacities)
Treatment: through medicine and bio-technology **Prevention:** through biological/ genetic intervention or screening **Social responsibility:** to eliminate or cure disability	**Treatment:** through rehabilitation services **Prevention:** through early diagnosis and treatment **Social responsibility:** to ameliorate and provide comfort
Social Pathology	
Environmental approach (consequence of environmental factors and service arrangements)	Human rights approach (consequence of social organization and relationship of individual to society)
Treatment: through increased individual control of services and supports. **Prevention:** through elimination of social, economic and physical barriers **Social responsibility:** elimination of systemic barriers	**Treatment:** through reformation of economic, social and political policy **Prevention:** through recognition of condition disability as inherent in society **Social responsibility:** to provide political and social entitlements

Figure 6.2 Formulations of disability

programmes and in human rights instruments. Two of them emanate from theories of disability that postulate it as a result of individual pathology (a deficit model) and two that postulate it as a result of social, legal and economic conditions. How disability is perceived, diagnosed and treated, scientifically and socially, is reflected in assumptions about the social responsibility towards people with disabilities as a group. The assumptions or postulates about disability are not mutually exclusive nor have they been temporally chronological.

Scientific formulations of disability based on an individual pathology have a number of common characteristics:

- they approach disability as a field of professional expertise
- they use, primarily, a positivist paradigm
- they emphasize primary prevention including biological and environmental conditions
- they characterize disability as incapacity in relation to non-disabled persons; a comparative incapacity they distinguish disability and its attached costs as an anomaly and social burden
- they portray the inclusion of people with disabilities as a private responsibility
- they depict the individual condition as the primary point of intervention.

The social obligation attached to the characterization of disability as a biomedical or biological condition has conventionally been limited to medical diagnosis and treatment, including medical or genetically directed therapeutic interventions. For those who cannot be cured or rehabilitated, the conventional models of care have been institutions and other segregated housing and all-encompassing service provision centres. Until quite recently, people with disabilities were expected to make no contribution to society. They were in many cases considered a danger to society (see Cohen 1985: Cohen and Scull 1983; Canada 1979; Sutherland 1976), and because they were characterized as without potential, families were encouraged to place their children in institutions. Their well-being would be provided but limited to the basic necessities of food, shelter and clothing. The alternative for families was to keep their children at home where they would have familial contact and care but the state was under little obligation to provide services, supports or financial resources.

The second of the two formulations of disability as an individual pathology is a bio-functional or rehabilitation approach. Like the bio-medical approach, the underlying presumption is that the deficit stems from an individual condition or pathology. The feature that distinguishes this approach from the biomedical is that the way of understanding the condition is in relation to the impact that the biological condition has on the individual's functional capacity.

The social responsibility in dealing with disability as a functional abnormality is to provide ways to ameliorate the condition to the extent that the negative effects can be reduced and incapacity to function can be reduced. This leads to the development of systems of assessment, habilitation and measures to improve self-care and social skills. This social responsibility derives principally from a sense of charity and benevolence (and in some cases, an economic calculation of the social cost that attaches to being dependent in society). The definition of the hierarchy of needs to ameliorate the functional inability is left to professionals, who are attributed, with the skills and knowledge to determine what is in the best interests of the individual and what will be most beneficial.

Table 6.1 (Mackelprang 1999) shows the role of professionals within a context of a formulation of disability grounded in individual pathology in both the bio-medical and functional approaches.

Table 6.1 Professional responses to disability

Perspective	Problems	Role and definitions of the person	Professions	Controls	Expectation of the person
Medical	Illness, sickness	Patient	Medicine, nursing, physical therapy	Physician with consultation of allied health professionals	Passive recipient of treatment
Mental Health	Mental illness, personality deficits	Patient, client	Psychiatry, psychology, mental health, social work	Psychiatrist, clinical psychologist with consultation of other professionals	Passive recipient of treatment, compliance with treatment plans
Vocational	Unemployment ability due to personal problems	Client, student	Educational psychology, vocational rehabilitation, rehabilitation psychology	Rehabilitation counsellor, job coach	Follow vocational plans
Educational	Learning, attention and/or behavioural deficits	Student	Special education, behavioural therapy, educational psychology	Resource/special education counsellors, educational psychologists	Remedial learning and improving behaviour
Social service	Social worker, social service worker, financial worker	Client	Social work, social services	Social worker, financial worker, eligibility worker	Being compliant and remaining eligible

Source: From: Mackelprang (1999: 12).

In both formulations of disability originating in an individual pathology, labelling or diagnosing the physiological or psychological state is important. It is a means of determining the individual pathology or functional disabilities, and a basis for undertaking curative or remedial treatment. And it provides both the market and the public sector with the means to confine or delimit its financial commitment. Given the 'medicalization' of disability, many instruments have been developed for the purpose of diagnosis such as the International Classification of Impairment, Disability and Handicap (ICIDH), the Diagnostic Statistical Manual (DSM 3), the International Classification of Disease (ICD 10), and various IQ tests. On the basis of such diagnostic tools, medical or alternatively rehabilitation therapy is initiated to address the diagnosed problem, which, if cured medically or remediated, will enable a person to function as independently as possible – within the social and economic environments designed and used by able-bodied persons.

There is a presumption that it is a public good to address social justice and citizenship but only to the extent that it is feasible within the values of the marketplace. Otherwise it belongs to the public domain. But as Mr Juan Somavia, Director-General of the International Labour Organization (ILO) asked in a recent address, 'Why should the macroeconomic balance be achieved on the basis of unbalancing the lives of people already living in the margins of society?'

As well as the two approaches to disability based on individual pathology, there are two identifiable approaches to disability based on 'social pathology'. They both start from a presumption that disability is not inherent to the individual. Rather they assume that the disability is a function of the social structure. It is a structural model rather than an individual model, recognizing the pathology as a consequence of social and economic conditions rather than the individual impairment.

The shared characteristics of these are:

- they assume that disability is not inherent to the individual independent of the social structure;
- they give priority to political, social and built environment;
- they emphasize secondary prevention rather than primary treatment;
- they recognize disability as difference rather than as an anomaly;
- they portray the inclusion of people with disabilities as a public responsibility;
- they depict the social, environmental and economic structures as the primary point of intervention.

Disability as social pathology

Advances in knowledge, based on an understanding of disability as a social pathology, have shown that personal abilities and limitations are the result not only of factors residing in the individual, but also of the interaction between individuals and their environments. This, recognizably, moves disability into the public domain, making problematic the argument that disability is a private responsibility and therefore ought to be privately ameliorated. Social justice would demand that the needs of people who are disadvantaged by social, economic, legal and political conditions be met through the public domain as part of a package of socially expected public goods.

From an environmental perspective on disability, the policy and programme focus is placed on the way the environments are arranged. Increasingly, there is evidence in policy research that the impact of disability can be reduced, as environments are adapted to enable participation.

The handling of disability from this approach is to identify the barriers in society that restrict the participation of people with impairments or disabilities in economic and social life. Structural barriers to independent living or community living become the sites for state intervention (*Canadian Association for Independent Living Centres* 1994; Roeher 1988). Prevention then is through the elimination of social, economic and political barriers. The elimination of physical barriers, for example, the building of ramps or the adoption of employment equity or affirmative action policies would be methods of prevention.

The second of the two systemic approaches presumes that disability has social causes and is a consequence of how society is organized and the relationship of the individual to society at large (see Roth 1983; Beresford and Campbell 1994; Roeher 1993; Rioux 1994; ICIDH 1991). Research, policy and law from a rights-outcome approach, look beyond particular environments to focus on the broad systemic factors keeping some groups of people from participating as equals in society.

From a rights-outcome approach, wide variations in cognitive, sensory and motor ability are seen as inherent to the human condition and consequently, the variations should not limit the potential to contribute to society. It frames disability issues through the lens of principles of social justice. It recognizes that it is a public good to reduce civic inequalities and address social and economic disadvantage. People will need supports (e.g., personal services, aids and devices) in order to gain access to, participate in, and exercise self-determination as equals in society. Recognition of social and political entitlements is based on social justice rather than economic contribution and rights are equated with those of all others in society. There is a social good in enabling inclusion and the exercise of citizenship rights (see Figure 6.3).

Policy from a rights-outcome approach constructs an analysis of how society marginalizes people and assumes that social institutions can be adjusted to respond effectively to the participation and the needs of those who have been systemically marginalized. Treating the disadvantage is the result of reformulation of social and political policy and of recognizing the condition of disability as inherent to society, not some kind of anomaly to normalcy.

The impact on social policy of how the disadvantage that attaches to disability is characterized is significant. Relieving the state of responsibility for

1. Individual Pathology (IP): 'Can you tell me what is wrong with you?'

Social Pathology (SP): 'Can you tell me what is wrong with society?'

2. IP: 'What complaint causes your difficulty in holding, gripping or turning things?'

SP: 'What defects in the design of everyday equipment like jars, bottles and tins causes you difficulty in holding, gripping or turning them?'

3. IP: 'Are your difficulties in understanding people mainly due to a hearing problem?'

SP: 'Are your difficulties in understanding people mainly due to their inability to communicate with you?'

4. IP: 'Do you have a scar, blemish or deformity, which limits your daily activities?'

SP: 'Do other people's reaction to any scar, blemish or deformity you may have limit your daily activities?'

5. IP: 'Have you attended a special school because of a long-term health problem or disability?'

SP: 'Have you attended a special school because of your education authority's policy of sending people with your health problem/disability to such places?'

6. IP: 'Does your health problem/ disability prevent you from going out as often or as far as you would like?'

SP: 'What is it about the local environment that makes it difficult for you to get about in your neighbourhood?'

7. IP: 'Does your health problem/disability make it difficult for you to travel by bus?'

SP: 'Are there any transport or financial problems which prevent you from going out as often or as far as you would like?'

8. IP: 'Does your health problem/disability affect your work in any way at present?'

SP: 'Do you have problems at work because of the physical environment or the attitudes of others?'

9. IP: 'Does your health problem/disability mean that you need to live with relatives or someone else who can help or look after you?'

SP: 'Are community services so poor that you need to rely on relatives or someone else to provide you with the right level of personal assistance?'

Figure 6.3 Understanding disability from a societal and individual perspective
Source: Adapted from Barnes *et al.* (1999: 29).

providing for the social well-being of people with disabilities, would mean that social well-being loses the characteristics of public goods of non-excludability and non-rivalness. But if the difference is biology, an argument can be made that the nature of the class of people itself provides justification for the well-being of those in that class to be distinguished from that of others. The public good of well-being can, arguably, still be recognized.

If the difference attached to disability is attributed to social conditions and the social relations in which biology exists, then there is an increased public responsibility to better the conditions through redistributive policies assuming social well-being and social justice are public goods. It then falls within the public domain to reduce civic inequalities, that is, to address social and economic disadvantage by providing supports to enable social and economic integration, self-determination and legal and social rights. Social justice and equity are interpreted as political demands that social policy should focus on the disabling aspects of society, on supporting human diversity and on empowering disadvantaged individuals in order to provide well-being.

These social and scientific formulations of disability provide a means to recognize how scientific rationalism has been used to justify political policies and programmes that maintain disability as a private rather than a public responsibility – a matter of opportunity cost or economic drain (see Figure 6.4).

The recognition and elaboration of what determines the lives of those with disabilities and others is useful as a barometer of the construction of the demarcation between the public and private domain and of the impact of economic pressures to reduce redistributive policies. If disability is interpreted as a biological condition, an individual pathology, then there is less imperative for the state to make it an expenditure priority and a necessary condition of social well-being – that is, for it to be treated as a public good. More importantly, policy that provides for the humane treatment of people with disabilities can be characterized as beneficence, which rather than social justice, and falls outside the parameters of the social good, social justice and social well-being. The demand to address it through programmes and policies is weakened.

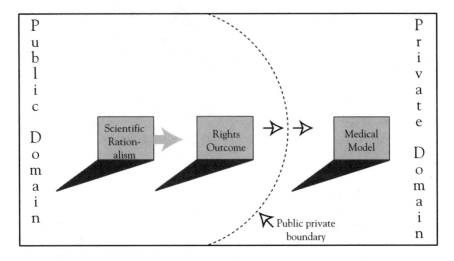

Figure 6.4 Scientific rationalism as a legitimizing mechanism for determining the public/private boundary

Rethinking the social

When disability is recognized as a condition resulting from the social conditions in which biology exists, then the social inequity and the public policy created to respond to it has to take into account state responsibility for social justice and well-being to be recognized as public goods. There are examples of circumstances of disability being recognized as a public responsibility even while the same disabilities are privatized in other circumstances. Disabilities resulting from identifiable conditions such as workplace accidents, are generally interpreted as the responsibility of the state in the sense that disability insurance (workers compensation) is regulated and administered by the state. Further, programmes have been established and paid for by the government to enable return to work. Entitlements to such state programmes are commonly dependent on the cause of the disability rather than either the need or the type of disability. There is an inequity built in to social programmes for people with disabilities based on the cause of the condition. Some particular medical conditions have led to the acknowledgement of state accountability. For example, the state has, in some cases, been held accountable for the disabled children of mothers who used thalidomide. It is possible that this attaches to health as a social good, rather than social justice or social well-being.

The important point is that the same condition might, in one case, bring a duty on the state to put in place redistributive policies to ameliorate the disability and in another leave the state with no duty. It may depend on the time of the conditions' occurrence (at birth versus in the workplace) or its cause (genetic versus non-genetic).

If individual biology, for which the state allegedly has neither culpability nor influence, is the determining factor in disability, then it limits the liability and shifts the boundary towards privatization of responsibility and limiting entitlement. It delimits the public domain and increases the private domain. On the other hand, if disability is a consequence of social conditions and social relations in which biology exists, the social disadvantage attached to disability becomes part of the public domain with corresponding duties and obligations to respond. Ensuring the social well-being of those with disabilities is then an intrinsic part of the state's responsibility to ensure social well-being for all citizens. It is a public good.

Consequently, how a group is differentiated and how the difference is formulated has had an effect on where governments have differentiated between the public and private domains and their consequent social policy. How people are characterized is used as a rationale to shift the boundary between the public and the private domains and the role of the state in ensuring social well-being. Whether the cause of their disadvantage is a result of their own actions or can be characterized as an individual circumstance rather than recognizing the social, political, and economic conditions contributes to the extent the government responds to the disability. Thus social conditions such as inequality, unemployment, social cohesion, health, marginalization and so on can fall into either domain depending on which values predominant.

If the failure of the market, which contributes to inequality, is attributed to individual circumstance, the argument is made to limit the size and role of the state. The legitimization of difference is used to limit the public obligation, through privatizing public misfortune and reduce public costs and expenditures.

On the other hand, if the role of the market in creating social exclusion and reducing social well-being is recognized, then it is less feasible for governments to legitimize not building it into the relationship between the economic and social aspects of development. The market cannot be relied upon to correct the imbalances inherent in these values.

The issue of how disability is treated suggests a number of trends. First, the economic pressures of globalization and deficit reduction result in the limitation of government to a minimal agenda of social equilibrium between the individual and the public interest. Second, social policy is being motivated by deficit reduction that diminishes principles of democratization, equality and self-determination. It is a continuing trend towards a narrowing definition of worthy poor and has two impacts: it minimizes state responsibility and in the process increases the inequality in SES (socio-economic status), social entitlement and citizenship rights. Third, there is a commodification of resources, including people, which limit the provision of social well-being as a public good. Standards of economic efficiency and scientific rationality are used to set the barrier of what the state is prepared to recognize within the context of social justice and well-being as public goods.

Conclusion

The ambiguities involved in efforts to determine what is public and what is private are not insignificant. And because where the boundary falls is a consequence of economic, social and legal pressures, the boundary between the public and private domain is dynamic. Attempts to clarify, by definition, what is a public good have simply highlighted the ambiguity. The politics of welfare and of provision for the disabled population has been about shifting responsibilities from one sector to another. The achievement of social well-being as a public good and the consequent provision of welfare are the products of struggle by various interests and are the result of the balance that emerges from a struggle for recognition, legitimacy, resources and autonomy. However, if social well-being and social justice are public goods, then there is a need to be cautious about assumptions that shifting the responsibility for some functions of welfare and for some disability from the public sector to the private sector will not result in inequalities, reduction of health status, and limitation of social citizenship. Retrenchment and disentitlement can have serious consequences, even where legitimized by economic determinism, utilitarianism and scientific rationalism.

As governments shift the boundaries of what is within the public domain, they legitimate their decisions as having some objective claim. The pressures of globalization have had a significant impact in shifting understanding of what is the content of a public good and ought therefore to be public responsibility.

Disability is an area that is particularly sensitive to the changing position of the boundary between the public and private domain. It is an indicator of how states conceive of social justice as a public good and the economics of social responsibility. There are two forces that underlie the shift. The first is economic determinism (that is a function of such phenomena as market values) and the second is a function of scientific rationalism (that is a function of the belief in the ability of the 'technological' sector to solve both physical and social problems). The pressures to define the public domain within the framework of globalization, deficit reduction and market dominance raise serious issues about social well-being as a public good. Not only have governments shown themselves willing to adopt an international economic agenda but also they have quite creatively legitimized the privatization of individual misfortune. Collective responsibility is sacrificed to an economic agenda that offers up the social good as a dispensable commodity.

Globalization has not succeeded in making markets work for all. The benefits have been unevenly distributed both between and within states and among various groups. Juan Somavia, Director-General of the ILO concluded in a recent speech:

> globalization's failure to deliver a steadily increasing number of productive jobs is the result of inadequacies in international and national policies and implementation. The solution must recognize that improved financial system architecture cannot replace the need for effective domestic policies.
>
> (Somavia 2000)

The notion of public goods, in cohesive societies, has, historically, been articulated in values and policies distinct from, and that may even conflict with, those of the individual interests in the marketplace. There are however compatibilities of social well-being and economic well-being. Managing markets should not come at the expense of the common goods of social justice and social well-being.

Notes

1   A realist view dominated this Cold War period in which the national interest was defined as the acquiring of sufficient power to ensure survival.
2   Government bureaucrats began to acknowledge the role that continuous economic development, human rights, social equity and essential freedoms had in the maintenance of peace and provision of security.
3   In the nineteenth century, alternatives to *laissez-faire* and the status quo of widespread poverty and suffering had led to the promotion of alternate political and economic models.
4   Well-being is a dynamic relationship between, on the one hand, an individual's developing capacities and sense of purpose and, on the other, the changing social, cultural and economic conditions that affect the pursuit and achievement of a person's aims. At an individual level, well-being entails the support by other individuals, communities and society to exercise self-determination, to recognize respect and to accommodate the aims of others. Individuals cannot attain well-being by themselves but do so in the context of the communities to which they belong, communities defined by common heritage, language, culture, gender, geography or interests.
5   The 1834 revision of the Elizabethan Poor Laws. This principle required that the public support for an individual guaranteed a lower standard of living than that of the poorest paid labourer.
6   The cracks in the post-war framework and subsequent pressure for its restructuring gained momentum from the 1960s to the 1980s – first from the civil rights movement, from the women's movement and later from other movements of marginalized people. The obligations found in statutory and regulatory human rights protections contributed to a new understanding of what constituted social well-being as a public good. It built on the post-war framework and expanded the understanding of social well-being. This brought into question some of the underlying assumptions about what was private and what was public, in particular that of the worthy/unworthy poor distinction. The reinvented notion of social well-being and progress that was articulated as a public good incorporated the importance of social justice, human rights and social solidarity. The 1980s saw a retrenchment of this trend.

Bibliography

Barnes, C., Mercer, Geof and Shakespeare, Tom (1999) *Exploring Disability: A Sociological Introduction*, Cambridge: Polity Press.
Beresford, P. and Campbell, J. (1994) 'Disabled People, Service Users, User Involvement and Representation', *Disability and Society*, 9: 315–25.
Bowles, G. and Gintis, H. (1986) *Democracy and Capitalism: Property, Community and the Contradictions of Modern Thought*, New York: Basic Books.
Canada, Law Reform Commission (1979) *Sterilization: Implications for Mentally Retarded and Mentally Ill Persons*, Ottawa: Minister of Supply and Services Canada.

Canadian Association for Independent Living Centres (1984) Ottawa: Canadian Association for Independent Living Centres.

Cohen, S. (1985) *Visions of Social Control: Crime, Punishment and Classification*, Cambridge: Polity Press.

Cohen, S. and Scull, Andrew (ed.) (1983) *Social Control and the State*, Oxford: Martin Robertson.

Drache, D. (2001) – this volume.

Esping-Andersen, G. (1985) *Politics Against Markets: The Social Democratic Road to Power*, Princeton, NJ: Princeton University Press.

European Information Service (1993) 'Social Sciences Get Star Billing at "EC Science Summit"', *European Social Policy*, 35.

Grayson, K. (2001) 'Human Security in the Global Era', in Daniel Drache (ed.) *The Market or the Public Domain? Global governance and the asymmetry of power*, London: Routledge.

Guest, D. (1980) *The Emergence of Social Security in Canada*, Vancouver: University of British Columbia Press.

Holden, Chris (1999) 'Globalization, Social Exclusion and Labour's New Work Ethic', *Critical Social Policy*, 19, 4, November.

ICIDH, Canadian Society for (1991) 'The Handicap Creation Process', *ICIDH International Network*, 4.

Kapstein, E. B. (1999) 'Distributive Justice as an International Public Good: A Historical Perspective', in Inge Kaul, Isabelle Grunberg, and Marc A. Stern (eds), *Global Public Goods: International Cooperation in the 21st Century*, Oxford: Oxford University Press, pp. 88–115.

Katz, M.B. (1986) *In the Shadow of the Poor House: A Social History of Welfare in America*, New York: Basic Books.

Kaul, Inge., Grunberg, Isabelle and Stern, Marc A. (eds)(1999) *Global Public Goods: International Cooperation in the 21st Century*, New York: United Nations Development Program.

Korpi, W. (1983) *The Democratic Class Struggle*, London and Boston, MA: Routledge and Kegan Paul.

Kuttner, R. (1984) *The Economic Illusion: False Choices Between Prosperity and Social Justice*, Boston, MA: Houghton Mifflin.

Laurell, A.C. and Wences, M.I. (1994) 'Do Poverty Programs Alleviate Poverty? The Case of the Mexican Solidarity Program', *International Journal of Health Services*, 24: 381–401

Lukes, S. (1980) 'Socialism and Equality', *Justice Alternative Political Perspectives*, ed. J. Sterba (ed), Belmont, CA: Wadsworth Publishing House.

Mackelprang, R. and Salsgiver, R. (1999) *Disability: A Diversity Model Approach in Human Service Practice*, Toronto: Brooks/Cole Publishing Company.

Marshall, T.H. and Bottomore, T.B. (1992) *Citizenship and Social Class*, London, Concord, MA: Pluto Press.

Mishra, R. (1984) *The Welfare State in Crisis: Social Thought and Social Change*, Brighton, Sussex: Wheatsheaf Books.

—— (1990) *The Welfare State in Capitalist Society: Policies of Retrenchment and Maintenance in Europe, North America and Australia*, New York Hempstead: Harvester: Wheatsheaf.

Moran, M. and Wood, B. (1996) 'The Globalization of Health Care Policy', in Philip Gummet (ed) *Globalization and Public Policy*, Cheltenham Brookfield, VT: E. Elgar.

Myles, J. (1991) 'Post-industrialism and the Service Economy', in Daniel Drache and Meric Gertler (eds) *The New Era of Global Competition: State Policy and Market Power*, Montreal: McGill-Queen's University Press.

Osberg, L. (1990) 'Is it retirement or unemployment? Constrained labour supply and induced retirement among older workers'. Working paper, Dalhousie University: Department of Economics, .

Portella, E. (2000) 'Cultural Cloning of Hybrid Cultures', *Unesco Courier*, 9.

Rao, M. (1999) 'Equity in a Global Public Goods Framework', in Inge Kaul, Isabelle Grunberg and Marc A. Stern (eds),*Global Public Goods: International Cooperation in the 21st Century*, New York: United Nations Development Program, pp. 7, 70.

Rawls, J. (1971) *A Theory of Justice*, Cambridge, MA: Belknap Press of Harvard University Press.

Rioux, M.H. and Bach, Michael (ed.) (1994) *Disability is Not Measles: New Research Paradigms in Disability*, North York: Roeher.

Roeher, I. (1988) *Income Insecurity: The Disability Income in Canada*, Toronto: Roeher.

—— (1992) *Social Well-Being*, Toronto: Roeher.

—— (1993) *Social Well-Being: Paradigm for Reform*, Toronto: Roeher.

Roth, W. (1983) 'Handicap as a Social Construct', *Society*, 20.

Ruggie, M. (1984) *The State And Working Women: A Comparative Study of Britain and Sweden*, Princeton, NJ: Princeton University Press.

Schoenblum, J.A. (1995) 'Tax Fairness or Unfairness? A Consideration of the Philosophical Bases for Unequal Taxation of Individuals', *The American Journal Of Tax Policy*, 12, 221.

Sen, A. (1999a) *Development as Freedom*, Oxford: Oxford University Press.

—— (1999b) 'Global Justice: Beyond International Equity', in Inge Kaul, Isabelle Grunberg and Marc A. Stern (eds) *Global Public Goods: International Cooperation in the 21st Century*, New York: United Nations Development Program, pp. 116–25.

Somavia, J. (2000) *Roundtable on Disability and Social Development*, Geneva: International Labour Organization.

Sutherland, N. (1976) *Children in English-Canadian Society*, Toronto: University of Toronto Press.

Taylor, C. (1992) *Multiculturalism and the Politics of Recognition: An Essay*, Princeton, NJ: Princeton University Press.

Section 3

Rethinking public goods in an era of globalization

Polarized societies, market intrusiveness and social well-being in highly unstable market settings

7 The informational commons at risk

Alasdair Roberts

The public right to know

Conventional wisdom says that we are witnessing the emergence of a global information society, in which new technologies will provide citizens with unprecedented access to information. This is an appealing but flawed vision of the future. Governments are still reluctant to disclose information about core functions. At the same time, neo-liberal reforms have caused a diffusion of power across sectors and borders, confounding efforts to promote governmental openness. Economic liberalization has also made it more difficult to enforce corporate disclosure requirements. Meanwhile, technological change has spurred efforts by businesses and citizens to strengthen their control over corporate and personal information. Efforts to defend the borders of the 'informational commons' – the domain of publicly accessible information – will also be complicated by problems of policy design and political mobilization. Imposing transparency requirements was easier when national and sub-national governments closely held authority. The task is more difficult when power is widely diffused.

Our first impression of the public domain is territorial. We imagine it as a space – an agora, square or commons – that is accessible to everyone as a right of citizenship, and in which important public business, such as the governance of the community, can be undertaken.[1] But the public domain is obviously more than this. It also includes commonly held intangibles without which the commons or agora would be unusable. These include a sense of shared identity and trust, as well as norms and rituals that regulate collective deliberations (Fukuyama 1995; Putnam 2000). There is another, critically important intangible: the pool of information about community affairs that must be publicly accessible for citizens to engage intelligently in the act of self-government. The territorial commons is paralleled by an ephemeral but equally important 'informational commons', comprised of all the information that is accessible as a matter of right to all citizens.[2]

Conventional wisdom says that the informational commons is broader than ever before. Technological improvements have given citizens an unprecedented capacity to retrieve government information, such as local crime statistics, the discharge records of local polluters, and test results for neighbourhood schools. They can download transcripts of that day's legislative hearings, the text of proposed laws, budget proposals from government departments, and policy analyses from non-government groups. Better communication technologies are said to give citizens and non-governmental organizations an unparalleled capacity to

What is the informational commons?

The idea of an informational commons has been developing in American intellectual property law for a half-century. William Carman observed, in 1954, that American courts:

> wholeheartedly recognize that ideas, new or old, when once disclosed must be kept 'free as air' for all to use. [Such ideas] are the universal heritage, the public commons, from which all may freely draw sustenance and which all may use as seems most satisfactory to them.
>
> (Carman 1954: 57)

A related concept in American intellectual property law is the 'public domain'. 'The public domain', says Jessica Litman,

> is an import from the realm of property. In the intellectual property context, the term describes a true commons comprising elements of intellectual property that are ineligible for private ownership. The contents of the public domain may be mined by any member of the public.
>
> (Litman 1990: 975)

David Lange suggests that 'the public domain in the field of intellectual property can be compared to the public grazing lands on the Western plains of a century ago ... [It is] the territory of the creative subconscious'

> (Lange 1981: 176).

Similarly, Yochai Benkler divides our 'information environment' into two parts: a public domain, in which 'all users are equally privileged to use information', and an enclosed domain, in which we 'expect information to be owned, and to be controlled by its owner'

> (Benkler 1999: 354–64).

Donald Gutstein has recently defined the information commons as the 'common store of facts, information, and knowledge that exists in the public domain in reference books, libraries, schools, government documents, and the news media, as well as in society's stories, myths and public talks'

> (Gutstein 1999: 138).

monitor the activities of governments and corporations anywhere in the world, often provoking government action or consumer boycotts to protect human rights (Giddens 2000: 144 and 154). And longstanding restrictions on distribution to information appear to have broken down. On the Internet, citizens seem to violate copyright laws with impunity. Government's capacity to enforce secrecy laws appears to be undermined when sensitive documents are quickly replicated on websites the world over (Norton-Taylor and Pallister 1999; Loeb and Struck 2000).

This technological revolution has happened so quickly that we imagine it to be limitless. 'Information wants to be free', the saying goes;[3] the pace of liberation depends only on our willingness to invest in better hardware and fibre-optic cable. Our ultimate destination, leaders of the G8 nations announced in July 2000, will be a global information society, in which improved access to information will 'strengthen democracy, increase transparency and accountability in governance, promote human rights, enhance cultural diversity, and foster international peace and stability' (G8 2000). 'Anyone with a modem', says Alan Murray, will be able to 'gather nearly as much intelligence as the CIA' (Long 2000).

This is an appealing but flawed vision of the future. It overestimates the power of new technologies and ignores other trends that may actually restrict public access to information. The informational commons is contested terrain. Governments and corporations – and citizens themselves – have all taken steps to preserve secrecy, often spurred to do so by the power of new modes of surveillance, or by the desire to gain economic advantage by asserting their property rights over the central commodity of the new information economy.

The argument in brief

The purpose of this chapter is to canvass current threats to the informational commons. It makes three broad points. First, there is no evidence that new information technologies have altered the willingness of governments to improve transparency for their most sensitive functions, such as policy formulation or law enforcement activities. Second, technological advances have been offset by neo-liberal reforms that have reduced transparency, either by shifting power to private and supranational institutions, or by enabling corporate flight to jurisdictions with weaker disclosure requirements. Finally, the second-order effects of technological change have been neglected. Corporations and individuals are already reacting to the impact of new technologies by strengthening legal and technical controls over information, thereby restricting the realm of publicly accessible information.

As our euphoria about the power of new information technologies fades, we will begin to see that the boundaries of the information commons are contested, and in some places have already receded. This should alarm advocates of strong democracy. The informational commons, as much as a territorial commons, is essential to self-government. But the fight to reclaim the informational commons will also be complicated by problems of policy design and political mobilization. Imposing openness codes was easier when authority was closely held by national and sub-national governments. The task is more difficult when power has diffused away from governments and across borders.

Secrecy at the heart of government

Technological advances have led to dramatic improvements in public access to some kinds of government information. Documents that were once found only in legislative or depository libraries can now be quickly retrieved through the Internet – at least by citizens who can afford the technology and understand the structure of government. But the improvement in openness is also qualified in another and more important way. The Internet has transformed information that was already publicly accessible as a matter of principle, and made it accessible as a matter of fact. However, it has not caused governments to abandon old habits of protecting many key documents under the mantle of official secrecy.

Since 1997, advocates of governmental openness in the United Kingdom have realized how much strength remains in the old doctrine of official secrecy. Britain is one of the few Commonwealth democracies that does not have a freedom of information (FOI) law, which establishes a legal right of access to some government documents. In Opposition, Britain's Labour Party repeatedly promised to adopt a strong FOI law as part of a broader programme of constitutional modernization. A new law, party leader Tony Blair said in March 1996, would 'end the obsessive and unnecessary secrecy which surrounds government activity' (Blair 1996).

After its election in May 1997, the Blair government began a retreat from its earlier commitments. A White Paper released in December 1997 was hailed for its 'surprisingly radical approach' (Frankel 1997); nevertheless, there were significant limits on the proposed new right of access to information. The new FOI law would not affect security and intelligence services, some defence functions, law enforcement functions of police and regulatory agencies, or legal advice to government. The burden of proof imposed on officials who wanted to withhold information would be less onerous if information related to 'decision-making and policy advice processes in government' (United Kingdom 1997).

These restrictions were criticized in a May 1998 parliamentary review (Select Committee on Public Administration 1998), without effect. On the contrary, there was intense lobbying by key government departments for the FOI proposals to be further restricted or entirely abandoned. In July 1998, the minister who had developed the proposals was removed from Cabinet, and responsibility was given to the Home Secretary, who was known to favour a more limited law. A draft bill released in May 1999 would have denied any access to information relating to policy development or information whose disclosure would 'prejudice the effective conduct of public affairs'. The burden of proof on officials for most other exemptions to the right of access was also reduced (Home Office 1999). Despite continued criticism from parliamentarians, many of these restrictions were retained in a second draft bill introduced in the House of Commons in November 1999.[4] The bill languished in Parliament, but was eventually adopted in December 2000.[5]

The deficiencies of the British bill are matched in most of the Commonwealth FOI laws. Several, including the new Irish law, allow ministers to issue directives that prohibit any independent review of their decisions to withhold sensitive information.[6] Among the restrictions in Canada's FOI law are a broad ban on access to records relating to policy-making and management, as well as a limit on judicial review of decisions relating to sensitive state interests.[7] The Chretien government has delayed on ministerial promises to undertake a review of the law,[8] and opposed back-bencher efforts to broaden the ATIA (Bronskill 2000). It has also sought new restrictions on access to information. For example, the proposed Money Laundering Act will completely eliminate a right of access to much information held by a new law enforcement agency, the Financial Transactions and Reports Analysis Centre.[9]

In the United States, the end of the Cold War briefly seemed to provide an opportunity to reverse secrecy rules intended to protect national security. Shortly after his inauguration, President Clinton issued a memorandum to government departments directing them to 'renew their commitment' to the Freedom of Information Act (Clinton 1993). While Attorney General Janet Reno reversed a Reagan-era policy on interpretation of FOIA and urged departments to resolve thousands of backlogged requests (Reno 1993); Clinton also appointed a taskforce to review government policy on classified information. Heads of the Central Intelligence Agency and the Department of Energy (which operates the government's nuclear weapons complex) promised to 'come clean' with the public about their activities during the Cold War (Gruenwald 1993).

These efforts had a limited impact. Because FOIA administration is highly decentralized, Reno's efforts to liberalize interpretation of the law and clean up backlogs had little influence. As new national security concerns arose at the end of the decade, defence and intelligence agencies lobbied for statutory amendments that would weaken FOIA by excluding many records from the law.[10]

Defence and intelligence agencies also succeeded in undermining proposals for reform of classification policies drafted by Clinton's task force (Smith 1994; Weiner 1994). Nevertheless, an executive order signed by Clinton in 1995 did require federal agencies to declassify millions of pages of records from the Cold War era.[11] However, implementation did not proceed smoothly. The Central Intelligence Agency claimed that budget cuts made it impossible to declassify old records quickly (Lardner 1998). Declassification efforts at the Department of Defence were also hampered by cutbacks (Aftergood and Blanton 1999).

Conservatives alleged that the Department of Energy's attempt to promote openness had encouraged espionage, prompting the department to adopt more meticulous procedures for declassification of records (Department of Energy 2000). A recent executive order has extended the 1995 deadlines for declassification of old records.[12]

The Clinton task force's proposed rules for classifying new records were also compromised by attacks from defence and security agencies. While the classification rules contained in the 1995 executive order are more liberal than the Reagan policy which they displaced, critics argue that the rules are more restrictive than the Carter administration's policy, which explicitly required agencies to balance the public's right to know against national security concerns (Quist 1989: chap. 3). The Department of Energy also considered new rules that would limit the range of classified information, but these have been shelved because of worries about spying (Weeks 2000).

Senator Daniel Moynihan's experience in battling for openness provides evidence of the continuing power of the national security community. In 1994, Moynihan lobbied successfully for a special commission that would look for 'a new way of thinking about secrecy' (Moynihan Commission 1997) in the post-Cold War era. The Commission eventually recommended a new Government Secrecy Reform Act that would codify and limit classification practices. The Clinton administration opposed the bill, arguing that it would restrict presidential discretion (Berger 1998), and it died in 1999.[13] Moynihan then introduced a more limited bill to encourage declassification of old records.[14] It has also been weakened in response to administration concerns, and has not yet been adopted (Aftergood 2000). The Cold War has ended, Moynihan recently observed, but the 'vast secrecy system … shows no signs of receding' (Moynihan 1998: 214).

Freedom of information – still not a citizen's fundamental right

The historic tendency of governments to preserve secrecy for the most sensitive governmental interests has been aggravated by a second trend: efforts to restructure or 'reinvent' national and sub-national governments. These restructuring efforts are part of a broader neo-liberal reform programme that is intended to limit the role of government in social and economic life. Restructuring is often presented as an unavoidable response to fiscal stresses. However, it is also motivated by a desire to restore the 'governability' of western democracies (Crozier *et al.* 1975; Rose 1980), by restricting the capacity of citizens to exert influence over policy in key sectors. The erosion of information rights as a consequence of domestic governmental restructuring is neither temporary nor inadvertent: on the contrary, it is a critical part of the effort to make policy processes more manageable.[15]

One of the most prominent components of domestic neo-liberal reform has been the privatization of state-owned enterprises. Privatization did not always erode information rights, since government practice in allowing access to records held by state-owned enterprises was mixed. (Canada, for example, usually excluded its crown corporations from its FOI law.) But in some circum-stances, where state-owned enterprises delivered critical services or monopolized the market, information rights were recognized and consequently eroded through privatization. In Ontario, environmental advocates protested when the provincial utility, Ontario Hydro, was reorganized and largely priva-tized; while Hydro had been subject to provincial FOI law, its successors are not (*Toronto Globe and Mail* 1999). Similar complaints were voiced when Australia's federal government proposed the privatization of Telstra, the national telecom-munications monopoly (Australian Law Reform Commission 1996: para. 16.7), and its state governments privatized electricity, gas, and water utilities. After intense lobbying, the British government backed away from its 1997 proposal to include privatized utilities in its new FOI law. The current bill contains a weaker provision giving the Cabinet the discretion to include private organiza-tions that perform a public function (Parker and Parker 1998; Milne 1999).

The increased popularity of contracting-out has also jeopardized information rights. Cash-strapped governments have outsourced 'non-core' or ancillary activi-ties for many years. More recently, they have broadened the scope of contracting, by enlisting the private sector to finance, build and operate major components of infrastructure. Britain's Private Finance Initiative (PFI) represents the most systematic effort at this sort of outsourcing. By December 1999, the British government had signed more than 250 PFI contracts, initiating £16 billion of private investment in roads, hospitals, schools, prisons, government offices, and computer systems (Arthur Andersen and Enterprise LSE 2000). Canadian governments have also experimented with private financing, particularly in the transportation sector. An industry group says that these 'public–private partner-ships' will soon produce a 'minor revolution' in the structure of Canadian government (Canadian Council for Public–Private Partnerships 1999).

No Canadian FOI law – and few laws in other jurisdictions[16] – preserves a right of access to information when activities are transferred to private sector contractors. Governments could draft contracts to maintain information rights, but they have no strong incentive to do so, and usually do not. Furthermore, citizens may be unable to obtain information that is held by government agen-cies that relates to the negotiation or management of those contracts. Although a citizen's right of access to this information persists; contractors have a coun-tervailing right to insist on the withholding of commercial information provided in confidence to government. Contractors may also have a right to make a judicial appeal of government decisions to release contract information. Critics in many countries have complained that the power of contractors to delay or block the release of information weakens the ability of citizens to hold governments and contractors accountable for contract performance.[17]

The reforming of information access

Government's reliance on contractors is one aspect of the new 'structural pluralism' (Giddens 2000: 55) that now typifies the organization of public services. Another is the proliferation of quasi-independent organizations that are established by government but which refuse to be described as governmental. Many of these organizations have corporatist governance structures, with boards that include representation from major client groups. Many are also excluded from FOI laws. In Canada, these include the new air traffic services corporation, Nav Canada; several new airport authorities; the St Lawrence Seaway Management Corporation; the reorganized Canadian Wheat Board; Canadian Blood Services; the Canadian Foundation for Innovation; the Canadian Millennium Scholarship Foundation; and the Canada Pension Plan Investment Board. The British government has experimented with similar structures for its air navigation services. Several Canadian provinces have delegated regulatory functions to comparable quasi-independent agencies, which are also excluded from FOI law (Roberts 2000: 313).

Restructuring also affected access to government information in more prosaic ways. Fiscal retrenchment implied a reduction in 'non-essential' spending within government; for many policy-makers, this included a reduction in resources dedicated to administration of FOI laws. The natural result was a lengthening in the time required to process FOI requests. Budget cuts also weakened offices responsible for enforcement of FOI laws, encouraging departments to engage in other forms of non-compliance, such as the unjustified withholding of information. In addition, governments increased the fees charged for processing FOI requests, sometimes with dramatic effect. In Ontario, fee increases that were justified as part of an effort to make government 'more affordable and efficient' caused a 35 per cent drop in FOI requests (Roberts 1999).

Governments also began raising fees for access to information that had previously been distributed at low or no cost. In the early 1980s, policy-makers began to realize that the vast 'data stockpile' held within government agencies could be exploited as a source of new revenues (Schiller 1989). In the United States, many federal agencies entered into partnerships with private firms to package and sell government information (Grossklaus 1991; Gellman 1995; Kelley 1998). Recent attempts to introduce legislation that would regulate these partnerships and preserve public access to information were defeated after lobbying from the database industry (Prophet 1999). In Canada, federal agencies have sharply increased the price of information products or entered into licensing agreements that allow the private sector to sell government information (Morton and Zink 1991; Nilsen 1996: 7–8; Hubbertz 1999). 'The concept of government information as a *corporate resource*', says Kirsti Nilsen, 'appears to be overriding the concept of public *rights* to that information' (Nilsen 1994: 205).

Supranational governance

The neo-liberal agenda includes other reforms that have also impaired governmental openness. Efforts to liberalize international trade and capital flows have required the invention or elaboration of supranational institutions to serve as fora for policy-making and dispute resolution, and instruments for crisis management. These institutions often impose substantial constraints on policy-making by national and sub-national governments; indeed, many critics suggest that these supranational institutions constitute an emerging system of global governance. At the same time, these institutions lack many of the structural features that have legitimized lower orders of government, including a comparable level of transparency. Indeed, the secretiveness of supranational institutions is frequently cited, even by proponents of economic integration, as one of the factors contributing to the 'crises of legitimacy' afflicting supranational institutions.

Complaints about 'secretive and autocratic' negotiations (Nader 1993) fuelled protests against the 1993 North American Free Trade Agreement and contributed to the eventual defeat of a Clinton administration proposal to renew 'fast track' negotiating authority in November 1997. The next year, similar complaints led to the abandonment of negotiations over a new treaty on the treatment of foreign direct investment. Formal discussions on the proposed Multilateral Agreement on Investment (MAI) began within the Organization for Economic Cooperation and Development (OECD) in May 1995, but attracted little publicity until non-governmental organizations obtained a confidential negotiating text in January 1997. Protests against the treaty and the 'veil of secrecy' (AAP Newsfeed 1998) that had cloaked negotiations erupted world-wide. The OECD attempted to rebut the complaints, meeting directly with non-governmental organizations and delaying MAI talks to allow 'further consultation between the negotiating parties and interested parts of their societies' (*Financial Post* 1998). But these belated attempts at transparency proved ineffective, and negotiations were formally abandoned in October 1998.

Protestors at the World Trade Organization's Seattle conference in November 1999 launched similar complaints about secrecy. The WTO, which is responsible for enforcement of trade rules adopted after the Uruguay Round negotiations, adopted a code on access to information shortly after its establishment in 1995, but it had many limitations. Chief among these was the exclusion of documents produced within the WTO's dispute settlement procedures, including submissions by nations involved in a dispute and preliminary decisions by WTO panels. In addition, non-governmental organizations were barred from observing or reading transcripts of hearings on trade disputes (Debevoise 1998). The rules, Ralph Nader complained in 1996, meant that important trade policy decisions were made by 'a group of unelected bureaucrats sitting behind closed doors in Geneva' (Nader and Wallach 1996: 94).

By fall 1999, governments of many advanced economies had recognized that these complaints were undermining the credibility of the trade regime among their citizens. The United States called improved openness 'a priority issue', conceding that 'transparency in the operation of the WTO itself has become a critical factor in ensuring the long-term credibility of the multilateral system' (United States Trade Representative 1998: 37; US Mission 1999). But the Seattle meeting did not produce agreement on reforms to improve transparency.

Many nations – including some developing economies – oppose the American proposals, arguing that they would subject the WTO to undesirable 'external non-legal pressures' and destabilize its dispute settlement procedures (WTO General Council 1998; Raghavan 2000).

New international barriers

The International Monetary Fund (IMF) also suffers legitimacy problems that are rooted in perceptions of excessive secrecy. There is an irony in such criticisms, because the IMF is itself a mechanism for promoting access to information: it facilitates international economic policy coordination through its surveillance of domestic policy decisions by member countries (Pauly 1997).[18] But the IMF also plays a growing role in providing conditional aid to nations with balance of payments difficulties and in managing global financial crises. Observers on both ends of the political spectrum attacked the Fund for its response to the East Asian financial crisis that began in summer 1997, and related crises in Russia and Brazil. Joseph Stiglitz, chief economist of the World Bank during the crisis, later said that 'excessive secrecy' had allowed the Fund to pursue indefensible policies (Stiglitz 2000: 60). In 1998, Conservatives in the US Congress, frustrated by their inability to obtain internal reports that were said to be critical of the IMF's handling of the crisis, refused to provide $18 billion in emergency aid for the Fund (Saxton 1998). The impasse was resolved in October 1998, when the IMF agreed to release some key documents on lending activities and policy changes.[19]

However, there are clear limits to the IMF's willingness to improve transparency. Some members of Congress unsuccessfully advocated broader disclosure requirements, with stronger mechanisms for ensuring compliance.[20] Since 1998, legislators have also attempted without success to tie US support to disclosure of IMF operating budgets and improved financial statements.[21] The IMF continues to regard the disclosure of staff reports relating to the Fund's surveillance function as an experiment, undertaken only with the consent of countries whose policies are being reviewed (International Monetary Fund 2000). The IMF's managing directors have warned that it is accountable only to the governments of its member countries, and that increased openness will require a consensus among those governments (Camdessus 1998; Köhler 2000: 260).[22]

Another effort at economic integration – the European Union – has also been hobbled by complaints about the secretiveness of its main institutions. Such complaints contributed to the rejection of the Maastricht Treaty by Danish voters in June 1992, and more recently to the attempt by the European Parliament to censure the European Commission in January 1999, and the eventual resignation of the Commission in March 1999 (*Guardian* 1999). Attempts to improve transparency have had limited impact. An administrative FOI code adopted in December 1993[23] is widely thought to be ineffective; disagreements among the Union's member nations about appropriate levels of transparency have led to delays and inconsistent decisions. A commitment to stronger FOI rules was included in the 1997 Treaty of Amsterdam. However, a draft of the proposed new rules prepared by the Commission and released in January 2000 has been heavily criticized. The EU Ombudsman says the proposed rules contain 'a list of exemptions without precedent in the modern world' (Söderman 2000).

Corporate control of information

The achievement of an open society does not depend only on improved access to government information. It also depends on appropriate rules to regulate access to information that is controlled by the private sector. Some observers have suggested that corporate control of information is weakening, primarily because of the impact of new technologies. They note that intellectual property law, which gives corporations the capacity to restrict dissemination of information, has been undermined. At the same time, governments have begun using the Internet to disseminate information collected from the private sector through regulatory processes.

There are two major difficulties with this argument. The first is its inattention to the second-order effects of technological change – that is, the ways in which corporations react to technological change by finding new ways of controlling the flow of information. The second is its inattention to the impact of neo-liberal reforms on the capacity of governments to impose disclosure requirements on the private sector.

In summer 2000, the high-profile Napster lawsuit seemed to provide further evidence of the 'crisis in intellectual property' (Barlow 1994) that had been caused by advances in information technology. The Recording Industry Association of America claimed that Napster software encouraged copyright violation by allowing individuals to retrieve music from other personal computers. Although courts supported the RIAA's attempt to block Napster, many other 'peer-to-peer computing' programs designed to evade legal challenges quickly emerged to replace it (Berman 2000).

The severity of this 'crisis' can be overstated.[24] Industries that rely heavily on intellectual property have attained significant improvements in legal protection over the last decade. One of the most notable gains has been through the expansion of international trade agreements to include provisions for strengthening intellectual property rights, particularly in the developing world, where patent and copyright laws have been less stringent or weakly enforced. The 1994 Agreement on Trade-Related Aspects of Intellectual Property Rights (TRIPS) compels nations to adopt intellectual property standards comparable to those in the United States and some other developed nations. Furthermore, it allows governments to use the World Trade Organization's dispute settlement procedures to impose trade sanctions on nations that fail to comply (Long 2000).[25]

Even in the United States, legal protection has been improved in response to the perceived threat from new technologies. The 1998 Digital Millennium

Copyright Act (DCMA) makes it an offence for citizens to break software or hardware 'locks' that restrict access to information distributed in digital form, even if the consumer's use of that information would normally be considered a fair use under copyright law (Benkler 1999: 419–20). The Motion Picture Association of America recently relied on the DCMA to block dissemination of software that breaks the encryption system on digital versatile disks (DVDs). The court conceded that its judgment prevented some fair uses of material on DVDs (US District Court for the Southern District of New York 2000: 49). Another judgment allowed the on-line auctioneer EBay to invoke the common law of trespass to restrict efforts to collect information on its website (US District Court for the Northern District of California 2000). The US Congress is also considering legislation that would prohibit extraction of non-copyrighted information from databases if it harms the commercial value of a database.[26]

These legal protections will soon be complemented by technical improvements that give producers of intellectual property more control over the use of their products. These new digital-rights-management (DRM) systems include software and hardware designed to enhance the value of digital data by impairing the capacity of consumers to reproduce or manipulate information (*The Economist* 1999; Solomon 2000). Commentators have suggested that DRM systems will eventually displace copyright law as the principal method of regulating the use of information (Lessig 2000: 126–7). The influence of DRM systems will be felt more heavily as print is supplanted by new technologies as the dominant form of information distribution.

Broadening intellectual property rights?

Advocates of the information society suggest a second reason why corporate control of information might be weakening: the improved capacity of governments to disseminate information collected through regulatory processes over the Internet. For example, residents of the United States can now easily retrieve information about the use of toxic chemicals by industries in their neighbourhood; the information is collected and distributed through an on-line database – the Toxics Release Inventory – maintained by the Environmental Protection Agency.[27] In fact, many students of regulation have begun to argue that disclosure of this sort of information can be a simple but effective tool for regulating corporate conduct (Tietenberg 1998). The publication of information about business practices enables communities to mobilize for political action and has a sharp impact on investors' assessment of the value of firms (Khanna et al. 1998).

For these reasons, improved access to information can also spawn a powerful backlash from affected industries. The distribution of TRI data over the Internet caused 'spasms' in the chemical industry, which engaged in litigation and lobbying to thwart proposals to broaden the TRI database (Fairley 1997b; Fairley and Mullin 1998).[28] The conflict over TRI is only one of several battles waged by US industry to restrict the flow of environmental information. Businesses have also resisted implementation of an EPA pilot project to create on-line risk profiles of major industrial facilities (Fairley 1997a);[29] lobbied law enforcement and intelligence agencies to block the EPA's proposal to publish their crisis management plans, arguing that the plans would be misused by terrorists (Matthews 2000); and sought new restrictions on access to internal audits of compliance with environmental laws.[30]

The capacity of businesses to resist disclosure requirements has been enhanced as a result of economic liberalization. If the government of one jurisdiction is reluctant to shield industries from requirements to release information, it is easier than ever before for industries to relocate to jurisdictions whose governments will be less demanding.

The phenomenon of inter-jurisdictional flight is not new. Within the United States, Delaware is a home for many businesses partly because of its weak rules on disclosure of information on corporate governance (Cary 1974). Recently, the Russian Mafia was alleged to have exploited Delaware's corporation law to cloak an elaborate money-laundering scheme (*Village Voice* 1999). An even more dramatic illustration of the potential danger of inter-jurisdictional flight is provided by the burgeoning speculative prison industry. Private operators build speculative prisons to house prisoners from other states whose own prisons are overcrowded. Because there is no contractual relationship between prison operators and governments of the states in which they operate, there is no guarantee that governments or citizens will have access to information relevant to public safety, such as the number or classification of inmates, staffing policies, or emergency response plans. Attempts by state legislatures to impose disclosure requirements are often met with threats to relocate facilities – threats that are compelling to the economically disadvantaged jurisdictions in which such prisons are typically located (Collins 1999).[31]

Economic liberalization has already encouraged business flight across national borders, to countries whose incorporation and banking laws contain weaker disclosure requirements. In 1998, the OECD argued that transnational flight of 'geographically mobile activities, such as financial or other service activities' posed an urgent challenge for governments of the developed nations, because of increased risk of tax evasion or money laundering (OECD 1998: 9, 24). It recently issued a blacklist intended to encourage reform by nations that were judged to engage in 'harmful tax practices', including inadequate levels of corporate disclosure (OECD 2000). In addition, the G7 nations operate a task force on money laundering that pressures 'non-cooperative countries' for reform (Financial Action Task Force 2000). The OECD and G7 nations have also attempted to pressure nations whose lax disclosure requirements are said to aggravate global financial instability.[32]

Disclosure requirements for other sectors might also be eroded as a consequence of liberalization. Environmental groups have protested that trade liberalization will encourage industry flight to nations with weaker rules on environmental protection, initiating a global 'race to the bottom' on environmental standards.[33] Similarly, labour unions complain that liberalization has undermined their ability to monitor working conditions in factories that produce apparel and other consumer goods for the advanced economies; they have called for new programmes to compel disclosure of factory locations and audits of working conditions (Bernstein 1999).[34] Persuading western governments to take coordinated action that will improve transparency in these areas may be difficult. There is no immediate and concrete threat to their interests, comparable to the threat posed by tax evasion or economic instability that outweighs their reluctance to intrude on the sovereignty of other nations.

Hyper-privacy?

Individual citizens can also encroach on the boundaries of the informational commons. Much of the information that communities use in the process of self-governance is *personal* information – that is, information about another identifiable individual[35] – or is constituted of knowledge derived through the manipulation of aggregated personal information by researchers or administrators. However, the right of access to personal information is now being strictly limited, as citizens assert a countervailing right to privacy.

The movement to strengthen legal protection for personal information is, in part, another second-order effect of technological change. It has been given momentum by fears about the ability of businesses to use new technologies, including web-based commerce, to collect and manipulate consumer information,[36] and by fears about the improved surveillance capacity of law enforcement and intelligence agencies.

However, the movement is not purely a reaction to technological change. It is also part of a larger, decades-long effort to obtain legal recognition for an array of basic rights, and a concomitant tendency to use 'rights discourse' to frame policy discussions (Glendon 1991). A right to privacy is included within the United Nations Declaration of Human Rights, the International Covenant on Civil and Political Rights and several other international and regional treaties. Many national constitutions also recognize the right to privacy. The privacy movement is also bolstered by the steep decline in popular trust of major institutions (Etzioni 1999: 75–102).

Fears about the loss of privacy are often justified. However, the doctrine of personal privacy can also be employed in unexpected ways, often with significant social costs.

One of these unintended effects may be a restriction in the public's capacity to oversee the conduct of government agencies. Traditional arguments about the need to protect sensitive governmental interests can now be bolstered by new arguments about the need to protect the privacy of officials within public agencies. In Canada, the mayor of a Quebec City suburb recently declined to release details of her expenses, arguing that this would violate her personal privacy; Quebec's information commissioners supported the mayor's decision (Cobb 1999). Earlier, the Canadian Department of Finance cited privacy concerns as the reason for its refusal to release sign-in logs for its employees; the information was only released after a slim majority of the Supreme Court of Canada rejected the department's arguments (Supreme Court of Canada 1997). The Nova Scotia Court of Appeal recently upheld a government decision to deny a request by a patient of a drug treatment facility for records of the investigation into her allegations of sexual assault, arguing that it would invade the privacy of the employee who was the subject of the allegations (Cahill 1999).

The tension between accountability and privacy is felt in other countries as well. In Europe, human rights organizations have complained that new privacy laws may compromise their ability to report on allegations of human rights violations by police and security forces (HURIDOCS 1993). In March 2000, the Spanish Association Against Torture was investigated for privacy abuses after it published names of prison officials who were alleged to have committed acts of torture (Nodo 50 2000). In the United States, senior federal judges recently resisted public disclosure of their conflict-of-interest statements, claiming that Internet publication of the statements would violate their privacy (Pringle 2000).

Privacy claims may infringe on public accountability in other ways. Under proposed amendments to French criminal law, the media would be prohibited from showing pictures of a person wearing handcuffs before conviction, as well as crime scene photos that would 'harm the dignity of the victim' (Guerrin 2000). The French proposals exemplify a growing ambivalence about the openness with which judicial proceedings have typically been conducted. Some US courts are considering new restrictions on access to court case files, noting that personal information that had once been 'practically obscure' might now be easily retrieved over the Internet (AOUSC 1999). In Canada, the federal government promised to reconsider its policy of publishing employment insurance appeal decisions on the Internet after legislators complained about the violation of privacy.[37]

Personal information disclosure

The unwillingness of citizens to surrender personal information has also been evidenced in popular protests against national censuses. The most dramatic protests occurred in West Germany in 1987, when census-taking was marred by mass protests and rioting. Before the 2000 US census, libertarians appealed to citizens to 'strike a blow for privacy' by refusing to answer census questions (Sylvester 2000). Senior Republicans suggested that citizens would be justified in ignoring census questions, and the US Senate called on the Census Bureau to ensure that citizens would not be 'prosecuted, fined or in anyway harassed for failure to respond'.[38] Recent Canadian censuses have provoked protests as well (Privacy Commissioner 2000: 49–56). The federal government is planning a public relations effort to 'proactively deal' with privacy concerns before the 2001 census, including a reminder about penalties for non-compliance (Statistics Canada 2000).[39]

In early 2000, worries about privacy triggered an extraordinary public protest against the Longitudinal Labour Force File (LLFF), a database built by policy analysts within the federal Department of Human Resources Development for research on departmental programmes. The database combined information from several other sources, including federal tax returns, unemployment insurance files, and federal pension files. The database conformed to requirements of the federal Privacy Act, which regulates the use of personal information by government, and there was no evidence of misuse by officials. Nevertheless, Canada's Privacy Commissioner protested that the LLFF was 'a citizen profile' that could easily be abused by government (Privacy Commissioner 2000: 64–70). Prodded by the media, more than forty thousand citizens submitted requests for personal information contained in the LLFF. Within weeks, the database had been dismantled.

The potential conflict between demands for privacy and the public interest in sound management of government programmes is also evident in debates over the use of personal health information. In Canada, healthcare consumes about 10 per cent of national income. Governments and researchers argue that their capacity to assess the effectiveness of health programmes, and new treatments and technologies, may be undermined if tight constraints are put on the use of personal health information. Rules that require explicit consent to these secondary uses of information might prove administratively cumbersome. Individuals might also deny consent for secondary uses of their health information, undermining the reliability of databases and results that are drawn from them (Lowrance 1997).

The next informational frontier

The controversy over Canada's new Personal Information Protection and Electronic Documents Act[40] was largely grounded in disagreements about the limits that should be put on use of personal health information. The bill proposed by the federal government required many health care organizations to obey strict rules on the use of personal information. Provincial governments, which operate Canada's health care systems, argued that the rules should not apply to organizations who collect and use information for 'the purposes of health research or management of the health system' (Lindberg 1999).[41] Parliament eventually gave health organizations a one-year reprieve, with the expectation that provincial governments would use the time to develop their own policies for the handling of personal health information. Several provinces have now drafted health information laws, provoking the same debate about the balance between private and public interests.[42]

The controversy transcends national borders. Critics say that a recent Australian privacy bill is also 'too generous in relation to management and research uses without consent' (Australian Privacy Charter Council 2000). The US government has proposed new privacy standards for health care providers that would allow disclosure of personal health information without explicit consent for 'health care operations' and for some 'national priority purposes' such as research or public health. The proposed rules have been heavily criticized by privacy advocates who argue that a citizen's 'right to choose' should trump 'governmental or national purposes' (Sobel 2000).

Amitai Etzioni worries that a desire to achieve 'hyper-privacy' may also compromise the ability of government agencies to investigate crimes and protect national security (Etzioni 1999: 75–102). In the United States, privacy advocates have successfully resisted efforts by federal agencies to create 'backdoors' in new technologies that would allow surveillance (Sykes 1999: 167–82) and limit availability of strong encryption technologies, such as the software program Pretty Good Privacy (Garfinkel 1995: 109–12). An attempt by the Federal Bureau of Investigation to adopt new technology for monitoring e-mail communications has also been delayed because of privacy concerns (Schwartz 2000).[43] The British government was harshly criticized for adopting a new law that would authorize similar initiatives to improve surveillance by law enforcement agencies.[44]

For libertarians, the challenge to governmental capabilities that is posed by hyper-privacy is not problematic. On the contrary, libertarians recognize that the expansion of government responsibilities in the post-war period depended in large part on improved capacity to collect and manipulate information from citizens. Restricting that capacity becomes one method of restricting government's role (Southestern Legal Foundation 2000).[45] But most citizens in the advanced democracies do not take so consistent a position: distrust of government is matched by a desire for continued governmental activism, and impatience with badly managed public spending.[46] For these citizens, the insistence on very strong privacy protections may be less defensible.

Protecting the informational commons

In the last twenty years we have witnessed a dramatic improvement in information and communication technologies. On its own, this technological revolution might seem likely to lead us to an era of unprecedented broadening of the informational commons, and the emergence of a true 'global information society'. But this would be a misguided view, for two reasons.

First, we have not yet realized the second-order effects of technological change. The fact that new technologies allow easier access to information will lead to a reappraisal of what sort of information ought to be contained within the informational commons. The struggle to adopt stronger protection for personal information, partly driven by a fear of what new technologies can do, is one such second-order effect. So, too, is the attempt by businesses to eke profits out of new technologies by strengthening their legal and technical control over information, these second-order effects will undo some of the improvements in access initially provided by new technologies.

In addition, there are other powerful social changes that must be accounted for, Fiscal stresses, and the rising popularity of neo-liberal politics, have led to profound changes in the structure of our governments. A world economy, distinguished by freer trade and improved capital mobility and regulated by a new superstructure of financial and trade institutions, has emerged. Citizens have become more adept in demanding protection for basic human rights, including the right to privacy. These other social changes may also shrink the boundaries of the informational commons, offsetting the gains realized by technological change.

As a consequence, the struggle to broaden the information commons is far from over. Indeed, there is good reason to think it may become even more difficult, again for two reasons.

The task of designing policies to promote openness is likely to become more complex. In the big-government, pre-globalization era, designing policies to improve access to information was relatively straightforward. Many critical functions were performed by a homogeneous group of organizations directly owned and controlled by government. The result was that one regulatory tool – the comprehensive FOI law – could be highly effective in promoting openness. This no longer holds true. Social power has leaked away from governments. It has diffused among an array of private, quasi-private, and governmental bodies, some of which are wholly contained within single jurisdictions, and some of which span jurisdictions. Heterogeneity is the order of the day, and old FOI laws no longer seem to cover the most important loci of social power. New statutes to promote access to information held by the whole agglomeration of private and public institutions will have to be crafted.[47] Non-legislative methods of promoting transparency among supranational institutions must be developed, as well as methods of counteracting the corrosive effect of inter-jurisdictional corporate flight.[48]

Accompanying these challenges in policy design are new difficulties in building coalitions that are powerful enough to push for adoption of policies that promote openness. It was once easy to build an alliance of citizens, businesses and non-governmental organizations, all of whom shared a common interest in foisting strong openness rules on big government. But it is harder to build powerful alliances when power has diffused, and members of the old coalition – citizens, businesses, or non-governmental organizations – are transformed into the objects of regulatory action. Coalition building is also complicated when power is transferred to supranational institutions, and effective campaigns for openness require cross-border coordination.

In short, the informational commons is still contested terrain, and there is no assurance that its advocates will muster forces adequate to preserve its borders. Nevertheless, the struggle for an informational commons remains crucially important. Without the right of access to information, more basic human rights cannot be fulfilled. The right to participate in the governing of one's country, and live in a society built on informed consent,[49] presumes the availability of information about the operation of powerful public and private institutions. The rights to due process and protection against arbitrary interference[50] cannot be adequately defended without a right to know about the motives of powerful institutions and their intrusive capacities. The right to freedom of opinion, and the concomitant recognition that individuals are endowed with reason,[51] implies the availability of the information needed to exercise one's reason and form sound opinions. A failure to preserve the informational commons would threaten all of these rights, producing a technologically sophisticated but nonetheless poorer society.

Notes

1 For example, Kunstler defines the public realm as 'pieces of terrain left between private holdings' (Kuntsler 1996). In this volume, Daniel Drache observes that the public domain is often thought to be 'synonymous with the public park, the skating rink, the local library, music halls, art galleries, bus and subway routes, and the local post office'.
2 The metaphor is not original: Benkler 1999.
3 The phrase was first used by Stewart Brand. A co-founder of the Well, one of the first on-line discussion fora.
4 Freedom of Information Bill, Bill 5 of Session 1999–2000.
5 British governments have also been vigorous in their use of the Official Secrets Act to discourage the publication of information by former officials. Stephen Dorril observes that 'Labour politicians ... have been easily seduced by the magic of secrecy and privileged access to special sources' (Dorril 2000: 758–800).
6 The Australian and New Zealand laws also include provisions for ministerial certificates.
7 Access to Information Act, R.S.C. c. A-1, ss. 21, 50 and 69.
8 Justice Minister Allan Rock promised a review in 1994 (Calamai 1994). His successor Anne McLellan made a similar commitment in March 2000 (Durkan 2000). In August 2000, McLellan announced that an internal committee had been set up to review the law (McLellan 2000), but this was regarded sceptically by many observers.
9 Proceeds of Crime (Money Laundering) Act, Bill C-22, 36th Parl., s. 55.
10 The current defence authorization bill would exclude operational files of the Defense Intelligence Agency, as well as unclassified information provided by foreign governments: S. 2549, 106th Cong., ss. 1044–5. The proposed Cyber Security Information Act of 2000, HR 4246, 106th Cong., would exclude information collected from the private sector relating to potential 'cyber attacks' on critical infrastructure.
11 E.O. 12958, 17 April 1995.
12 E.O. 13142, 19 November 1999.
13 The Government Secrecy Reform Act was introduced as S. 712, 105th Cong. It was re-introduced as S. 22, 106th Cong.
14 Public Interest Declassification Act, S. 1801, 106th Cong. Introduced in October 1999.
15 In addition to FOI laws, governments adopted several other instruments to promote public accountability in the post-war period, including administrative procedures laws, ombudsmen and special commissioners, public consultative mechanisms, and interest group funding. Many of these instruments have also been limited as a consequence of governmental restructuring.
16 The Irish FOI law is one of the exceptions. Some US State laws also maintain a right of access.
17 Canadian experience is briefly described in Roberts (2000). For a sense of the Australian debate, see Administrative Review Council (1997). For the American debate, see Fitzgerald (1995); Bunker and Davis (1998). For a view of the British debate, see Campaign for Freedom of Information (1994).

18 The same might be said of the World Trade Organization, whose Trade Policy Review Mechanism serves a comparable surveillance function (Hoekman and Mavroidis 1999).

19 The conditions were stipulated in the Omnibus Appropriations Act, PL105–277, passed by Congress on 21 October 1998. Executive Directors representing the major donor countries agreed to implement similar reforms in a memorandum to the IMF Managing Director on 30 October 1998.

20 See IMF Transparency and Efficiency Act, HR 3331, 105th Cong. and Saxton (1998).

21 Debt Relief and IMF Reform Act of 1999, HR 2939, 105th Cong. (September 1999); IMF Reform Act of 2000, H.R. 3750, 105th Cong. (February 2000). See also HR 3425, 105th Cong., section 504, which was adopted by reference in the FY Omnibus Appropriations Act, PL 106–113.

22 These comments give a hint of the broader question underlying the debate over transparency of the WTO and the IMF: can these organizations be 'democratized', through the recognition of certain rights given directly to citizens, and exercised through non-governmental organizations; or must they remain as 'bureaucratic bargaining systems', in which procedural rights are given only to participating governments? (Dahl 1999).

23 Council Decision 93/731/EC.

24 Practical difficulties may also undermine Napster (Adar and Huberman 2000; Greenman 2000).

25 For a discussion of the impact of TRIPS in Latin America, see Correa 2000.

26 Collections of Information Antipiracy Act, H.R. 354, 106th Cong. see also Benkler 1999: 440–6.

27 The Toxics Release Inventory (TRI) was established by the Emergency Planning and Community Right-to-Know Act of 1986, 42 USC 11023. For an illustration of how environmental activists have used the database, see http://www.scorecard.org.

28 The most recent legislative proposal is Rep. Waxman's Children's Environmental Protection and Right to Know Act, H.R. 1657, 106th Cong.

29 The plan is known as the Sector Facility Indexing Project. A modified database went on-line in May 1998.

30 See the Environmental Protection Partnership Act, S. 1661, 106th Cong. Many states have adopted comparable 'audit privilege' laws (Koven 1998; Arlen and Kraakman 2000).

31 State legislators complained that they were 'stonewalled' by the Corrections Corporation of America after a mass escape from its Youngstown, Ohio facility in 1998 (Morse 1998).

32 The OECD has established a Task Force on Corporate Governance (OECD 1999: 3), while the G7's Financial Stability Forum has established a Working Group on Offshore Centres (Financial Stability Forum 2000: 1).

33 However, there is no clear evidence that such flight has occurred, see Jaffe and Peterson (1995); Neumayer (2000).

34 Labour unions have been supported by a coalition of student groups and other non-governmental organizations (Klein 2000: 343 and 409; Lee and Bernstein 2000). This coalition may provide a model of how effective movements for transparency can be established in a world in which power has diffused across national borders.

35 For a review of the definitions used in Canadian privacy laws, see McNairn and Woodbury (1998): 7(2)(a).

36 See Garfinkel (2000). The depth of public concern was illustrated in Fall 1999, when the American firm DoubleClick announced that it intended to combine its own databases, containing data on Internet surfing habits, with recently purchased databases containing the purchasing histories of 88 million US households. DoubleClick eventually retreated from the plan (Tynan 2000: 106).

37 See Hansard, 31 May 2000.

38 H.Con.Res. 290, 106th Cong., section 344.

39 A related question is whether historians and other researchers should have access to returns from earlier censuses. Statistics Canada has resisted researchers' requests for access to returns from the 1906 and 1911 censuses, arguing that disclosure would breach promises of confidentiality made by the government at that time. The Privacy Commissioner has endorsed this position (Privacy Commissioner 2000: 49–56). A preferred approach, privacy advocates claim, is the eventual destruction of census records.

40 Personal Information Protection and Electronic Documents Act, S.C. 2000, c. 5. The Act received royal assent in April 2000.

41 The Canadian Healthcare Association, representing hospitals and other healthcare agencies took a similar position.

42 Alberta's Health Information Act allows the use of personal information without consent for internal management and policy development, and authorizes disclosure without consent to the provincial government for 'health system purposes'. Critics complain that law 'destroys the right to information privacy' by giving citizens' records to 'people they do not know and for purposes for which they have never given consent' (Alberta Liberal Caucus 1999). Ontario's draft Personal Health Information Protection Act has also been derided as 'an access bill, not a privacy bill' (Public Interest Advocacy Centre 2000).

43 The technology, named Carnivore, is being reviewed by Congress. Another FBI programme named Digital Storm – which would employ 'data mining' techniques to improve monitoring of telephone and cellular calls – has also proved controversial.

44 The Regulation of Investigatory Powers Act (UK) 2000 c. 23, became law in July 2000. Another object of criticism has been the Council of Europe's proposed International Convention on Crime in Cyberspace, which would commit governments to developing methods of accessing computer systems for criminal investigations (Blumner 2000).

45 For a more general statement of the libertarian position, see Murray (1997).

46 A recent US survey found that nearly half of its respondents regarded their national government as a threat to their personal freedom; at the same time, a majority advocated an expansion of federal responsibilities in many areas (NPR 2000).

47 South Africa's new Promotion of Access to Information Act, which recognizes a right of access to information in both private and public sectors, may serve as a model in this regard.

48 Such as non-governmental projects to monitor behaviour of multi-national corporations: Sabel *et al.* (2000).

49 Article 21 of the United Nations Universal Declaration of Human Rights (1948).

50 Articles 7, 10, 12 of the United Nations Universal Declaration of Human Rights (1948).

51 Articles 1 and 19 the United Nations Universal Declaration of Human Rights (1948).

Bibliography

AAP Newsfeed (1998) 'Fischer Defends Negotiations after Mason Criticism', *AAP Information Services Pty. Ltd*, Canberra, 3 March.

Adar, Eytan and Huberman, Bernardo (2000) *Free Riding on Gnutella*, Palo Alto, CA: Xerox Palo Alto Research Center, August.

Administrative Review Council (1997) 'The Contracting Out of Government Services: Access to Information', Australian Government Printing Service, February, Issues Paper.

Aftergood, Steven (2000) 'E-mail: Moynihan Bill on Declassification', Listserver: foi-l

Aftergood, Steven and Blanton, Tom (1999) 'The Securocrats' Revenge', *The Nation*, 9–16 August: 20.

Alberta Liberal Caucus (1999) *News Release: Albertans' Right to Privacy Degraded by Klein*, Edmonton: Alberta Liberal Caucus, 10 December.

AOUSC (1999) *Privacy and Access to Electronic Case Files in the Federal Courts*, Washington, DC: Administrative Offices of the United States Courts, Office of Judges Programs, 15 December.

Arlen, Jennifer and Kraakman, Reiner (2000) 'When Companies Come Clean: Mitigation is Better than Environmental Audit Privileges', *Business Law Today*, 9, 3 (January–February): web edition.

Arthur Andersen and Enterprise LSE (2000) *Value for Money Drivers in the Private Finance Initiative*, London: Private Finance Initiative Treasury Taskforce, 26 January.

Australian Law Reform Commission (1996) *Open Government: A Review of the Federal Freedom of Information Act 1982*, Canberra: Australian Law Reform Commission, report no. 77.

Australian Privacy Charter Council (2000) *Submission on Privacy Amendment (Private Sector) Bill 2000 to the House of Representatives Committee on Legal and Constitutional Affairs*, Canberra: Australian Privacy Charter Council, May.

Barlow, John Perry (1994) 'The Economy of Ideas', *Wired*, 2, 3 (March): web edition.

Benkler, Yochai (1999) 'Free as the Air to Common Use: First Amendment Constraints on Enclosure of the Public Domain, *New York University Law Review*, 74, 2 (May): 354 *et seq*.

Berger, Samuel (1998) *Letter to Rep. Lee Hamilton on S. 712, the Government Secrecy Reform Act*, Washington, DC: National Security Council, 17 September.

Berman, Dennis (2000) 'With Technology Like This, Who Needs Napster?', *Business Week*, 3694, 14 August: 121.

Bernstein, Aaron (1999) 'Sweatshop Reform', *Business Week*, 3627, 3 May: 186.

Blair, Tony (1996) 'Speech at the Campaign for Freedom of Information Annual Awards Ceremony', London: Campaign for Freedom of Information, 25 March.

Blumner, Robyn (2000) 'Cyberfear Leading to International Invasion of Privacy', *Milwaukee Journal Sentinel*, Milwaukee, WI, 6 June: 17A.

Bronskill, Jim (2000) 'Senior Liberals Shoot Down Broader Access Act', *Ottawa Citizen*, Ottawa, 7 June: A3.

Bunker, Matthew and Davis, Charles (1998) 'Privatized Government Functions and Freedom of Information', *Journalism and Mass Communication Quarterly*, 75, 3: 464–77.

Cahill, Barry (1999) 'Are Freedom of Information and Protection of Privacy Mutually Exclusive? A Comment on *Dickie*', *Government Information in Canada*, 19, October: web edition.

Calamai, Peter (1994) 'Not Necessarily Between a Rock and a Hard Place', *Media*, 1, 2 (July): 28.

Camdessus, Michel (1998) 'Remarks to the World Affairs Council', Philadelphia, PA: International Monetary Fund, 6 November.

Campaign for Freedom of Information (1994) *Proceedings of a Seminar on Commercial Confidentiality*, London: Campaign for Freedom of Information, 18 October.

Carman, William (1954) 'The Function of the Judge and the Jury in the 'Literary Property' Law Suit', *California Law Review*, 42, 1: 52–76.

Canadian Council for Public–Private Partnerships (1999) 'About the Canadian Council for Public–Private Partnerships', web: http://www.inforamp.net/~partners, accessed 31 March.

Cary, William (1974) 'Corporate Law and Federalism: Reflections upon Delaware', *Yale Law Journal*, 83: 663–705.

Clinton, William J. (1993) 'Statement of the President Regarding Implementation of FOIA', in A.R. Adler, *Litigation Under the Federal Open Government Laws*, Washington, DC: American Civil Liberties Union, pp. A34.

Cobb, Chris (1999) 'Access Panel's Ruling Opposed', *Montreal Gazette*, Montreal, Quebec, 16 January: A6.

Collins, William C. (1999) *Privately Operated Speculative Prisons and Public Safety*, Washington, DC: Department of Justice, Office of Justice Programs.

Correa, Carlos (2000) 'Reforming the Intellectual Property Rights System in Latin America', *World Economy*, 23, 6 (June): 851–73.

Crozier, Michel, Huntington, Samuel P. and Watanuki, Joji (1975) *The Crisis of Democracy*, New York: New York University Press.

Dahl, Robert (1999) 'Can International Organizations be Democratic?', in I. Shapiro and Hacker-Cordón, (eds) *Democracy's Edges*, Cambridge: Cambridge University Press, pp.19–40.

Debevoise, Whitney (1998) 'Key Procedural Issues: Transparency', *International Lawyer*, 32 (Fall): 817.

Department of Energy (2000) *Special Historical Records Review Plan (Supplement)*, *Public Laws*, 105–261 and 106–65, Washington, DC: Department of Energy, 1 March.

Dorril, Stephen (2000) *MI6*, New York: The Free Press.

Durkan, Sean (2000) 'Chretien Pledges One-tier Health Care', *London Free Press*, London, Ontario, 19 March: A5.

Economist, The (1999) 'Digital Rights and Wrongs', London, 17 July, web edition.

Etzioni, Amitai (1999) *The Limits of Privacy*, New York: Perseus Books.

Fairley, Peter (1997a) 'EPA Plans On-line Report Cards', *Chemical Week*, 159, 10 (12 March): 13.

—— (1997b) 'Right-to-know Knocks: Will the Industry Open Up?', *Chemical Week*, 159, 32 (20 August): 19–21.

Fairley, Peter and Mullin, Rick (1998) 'Scorecard Hits Home', *Chemical Week*, 160, 21 (3 June): 24–6.

Financial Action Task Force (2000) *Annual Report 1999–2000*, Paris: Financial Action Task Force, 22 June.

Financial Post (1998) 'Flak Prompts Delay in MAI Negotiations', *Financial Post*, 29 April. 16.

Financial Stability Forum (2000) *Report of the Working Group on Offshore Centres*, Washington, DC: Financial Stability Forum, 5 April.

Fitzgerald, Mark (1995) 'Should Government Information be Privatized?', *Editor and Publisher*, 128 (11 November): 30–1.

Frankel, Maurice (1997) *Unlocking the Truth: The Government's FOI White Paper*, London: Campaign for Freedom of Information, 16 December.

Fukuyama, Francis (1995) *Trust*, New York: The Free Press.

G8 (2000) *Okinawa Charter on Global Information Society*, Okinawa, Japan, 22 July.

Garfinkel, Simson (1995) *Pretty Good Privacy*, Cambridge: O'Reilly.

—— (2000) *Database Nation*, Beijing, Cambridge: O'Reilly.

Gellman, Robert (1995) 'Twin Evils: Government Copyright and Copyright-like Controls Over Government Information', *Syracuse Law Review*, 45, 3: 999–1072.

Giddens, Anthony (2000) *The Third Way and Its Critics*, Cambridge: Polity Press.

Glendon, Mary Ann (1991) *Rights Talk*, New York: The Free Press.

Greenman, Catherine (2000) 'Taking Sides in the Napster War', *New York Times*, New York, 31 August, web edition.

Grossklaus, D. (1991) 'Byting the Hand That Feeds Them', *Washington Monthly*, 23, 11 (November): 37–42.

Gruenwald, Juliana (1993) 'Wire Story: Delay in Declassifying Radiation Documents', *United Press International*, Washington, 30 December.

Guardian (1999) 'Santer Has to Take Notice', *Guardian*, London, 16 January: 20.

Guerrin, Michel (2000) 'French Media Angered by New Privacy Law on Pictures', *Guardian Weekly*, London, 8 June: 29.

Gutstein, Donald (1999) *e.con*, Toronto: Stoddart.

Hansard (2000) Parliament of Canada, Houses of Commons, 31 May.

Hoekman, Bernard and Mavroidis, Petros (1999) '*WTO Dispute Settlement, Transparency and Surveillance*, Washington, DC: World Bank, WTO 2000 Capacity Building Project background paper.

Home Office (1999) *Freedom of Information: Consultation on Draft Legislation*, London: Home Office, May, Cm 4355.

Hubbertz, Andrew (1999) 'Response to "Closing the Window"', *Government Information in Canada*, 17 (March), web edition.

HURIDOCS (1993) *HURIDOCS Standard Formats: A Tool for Documenting Human Rights Violations*, Versoix, Switzerland: Human Rights Information and Documentation Systems International.

International Monetary Fund (2000) *IMF Reviews the Experience with the Publication of Staff Reports*, Washington, DC: International Monetary Fund, 20 September, Public Information Notice No. 00/81.

Jaffe, Adam and Peterson, Steven (1995) 'Environmental Regulation and the Competitiveness of US manufacturing', *Journal of Economic Literature*, 33, 1 (March): 132–64.

Kelley, Wayne (1998) 'Keeping Public Information Public', *Library Journal*, 123 (15 May): 34.

Khanna, Madhu, Quimio, Rose Wilma *et al.* (1998) 'Toxics Release Information: A Policy Tool for Environmental Protection', *Journal of Environmental Economics and Management*, 36, 3 (November): 243–66.

Klein, Naomi (2000) *No Logo*, Toronto: Knopf Canada.

Köhler, Hans (2000) 'IMF Must Adapt and Reform', *IMF Survey*, 29, 16 (14 August): 258–60.

Koven, Lisa (1998) 'The Environmental Self-audit Evidentiary Privilege', *UCLA Law Review*, 45, 4 (April): 1167–200.

Kuntsler, J.H. (1996) *Home from Nowhere*, New York: Simon and Schuster.

Lange, David (1981) 'Recognizing the Public Domain', *Law and Contemporary Problems*, 44, 4: 147 *et seq.*

Lardner Jr, George (1998) 'CIA Won't Declassify Files, Blames Budget', *Washington Post*, Washington, DC, 17 July: A15.

Lee, Louise and Bernstein, Aaron (2000) 'Who Says Student Protests Don't Matter?', *Business Week*, 3685 (12 June): 94–6.

Lessig, Lawrence (2000) *Code and Other Laws of Cyberspace*, New York: Basic Books.

Lindberg, Mary (1999) *Statement on Behalf of the Ontario Ministry of Health on Bill C-6*, Ottawa, Ontario: Senate Standing Committee on Social Affairs, Science and Technology, 2 December.

Litman, Jessica (1990) 'The Public Domain', *Emory Law Journal*, 39, 4: 965–1023.

Loeb, Vernon and Struck, Doug (2000) 'Web Site Posts Secret CIA Briefing Papers', *Washington Post*, Washington, DC, 23 July: A2.

Long, Clarisa (ed.) (2000) *Intellectual Property Rights in Emerging Markets*, Washington, DC: American Enterprise Institute.

Lowrance, William W. (1997) *Privacy and Health Research*, Washington, DC: Department of Health and Human Services, Office of the Assistant Secretary for Planning and Evaluation, May.

Matthews, William (2000) 'Access Denied', *Federal Computer Week*, 29 May, web edition.

McLellan, Anne (2000) *Notes for an Address to the Canadian Bar Association*, Halifax, Nova Scotia: Department of Justice, 21 August.

McNairn, Colin and Woodbury, C.D. (1998) *Government Information: Access and Privacy*, Toronto: Carswell.

Milne, Roger (1999) 'A Question of Freedom', *Utility Week*, 11 June: 17.

Morse, Janice (1998) 'Guards Faulted in Escapes', *The Cincinnati Enquirer*, Cincinnati, OH, 5 August: B1.

Morton, Bruce and Zink, Steven (1991) 'Contemporary Canadian Federal Information Policy', *Canadian Public Administration*, 34, 2 (Summer): 312–28.

Moynihan Commission (1997) *Report of the Commission on Protecting and Reducing Government Secrecy*, Washington, DC, 3 March. S.Doc. 105–2, 103d Congress.

Moynihan, Daniel (1998) *Secrecy: The American Experience*, New Haven, CT: Yale University Press.

Murray, Charles (1997) *What it Means to Be a Libertarian*, New York: Broadway Books.

Nader, Ralph (1993) 'NAFTA vs. democracy', *Multinational Monitor*, 15, 10 (October): web.

Nader, Ralph and Wallach, Lori (1996) 'GATT, NAFTA, and the Subversion of the Democratic Process', in J. Mander and E. Goldsmith (eds) *The Case Against the Global Economy*, San Francisco, CA: Sierra Club Books, pp. 92–107.

Neumayer, Eric (2000) 'Trade and the Environment: A Critical Assessment', *Journal of Environment and Development*, 9, 2 (June): 138–59.

Nilsen, Kirsti (1994) 'Government Information Policy in Canada', *Government Information Quarterly*, 11, 2: 191–209.

—— (1996) 'The Effects of Electronic Publication on Social Science Researchers in Canada', in C. Meadow, M. Weaver and F. Hébert (eds) *Electronic Publishing: Its Impact on Publishing, Education, and Reading*, Toronto: Faculty of Information Studies, University of Toronto, pp.1–25.

Nodo 50 (2000) *No Data Privacy for Top Torturers*, Nodo 50, 15 April.

Norton-Taylor, Richard and Pallister, David (1999) 'MI6 Tries to Limit Internet Damage', *Guardian*, London, 15 May: 6.

NPR (2000) *Americans Distrust Government, But Want It To Do More*, Washington, DC: National Public Radio, 28 July.

OECD (1998) *Harmful Tax Competition: An Emerging Global Issue*, Paris: Organization for Economic Cooperation and Development, April.

—— (1999) OECD *Principles of Corporate Governance*, Paris: Organization for Economic Cooperation and Development, Ad Hoc Task Force on Corporate Governance, 19 April, SG/CG(99)5.

—— (2000) *Towards Global Tax Cooperation: Progress in Identifying and Eliminating Harmful Tax Practices*, Paris, France: Organization for Economic Cooperation and Development, Committee on Fiscal Affairs, 26 June.

Parker, Andrew and Parker, George (1998) 'Utilities Win Fight to Curb Freedom Act Impact', *Financial Times of London*, London, 22 July: 8.

Pauly, Louis (1997) *Who Elected the Bankers?*, Ithaca, NY: Cornell University Press.

Pringle, Kenneth (2000) 'Judges Release Financial Records', *APBnews.com*, New York, 21 June, website.

Privacy Commissioner (2000) *Annual Report, 1999–2000*, Ottawa: Office of the Privacy Commissioner.

Prophet, Katherine (1999) 'Threats to Public Access to Federal Government Publications in Canada and the United States', *Government Information in Canada*, 18, August.

Public Interest Advocacy Centre (2000) *Fact Sheet on the Personal Information Protection Act*, Ottawa: Public Interest Advocacy Centre, 11 April.

Putnam, Robert (2000) *Bowling Alone*, New York: Simon and Schuster.

Quist, Arvin (1989) *Security Classification of Information*, Oak Ridge, TN: Oak Ridge National Laboratory, September.

Raghavan, Chakravarthi (2000) *Continuing Conceptual Divides at the WTO*, Penang, Malaysia, 2 March.

Reno, Janet (1993) 'Statement of the Attorney General Regarding Implementation of FOIA', in A. Adler (ed.), *Litigation Under the Federal Open Government Laws*, Washington, DC: American Civil Liberties Union, pp. A35–6.

Roberts, Alasdair (1999) 'Retrenchment and Freedom of Information: Recent Experience Under Federal, Ontario, and British Columbia Law', *Canadian Public Administration*, 42, 4 (Winter): 422–51.

—— (2000) 'Less Government, More Secrecy: Reinvention and the Weakening of Freedom of Information Law', *Public Administration Review*, 60, 4 (July–August): 298–310.

Rose, Richard (1980) *Challenge to Governance*, Beverly Hills, CA: Sage Publications.

Sabel, Charles, O'Rourke, Dara and Fung, Archon (2000) *Ratcheting Labor Standards: Regulation for Continuous Improvement in the Global Workplace*, New York: Columbia Law School, 23 February.

Saxton, Jim (1998a) *News Release: Hearing to Discuss IMF Transparency*, Washington, DC: Joint Economic Committee, US Congress, 19 February.

—— (1998) *News Release: New IMF Reform Rooted in Transparency and Efficiency Act*, Washington, DC: Joint Economic Committee, US Congress, 20 October.

Schiller, Herbert (1989) *Culture, Inc*, New York: Oxford University Press.

Schwartz, John (2000) 'FBI Internet Wiretaps Raise Issues of Privacy', *Washington Post*, Washington, DC, 12 July: E1–E4.

Select Committee on Public Administration (1998) *The Freedom of Information White Paper*, London: House of Commons, 19 May, Third Report, Session 1997–98.

Smith, R. Jeffrey (1994) 'CIA, Others Opposing White House Move to Bare Decades-old Secrets', *Washington Post*, Washington, DC, 30 March: A14.

Sobel, Richard (2000) *Comments on Proposed HHS Rules on Medical Records*, Washington, DC: National Coalition for Patient Rights, 17 February.

Söderman, Jacob (2000) 'The EU's Transparent Bid for Opacity', *Wall Street Journal Europe*, 24 February.

Solomon, Karen (2000) 'Toward Fewer Free Lunches', *The Industry Standard*, 26 June: 212–26.

Southeastern Legal Foundation (2000) *Census in Crisis*, Atlanta, GA: Southeastern Legal Foundation, 3 April.

Statistics Canada (2000) *Census Communications Program, 2001 Census*, Ottawa: Statistics Canada.

Stiglitz, Joseph (2000) 'What I Learned at the World Economic Crisis', *The New Republic*, 222, 16 (17–24 April): 56–60.

Supreme Court of Canada (1997) *Dagg v. Minister of Finance*, S.C.J. No. 63.

Sykes, Charles (1999) *The End of Privacy*, New York: St. Martin's Press.

Sylvester, Sherry (2000) 'Libertarians Oppose Census Questions', *San Antonio Express-News*, San Antonio, TX, 12 February: 1B.

Tietenberg, Tom (1998) 'Disclosure Strategies for Pollution Control', *Environmental and Resource Economics*, 11, 3/4 (April): 587–602.

Toronto Globe and Mail (1999) 'Editorial: Free up Ontario Hydro', Toronto, 26 February: A10.

Tynan, Daniel (2000) 'Privacy 2000: In Web We Trust?', *PCWorld*, June: 103–16.

US District Court for the Northern District of California (2000) *EBay, Inc. v. Bidder's Edge, Inc.: Order Granting Preliminary Injunction*, San Jose, CA, 24 May, Whyte, J.

US District Court for the Southern District of New York (2000) *Universal City Studios, Inc., et al., v. Shawn C. Reimerdes, et al.*, New York, 17 August, Kaplan, J.

US Mission (1999) *Communication to the Working Group on the Interaction between Trade and Competition Policy*, Geneva: United States Permanent Mission to the WTO, 13 July.

United Kingdom (1997) *Your Right to Know: The Government's Proposals for a Freedom of Information Act*, London: Stationery Office, December, Cm 3818.

United States Trade Representative (1998) *1998 Annual Report of the President of the United States on the Trade Agreements Program*, Washington, DC: Office of the United States Trade Representative.

Village Voice (1999) 'Russian Cons and New York Banks', New York, 7 December: 57–61.

Weeks, Jennifer (2000) 'Keeping Secrets', *Washington Post*, Washington, DC, 25 June: B3.

Weiner, Tim (1994) 'US Plans Overhaul on Secrecy', *New York Times*, New York, 18 March: A1.

WTO General Council (1998) *Minutes of Meeting of the General Council*, Geneva: World Trade Organization, 24 April, WT/GC/M/28.

8 Avoiding the tragedy of the commons

Greening governance through the market or the public domain?

Keith Stewart[1]

Contemporary environmental policy is torn between a corporate-led attempt to privatize the commons, and efforts to build a vibrant public domain capable of governing the commons in a more democratic, equitable and ecologically sustainable manner. To date, it is the former political project, which has prevailed. The 'tragedy of the commons', i.e., the destruction of collective assets, such as eco-systems, through the pursuit of private gain, continues unabated while the institutions capable of defending the environmental commons against new enclosures and encroachments are being systematically weakened.

To understand this situation, we must examine how the promise of the second wave of environmental concern, which arose in the late 1980s and early 1990s has been betrayed by the shifting of environmental governance out of the public domain and into the private sphere. This shift has been accomplished through the adoption of 'market environmentalism' and the creation of a privatized commons in order to de-politicize and thus mute environmental concern. The response to the environmental crisis is thus shifted away from collective responses to the challenges posed by ecological interconnectedness and into the privatized world of individualistic consumer choice among a range of options governed by corporate investment decisions.

While the empirical evidence presented below is drawn primarily from the Canadian experience, market environmentalism is not limited to Canada. The Canadian case is, however, an interesting one for two reasons. First, Canada has portrayed itself as an environmental leader, yet the enthusiastic endorsement of sustainable development by Canadian political and economic elites has not resulted in significant environmental improvements. Second, Canada has a tradition of a strong public regulatory system (at least relative to the United States) but since the mid 1980s, its state agencies have been downsized and restructured along market lines. Not surprisingly, this 'marketization of the state' has spilled over into the realm of environmental governance.

The principal argument of this chapter is that 'market environmentalism' represents a profoundly mistaken response to the environmental problematic. It will, in fact, replicate and entrench ecologically and socially destructive dynamics. To truly avoid the tragedy of the commons, we must build the institutions, norms and social relations capable of integrating ecological criteria and concerns into all aspects of collective and private decision-making. This, in turn, can only be achieved through a 're-embedding' of market relations within the public domain.

Defending the commons

The evidence of ecological crisis is compelling. As detailed in the latest *State of the World* report, humans are using fresh water, forests, range-lands and oceanic fisheries at a rate which is undermining the ecological processes which support these resources. We are also in the early stages of the greatest loss of plant and animal species in 65 million years: 14 per cent of known plant species are threatened with extinction, while two thirds of all animal species are now in decline and 11 per cent are threatened with extinction. Synthetical chemicals can be found in all parts of the globe and in concentrations which may disrupt human and animal hormonal systems with serious consequences for health. Global climate change is under way as a consequence of the burning of fossil fuels with consequences, which are difficult to predict, but which are potentially devastating. There are also emerging concerns over the long-term implications of genetic engineering on the already-declining levels of biodiversity (Brown et al. 1998). Taking action to counter these trends is particularly important in the industrialized nations, which use the majority of the world's resources.

Addressing this crisis is fundamentally a question of protecting the commons, where the commons is understood as the web of ecological interconnectedness which links and supports all life.[2] It is this character of interconnectedness, which has made environmental governance so difficult for the modern administrative state. Environmental governance consists of the establishment and operation of social institutions for resolving conflicts, facilitating cooperation and alleviating collective action problems related to ecological processes in a world of interdependent actors (Environment Canada 1999: 2).[3] The effect of many of the regulatory measures adopted to capture contaminants at the 'end-of-pipe' has been not to reduce pollution so much as to move it from one medium to another (e.g. from the air into the soil or water), to send it somewhere else (e.g. shipping the toxic waste to Africa) or to shift the costs forward in time so that our descendants will pay the costs (Dryzek 1987).

Pollution and the overexploitation of natural resources are rooted in the conflict between the pursuit of private interests (profit) and collective interests (protecting the commons, be it the ozone layer, clean water, breathable air or genetic diversity). It is this conflict between private rationality and collective responsibility which is captured in Garrett Hardin's influential metaphor of the tragedy of the commons:

> Picture a pasture open to all. It is to be expected that an individual herdsman will try to keep as many cattle as possible on the commons. Unfortunately, this is the conclusion reached by each and every rational herdsman sharing a commons and therein is the tragedy. Each is locked into a system that compels them to increase their herd without limits and yet the world, the commons are limited. Ruin is the destination toward which

all men rush, each pursuing his own best interest in a society that believes
in the freedom of the commons. Freedom in the commons brings ruin to all.

(Hardin 1968: 1244)

A modern tragedy: market environmentalism

Written at a time when environmental problems were still relatively new on the
political agenda, Garrett Hardin's metaphor of the 'tragedy of the commons'
helped to shape our collective understanding of, and response to, the ecological
crisis.[4] Hardin used this simple parable, borrowed from a pamphlet written in
1833, to argue that the only way to avert the 'tragedy of freedom in the
commons' was through strong state intervention, i.e. 'mutual coercion, mutually
agreed upon' (Hardin 1968: 1244–7). This echo of Hobbes' call for a Leviathan
– a sovereign state capable of imposing order on the 'state of nature' – struck a
sympathetic chord with policy-makers and analysts, resulting in the construction of an elaborate administrative state to undertake environmental regulation
(Paehlke and Torgerson 1990).

Thirty years later, the metaphor of the commons still has a hold on the
collective imagination but now the 'invisible hand' of the market has replaced
the 'heavy hand' of state intervention as the favoured means of averting tragedy.
In contrast to Hardin's call for a redefinition of morality, the tragedy of the
commons, for many contemporary policy-makers and corporate lobbyists, lies
not in our moral character or in freedom, *per se*, but rather in poorly defined
property rights. Their solution is to privatize, as far as possible, environmental
regulation through the creation of markets in pollution, the privatization of
collectively held resources, and the shift towards corporate self-regulation and
'voluntary' environmental governance regimes. The advocates of this form of
'market environmentalism' argue that it will ensure the most efficient allocation
of resources, provide environmental protection at the least cost, and use the
power of the marketplace to stimulate entrepreneurial innovation, so as to
develop technological solutions to our environmental problems.

This shift from the state to the market as the central mechanism for regulating
humanity's relation to non-human nature must be understood in light of the two
waves of environmental concern, which have occurred in the industrialized
countries, and the different political-economic situations in which they arose.

Two waves of environmental concern

Popular concern over the environment and the resulting forms of environmental regulation are commonly divided into two waves or generations, which
can be distinguished in terms of the substantive focus of environmental policy,
the dominant political actors, the policy instruments employed and the
prevailing ideas on the relationship between the environment and the economy
(Paehlke 1997; Hoberg 1993; Skogstad 1996).

The origins of the first wave are often traced to the publication of Rachel

Carson's *Silent Spring*, reaching its high point on Earth Day 1970. First wave environmentalism extended the older conservationist agenda of wilderness preservation and scientific resource management to incorporate a concern for industrial pollution and more urban-oriented concerns, such as air and water quality, occupational and environmental health, hazardous waste, nuclear power, and resource depletion, particularly oil (Paehlke 1997). It was initially linked to the radical democratic and participatory politics of the New Left, but it also included a more apocalyptic concern for the very possibility of survival, as highlighted by the oil crisis of 1973 (Eckersley 1992: 8–11). In Canada, it resulted in the emergence of an environmental movement embodied in groups like Pollution Probe (established in 1969), the Canadian Environment Law Association (1970), Greenpeace (1971) and the transformation of the Sierra Club of Canada from a conservation group into an environmental group.

The rise of the environmental movement was significant, not only for its role in bringing new issues onto the political agenda, but for the way in which it (along with other social movements such as the women's movement, the peace movement, and civil rights movement) challenged the conventional definition of politics. These new collective actors protested 'not against the failure of the state and society to provide for economic growth and material prosperity, but against their all-too-considerable success in having done so, and against the price of this success' (Berger 1979: 32). Rather than organizing themselves into political parties and arguing over the fairest distribution of an ever-larger pie, these new collective actors rejected the issues, identities and institutional modes of the post-war class compromise, as embodied in the Keynesian Welfare State in favour of the politics of civil society:

> From this observation [that political parties only allow citizens to select from among the elites who are to govern them], some movement activists concluded that the foremost site of political activity must be civil society itself. Here, outside the party system, and beyond the reaches of the centres of state power, public spheres of interacting citizens could project into the political arena problems and issues untreated or compromised by the party system and the state. Here, in what remained of civil society, the movements demanded that hitherto neglected interests be articulated and served. It was also here that individual pleasure and the self-confidence gained through participation in the public sphere could be maximized.
>
> (Keane 1988: 136)

For social movement activists, these 'public spheres of interacting citizens' (a key element of the public domain) represented a space from which both the political sphere (the state) and the economic sphere (corporations) could be democratized and thus re-embedded within social and ecological processes. In the case of the environmental movement, this meant challenging the idea that economic growth, in and of itself, furthers the public good and pointing to the ecological costs and ultimate unsustainability of this form of growth.

The command and control model

In contrast to the often-radical demands coming from the environmental movement, the institutional response to the first wave of environmental concern was to create in the early 1970s, largely on an *ad hoc* basis, Ministries of the Environment and a patchwork of environmental legislation across the country. The form of regulation, which emerged in this period, is often referred to as 'command and control'. The label is misleading, however, for environmental ministries in Canada have typically not only had difficulty 'controlling' corporate practices but have often lacked the scientific and legal capacity to issue 'commands' (Conway 1990; Paehlke and Torgerson 1990). Business, in turn, was largely successful in its attempts to 'resist' environmental regulation (Schrecker 1990).

In practice, the first wave regulatory approach was technology focused and had three principal characteristics: 'a preference for regulatory [as opposed to legislative] standards-setting, a tendency to negotiation and exhortation as a substitute for strict legal enforcement of standards, and spending to facilitate industrial adjustment' (Conway 1990: 27). Nevertheless, the 'command and control' variety of environmental regulation has been extensively criticized from the right as overly bureaucratic (e.g., Block 1990). Environmentalists have also criticized it for addressing the symptoms rather than the causes of ecological degradation. According to this critique, it promoted an end-of-pipe approach, an expert-driven discourse, anti-democratic processes and it failed to challenge the equating of capital accumulation with human development (not to mention the fate of non-humans) (Paehlke and Torgerson 1990; Harvey 1996).

North America and Europe experienced a second wave of environmental concern in the late 1980s and early 1990s, which once again brought environmental issues to the forefront of citizens' concerns and government policy agendas. The defining moments of second wave environmentalism have been the 1987 publication of the World Commission on the Environment and Development's *Our Common Future* and the 1992 Earth Summit in Rio, which introduced and then entrenched 'sustainable development' as the new goal of both environmental and economic policy.

The most prominent definition of sustainable development is 'development that meets the needs of the present without compromising the ability of future generations to meet their own needs' (World Commission on Environment and Development 1987: 43). The concept of sustainable development is, however, a notoriously ambiguous one, with dozens of definitions in circulation. The popularity of the term is, in fact, largely a consequence of this intentional ambiguity and the resultant political flexibility (Daly and Cobb 1989: 75). As one commentator remarked:

Sustainable development is a 'metafix' that will unite everybody from the profit-minded industrialist and risk minimizing subsistence farmer to the equity seeking social worker, the pollution-concerned or wildlife loving First Worlder, the growth maximizing policy maker, the goal orientated bureaucrat, and, therefore, the vote counting politician.

(Lele in O'Riordan 1997: 8)

Second wave environmentalism at bay

In second wave environmentalism, new 'global' issues, such as climate change, the ozone layer and biodiversity are at the top of the political agenda. At the same time though, the political-economic processes of globalization have restructured economies, societies and eco-systems around the world. Globalization poses particular problems for analyzing and addressing environmental problems. On the one hand, the environmental problems which rose to prominence in the 1980s, such as global warming, the hole in the ozone layer, ocean and air-transported toxic pollution, or the loss of biodiversity have been increasingly constructed as global in character and thus beyond the purview of individual sovereign states. And yet, in spite of the plethora of international institutions addressing environmental problems,[5] the capacity of these institutions to prevent ecological degradation is relatively weak.

Environmental groups, which are now better integrated into (and some would say co-opted by) policy-making processes, have organized themselves at the international level in order to use international fora to criticize their own governments and corporate sectors in what is 'a mirror-image, though usually from a weaker base of power, of what business and corporate interests do in using international alliances and agreements to "discipline" their national social sectors' (Doern *et al.* 1996: 10).

It is this other half of globalization – economic globalization – which undermines environmental policy-making. On the one hand, globalization promotes patterns of economic growth which put increasing pressure on eco-systems as they extract ever more resources and put out increasing amounts of waste into ecological 'sinks' at ever-faster rates (Altvater 1993; Lipietz 1992). On the other hand, even as the trans-boundary and global character of ecological relationships greatly complicates political responses to the crisis, economic globalization has transformed the structure and role of nation-states, i.e. the principal institutions through which social, economic and environmental problems have been 'regulated' in the post-World War II era. Although the need for collective intervention to address the environmental crisis is increasingly recognized, the capacity of states to do so has been limited in the 'new' global world of powerful transnational corporations and free capital mobility.

Even the Organization for Economic Cooperation and Development, one of the most ardent institutional promoters of globalization, has recognized that globalization poses significant problems for environmental governance:

Market-based policy responses might not even be sufficient to address the *ecological* bases of globalization/environment problems. This is because: i) markets often do not capture environmental externalities at all; ii) even where they *do* capture some of these externalities, markets are typically not sensitive to *local* ecological conditions; and iii) countries have even less reason to use markets as a vehicle for internalizing trans-frontier/global externalities than they do for internalizing domestic ones.

(OECD 1997a: 9)

Environmental governance

The regime of environmental governance which has emerged out of the inter-section of sustainable development and the changing political-economic context in the 1990s has been labelled 'ecological modernization' (Hajer 1995; Harvey 1996). Ecological modernization rests upon a new vision of the relation-ship between the environment and economy, wherein the economy is seen as systematically producing environmental harms. Thus, society should adopt a proactive stance with regards to ecological protection. In contrast to the older view, which saw the trade-offs between environment and economy as a zero-sum game, ecological modernization stresses the possibility of 'win-win' scenarios wherein enhanced efficiency contributes to the emergence of environ-mental industries and technologies.

Although the precise meaning of ecological modernization varies signifi-cantly depending on author and context, certain core features can be identified (Mol 1996). First, ecological modernization identifies science and technology as central institutions for ecological reform and seeks to re-orient technological innovation towards solving environmental problems rather than creating them. This is to be accomplished through the replacement of end-of-pipe technological regimes by pollution prevention and through changes in production processes and in the products produced. Second, it stresses the increasing importance of economic and market dynamics in attaining ecological reform and further it grants an important role to innova-tors and entrepreneurs alongside state agencies. There is also recognition that social movements can play a key role in informing and implementing ecolog-ical modernization strategies. There had been, as a result, a widespread adoption of the 'multi-stakeholder' model where environmentalists, govern-ment bureaucrats and industry representatives negotiate directly (albeit from highly unequal bases of power) over the content of policy. Third, it stresses the need for political reforms which would transform the role of the state in environmental policy-making from curative and reactive to preventative, from centralized to decentralized, and from a directing role to one of contex-tual steering.

Ecological modernization is significantly more advanced in Europe than in North America due to the stronger social-democratic tradition and acceptance of the 'social market'. It is most advanced in Germany and The Netherlands where, for example, the success of the Dutch National Environmental Policy Plan has been linked to:

> the highly corporatist nature of Dutch politics and planning, the Dutch state's acceptance of a significant role in facilitating and directing industrial development and environmental protection, and also the timing of the Plan's release in 1989, during a high point of international and national environmental concern.
>
> (Christoff 1996: 479; see also Neale 1997)

The key distinctions between first- and second-wave environmentalism and environmental governance regimes are presented in Table 8.1.

Market environmentalism

This integration of ecological concerns into economic policy has taken place concurrently with the trend towards a smaller and more market-driven state.[6] The product of this confluence of second wave environmentalism and the 'triumph of markets' (Drache, present volume) is market environmentalism – a political/policy project which adopts the principles of ecological modernization but seeks to incorporate, and ultimately subordinate, these concerns within a broader project of governance by and through the market.

It is important to recognize that the political response to second-wave environmentalism has been shaped in profound ways by a more proactive and class conscious corporate leadership. In the words of one CEO, 'The environment is too important to be left to environmentalists' (Willums 1990). Today's industry associations do not simply oppose new regulatory policies (although they also do this), but actively campaign for a new model of environmental regulation. What they support is an interpretation of 'ecological modernization' which emphasizes the market-enhancing aspects of the new governance paradigm, while downplaying the role of public accountability and participation in advancing environmental protection. Within market environmentalism, private corporations are portrayed as the central actors in designing and implementing public policy *vis-à-vis* the environment.

This is perhaps clearest in the creation of bodies such as the Business Council on Sustainable Development, which coordinated industry's input to the Rio Earth Summit, and national counterparts such as the 'Friday Club'[7] in Canada. It is also evident in the adoption by some environmental groups of a reformist agenda of trying to work with corporations.[8]

For market environmentalists, the environmental crisis calls not for a questioning of the entire capitalist growth model, but rather for its intensification via an extension of the neo-liberal model.[9] And yet because nature is not produced as a commodity, to treat it as such, paradoxically, requires an active state, although one which intervenes so as to create markets rather than replace them.

Table 8.1 Contrasting first- and second-wave environmental governance

	First wave (1968–76)	Second wave (1986–94)
Discourse on environment and economy	Limits to growth: environmental protection hurts economic growth (zero-sum game).	Sustainable development: emphasis on win-win scenarios where what is ecologically sound is also profitable.
Governance regime	'Command and Control' – *ad hoc*, fragmented and bureaucratic approach to environmental regulation; react-and-cure strategy using end-of-pipe technological solutions.	Ecological modernization – attempt to integrate environmental concerns into overall policy; pollution prevention: adoption of the precautionary principle and an emphasis on changing production processes to prevent pollution rather than clean it up.
Issues	Urban-based air and water pollution concerns; nuclear power; population; resource depletion; urban neighbourhood preservation.	New 'global' problems such as climate change, ozone depletion and biodiversity (old-growth forest, tropical rain forests, animal rights); waste recycling, landfill siting; hazardous waste, carcinogens; urban planning, cars and land use.
Characteristics and emphases	Environmental concern tended to be linked to alienation, detachment from social, political and economic order; anti-technological inclinations and attitudes.	Globalized focus of concern; re-emergence of 'preservationist' issues; acceptability of some environmental ideas within political and economic elites; professional character of major environmental organizations.
Key actors	The administrative state (in closed-door consultation with industry), Ministry of the Environment is the lead actor in environmental regulation.	Multi-stakeholder negotiations (government, business, environmentalists and sometimes labour, academics or Aboriginals); green plans, environmental bills of rights, and the 'greening' of taxation or budgets attempts to integrate environmental concern into all aspects of government policy.
Policy instruments to regulate pollution	Environmental regulations which specify which technologies must be used; uneven enforcement and tendency towards moral exhortation and spending rather than strict legal application of regulations.	Environmental regulations specify standard to be met and allow for entrepreneurial innovation to meet these in the cheapest way possible; greater use of legal processes; greater use of economic instruments (taxation, tradable permits, etc.); corporate self-regulation.

Source: based on Paehlke (1997), Hoberg (1993), Skogstad (1996) and Stewart (1998).

In short, governments, in 'partnership' with industry, have been actively shifting environmental governance out of the public domain and into the realm of privatized decision-making through the market. Since 1984, the Organization for Economic Cooperation and Development has played an important role in generalizing a market-driven response to second-wave environmentalism through its championing of the use of economic instruments in environmental policy (see OECD 1997b for a recent summary), for example, in its work on the win-win possibilities inherent in harmonizing environmental and employment policies (OECD 1997c), green taxes (OECD 1997d), the reform of energy and transport subsidies (OECD 1997e), and in its promotion of 'eco-efficiency' (OECD 1998).

An explicit policy statement of second-wave environmentalism can also be found in the federal Liberal party's 1993 Red Book – the policy platform for the political party, which has governed Canada since 1993 (Juillet and Toner 1997: 179–80). In Ontario, Canada's largest province, the New Democratic Party government in Ontario (1990–95) enthusiastically adopted the discourse of ecological modernization. Ultimately, however, even this social democratic party implemented the market-environmentalism version of ecological modernization (Stewart 1998).

Market environmentalism, broadly speaking, is comprised of four interrelated elements: an overall development model, a critique of the state and proposals for corporate self-regulation, privatization as a solution to the tragedy of the commons, and a shifting of responsibility within environmental governance from the citizen to the consumer through market-based mechanisms of environmental regulation.

The limits of market environmentalism: the goal of development

At the most general level, it is argued that the neo-liberal, market-driven development model should be applied as fully as possible because market competition promotes innovation and efficiency. Efficiency allows for 'doing more with less' which in turn promotes competitiveness. In the words of the blue-ribbon, multi-stakeholder Ontario Round Table on the Environment and Economy 'sustainable development can lead to economic prosperity: as efficiency and innovation become the engines of our economy, they provide direct economic returns here, and provide the basis for marketing goods and services abroad as well as at home' (ORTEE 1992: 1).

If ecological degradations were simply unwanted 'externalities', then a market-driven strategy might be effective. But ecological catastrophes, such as climate change, the destruction of biodiversity and toxic contamination are not an accidental side effect of our contemporary capitalist civilization. Rather they are a consequence of its formal mechanism of development (Altvater 1993). Ecological degradation thus provides a powerful point of departure for critiques of the neo-liberal model of development. The question in the OECD countries is not simply one of 'doing more with less', but of 'doing less', i.e. reducing the throughput of materials and energy in the economy.

More efficient and cleaner forms of production are, without a doubt, important. Yet if we simply follow the logic of the marketplace, then the rebuilding of the environment becomes simply a new market niche. Environmentalists have argued that this limits environmental policy to what is profitable for the transnationals and locks us into continuous growth without reflecting on what *kind* of economic activity is being encouraged.

The ecological critique thus goes beyond the conservationists' call for the rational and scientific exploitation of natural resources to encompass a critique of contemporary society. The debate on the ecological crisis is:

> one of the few remaining places where modernity can still be reflected upon. It is in the context of environmental problems that we can discuss the new problems concerning social justice, democracy, responsibility, the preferred relation of man [sic] and nature, the role of technology in society, or indeed, what it means to be human.
>
> (Hajer 1996: 265)

To engage in such a reflection requires a strong public domain. We must engage in public, democratic debate on the goals of development and what constitutes 'the good life' rather than leave these key questions to the marketplace:

> The objective [is] to limit the field in which economic rationality may find expression – or, in other words, to limit the logic of profit and the market. The point is to subject economic and technical development to patterns and orientations which have been thought through and democratically debated; to tie in the goals of the economy with the free public expression of felt needs, instead of creating needs for the sole purpose of enabling capital to expand and commerce to develop.
>
> (Gorz 1994: 8)

A broadly based political project of education and institutional creation will be required to limit economic rationality along these lines and tie the goals of the economy to the free public expression of felt needs. This involves strengthening certain aspects of the public domain, e.g., the public sphere of democratic debate, as a means to protect other aspects of the public domain, e.g., collectively held resources and eco-system integrity.

The limits of market environmentalism: corporate self-regulation versus citizen participation

In response to the perceived limitations of state environmental regulation, both market-environmentalists and public-domain advocates have sought to involve the institutions of civil society directly in environmental regulation. These proposals take two forms. Coming out of a perspective of promoting a vibrant public domain, environmentalists demand more democratic forms of regulation in which citizens and/or environmental groups participate directly in environmental decision-making. Participation is framed as both a democratic right and as a means of reaching better decisions. The market environmental approach, on the other hand, calls upon corporations as the representatives of civil society to undertake voluntary/self-regulation. Corporate self-regulation is depicted as being more flexible and cost-effective, capable of being strategically targeted, and as encouraging creativity and innovation.

Both approaches are rooted in the widespread perception of the failure of the Keynesian welfare state. While the state continues to be the central democratic institution for determining who gets what, when and how within society, the national Keynesian welfare state is undergoing an unprecedented assault. This challenge comes from below, as new social movements demand greater openness from the state's institutions and seek to participate more directly in the development and implementation of public policy. It also comes from above, as trade agreements and international organizations are created to administer the rights, rules, decision-making procedures and compliance mechanisms of the global trade, monetary, investment, environmental and other regimes. These regimes organized by states themselves, enhance capital mobility and limit the state's capacity to regulate capital.

Market environmentalism has a well-developed critique of what it refers to as 'command and control' forms of environmental regulation, which are depicted as overly bureaucratic and an impediment to innovation (see Doern 1990a and 1990b; Block 1990). In light of this critique, the emphasis on pollution prevention within ecological modernization discourse and the budget crisis faced by the state, corporate self-regulation and voluntary programmes have been adopted by Canadian governments within a 'new politics of greening'. The programmes are said to provide incentives for industry to initiate environmental clean-up measures and to be more cost-effective than regulations because they cost less to implement and enforce. They are believed to be capable of being designed and implemented more quickly than regulations or legislation, and to encourage technological and organizational innovation.

Voluntary corporate environmental initiatives are usually contrasted with the supposed heavy hand of regulation. As such, they are said to 'signal a movement away from traditional adversarial relationships between industry and government towards those which are more cooperative in nature and involve varying degrees of government intervention' (Labatt and Maclaren 1998: 191). Voluntary initiatives include: the establishment of an industry-based regulatory body with responsibility for monitoring its members' compliance with laws (e.g. the chemical industry's Responsible Care programme), government challenge programmes where polluters are encouraged to improve their performance and report their results publicly (e.g. the Voluntary Challenge Program described below), environmental management systems (e.g. the ISO 14000 series), the adoption of new methodological norms (environmental accounting and environmental audits), eco-labelling (Canada's Eco-Logo Program), memoranda of understanding between companies and government, as well as a range of self-monitoring and reporting programmes. In general, these initiatives are intended to influence and shape the actions of the affected industry without having to rely on the traditional regulatory approach of command and control inspection and enforcement, with its subsequent increased government involvement.

Voluntary compliance codes: are they effective?

Virtually all analysts would agree that when combined with the full use of regulatory tools and effective forms of public scrutiny, such initiatives are potentially a useful complement to the regulatory system, as a means of forcing and facilitating environmental improvements in the private sector (Gibson 1999). Yet there are also fears that voluntarism is being adopted as an alternative to public action by governments and as part of a movement towards corporate self-regulation. When implemented in tandem with the cut-backs in government ministries identified in Table 8.2, there is a very real fear that this is a form of *de facto* de-regulation.[10]

The failure of the most high-profile voluntary initiative in Canada, i.e. the National Climate Change Voluntary Challenge and Registry Programme (VCR), is indicative of the broader limits of voluntarism. Governments around the world have recognized climate change as one of the most important environmental issues facing us today. In signing the 1997 Kyoto protocol on climate change, the federal government committed itself to reducing Canada's greenhouse gas emissions by 6 per cent from 1990 levels by the year 2000. Yet, thus far its principal strategy has been to stall. First, by establishing an eighteen-month climate change process involving fifteen issue tables and 450 members in order to further study the problem (which is already one of the most studied of contemporary public policy issues), the government put off the possibility of

Table 8.2 Downsizing of environmental ministries in Canada

	Reduction in ministry budget	Resource reductions ($ millions)	Staff reduction
Federal government	30 (1993–96)	737 to 503	5,700 to 4,300
Ontario	63 (1995–98)	529 to 194	2,208 to 1,494
Alberta	31 (1993–97)	405 to 317	1,550 cut between 1993–2000
Newfoundland	60 (1995–97)	10.6 to 3.6	n/a

Source: Stefanick and Wells 1998; Winfield and Jenish 1998; and Muldoon and Winfield 1997.

This question of choice is crucial, for it shifts responsibility for ecological degradation away from profit-seeking corporations and onto the sovereign consumer, who is envisaged as the utility-maximizing rational individual of neo-classical economic theory. Here we can see the co-optation of the language of empowerment, whereby individuals are empowered not as citizens or as part of an ecological and social community, but as sovereign consumers who can save the world by buying green products.

This reflects a broader change in political discourse on the nature of citizenship. The 'citizen' was previously constituted as a social being whose powers and obligations were articulated in the language of social responsibility and collective solidarities. Citizens are now being reconstituted as active individualists exercising free political choices whose most vital economic role is not as a producer but as a consumer, i.e. as entrepreneurs of themselves who maximize their quality of life through the artful assembly of a lifestyle (Miller and Rose 1990).

Within this governance regime, the individual is seen not as a democratic citizen, but as a consumer reacting to price signals. The atomistic model of society as made up of free and individual consumers is reinforced and deepened by the attempt to reassert control over the environment through the extension of forms of economic calculus to the environment, i.e. the capitalization of nature and the further colonization of the natural world (O'Connor 1994). This social construction of nature as 'natural capital' is ideologically important for natural capital is interchangeable with other forms of capital through the medium of money.

The central point, from the perspective of strengthening the public domain, is that the equation of nature with natural capital leads to decisions being framed as 'technical' rather than as issues subject to democratic choices. They should, it is then argued, be at 'arms-length' from democratically accountable governments. This is a key moment in the political project of de-politicizing environmental concerns:

> Thus, [the transformation of the public space of politics into a pseudo-space of interaction in which individuals no longer 'act' but 'merely behave' as economic producers, consumers and urban city-dwellers] does not represent simply a blurring of the boundaries between public and private life – something many social movements might want to preserve as part of the democratization of everyday life – but the replacement of both by a particular configuration of social life in which the commodity is king, and in which bureaucratic, administrative and instrumental logic have largely replaced democratic conversations.
>
> (Sandilands 1997: 81)

This process of narrowing the boundaries of collective discussion and contestation can be attractive to some environmentalists. It offers the promise of swift action and direct negotiation with key decision-makers within existing structures of power, alongside the possibility of exhorting individuals to 'do

something' in their individual lives without the difficulties inherent in collective organization. Yet many environmentalists and theorists such as Hannah
Arendt, Jürgen Habermas and Nancy Fraser have put forward strong arguments
in support of approaching environmental problems as *public* and *political*:

> There is no reason to doubt our present ability to destroy all organic life on
> earth. The question remaining is whether we wish to use our new scientific
> and technical knowledge in this direction. This question, in turn, cannot
> be decided by scientific means; it is a political question of the first order
> and therefore can hardly be left to the decision of professional scientists or
> professional politicians.
>
> (Arendt, in Sandilands 1997: 91)

Conclusion: strengthening the public domain as a means of environmental governance

The attempt to avert tragedy by privatizing the commons is doomed to failure.
While compelling as an intellectual model, market environmentalism is unable
to avoid the tragedy of the commons for four main reasons. First, in treating the
ecological crisis as primarily a quantitative problem of allocating 'public bads'
(pollution) in the most efficient way possible, it ignores the importance of
collectively reflecting on the qualitative issues of what constitutes 'the good life'
and how we, as a society, can live within ecological limits.

Second, the push towards voluntarism and corporate self-regulation masks an
attempt to dismantle the institutions of public involvement and oversight in
environmental regulation. This is evident not only in the proactive attempt by
corporations to set the terms for environmental policy-making but also in the
dramatic cutbacks in those state institutions whose role it is to make and
enforce environmental regulations. The elimination or bypassing of mechanisms for the participation of civil society through the adoption of voluntary
initiatives is a reaction to the success of the environmental movement in
forcing environmental governance into the public domain.

Third, market environmentalism's attempt to privatize the commons cannot
address the interconnectedness of ecological systems. It literally seeks to value
the fish independent of the water in which they swim. Analysts working from
the perspective of contemporary microeconomics reflect this misunderstanding.
For them, the 'tragedy of the commons' was a consequence of the fact that the
collective resource was un-priced, hence the need to assign strong private property rights to natural resources and sinks. Historical analysis, however, shows that
the tragedy of the commons ensues when the system of reciprocal rights and obligations, which govern the 'public domain' of the commons and regulate
individual and collective access to resources, is destroyed through the introduction of the market logic of private property and profitability.

And finally, market environmentalism seeks to empower individuals not as
citizens or as part of an ecological and social community, but as sovereign

Muldoon, Paul and Winfield, Mark (1997) *Brief to the House of Commons Standing Committee on Environment and Sustainable Development Regarding the Canadian Council of Ministers of the Environment (CCME) Environmental 'Harmonization' Initiative*, Toronto: Canadian Environmental Law Association and the Canadian Institute for Environmental Law and Policy.

Neale, Alan (1997) 'Organising Environmental Self-Regulation: Liberal Governmentality and the Pursuit of Ecological Modernisation in Europe', *Environmental Politics*, 6 (4): 1–24.

O'Connor, Martin (1994) 'On the Misadventures of Capitalist Nature', in M. O'Connor (ed.) *Is Capitalism Sustainable: Political Economy and the Politics of Ecology*, New York: Guildford Press, pp. 152–75.

Olson, Mancur (1965) *The Logic of Collective Action*, Cambridge, MA: Harvard University Press.

Ontario Round Table on the Environment and Economy (1992) *Restructuring for Sustainability*, Toronto: Ontario Round Table on the Environment and Economy.

Organization for Economic Cooperation and Development (1995) *Governance in Transition: Public Management Reforms in OECD Countries*, Paris: OECD.

—— (1997a) *Economic Globalization and the Environment*, Paris: OECD.

—— (1997b) *Evaluating Economic Instruments for Environmental Policy*, Paris: OECD.

—— (1997c) *Environmental Policies and Employment*, Paris: OECD.

—— (1997d) *Environmental Taxes and Green Tax Reform*, Paris: OECD.

—— (1997e) *Reforming Energy and Transport Subsidies: Environmental and Economic Implications*, Paris: OECD.

—— (1998) *Eco-Efficiency*, Paris: OECD.

O'Riordan, Timothy (1997) 'Ecotaxation and the Sustainability Transition', in T. O' Riordan (ed.) *Ecotaxation*, New York: St. Martin's Press.

Paehlke, Robert (1990) 'Democracy and Environmentalism: Opening a Door to the Administrative State', in R. Paehlke and D. Torgerson (eds) *Managing Leviathan: Environmental Politics and the Administrative State*, Peterborough: Broadview Press, pp. 35–58.

—— (1997) 'Green Politics and the Rise of the Environmental Movement', in T. Fleming (ed.) *The Environment and Canadian Society*, Toronto: Nelson, pp. 252–74.

Paehlke, Robert and Torgerson, Douglas (eds) (1990) *Managing Leviathan: Environmental Politics and the Administrative State*, Peterborough: Broadview Press.

Pearce, David, Markandya, Anil and Barbier, Edward B. (1989) *Blueprint for a Green Economy*, London: Earthscan.

Pierre, Jon (1995) 'The Marketization of the State: Citizens, Consumers, and the Emergence of the Public Market', in G.B. Peters and D. Savoie (eds) *Governance in a Changing Environment*, Montreal: McGill-Queens University Press

Sandilands, Catriona (1997) 'Is the Personal Always Political? Environmentalism in Arendt's Age of "The Social"', in W. Carroll (ed.) *Organizing Dissent: Contemporary Social Movements in Theory and Practice*, 2nd edn., Toronto: Garamond Press, pp. 76–93.

Schrecker, Ted (1990) 'Resisting Environmental Regulation: The Cryptic Pattern of Business–Government Relations', in R. Paehlke and D. Torgerson (eds) *Managing Leviathan: Environmental Politics and the Administrative State*, Peterborough: Broadview Press, pp. 165–200.

Skogstad, Grace (1996) 'Intergovernmental Relations and the Politics of Environmental Protection in Canada', in K. Holland, F. Morton and B. Balligan (eds) *Federalism and* the Environment: Environmental Policymaking in Australia, Canada and the United States, Westport, CT: Greenwood Press, pp. 103–34.

Spears, Tom (1997) 'The Friday Group: Industry Association Takes Aim at Environmental Regulations', *Ottawa Citizen*, 28 July.

Stefanick, Lorna and Wells, Kathleen (1998) 'Staying the Course of Saving Face?: Federal Environmental Policy Post-Rio', in Leslie A. Pal (ed.) *How Ottawa Spends 1998–99: Balancing Act: The Post-Deficit Mandate*, Toronto: Oxford University Press, pp. 243–69.

Stewart, Keith (1998) 'Greening Social Democracy? Ecological Modernization and the Ontario NDP', Ph.D. dissertation, Department of Political Science, York University.

Toner, Glen and Conway, Tom (1996) 'Environmental Policy', in G.B. Doern, L. Pal and B. Tomlin (eds) *Border Crossings: The Internationalization of Canadian Public Policy*, Toronto: Oxford University Press.

Walkom, Thomas (1997) 'Hydro Thorn Energy Probe Rooted on the Right: Pro-Privatization Empire not part of Environmentalism's Whole-Grain World', *Toronto Star*, 23 August.

Warriner, G. Keith (1997) 'Public Participation and Environmental Planning', in T. Fleming (ed.) *The Environment and Canadian Society*, Toronto: Nelson.

Williamson, John (ed.) (1994) *The Political Economy of Policy Reform*, Washington, DC: Institute for International Economics.

Willums, Jan-Olaf (ed.) (1990) *The Greening of Enterprise: Business Leaders Speak out on Environmental Issues*, Aurskog, Norway: International Chamber of Commerce.

Winfield, Mark and Jenish, Greg (1998) *Ontario's Environment and the 'Common Sense Revolution': A Third Year Report*, Toronto: Canadian Institute for Environmental Law and Policy.

World Bank (1997) *World Bank Development Report 1997: The State in a Changing World*, New York: Oxford University Press.

World Commission on Environment and Development (1987) *Our Common Future*, Oxford: Oxford University Press.

Yacoumidis, James (2000) *Ontario: Open for Toxics: Hazardous Waste Disposal Becomes a Growth Industry for Ontario*, Toronto: Canadian Institute for Environmental Law and Policy.

9 Human security in the global era

Kyle Grayson

Introduction[1]

The end of the Cold War has forced us to rethink state security. Nowhere is this more apparent than in the relationship with human well-being. Public authorities now are starting to acknowledge that sustained economic development, human rights and fundamental freedoms, the rule of law, good governance, sustainable development, and social equity are as important to global peace as arms control and disarmament (Axworthy 1997: 184). With the 'clear and present dangers' of the Cold War no longer possessing its former rhetorical power, the national interest is no longer as effective in justifying actions that are driven by Machiavellian and Hobbesian imperatives. While one cannot deny that there may have been other reasons than the high politics of humanitarianism, missions to the former Yugoslavia, Cambodia, Rwanda, Somalia, and East Timor do reflect a profound change in the security outlook for many states of the world. Security is beginning to be reconceptualized both above the state as international security and below as human security. Many medium-sized countries like Canada, Norway, The Netherlands, Denmark, and Switzerland are attempting to meet these challenges by being at the forefront of the human security movement. A people-centred conception of security provides the best opportunity for the generation of a new kind of public good.

This chapter will argue that if public goods theory is going to be coherent, it needs to be rethought in a political, rather than economic, framework that stresses demands by citizens/groups and supply by political institutions. At the same time, it will be demonstrated that viewing public goods in this manner will have fundamental consequences for how we understand human security.

Although a strong case for human security as a public good is presented, it still must be acknowledged that many obstacles exist in the way of broadening the security agenda to encompass an expanded and meaningful notion of human rights. The next section will outline some of these challenges: including who should provide the bulk of the resources and services needed if human security is to become a global reality in the post-Washington consensus era, overcoming the problems of cooperation in the international arena, the potential reordering of the international system, globalization, and establishing new international norms.

The case will be made that the provision of human security will involve an ever-changing mixture of 'public' (i.e., the state) and 'private' (e.g., non-governmental organizations and multinational corporations), depending on the time and place. Therefore, the global public domain, best represented in this instance as the area both between and interlinked to the state, market, and civil society, will be the site where many of these issues are discussed, debated and ultimately resolved.

The final section contends that human security is here to stay. Despite concerns that the combination of being proactive and concentrating on the well-being of individuals will erode state sovereignty, human security and the state are not necessarily antithetical. Although an increasing number of other actors will be involved, strong states will be needed in order to provide the essential public goods required for human security to be fully realized at a global level.

The transformation of security: from states to people

Although human security has been a term bandied about in discussions of security during most of the post-Cold War era, the *United Nations Development Report*, 1994 is regarded as the venue, which introduced human security and its allocative spirit. The United Nations Development Program (UNDP) definition of human security is broad and far-reaching. In retrospect, it best reflects a call for a change in thinking, rather than a practical plan for the implementation of human security and its underlying principles in international affairs. While the UNDP articulation has been called 'unwieldy' by some, it provides the most ambitious reconceptualization of what human security might come to be in the global era.

In the *United Nations Development Report*, human security is distinguished from traditional security in five key ways. First, rather than being concerned with weapons, human security is tied to *notions of human life and dignity*. Second unlike traditional security which was bounded by the borders of individual states, human security is presented as a universal concern *unconstrained by territorial borders*. Most threats, which endanger human security are common to most people, although it is acknowledged that the intensity of the threat may differ. Third, it is argued that all of the components of human security are *interdependent*. Different threats to human security are related, mutually enforcing, and likely to have global repercussions. Fourth, the provision of human security is thought to be much easier to achieve through *early prevention* rather than through intervention at later stages. Finally, unlike realist security, which is state-centred, human security focuses on *individuals* (UNDP 1995: 229).

The converse to human security is human insecurity and can be equated with extreme vulnerability to conflict, violence, environmental degradation, and perhaps even market forces (Suhrke 1999). More importantly, Caroline Thomas has asserted that human insecurity should be viewed not as the result fying side-effects for many people of the world including astounding human rights violations of workers and those opposed to unregulated markets (e.g., the murder of Ken Saro Wiwa, a Nigerian activist critical of Shell Oil). Another serious threat is environmental degradation, which may not only threaten a people's livelihood, but also their culture (e.g., indigenous groups in the Amazon). Known as 'social dumping', these fears are generated by the deliberate practice of reducing labour and environmental standards in order to attract foreign corporations. (Stanford *et al.* 1993: 1).

For this vision of human security to be viable, the international community must be prepared to endorse the concept. It needs to make full contributions to human security, maintain group solidarity in crises, demand that all countries adopt policy measures for human security, develop new networks of global and regional cooperation, increase preventive diplomacy efforts, and redesign existing global and regional institutions in order to make them better able to deal with the challenges at hand (UNDP 1995: 236). None of this is easy to accomplish, yet it is hoped that a fresh perspective on public goods may offer potential solutions to the challenge of ensuring the viability of human security.

Public goods: the search for a new theory

Like security in international relations, public goods in economics are a powerful theoretical concept with a long history and much baggage. Unfortunately, the way that public goods have been theorized in mainstream economics (i.e., neo-liberal economics) is both strange and confusing. First, the language used is arcane and limited. Second, public goods are seen as an aberration rather than as a 'natural' result of social living. Third, the criteria required for a good to be considered public are highly unrealistic and analytically imprecise. Therefore, a new theory of public goods is needed, one that is able to break free of its neo-liberal prison. It will be argued that public goods should be thought of as the result of political factors rather than market conditions; however the economic criteria can be saved if they become normative rather than descriptive. From rethinking how we view public goods, potential sources for solutions to ensuring the viability of human security will be revealed.

Public goods are not a new concept in economics. Early liberals like Adam Smith who promoted the merits of *laissez-faire* capitalism, were also faced with the problem of being able to account for why the market might not be able to supply efficiently and effectively every good needed for the well-functioning of society. Smith recognized that government intervention and provision were needed in a number of select areas including the establishment of a justice system, the enactment and enforcement of laws, protection against invasion (i.e., realist security), and the provision of schools and other public goods (Cornes and Sandler 1986: 3). The legacy of viewing public goods as a failure of the market has stunted public goods theory to this day (see Kaul this volume).

Early liberals like Smith failed to understand that public goods historically predated the capitalist market system. For example in Rome, aqueducts and bathhouses were public goods often constructed and financed by the state for the use/benefit of citizens. By assuming the universality of their 'Leviathanesque' conception of markets, neo-liberals continue to view public goods as a symbol of the failure of markets to encompass every area of economic and social activity (Foldvary 1994: 1). The important question according to mainstream economics is what are the necessary conditions for market failure and how do they encourage the production of public goods rather than the more logical question of how have markets taken over the provision of so many goods and services?

Private goods in mainstream economics are not problematic because they exhibit the characteristics of 'excludability' and 'rivalness/competitive consumption', which allows them to be demanded and supplied through market mechanisms. 'Excludability' refers to the requisite conditions that allow a producer to prevent others from consuming a good or service whether it is a monetary barrier such as price or some kind of physical barrier. 'Rivalness/competitive consumption' signifies the normal market situation where one person's consumption of a good or service necessarily reduces the possible consumption available for another of the same good or service. In other words, 'rivalness/competitive consumption' is a term that denotes the causes of scarcity from the demand side of the market equation. Thus, to have a public good, one must have open and continual access, a trait that economists have failed to acknowledge.

The unproblematic nature of private goods for economics hides a very important fact; while private goods are consumed by individuals they are produced within social communities and therefore are inextricably embedded within community structures and relationships. The downplaying of the social in economics, which allows for the assumption of atomistic producers, gives the misleading impression that private goods are more private than really is the case.

Like private goods, economics has declared that public goods have two defining characteristics. Not surprisingly, in contrast to private goods, these characteristics are 'non-excludability' and 'non-rivalness'. It is these two conditions that contribute to market failure. But the real story of public goods is not the conditions necessary for the occurrence of market failure but the more illusive story of how public goods may be created in these situations.

The first characteristic of public goods, non-excludability, which will be renamed 'inclusiveness' for this chapter, refers to the inability of a producer to prevent people from consuming a good. For example, fresh air would be an inclusive good in that it would be extremely difficult for a firm to charge for its consumption and prevent those who would not pay from breathing air.

Non-rivalness, the second characteristic of public goods which will be called 'cooperative consumption' in this chapter, refers to the fact that consumption of the good by an individual will not necessarily reduce the quantity or the utility of the good available for others. In other words, cooperative consumption will not necessarily create scarcity. The classic cooperative consumption example function is only a reflection of ethical preferences held by group members (i.e., society) and can therefore vary with the code of ethics in place (Samuelson 1954; Margolis 1955; Colm 1956). Buchanan's definition is also congruent with Eden and Osler Hampson's emphasis on failures in redistribution as a root cause of public goods and the implicit role granted to human agency within their framework.

There are, of course, some conceptual shortcomings in viewing public goods as the result of political demands. The first is the demand variable of the definition, how much demand is necessary? Does it require unanimity, a majority, or a sizeable minority? I would take the position that all that is required to meet the demand criterion is that a sizeable minority need to engage a political institution with demands for some good or service. This reflects the contemporary nature of politics at all levels, including the local, national, regional, and international, where coherent unanimous or majority positions are exceedingly rare on any issue.

The second problem with the demand criterion is that just because something is being demanded does not necessarily make it 'good' in a utilitarian or moral fashion. However, Buchanan's political definition is only meant to be a descriptive device, not a normative standard. As Olson has argued:

> There is no necessity that a public good to one group in a society is necessarily in the interest of the society as a whole. Just as a tariff could be a public good to the industry that sought it, so the removal of the tariff could be a public good to those who consumed the industry's product. This is equally true when the public good concept is applied only to governments; for a military expenditure or a tariff, or an immigration restriction that is a public good to one country could be a public bad to another country and harmful to world security as a whole.
>
> (Olson 1971: 15)

Therefore, the establishment of a normative standard for public goods is needed.

The third potential problem with the political definition is the term political institution. The first key question (and a staple of much political-economy analysis) is where do political institutions come from? Political institutions do not appear out of thin air; they are the result of human action often based on demands for certain forms of representation, such as parliaments, or demands for the provision of particular services, for example in the form of education systems. The second question, which follows from the first, is, does this mean that only governments or inter-governmental organizations can provide public goods as is implicitly assumed by mainstream economic definitions? Is it possible for institutions traditionally considered 'private' like multinational corporations (MNCs) or groups considered to be 'semi-public' like non-governmental organizations to supply the goods and services that are demanded? For example, do voluntary codes against the employment of child labour adopted by several

MNCs under pressure from advocacy groups constitute a public good? The answer is yes; in any instance where MNCs and NGOs are involved in processes of debate, discussion, and negotiation within the public domain, these groups should be considered political institutions (see Hodess this volume). This is especially true in circumstances where governments may be unwilling or unable to directly supply a public good (for whatever reason) that is being demanded by a particular group of people.

The ability of non-government institutions to supply public goods demonstrates that many institutions that have been considered private have vibrant public elements willing to address issues of redistributional failures. Therefore, the creation/establishment of political institutions should be seen as the catalyst for further public goods production. This is particularly true in the case of human security because its implementation, which is often difficult for typical state institutions to provide, demands the introduction of new approaches and the application of new expertise in order to meet its objectives (Simmons 1998: 94–5).

Despite the potential shortcomings outlined above, Buchanan's political definition of public goods is the best analytic tool to determine whether or not a good is public in a descriptive sense. This definition though (as explained above) can put the analyst in the uncomfortable position of having to declare that a good, policy, or service that may be immoral and/or concentrates benefits to one group is a public good. Therefore, it is important to establish a normative standard by which goods that meet the descriptive criteria can be judged. This normative standard is offered by the economic definitions of public goods. In other words, while all that is needed for a good to be declared public is that it be demanded and supplied through political institutions, ideally it should also exhibit inclusive and cooperative consumption features. The astute reader may find this position to be in opposition to earlier remarks; however, this is consistent with the earlier statement that inclusiveness and cooperative consumption are muddled economic criteria. From an economic perspective, which requires clear classification, inclusiveness and cooperative consumption are not effective because they are open to interpretation. As ethical criteria, their subjective nature is less problematic.

It is also important that if one is analyzing a public good at the international level, inclusiveness and cooperative consumption should be trans-generational so that the enjoyment of a good today does not exclude or take away enjoyment from future generations. For example, a policy designed to reduce poverty that contributes to long-term ecological degradation should not be considered a public good for this normative position. Furthermore, a public good should be universal in the sense that other countries or people will also be able to enjoy any benefits (Kaul *et al.* 1999: 2–3). The closer a good or service is to this ideal, the more value it has to the group as a whole. It is important then to evaluate human security (as put forth in this paper) using the public goods criteria because public goods theory can help to determine if human security is a global public good.

Human security: a new public good?

Given the definition of human security argued for in this paper, is it possible for human security to meet the descriptive criteria of a public good?[6] There is little question that human security responses to fears produced by violent conflicts have been demanded for some time, including the establishment of an International Criminal Court and moves to regulate the flows of light weapons. Responses to these types of human security demands are being supplied by several different forms of political institutions including governments, NGOs, and MNCs. Novel arrangements between governments and NGOs have already helped to produce global public goods like the international ban on landmines. In addition, recent events including the protests against the World Trade Organization in Seattle demonstrate that the fear of social dumping aspect of human security is also being demanded by groups and states, both from the developed and developing worlds. However, governments and MNCs have been less willing to supply human security in this issue area, leaving NGOs in isolation as the only political institutions trying to adequately address the problem.

When judged from a normative standpoint using the economic definition, human security theoretically is a solid global public good; however, human security as it has been and is currently being practised runs into some difficulties. This is quite apparent when the universal and trans-generational aspects of inclusiveness and cooperative consumption are demanded. Many operations undertaken in the name of human security still seem to exhibit the exclusionary and competitive consumption characteristics of traditional security. For example, recent operations in the former Yugoslavia have offered, at best, short-term security for people involved in disputes by separating conflicting sides with little effort exerted to ensure that the sources of conflict in the region are adequately addressed in order to guarantee peace for the future. Human security issues like the international drug trade have continued to target certain segments within western societies leading to record prison populations, as well as targeting countries of the developing world without seeking to alleviate the underlying structural inequalities that have allowed the trade to flourish. While there is much talk surrounding environmental issues, far too little progress has been made at the global level in order to ensure that future generations will have access to natural resources.

For these reasons, it might be best from the normative standpoint to see human security as a work in progress. Currently, while human security may be a public good in the descriptive sense of the term, from a normative standpoint, it still appears to have some of the exclusionary and competitive consumption baggage of traditional security. Human security represents a move in the right direction, by seeking to address problems that would have been ignored during the Cold War, but its practices are not as public as they should be. In part, this is a direct result of the cross-breeding of realist security and human security in many policy-making circles like the United States where human security is invoked in some instances, such as involvement in Haiti, and realist security is utilized in others, like the American rejection of the nuclear test ban treaty.

All hope should not be abandoned though. If the type of human security that is being advocated by those countries known as the 'moral minority', including Canada, Sweden, Netherlands, Denmark, Norway, and Australia can entrench itself in the global security agenda, it is likely that the normative criteria of inclusiveness and cooperative consumption, including the requirements of trans-generationality and universality for each, will be better reflected in security policy at all levels. To date human security has displayed a tendency to pursue short-term easy-fix solutions, which do not involve structural transformations. In the future, the requirement that all underlying issues of a human security agenda be considered and managed in order to prevent the continuation of current threats and/or the debut of new threats may be realized. Table 9.2 presents policy examples of the two different approaches outlining the kinds of policies needed for robust human security. For example, in the case of environmental degradation, robust human security requires more than simply going through the motions of trying to manage a problem by developing international

Table 9.2 Short-term and robust responses to human security issues

Threat	Short-term response	Robust response
Light arms transfers	Non-proliferation, arms control, and disarmament treaties	Targeting producers and suppliers of light arms as well as consumers
Social dumping	Bilateral, regional, and multilateral agreements on minimum labour and environmental standards	Re-examining the principles of free trade with respect to the social costs of increased productivity, production, and wealth
Migration pressures	Allowing short-term increases in levels of immigration. Building refugee camps	Tackling the problems which spur migration (e.g. economic inequality, ethnic tensions, environmental degradation)
Environmental degradation	International treaties and protocols	Rethinking the relationship between modes of production, consumption patterns, and the environment
Drug trafficking	Declaring a 'war on drugs'	Addressing the issue of poverty brought on by falling agricultural commodity prices
International terrorism	Increased training and resources for anti-terrorist security forces worldwide	Providing more venues and greater access for sub-state groups in national and international politics

treaties and protocols; it necessitates a complete rethinking of the current economic system. If the transformation of security, which has already generated a shift from realist security to a partial form of human security, is to continue several major obstacles will have to be overcome.

Human security as a public good: the role of the public domain

For human security to be thought of as a public good, in both a descriptive and normative sense, answers to at least five major questions regarding its provision will have to be developed by the international community. The answers to these questions will be generated by the public domain, which can be thought of as the area between the state, the market, and civil society, as well as being interlinked to these three structures. Because the public domain will be the site of debate, discussion, negotiation, and compromise in trying to find solutions to the human security provision problem, it is very likely that in the end, human security will involve an ever-changing mixture of public (i.e., the state or inter-state) and private (e.g., non-governmental organizations, multinational corporations) providers depending on the time, the place, the international situation, and the issue(s) involved.

According to Daniel Drache (this volume), the notion of the public domain derives from the pre-neo-liberal view of the market economy, which did not see markets as all encompassing and argued that civil society was a critical non-market sector. This older view of the market economy argued that there were goods and services available to civil society that could not be bought or sold. It was asserted that not only did people enjoy the 'consumption' of these goods and services, but that they often attributed their well-being to the existence of such goods and services. Therefore, the public domain was conceived as assets that were held in common which could not be bought or sold on the open market. Drache argues that:

> Its unique location makes it a privileged site, where the price mechanism of the market and the regulatory power of the state constantly clashes and vies for dominance. … In this complex process, it is possible to see that the public domain may be strengthened, weakened or transformed depending on the outcomes reached and that the strength, vitality and organizational capacity of civil society are directly related to the resources it can access from 'the assets shared in common'(this volume).

The adequate provision of human security will necessarily depend on the balances reached within the global public domain between the market, state, and civil society. In turn, these shifting balances will be a result of the negoti-ated solutions reached within the public domain in response to the problems of international cooperation, resource provision, reordering of the international system, globalization, and international norms.

Five challenges to the future provision of human security

The ability of states to cooperate in the international system has been a staple topic of international relations since the 1970s and while the basis of international cooperation may be a fascinating line of inquiry, the relevant problem for human security is how to get all of the players involved in the international system (e.g., states, sub-state groups, interstate groups, multinational corporations, NGOs) to agree to use human security as the guide-post for their actions? This is, of course, required if human security is going to meet the normative criteria of a public good. In addition, the multifaceted nature of human security will demand that diverse groups of states and private organizations be able to work with one another. Any attempt to build greater international cooperation will therefore involve the public domain and interactions between the state, markets, and civil society.

The second major question that will have to be answered (probably on an issue by issue basis), in order for human security to become a reality, is who will provide the necessary resources? The provision of human security is obviously a massive international undertaking. As discussed earlier, both the private and public sectors have the ability to contribute resources for human security. Moreover, because human security seeks to be a global public good, the private/public sector question is transposed onto which country(ies), region(s), or international organization(s) should be contributing. Before the introduction of human security, Robert Keohane had addressed the contribution issue by arguing that any state which benefits from an institutional arrangement should pay their fair share (Keohane 1989: 109). Of course, this is not the way that things tend to work in the international arena. Therefore, the resource issue will still be quite contentious because, at least in the short term, the gains from an international commitment to human security would be perceived as likely to be more concentrated in underdeveloped countries with the required resources most likely coming from developed countries.

In the midst of such discussions, it is also important to determine who can most effectively provide the resources for human security. For example, in a case where food supplies need to be delivered to a remote rural region, it may be a combination of state(s) and business(es) who supply the food, with NGOs who already have people on the ground in the region, delivering the supplies. It is likely that those who can contribute and that those who can contribute most effectively will change depending on the human security issue involved. Therefore, once again, the public domain will serve as the arena where these decisions will be made.

The argument has been made that the provision of human security necessarily requires a reordering of the international political system and its concentration on interstate relations, to a new more inclusive international political system that recognizes the importance of new global actors like NGOs and MNCs (Coate *et al.* 1996; Lipschutz 1992; Rosenau 1992). Some have called for a rethinking of the privileged position of the state in international relations and the downgrading of the notion of national sovereignty (Makinda

1996). Some have argued that the United Nations must be redesigned in order for it to undertake the role of an effective world legislative body (Archibugi 1993). Others have focused on developing improved regional organizations which could undertake the activities necessary to ensure human security (MacFarlane and Weiss 1994: 283). Not surprisingly, states, interstate organizations, markets, and civil society all have a vested interest in advancing a structural design for the new international system which places them in the best possible, and therefore, most influential position. The final result will, of course, stem from actions and counter-actions within the public domain. It may be in vogue to lament that the market will inevitably come out on top, but this is far from certain, especially if human security is able to gain a foothold outside of the human security vanguard countries.

Related to this last point, the notion of globalization has become the 'boogie-man' for leftist scholars and the labour movement at the end of the twentieth century. Perceived as the lead horse of the pending world economic, social, and political apocalypse, globalization is blamed for the processes of 'global pillage' and the 'eclipse of the state'.[7] The pop culture definition of globalization, which sees it as being about 'borderless nations, stateless firms, infirm states, and a new frontier without frontiers' reflects the hysteria surrounding the concept (Copeland 1997: 17). Many forget that globalization is a double-edged sword and can provide benefits, such as increasing communication networks, spreading new ideas, and increasing transparency. The manifestations of these benefits are important, especially if human security is going to become a global reality.

While Daryl Copeland may argue that the policy of harmonization required by globalization translates into an agreement on the lowest common denominator, there is nothing inherent in the processes of globalization that prevents it from being an agent of positive change (from a human security perspective) and raising the bar on international standards. Already this has been seen with the global promotion and spread of democracy. Therefore, globalization is not inherently evil. If the state and civil society components of the public domain exert an effort to balance those with an interest in a 'global pillage' and make human security their end goal, the processes of globalization can in fact become something to be celebrated rather than reviled.

Human security will require that certain international norms be established for the behaviour of all actors at every level from the local to the global. Unlike realist security, which could recommend policies of inaction if an issue was deemed not to be a concern of the national interest, human security requires, at the most basic level, that appropriate action be undertaken any time that human life and dignity are threatened. This change from a state-centred to an individual-centred (though not in the neo-liberal sense of an individual) conception of security will involve changes to the norms of behaviour in international relations. No longer will the interests of the state be able to supersede those of its citizens or the citizens of other countries. Human security also demands that the principles of redistribution be adopted as an international norm. For example, peace-building initiatives require a transfer of funds and resources from a donor group to a receiving group in order to ensure that armed conflict is avoided. Given the current popularity of the neo-liberal doctrine and its distrust of non-market allocative functions, as embodied in the Washington consensus, establishing the principle of redistribution may be a hard sell, but that does not mean that it should be abandoned.

There is, of course, also a problem with how the international community can ensure compliance to the norms of human security. The legitimacy of armed conflict and other punitive actions, such as sanctions, will have to be re-examined from the human security perspective because recent history has shown that these actions often hurt those they are meant to protect. For example, sanctions against Iraq have adversely affected the general Iraqi population while Hussein remains firmly in power. If norms are to be changed, the process of changing them will take place within the public domain as all of the key sectors involved debate and negotiate (Ratner 1998: 79). Once again the results of these struggles within the public domain will have important consequences for human security.

Given that the public domain will have an enormous influence on the shape of human security (or if human security is even able to fully develop as a paradigm), and recognizing that the public domain is a site where both the private and the public interact, it is safe to assume that the provision of human security will be divided among states, markets, and civil societies. How the responsibility is divided will be in a constant state of flux, due to the fact that the most effective provider(s) will likely change with the issue involved. Human security then represents a new breed of public good, which is demanded and supplied through political institutions (whether they be public or private) and which uses the traditional economic concepts as a normative standard rather than as a *raison d'être* for government provision due to conditions of market failure.

Human security, the state, and sovereignty: combat or coexistence?

Although many analysts and policy-makers dismiss it as the sexy buzzword of the moment, events around the world will continue to demonstrate that human security is necessary. Major international players through false accusations and fear mongering have tried to derail human security at every possible opportunity. The potentially most damaging arguments are those that claim human security will erode the state and state sovereignty. While recent events have shown that non-state actors can contribute to the practice of human security, strong states are still necessary in order to contribute and coordinate indispensable public goods. Moreover, of what purpose is state sovereignty when a state's authority is not legitimate in the eyes of its citizens because it is unable to offer the most basic of protections against fear?

Whether one is prepared to admit it or not, human security is not going to fade away into the background. Ensuring that current world events and conditions have limited negative consequences demands that human security be the organizing concept of international relations for the foreseeable future. In particular, the rise of intrastate violence and the possibility of continuing interstate conflict, two issues that traditional views of security have been unable to contribute meaningful and satisfying solutions for, demonstrate that human security must establish, maintain, and strengthen the ability of people to live dignified lives free from fear. Although many academics have been able to adapt well to this changing security agenda, particularly those in Australia, Canada, and Great Britain, there have been problems convincing colleagues and policymakers within other countries, especially the United States, of the importance of human security even in the absence of Cold War-style strategic imperatives (Freedman 1998: 49). While adherence to human security may be guiding the foreign policy of countries like Canada, Norway, and Sweden, it is not making as big an impact on the global great powers like China, Russia, or the United States.[8] Of utmost importance is the perception that human security represents a downgrading of state sovereignty. Even a number of developing countries, like Indonesia, are concerned with the state sovereignty implications of human security having only been free from colonial rule for an historically short period of time.

There is a fear that because human security is able to justify outside interference in the internal affairs of states under particular circumstances, such as rampant human rights abuses, as was the case with Kosovo, that this power may be abused by the west with the 'White Man's Burden' reappearing with an updated agenda for the new century. Critics assert that many of the components of human security are in reality western values that are culturally relative and/or inappropriate for countries of the south. More importantly to the great powers, are worries within the policy-making elite that human security will interfere in the achievement of foreign and economic policy goals by constraining policy options. China would like to avoid any negative international costs from its horrendous human rights record. Russia does not want any outside interference in its dealings with its ethnic minorities or conflicts within members of the Commonwealth of Independent States. The United States does not want to completely dismantle its military-industrial complex supposedly weakening its international standing. This has been demonstrated in the recent American refusal to sign chemical weapons protocols or the landmines ban.

Being somewhat constrained in policy options, especially ones that may incorporate the threat or use of violence, does not mean that the age of the state is over or that state sovereignty is being overly compromised. In essence, human security demands that states be both responsible to their own citizens and to citizens of other states around the world by concentrating on the security issues that are affecting people directly with an emphasis on providing a lasting solution rather than a short-term quick fix. Long-term solutions to problems like the international drug trade, international migration, environmental degradation, crime, social dumping, and armed conflict will be global public goods. In order for such solutions to be possible, states must continue to play a vital role in international relations. States must be effective and strong. States must continue to provide public goods, give incentives and support to other actors like NGOs and MNCs in the provision of public goods, and actively engage in discussions with the market and civil society within the public domain. Rather than calling for the death of the state, human security demands a revitalization.

Conclusions

In the aftermath of the Cold War, with the emergence of new international actors and new international phenomenon, security has moved away from being a state-centric concept concerned with power, towards a notion of human security, which concerns itself with human life and dignity. Problems like environmental degradation and intra-state violence, which could be ignored previously are now increasingly being seen as global security threats that must be addressed for their consequences and their potential implications for every human being and state on this planet.

Human security can be described as a public good because it is being demanded by people and is starting to be supplied through political institutions both of the traditional state variety and non-traditional institutions like NGOs and MNCs. The economic criteria for public goods, inclusiveness and cooperative consumption, assume that market failure explains the public provision of goods and services. Such thinking is misguided. Instead it is often allocative failures, public demand, and/or the willingness of a political institution to supply a particular good or service that determines if it is 'public'. Rather than providing a formula to determine if a good should be 'private' or 'public', the economic criterion for a public good generates a normative standard which can be used as a benchmark. Ideally, public goods should include anyone interested and the consumption of the good by one individual should not subtract from another's enjoyment of the same good. In reality, few public goods can fully reach this standing. Human security has the potential to meet the normative criteria but thus far has fallen short. Therefore, it should be viewed as a work in progress.

If human security (or any other public good) is to realize the tough normative standard outlined by the economic definition, it will be a result of interactions within the public domain, the area which draws the forces of the state, market, and civil society into discussion, negotiation, and resolution. Because human security involves these three forces, its provision will necessarily involve a mixture of both public and private producers, depending on the issue and situation.

Fears that human security will compromise state sovereignty are greatly exaggerated by those with less than honest intentions. While adherence to the principles of human security may restrict particular types of policy options, it also requires an effective and strong state, which gains its legitimacy through responsibility to its own citizens and the citizens of other states. This will require that the state continue to provide and support the provision, by other political institutions, of public goods that seek to address allocative failures within various issue areas. Human security, the state, and public goods can be mutually intertwined and reinforcing.

Notes

1   Many thanks go out to the Robarts Centre for Canadian Studies at York University, Toronto, Ontario, Canada. This paper was written as a part of the 'Public Domain' project conceived and orchestrated by Robarts Director Daniel Drache. I greatly benefited from the combined wisdom of our numerous discussions over a year long period and the Public Domain Graduate Student workshops organized by the Centre. I would also like to thank Amitav Acharya and David Mutimer from the Centre for International and Security Studies at York University. Their comments and enthusiasm towards earlier drafts of this paper were greatly appreciated. Any errors though are my own responsibility.
2   The violence of the modern state towards its own citizens is taken up from a post-modern perspective in David Campbell's seminal book on foreign policy and national identity (Campbell 1992).
3   One wonders though how much of this theoretical division between human security and human development is a product of Canada having a separate government department, the Canadian International Development Agency (CIDA), for international development issues.
4   These initiatives are outlined in the Lyosen Declaration put forth by Canada and Norway.
5   It is important to remember that public goods can also be 'public bads' like pollution or the spread of disease which mainstream economics perceives as stemming from the 'tragedy of the commons'.
6   Although not the topic of this paper, human development could also be considered a public good as well, given the criteria that I am using.
7   Although he has coined the term the 'eclipse of the state', Peter Evans argues that the real danger of the global era is not that states will end up as marginal institutions but that meaner and more repressive ways of organizing the state's role will be the only way of avoiding the collapse of public institutions (Evans 1997: 64).
8   Unfortunately, critics point out that it is debatable even within the pro-human security countries how big a commitment to human security really exists. For example, in Canada, development aid budgets have been slashed throughout the 1990s and for the fiscal years of 1997 and 1998, only $10 million was directed towards peace building initiatives (Osler Hampson and Oliver 1998: 388)

Bibliography

Archibugi, Daniele (1993) 'The Reform of the UN and Cosmopolitan Democracy', *Journal of Peace Research*, 30 (3): 301–15.
Axworthy, Lloyd (1997) 'Canada and Human Security: The Need for Leadership', *International Journal*, 52 (Spring): 183–96.
—— (1999) *Human Security: Safety for People in a Changing World*, Ottawa: Department of Foreign Affairs and International Trade.
Birdsall, Nancy (1998) ' Life is Unfair: Inequality in the World', *Foreign Policy*, 111 (Summer): 76–93.
Bobrow, Davis B. and Boyer, Mark A. (1997) 'Maintaining System Stability: Contributions to Peacekeeping Operations', *Journal of Conflict Resolution*, 41 (6): 723–48.

Booth, Ken (1991) 'Security and Emancipation', *Review of International Studies*, 17 (4): 313–26.

Buchanan, James M (1968) *The Demand and Supply of Public Goods*, Chicago, IL: Rand McNally.

Buzan, Barry (1991) *People, States, and Fear*, 2nd edn, Boulder, CO: Lynne Rienner Publishers Inc.

Campbell, David (1992) *Writing Security: United States Foreign Policy and the Politics of Identity*, Minneapolis, MN: University of Minnesota Press.

Coate, Roger A., Alger, Chadwick F. and Lipschutz, Ronnie D. (1996) 'The United Nations and Civil Society: Creative Partnerships for Sustainable Development', *Alternatives* (January–March): 93–121.

Colm, Gerhard (1956) 'Comments on Samuelson's Theory of Public Finance', *Review of Economics and Statistics*, 38 (4): 408–12.

Connolly, William E. (1993) *The Terms of Political Discourse*, 3rd edn, Princeton, NJ: Princeton University Press.

Copeland, Daryl (1997) 'Globalization, Enterprise, and Governance: What does a Changing World mean for Canada', *International Journal*, 53 (Winter): 17–37.

Cornes, Richard and Sandler, Todd (1986) *The Theory of Externalities, Public Goods, and Club Goods*, Cambridge: Cambridge University Press.

Drache, Daniel (2001), this volume.

Eden, Lorraine (ed.) (1991) *Retrospectives on Public Finance*, Durham, NC: Duke University Press.

Eden, Lorraine and Osler Hampson, Fen (1997) 'Clubs are Trump: The Formation of International Regimes in the Absence of a Hegemon', in Robert Boyer (ed.) *Contemporary Capitalism: The Embeddedness of Institutions*, Cambridge: Cambridge University Press, pp. 361–94.

Elshtain, Jean Bethke (1995) 'Exporting Feminism', *Journal of International Affairs*, 48 (2): 542–57.

Evans, Gareth (1994) 'Cooperative Security and Intrastate Conflict', *Foreign Policy*, 96 (Fall): 3–20.

Evans, Peter (1997) 'The Eclipse of the State? Reflections on Stateness in an Era of Globalization', *World Politics*, 50 (October): 62–87.

Foldvary, Fred (1994) *Public Goods and Private Communities: The Market Provision of Social Services*, Aldershot: Edward Elgar.

Freedman, Lawrence (1998) 'International Security: Changing Targets', *Foreign Policy*, 110 (Spring): 48–63.

Heinbecker, Paul (1999) *Paul Heinbecker on Human Security. Canada's Arctic Foreign Policy. Canada, the USA and the World. CIDA Then and Now*, Toronto: Canadian Institute of International Affairs.

Kaplan, Robert (1994) 'The Coming Anarchy', *The Atlantic Monthly*, 273 (February): 44–76.

Kaul, Inge, Gruberg, Isabelle and Stern, Mark A. (1999) 'Defining Global Public Goods', in Inge Kaul, Isabelle Grunberg and Mark A. Stern (eds) *Global Public Goods: International Cooperation in the Twenty First Century*, New York: Oxford University Press, pp. 2–19.

Kegley, Jr, Charles W. and Wittkopf, Eugene R. (1995) *World Politics: Trend and Transformation*, 5th edn, New York: St. Martin's Press.

Keohane, Robert O. (1989) 'Closing the Fairness-Practice Gap', *Ethics and International Affairs*, 3: 101–16.

—— (1997) 'Problematic Lucidity: Stephen Krasner's "State Power and the Structure of International Trade"', *World Politics*, 50 (October): 150–70.

Krasna, Joshua S. (1999) 'Testing the Salience of Transnational Issues for International Security: The Case of Narcotics Production and Trafficking', *Contemporary Security Policy*, 20 (1): 42–55.

Lipschutz, Ronnie D. (1992) 'Reconstructing World Politics: The Emergence of Global Civil Society', *Millennium*, 21 (3): 389–420.

MacFarlane, S. Neil and Weiss, Thomas G. (1994) 'The United Nations, Regional Organisations and Human Security: Building Theory in Central America', *Third World Quarterly*, 15 (2): 277–95.

Makinda, Samuel M. (1996) 'Sovereignty and International Security: Challenges for the United Nations', *Global Governance*, 2: 149–68.

Margolis, Julius (1955) 'A Comment on the Pure Theory of Public Expenditure', *Review of Economics and Statistics*, 37 (4): 347–9.

Martin, Lisa (1999) 'The Political Economy of International Cooperation', in Inge Kaul, Isabelle Grunberg and Mark A. Stern (eds) *Global Public Goods: International Cooperation in the Twenty First Century*, New York: Oxford University Press, pp. 51–64.

Milner, Helen (1992) 'International Theories of Cooperation Among Nations: Strengths and Weaknesses', *World Politics*, 44 (April): 466–96.

Olson, Mancur (1971) *The Logic of Collective Action: Public Goods and the Theory of Goods*, Cambridge, MA: Harvard University Press.

Osler, Hampson Fen and Oliver, Dean F. (1998) 'Pulpit Diplomacy: A Critical Assessment of the Axeworthy doctrine', *International Journal*, 54 (Summer): 379–406.

Peterson, V. Spike (1992) 'Security and Sovereign States: What is at Stake in Taking Feminism Seriously?', in V. Spike. Peterson (ed.) *Gendered States: Feminist (Re) Visions of International Relations Theory*, Boulder, CO: Lynne Rienner Publishers, pp. 31–64.

Ratner, Steven R. (1998) 'International Law: The Trials of Global Norms', *Foreign Policy*, 110 (Spring): 65–80.

Rosenau, James N (1992) 'Citizenship in a Changing Global Order', in James. N. Roseneau and Ernst-Otto Czempiel (eds) *Governance Without Government: Order and Change in World Politics*, New York: Cambridge University Press, pp. 272–94.

Samuelson, Paul A. (1954) 'The Pure Theory of Public Expenditure', *Review of Economics and Statistics*, 37 (4): 387–9.

Sandler, Todd (1999) 'Intergenerational Public Goods: Strategies, Efficiency, and Institutions', in Inge Kaul, Isabelle Grunberg and Mark A. Stern (eds) *Global Public Goods: International Cooperation in the Twenty First Century*, New York: Oxford University Press, pp. 20–50.

Sens, Allen G. (1997) 'Somalia and the Changing Nature of Peacekeeping: The Implications for Canada', Ottawa: Commission of Inquiry into the Deployment of Canadian Forces to Somalia.

Simmons, P.J. (1998) 'Learning to Live with NGOs', *Foreign Policy*, 111 (Fall): 82–96.

Stanford, Jim, Elwell, Christine and Sinclair, Scott (1993) *Social Dumping Under North American Free Trade*, Ottawa: Canadian Centre for Policy Alternatives.

Stiglitz, Joseph E. (1988) *Economics of the Public Sector*, 2nd edn, New York: W.W. Norton and Company.

Stiglitz, Joseph E. and Squire, Lyn (1998) 'International Development: Is it Possible?', *Foreign Policy*, 110 (Spring): 138–51.

Suhrke, Astri (1999) 'Human Security and Interests of State', *Security Dialogue*, 30 (3): 265–76.

Thomas, Caroline (1999) 'Introduction', in Caroline Thomas and Peter Wilken (eds) *Globalization, Human Security, and the African Experience*, Boulder, CO: Lynne Rienner, pp. 1–23.

Tickner, J.-Ann (1988) 'Hans Morganthau's Principles of Political Realism: A Feminist Reformulation', *Millennium*, 17 (3): 429–40.

United Nations Development Program (1995) 'Redefining Security: The Human Dimension', *Current History*, 94 (592): 229–36.

Walker, R.B.J. (1990) 'Security, Sovereignty, and the Challenge of World Politics', *Alternatives*, 15: 3–27.

World Bank (1997) *World Bank Development Report 1997: The State in a Changing World*, New York: Oxford University Press.

Section 4

Global governance and new state practices

10 Public goods

Taking the concept to the twenty-first century

*Inge Kaul**

The past decades have witnessed major shifts in the boundaries between what is perceived as public and private. Economic liberalization and privatization have allowed markets to expand and integrate across national borders. In ever-larger numbers private corporations have gone public, i.e. floated shares on stock markets. Government programmes have been subjected to marketization, such as outsourcing of service provision. There are calls for public agents themselves to be more public, transparent and accountable. Labour and environmental policies of private firms can no longer be kept secret behind closed boardroom doors. The *public*, people at large, as consumers and investors, insists on knowing to what production principles companies adhere. Yet we also see signs of companies' self-regulation. Many now want to be good corporate citizens with a concern for the public welfare. Clearly, the lines between private and public have become blurred.

Assessments of these trends vary widely. Some analysts applaud the greater freedom granted to the invisible hand (Micklethwait and Wooldridge 2000). Others fear we are headed towards ruthless, property owner and shareholder-driven 'turbo-capitalism' (Luttwak 1999). And yet others waiver, recognizing in the present economic situation both risks and opportunities for all. As Giddens and Hutton (2000: 214) conclude, optimists and pessimists write about the current trends with equal fervour. They can probably do so, because they share the same preoccupation: getting the balance right between markets and states. Yet markets and states are mere mechanisms for the provision of goods. Sometimes one does a better job and sometimes the other. It all depends in the end on the basket of goods (and services) one has in mind. There is little, if any, debate in the present literature about the right balance between private and public goods.

Yet we all require for our well-being private goods as well as public goods – private goods such as bread, butter, shoes, or a house, and public goods such as law and order, street signs, an intact ozone layer, institutions to facilitate the efficient functioning of markets, or a healthy environment. Private goods and public goods cannot necessarily be equated with markets and states, respectively. Thus the key question is not how much market or state but rather what mix of private goods and public goods to aim at in order to realize our goals, be they poverty reduction, old-age security, or a sustainable environment, that is, how to distinguish private goods from public ones?

If we were to refer analysts to the standard economic textbooks, little if anything would be gained. Private goods are defined as excludable and rival in consumption. They thus meet the requirement for a market transaction. Their ownership can be transferred or denied, conditional on the offsetting exchange – the payment of the goods' price. Public goods are said to have the opposite properties. They are labelled 'market failures', and set aside as cases for government intervention. We are back to the market/state issue. The public domain appears as a residual category, comprised of things that are non-marketable.

The analysis in this paper suggests that the present standard definition of public goods is of limited analytical, and therefore also, limited practical political value. This is not a new insight. In effect, an extensive literature exists critiquing the standard definition of public goods. But so far, no revised definition has emerged. In the first part of this chapter we will, therefore, attempt such a redefinition. The proposal is to require public goods to be inclusive (public in consumption), based on participatory decision-making (public in provision) and offering a fair deal for all (public in the distribution of benefits).

The second part of this chapter tests the usefulness of the revised definition. It is applied to an examination of important and controversial global public goods, including such issues as the international trade regime, the international financial architecture and global environmental issues. The discussion reveals that these goods are marked by a sharp discrepancy between the goods' different dimensions of publicness. While they affect ever-larger population segments (becoming more public in consumption), they are lacking in terms of participatory decision-making and a just distribution of benefits. Thus, the revised definition allows us to see that public goods do not only face the long recognized risk of under-provision; they may also suffer from mal-provision – providing positive utility only for some and for others nothing, or sometimes even, only costs. A way to reduce the risk of such mal-provision could be to grant all concerned population groups a more direct say in selecting and shaping public goods, i.e. to better match publicness in consumption with publicness in decision-making. More issue-specific policy dialogue among all concerned actors and stakeholders could help achieve that.

In effect, the political realities throughout the world have begun moving in this direction. The growing number of civil society advocacy groups and public policy-networks, often composed of government, business and non-governmental organizations, bear testimony to that. The *public* is already taking more active charge of public policy issues. The challenge now is for our concepts and theories to catch up with the new realities. First and foremost, we need to update the notion of public goods. As the third part of this chapter shows, the redefinition suggested here raises many issues that need further research and policy debate. By implication this also means that the tool kit of policy-analysts and policy-makers is currently lacking critical instruments – a worrisome fact given the many crises facing us today, and a fact that deserves urgent attention.

Defining public goods

The literature on public goods (PGs) is quite extensive and diverse in its perspectives and conclusions.[1] Nevertheless, there exists what could be called a mainstream – or, standard – definition of PGs. We will begin by examining this standard definition in more detail. Then we will review some of the refinements and critiques of this definition suggested in the PG literature. In light of these commentaries, the final section will, then, suggest elements of a possible revised definition.

The standard definition

PGs are typically defined as counterparts of private goods. The latter tend to be excludable, with clearly defined property rights attached to them; and often, they are rival in consumption. For example, if one person consumes a glass of milk, others can't enjoy it any longer. It is then consumed. This rivalry in consumption lends added importance to the excludability of private goods. But it is especially the excludability that makes private goods tradable in markets. In a market transaction a buyer gains access to a private good in exchange for money, or sometimes, in exchange for another good or service.

PGs, on the other hand, are defined through non-rivalry in consumption, or indivisibility of their benefits, and non-excludability. Non-rivalry in consumption means that the consumption of a PG by one person does not detract anything from its consumption by other, additional persons. And non-excludability refers to the fact that it is impossible, or at least extremely difficult (and therefore most likely also economically undesirable) to exclude people from the good's consumption. This definition of PGs dates back to Samuelson's seminal article 'The Pure Theory of Public Expenditure', published in 1954. Today, it can still be found in most economic textbooks and throughout the economics literature on public goods and public finance.

There is full recognition in the literature that only a few goods qualify as purely private or purely public. Many have mixed properties. Goods that have non-rival properties but are excludable are referred to as club goods; and the public spillovers of largely private goods are termed externalities.[2] But the realization that many PGs fall into the category of impure PGs has not changed the basic policy argument in the literature. It suggests that due to their publicness in consumption PGs are subject to under-provision. People will have an incentive to attempt free riding: waiting for others to step forward to provide the good and then enjoying it for nothing. Another frequently mentioned reason for under-provision has become known as the prisoner's dilemma. It characterizes a situation in which the independent pursuit of self-interest makes both worse off than they would be, if they had cooperated.[3] Thus, 'underprovision' has, in the minds of many, become another, second, defining characteristic of PGs, leading to a third one, namely, the equation of PGs with being state-provided. Since PGs give rise not only to market failures, but also, as shown, to cooperation failures, the state is called in to solve their provision dilemma.

Critiques and refinements

The standard definition of PGs has given rise to numerous commentaries. As Shmanske (1991: 4) notes, the literature on the topic is vast and 'the mention of public goods brings to mind a dozen different issues, each of which brings along its own idiosyncratic model and relies on its own set of special assumptions'.[4] Yet despite the wide range of approaches and perspectives, there exists broad-based consensus on three points, which are of particular relevance in the present context, because they call into question the three core dimensions of the standard definition.

First, many analysts point out that 'public' and 'private' are not fixed but variable properties. Whether – and to what extent – a good is public or private is often not a given but a matter of policy choice. Second, a good's publicness in consumption, or being there for all, must not automatically mean that all population segments actually enjoy it and find that it has positive utility for them. And third, PGs are not necessarily state-provided. In many instances their provision is a complex process, involving besides the government also people at large, civil society, and business. More precisely, the arguments are as follows.

Publicness as a social construct

Of course, the economic desirability and feasibility of changing a good's position on the public-private continuum depends on a number of factors. Technology is one of them. If it had not become possible to scramble radio and TV waves, the issue of public or private programming would not have arisen. Now we do have to make a choice. Budget constraints also matter. For example, turning basic education, an essentially private good, into a PG by making it available for all entails resource implications for the state. Similarly, resource issues might come into play when determining public investments in, and the management of, physical infrastructure. Some goods, such as airports, require large initial investments, and hence, the government's support. Yet in later stages of their life cycle they can attract private enterprise. Knowledge is another interesting case in the present context. It often confronts societies and economies with a difficult choice between dynamic efficiency and static efficiency, growth of any type or growth with equity.[5]

Thus, for many possible reasons a good's properties might be changed, from private to public or the other way.[6] The choice to do so is a political one. Markets can provide important signals. But it is only people, individually and collectively, who can decide whether it is feasible and desirable to move into one or the other direction.

Publicness of utility

A second point of broad consensus among critics stresses that publicness in consumption must not necessarily mean that all persons value a good's utility equally, Mendez (1999), for example, illustrates this point by examining peace as a PG. Some policy-makers might opt for increased defence spending in order to safeguard peace. However, this decision could siphon off scarce resources from programmes in the areas of health and education. Other policy-makers might object to such a consequence and prefer to foster peace through just the opposite measure – improved health and education for all. Especially under conditions of extreme disparity and inequity, the first strategy could indeed provoke even more conflict and unrest, securing national borders by unsettling people's lives.

Or, consider the PG 'financial stability'. In order to ensure a well-functioning market, the government as well as private actors may have to allocate a large volume of policy attention, time, energy and financial resources to banking regulation, supervision or supporting the country's currency. Financial stability may rank high among investors' preferences. And in many respects, it is important even to the lives of poor farmers in emerging markets, because they, too, are likely to suffer when a financial crisis erupts. Nevertheless, financial stability may not be their top priority. Malaria control may rank higher in their list of preferences. But it may also be of interest to investors in industrial countries, because they may, off and on, have to visit emerging markets and be concerned about their health. Thus while both, financial stability and malaria control, are PGs; different population groups value them differently. One could also look at environmental regimes, let us say, at forest management regimes, or at legal systems. Yet the findings would be very similar.

A good's publicness in form does not automatically imply its publicness in substance, i.e. a fair and positive outcome for all. Yet publicness in form often means that people must consume the good. They cannot avoid being affected by it. This holds true especially in the case of national, and even more so, international PGs. In respect of local PGs (e.g. parks, school systems, police) people often do have a feasible exit strategy. Many might be able to move their residence, and as Tiebout (1956) put it, vote with their feet. Yet if we think of a governance regime that violates human rights and tolerates racial discrimination, people might be able to avoid the 'benefits' of such a PG only at high cost, by becoming refugees.[7] Public goods can – but must *not* – be sold or bought. People enter market exchanges voluntarily. But in the case of PGs they may not have an avenue for criticism nor a feasible exit opportunity. They may be compelled to consume a particular good. Therefore, it is important to ascertain whether a good's publicness in form goes hand in hand with publicness in substance – actual enjoyment of the good by all.

The role of non-state actors in the provision of PGs

Right from the writings of Hume and Smith, the concept of PGs has been linked to issues of public finance. Some authors have focused more on taxation questions, e.g. Pigou (1928), and others more on expenditure concerns, such as Samuelson's 1954 article. Even today, PGs are, in the minds of many, being equated with 'state-provided'. Yet in reality, many actors are involved, and many stakeholders claim a say in the decision-making process.

As Ostrom (1990) and others have shown, voluntary, community-based arrangements can, for example, offer effective and efficient solutions to the sustainable management of common pool resources. At least for local settings, 'Leviathan' is not the only possible policy response.[8] Some PGs have even emerged against the wishes of the state. Many aspects of environmental sustainability, gender equality, or human rights regimes fall into this category. As Sen (1999) argues, such concerns are often not state-mediated but an outcome of manifold other affiliations people have, including for example, those of being a lawyer, doctor or feminist. Acting in narrow self-interest, governments have, at times, tried to neglect these concerns, until put under public pressure. CSOs (civil society organizations) have been critical to their promotion.

Like civil society, private business can be an active promoter and shaper of PGs. Globalization has been accompanied by a world-wide trend of policy convergence behind national borders, aimed at increased harmonization of legal frameworks, technical norms and standards, banking regulation, and so on (see, on this point, for example, Birdsall and Lawrence 1999, and Zacher and Sutton 1996). Private corporations involved in international trade, finance or transnational production have been an important driving force behind this trend.

All this is not to say that the role of governments is unimportant. It continues to be critical and unique, because of the legislative and coercive powers of the state. Civil society and business can press for change in norms or adopt voluntary standards, but only governments can translate these demands into binding law. Markets for tradable pollution permits may function, but governments have to define the property rights. Or, education can be delivered through a voucher system. But state agencies may have to ensure the financing and monitor compliance with educational standards. The role of government is now often more focused on making agreements 'stick' and adjusting incentive structures. Civil society organizations (CSOs) and business play a role in pressing for policy decisions and helping in the delivery of PGs. Depicting PGs as state-provided would mean ignoring large and important parts of reality.

The finding that the provision of PGs is a complex, multi-actor and multi-stakeholder process could be perceived as 'bad news' for PGs. This, because the standard theory sees publicness as a major cause of cooperation failure. A larger and more diverse group of concerned parties might exacerbate the collective action problems that PGs are said to face. Yet several analysts have queried the validity of the assumptions that underpin many studies on free riding and the prisoner's dilemma. Runge (1984), for example, pointed out that non-cooperative attitudes are more typical of one-time interactions than reiterated ones. Prospects of longer-term, repeated relationships strengthen trust, confidence and cooperation among actors. Runge's research, in effect, suggests that fair-mindedness is often the preferred strategy, meaning that each person in a two-actor situation would rather that both either cooperate or not cooperate – than one trying to cheat and free-ride on the other.[9] With some effort, cooperation failures seem to be avoidable so that PGs stand a good chance, even in today's more open, diverse, pluralistic world.

To conclude, PGs are far more varied and complex than the standard definition suggests. In part, they have become so during the past decades – with the world's policy shifts towards enhanced economic and political liberalization, a better educated and informed general public, the growth of civil society, more differentiated market and state institutions, and increasing public-private partnerships. The question now is how to capture these new realities in the definition of PGs? How to take the concept out of the rarefied circles of public-finance experts and turn it into a notion that could effectively inform and guide today's policy-making?

Expanding the standard definition

In light of the foregoing, it seems that the standard definition of PGs requires modification in at least three respects. First, we need a positive – not just a negative – definition of publicness in consumption. Second, since many PGs are a social construct, and since we live in a world of inequity and disparity, 'public involvement in the design of PGs' should be among their defining characteristics. And third, publicness in consumption should be linked with publicness of benefits. We will now examine how each of these modifications could be made more precise and reflected in a revised definition of PGs.

From non-excludability to inclusiveness

As we saw, many goods have variable properties. In particular, we can think of them as items situated along a continuum stretching from 'fully excludable' to 'fully inclusive'. PGs are goods with significant qualities of inclusiveness, i.e. qualities of being non-discriminatory and there for all. If they discriminate (e.g. place a special emphasis on the poor or other population groups), that discrimination should be in the interest of inclusiveness. Otherwise, the good might be more appropriately classified as a club good, or even, a private good.

Inclusiveness pertains to the formal properties of the good (as opposed to its substantive properties, which we will discuss later). It can have three main origins, namely: one, a deliberate public-policy decision to place – or keep – a good's benefits in the public domain; two, non-excludability of the good's benefits, due to economic and/or technical reasons; and three, inadvertent existence of a good in the public domain. While the first two sub-categories are self-explanatory, the third one may need elaboration. To illustrate, for many years, the emission of CFCs had not been perceived as a negative externality. Nevertheless, it *de facto* had been one. It contributed to the emergence of a public bad, the thinning of the ozone layer. Similarly, there may today exist many things that we will only tomorrow acknowledge on a broader, consensual basis as public goods or bads, and this probably only after intensive political struggle and heated debates. It is often not easy to identify the nature of a good. Just think of the current controversies around the issue of genetic engineering.

Another example of an inadvertent public good is non-commercial knowledge. Many elements of that type of knowledge are available in the public domain, offering important insides into, let's say, the workings of policy change. But only a few aid agencies may care to assemble, sort, store and disseminate such knowledge systematically. Mostly it exists in a dispersed, unorganized and inaccessible way. It is being ignored, while people repeat past mistakes and are trying to 're-invent the wheel'. Thus, the sub-category of inadvertent public goods is an extremely important one, because it often contains goods with under-used positive utility or over-supplied public bads. It offers plenty of opportunities for enhancing efficiency.

Defining PGs through the broader criterion of inclusiveness changes the concept from a passive, residual category ('non-marketable') into an active, policy-guided one. PGs now clearly appear as the social constructs they are. They represent outcomes of human choice – or conversely, results of human failure, i.e. either political neglect or hesitancy caused by lack of knowledge and uncertainty.

Adding public choice

Just as an optimal allocation of private goods depends on well-functioning, competitive markets, an optimal provision of PGs depends on well-functioning, consultative and fair processes of political bargaining and decision-making. The existence of such a political regime of policy-making (just like the existence of efficient markets) constitutes an important PG in and by itself. It is indispensable to matching the preferences of different consumer groups with decisions about allocations (about which goods to provide and how much of each) and designs (about the shape and content of a good).

Adding this dimension to the definition of PGs leads us right into the deep, controversial waters of preference revelation. A vast literature exists on this issue, with few, if any, positive, practical–political results. Arrow's impossibility theorem represents one of the major conclusions of that strand of literature. It suggests that: 'There is no consistent method by which a democratic society can make a choice (when voting) that is always fair when that choice must be made from any three or more alternatives' (Arrow 1951: 5). [10]

However, the studies on preference revelation – and also those on the construction of a social welfare function – have typically chosen a technocratic approach rather than a participatory, political one. Their concern has been with making people reveal their preferences or defining rules for non-discriminatory political decision-making. Here, the focus is on giving people added opportunity to participate and bringing them more into the decision-making process. History and present-day reality show that the latter is needed and that it can work. Markets function on decentralized, continuous decision-making. And the provision of PGs can benefit from a similar approach. Throughout the world CSOs have sprung up to complement, through more issue-focused and continuous political advocacy, networking and lobbying, the democratic systems of periodic elections of legislatures and governments. Apparently, people find that the latter do not give them an adequate political voice. This not only because they fear government failures in the periods between elections but because they are keen to do more than just vote for political representatives. Many like to be actively involved in the political process – to reveal their preferences.

Of course, advocacy groups may overstate their concerns. But if all groups are properly and fairly represented, political bargaining – especially if it is institutionalized and set in a longer-term time frame – can, in large measure, take care of that. When push comes to shove, advocacy groups may also expect others to foot the bill. This not necessarily because they try to free-ride but because they represent 'voiceless' and 'penny-less' concerns, e.g. the poor or inter-generational issues such as environmental sustainability. But if the public agenda is not to reinforce but complement, or even, correct private consumption opportunities and decisions, then political persuasiveness and efforts to rescue society from a prisoner's dilemma should also count as a contribution, a contribution in kind. In effect, many times, political advocacy groups are able to demonstrate that society as a whole, including those who will pay the bill, can realize positive net gains from a suggested policy measure. The struggles of labour unions for enhanced working conditions – and increased workers' productivity – are a case in point. And so is the present struggle for poverty reduction and fighting growing global inequity. If disparities assume explosive magnitudes, the current political and economic systems will lose legitimacy and all will pay the price.

More concretely, the suggestion here is to ensure that major PGs be designed in a fully participatory way. All key actors and stakeholders should, on a PG-by-PG basis, have a fair opportunity to help shape the good in question, monitor its production, assess its impact and recommend if necessary, adjustments in its design. In many instances such consultations are already happening. 'Townhall meetings', for example, are a well-established practice in many local communities. But also at national and international levels policy-making has been opened up. Just think of the massive CSO involvement that marked such international conferences as the Earth Summit in 1992, the World Social Summit in 1995, or the 1999 WTO (World Trade Organization) meeting in Seattle. CSOs and other stakeholder groups are already claiming a more regular seat on the policy-making tables that were hitherto primarily reserved for governments. Similarly, consultations between governments and business actors are increasingly moving from behind the scenes into more open, public policy-making arenas. The Davos Forum and the Business Compact of the United Nations Secretary General, for example, bear testimony to that.[11] Increasingly one also hears calls for a new form of tripartite policy-making, involving governments, civil society and business (see, on this point, Kaul *et al.* 1999b: 478–85). The challenge now is to draw lessons from these and other such initiatives, which have so far mainly evolved in a spontaneous, *ad hoc* fashion, and to develop a more systematic approach to public policy partnerships.[12]

Building in fairness

The fairness and justice of public policy-making, and hence that of PGs, has troubled many authors. The contributions to this topic include such diverse body of thought as for example, represented by Buchanan, Musgrave, Rawls, Tullock, Sen and Wicksell. Recognizing that notions of fairness and justice vary widely across population groups, cultures, countries, times, issues, and other dimensions, the emphasis has been on devising rules to ensure a fair process of decision-making rather than defining the characteristics of a just policy outcome. To a certain extent, the foregoing discussion (see the previous section) reflects this concern with 'fairness of process'.

Certainly, fairness of process is in and by itself an important facilitator of justice. It provides people with a voice, and if they feel that they cannot make themselves adequately heard, they could even walk out of the consultations, demonstrating their dissatisfaction and exposing the problems they perceive. However, another important element of ensuring fairness and justice is transparency, and hence, information. Public policy-making should not be guesswork. It should be based on rigorous policy analyses, including disaggregated socio-economic impact assessments of PGs, *ex ante* appraisals as well as *ex post* analyses. People should know what benefits they can expect from a certain PG and whether their expectations have materialized. Again, reality seems to be ahead of our thinking on this point. Just consider the many so-called 'watches' that have emerged in the areas of human rights, social development and the environment. Increasingly, we also see impact assessments, notably on such issues as 'trade and human development' or 'trade and the environment'.[13] If these types of studies present sufficiently disaggregated measurements, people themselves would be able to decide whether and up to what point they consider a particular PG as a fair deal.

Thus, the revised definition of PGs characterizes these goods as inclusive (public in consumption), based on participatory decision-making and design (public in provision) and just (public in benefits).[14] PGs meeting these three requirements will be called 'genuine' (see Figure 10.1: Triangle of publicness).

Applying the revised definition to global public goods

So far, we have discussed PGs without specifying the geographical or jurisdictional reach of their benefits, i.e. whether their effects are local, national, regional or global in scope. In fact, much of the PG literature is silent on this issue, assuming implicitly that the benefits of PGs are of national reach and that

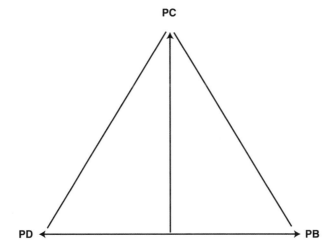

PB: Publicness in the distribution of benefits
PC: Publicness in consumption
PD: Publicness in decision-making

Figure 10.1   Triangle of publicness

their provision can be ensured through domestic actions. If the jurisdictional issue is raised, it is usually to highlight local PGs. However, with increasing globalization – openness of borders, a growing volume of border-transgressing economic activity and interdependence among countries – international (regional and global) PGs are gaining in importance.

In the following we will especially, focus on global PGs (GPGs), i.e. PGs whose benefits cut across several countries and generations, present and future (see Kaul *et al.* 1999a: 11). Some GPGs, such as the international trade regime, the international financial architecture or global environmental issues, are currently embroiled in considerable political turmoil and controversy. Can the revised definition of PGs help us understand the reasons for these conflicts?

Before attempting to answer this question, it is useful to take a closer look at GPGs, and in particular, to distinguish between the traditional class of GPGs and a new, emerging class of GPGs. It is mainly the latter group that is facing political problems today.

Traditional GPGs are largely external to countries and national borders. Dealing with them involves what is usually called 'foreign affairs'. Access to the oceans or the use of the sky is, for example, governed by *international* agreements *between* nations. The beginnings of these agreements date back to the seventeenth century. They proliferated as international economic activities – transport, communications, trade and investment – intensified during the nineteenth and twentieth centuries. If these agreements are multilateral and of worldwide coverage, they are, in PG parlance, public in consumption – inclusive, and even, non-rival. The traditional class of GPGs remains important, because the volume of international economic activity continues to be large and new means of interaction, such as the Internet, are emerging and calling for new rules and regulations.

Yet the global challenges figuring most prominently on the international policy agenda today are of a different nature. They are not just external to states, but crosscutting, and therefore, calling for increased policy harmonization and cooperation *behind* national borders. Examples are banking regulation, the recognition of property rights, investment laws, human rights, good governance, the protection of the ozone layer, the stability of the global climate, and control of infectious diseases. Providing these PGs requires joint, concerted policy-making among nations.[15]

Why then are these GPGs in trouble? Take, for example, the case of Seattle, i.e. the demonstrations and street battles, which accompanied the WTO meeting in Seattle in 1999. CSOs from around the world had spared no effort to travel to the meeting in order to voice concerns about the present international trade regime. Their messages were quite diverse, but all felt betrayed by the present shape and content of the GPG 'international trade regime'. It was perceived as unfair to poorer countries and poorer people, and as secretive – negotiated by technocrats from executive branches of governments, often without adequate inputs from politicians and the public at large.[16] Or, take as a further example, the present debates about a new international financial architecture, prompted in particular, by the harsh social costs of the Asian financial crises of the late 1990s. Many CSOs and other observers felt innocent by-standers, such as the poor, suffered while private investors often walked away 'without a hair-cut'. Now there are strong demands for involving all stakeholders in the policy debates, prevention and management of financial crises, and preferably, to agree *ex ante* on good social principles to respect, such as exempting basic social spending from any budgetary cuts that crises prevention and management may require.[17]

If we examine these policy events through the lens of the revised definition of PGs, it becomes evident that the GPGs in question are marked by an important discrepancy between their various dimensions of publicness. While ranking high in terms of inclusiveness (judging from the number of people and countries they affect), they are lacking in the view of many, in terms of publicness in decision-making as well as publicness of benefits. The international financial architecture reveals a similar picture. Looking at the negotiations pertaining to climate change, for example, at the issue of tradable pollution permits, we find that concerns about equity are decisive in holding back support from developing countries.

PGs, and GPGs are no exception, pose the challenge of ownership – just as private goods do. Yet ownership in their case is not defined through excludability and clearly established property rights. Rather, it is fostered through active participation, fairness of process and justice of policy outcome – through people having a stake in the good.[18]

Implications for future research and policy debate

Judging from the discussion in the second part of this chapter, the suggested redefinition of PGs – as goods that are inclusive (public in consumption), participatory in decision-making (public in provision) and offering a fair deal for all (public in benefits) seems to be a potentially useful one. It appears to shed new light on this category of goods and to help us better understand, and respond to, their provision challenges. At the same time, the proposed modifications raise a number of issues that warrant further study and debate.

First, it would be interesting to establish a *typology of PGs* based on the suggested, revised definition, categorizing goods according to the different criteria that establish their inclusiveness, or publicness in consumption. The distinguishing properties might include, for example: publicness by policy design (e.g. universal applicability, coverage or accessibility), non-excludability (innate properties of), inadvertent and contested publicness.

Second, the present paper recommends establishing for major PGs at least, consultative groups composed of representatives of the key actors and other stakeholders. As indicated, many such bodies have evolved in a spontaneous *ad hoc* fashion. There also exist extensive experiences with various consultative mechanisms at the local level. The time may be ripe to analyse the experiences gained and to develop best-practice recommendations on how to organize such consultative mechanisms. For example, of special interest in this connection might an exploration of how to ensure legitimacy of such consultative groups and how to relate their advice to the decisions taken by other bodies involved in the public policy-making process, notably those of legislative bodies. A further question could be whether and how the structure and functioning of consultative groups vary with the geographical/ jurisdictional reach of the PG's benefits. In other words, does it matter whether the benefits are local, national or international in scope?

Third, publicness in benefits has, here, been defined as positive utility for all, or *fairness* in the distribution of benefits. It has been suggested that the definition of what is fair and just should be left to the consultative groups themselves to decide (and one would hope that they would, in turn, do so in closest consultation with the groups they claim to represent). Yet their decision-making on this point can be facilitated in a number of ways. One would be to develop more operational definitions of fairness and justice and to illustrate how they could be applied to different issues and concerns and with what effects. Another facilitating step could be to develop easy-to-use but robust methodologies for social impact assessments of PGs. Some of the indices developed for example in the *Human Development Reports* (UNDP 1990–2000) could be of relevance in this context.

In addition, it may not always be appropriate to assess the fairness of public-policy bargains only on a good-by-good basis. A more cross-cutting perspective might, sometimes, be needed, and in particular, a clearer idea of facts and figures on the public domain as a whole. In many countries the public domain is probably huge – in size (or form). Yet it may be filled with a large volume of negative externalities, e.g. noise, pollution, risks, crime, or violence, i.e. matters that have been left there as public bads – either due to policy neglect or by policy design. In order to gain a clearer picture and understanding of local, national and international public domains, domain profiles could be a useful tool, listing PGs with (positive) benefits as well as those with costs.[19]

If some of the suggested concepts and instruments existed, we could re-introduce a concern about economic ends and goods, private and public, into our debates about where societies and economies are headed, and ought to be heading. We could move beyond the issue of balancing markets and states and discuss with fervour not just what means to employ but also what goals to pursue. Re-inserting into the discourse a recast notion of PGs, along the lines suggested here, would in particular, be critical. It would allow us to delineate more deliberately and clearly the boundaries of the public domain – the common ground which, if curtailed too excessively, will adversely affect social cohesion as well as economic efficiency, nationally as well as internationally. The fact that we are at present living in a world in turmoil might be a sign that recapturing a notion of PGs and of the public domain is a challenge that requires urgent attention.

Notes

*   The author is Director of UNDP's Office of Development Studies, New York. The views expressed here are hers and do not necessarily reflect those of the organization with which she is affiliated.

1   For an excellent overview of the literature, see, for example, Cornes and Sandler 1996; and for a discussion on the historical evolution of the concept, refer among others, to Musgrave 1985 and Musgrave *et al.* 1987.

2   To elaborate, a club good is an intermediate case between a pure public good and a pure private good. With a club good, exclusion is possible. An example would be a swimming pool or a film screening. In both cases it is possible to limit access to the good and to levy an entrance fee. An externality arises when an individual or firm takes an action (consumption or production) but does not bear all the costs or does not enjoy all the benefits. Air pollution through the use of a private vehicle is an example of a negative externality; and beautifying one's house not only to one's own enjoyment but also that of others is an example of a positive externality or spill-over of a private action into the public domain.

   It is also worth noting in this context that some authors, e.g. Demsetz (1970) and Kindleberger (1986) consider non-rivalry as the crucial determinant of publicness. Others, among them Olson (1965), take non-excludability as the hallmark. This author tends to associate herself with the latter view. In fact, Kaul *et al.* (1999b) show that the different causes of publicness entail quite different provision chal- lenges. See on this point, also Starrett (1988) and Stevenson (1991).

3   For a discussion of various collective action problems linked to different PGs, see for example, Sandler (1997).

4   Cornes and Sandler (1996) also provide a detailed account of the literature on which the discussion in this section draws. But the interested reader might also want to refer directly to some of the contributions to the debate, including for example: Bergstrom *et al.* 1986; Buchanan 1965; Coase 1960; Demsetz 1970; Heal 1999; Hirshleifer 1983; Kaul *et al.* 1999; Kindleberger 1986; Malkin and Wildavsky 1991; Margolis and Guitton 1969; Musgrave *et al.* 1970; and Olson 1965.

5   The publicness of knowledge resides in its non-rival benefits. Sharing a recent insight with others does not erase the newly won knowledge from the inventor's mind. At the same time, however, knowledge is a privately produced good. It is individuals who develop new ideas and insights. And therefore, knowledge is, at least in the shorter term, excludable. It can be withheld. Elaborating on the concepts of dynamic and static efficiency, Stiglitz (1999: 311), for example, writes that:

> Inventors obtain a return on their innovative activity either by charging through the use of a patent (licensing) or by charging a monopoly price on the product. In either case there is inefficiency. The gain in dynamic efficiency from the greater innovative activity is intended to balance out the losses from static inefficiency from the under-utilization of the knowledge or from the underproduction of the good protected by the patent.

As the current discussion about HIV/AIDS vaccines demonstrates, there are many ways of compensating for the short-run privatization of knowledge through other policy options. In the case of HIV/AIDS medicines, a vaccine-purchasing fund has, for example, been proposed to better balance dynamic efficiency (private R&D efforts) with static efficiency (the availability of pharmaceutical drugs). On the proposal for a vaccine-purchasing fund, see Sachs (1999).

6   Because of the variability of the goods' properties, some analysts, among them Malkin and Wildavsky (1991), suggest that the distinction between public and private goods be abandoned. Since their argument is close to the one developed here, it is important right from the outset, to clarify the differences in view between, for example, Malkin and Wildavsky and this author. Even though the properties of goods are – and should be – socially and politically determined, once a decision has been taken, the goods in question possess certain properties. Even though eventually only of a temporary nature, the properties affect actors' decisions, e.g. whether or not to reveal their true preferences for a particular good. Hence, a good's properties are critical to its provision, irrespective of their degree of permanence and durability. Also, as discussed later, non-rival goods, such as for example, knowledge, stay non-rival, even though they may temporarily fall under intellectual property rights protection. It would, for example, be difficult to judge the appropriateness of specific patents and their duration without the idea that essentially knowledge is a public, non-rival good and that the marginal costs of making it available to additional users tend to be zero, or at least, relatively modest. Hence, it is true that a good's qualities are social constructs. But at any point in time, a good possesses certain qualities that ought to be taken into account in determining its provision strategies.

7   In fact, PGs with negative utility or costs are often more appropriately called 'public bads'.

8   An extensive literature has emerged on the issue of private provision of PGs, some theoretical, others experimental or empirical. For an overview, refer again to Cornes and Sandler (1996), especially pp. 483–535. In addition, the literature on non-market or government failures has shown that state interventions may sometimes not only be unnecessary but unhelpful to the provision of public goods. For a brief overview of this literature, see, for example, Acocella (1998).

9   See, on this point of making cooperation work, also Axelrod (1984) and Ostrom (1990). Interestingly, it seems that international relations theory has, in general, been more interested in the issue of cooperation incentives than the literature that deals with PGs at the national level. The reason could be that the international relations theory examines cooperation among states, i.e. a case of cooperation, which does not offer the easy recourse to the coercive power of the nation-state that exists for analysts of national PG situations. In addition, as Sen (1969) noted, many studies

of cooperation are much better at explaining why cooperation fails than how it could succeed.

10 For other contributions to the theory of preference revelation and demand for PGs see, for example, Buchanan and Tollison (1984); Buchanan and Tullock (1962), Lindahl (1919, 1967), Wicksell (1896), and Vickrey (1961).

11 For information on the Davos Forum, see World Economic Forum www.weforum.org (accessed 23.04.01); and for information on the United Nations Secretary General's Business Compact, see www.unglobalcompact.org (accessed 23.04.01).

12 An interesting assessment of public policy partnerships is presented in Reinicke *et al.* 2000. As this study shows many partnerships are of a transnational nature, indicating the growing globalization of PGs which we will address in the second part of the present chapter.

13 See, for example: Ree 2000; Sampson and Pronk, 2000; UNDP 2000.

14 In effect, the provision process of public goods has two main dimensions, namely (1) the political process and (2) the production process. Both dimensions are closely interrelated. Yet the PG literature has in most part focused on the first aspect, the political process and how to reach incentive-compatible agreements on cooperation or coordination. Much less attention has been devoted to the second dimension, the production process of PGs. This probably because the production of the goods was often assumed to take on the form of government programmes and services. As we saw, in today's multi-actor world, the production process has become more complex and often poses significant management challenges. This in particular in the case of international PGs to which we will turn in the second part of this chapter. There are calls, nationally and internationally, suggesting to also accord preference to partici-patory production processes. For example, the emphasis often placed on the decentralized implementation of agreements is an indication of that. Yet, for the time being, publicness in production may not be as indispensable a requirement as publicness in decision-making. And therefore, it is not a part of the revised defini-tion. That may have to change one day; and right now, adjustments might have to be made for some select goods for which large population segments have a preference to be more directly involved.

15 For a more detailed discussion on the concept of GPGs and the policy implications see Kaul *et al.* 1999a and 1999b; and for an application of the concept of GPG to various issue areas – such as knowledge, health, peace and security, environment, equity, international trade and financial stability – see the collection of issue case studies in Kaul *et al.* 1999.

16 For more detail on CSO analyses of the international trade regime, see for example, the website of the International Forum on Globalization, www.ifg.org (accessed 23.04.01) or Focus-on-Trade at www.focusweb.org (accessed 11.04.01).

17 On the issue of the social costs of the Asian financial crises and possible policy responses, see among others, Griffith-Jones and Ocampo (1999).

18 This lesson also emerges from the aid literature, especially from studies on the effec-tiveness of conditionality and donor-driven policy change, see for example, Nelson and Eglinton 1993; Crawford 2000.

19 Kaul *et al.* (1999b: 469–73) recommend the design of country externality profiles to guide international cooperation and diplomacy. Such profiles could result from, and be a part of, the domain profiles suggested here.

Bibliography

Acocella, Nicola (1998) *The Foundations of Economic Policy: Values and Techniques*, Cambridge: Cambridge University Press.

Arrow, Kenneth (1951) *Social Choice and Individual Values*, New York: Wiley.

Axelrod, Robert (1984) *The Evolution of Cooperation*, New York: Basic Books.

Bergstrom, T., Blume, L. and Varian, H. (1986) 'On the Private Provision of Public Goods', *Journal of Public Economics*, 29, 1: 25–49.

Birdsall, N. and Lawrence, R.Z. (1999) 'Deep Integration and Trade Agreements: Good for Developing Countries', in I. Kaul, I. Grunberg and M.A. Stern (eds) *Global Public Goods: International Co-operation in the 21st Century*, New York: Oxford University Press.

Buchanan, James M. (1965) 'An Economic Theory of Clubs', *Economica*, 32: 1–14.

Buchanan, James M. and Tollinson, Robert D. (eds) (1984) *The Theory of Public Choice, II*, Ann Arbor, MI: University of Michigan Press.

Buchanan, James M. and Musgrave, Richard A. (1999) *Public Finance and Public Choice: Two Contrasting Visions of the State*, Cambridge, MA: The MIT Press.

Buchanan, James M. and Tullock, Gordon (1962) *The Calculus of Consent: Logical Foundations of Constitutional Democracy*, Ann Arbor, MI: University of Michigan Press.

Clarke, Edward H. (1977) 'Some Aspects of the Demand Revealing Process', *Public Choice*, 29: 37–49.

Coase, Ronald H. (1960) 'The Problem of Social Cost', *Journal of Law and Economics*, 3: 1–44.

Cornes, Richard and Sandler, Todd (1996) *The Theory of Externalities, Public Goods and Club Goods*, 2nd edn, Cambridge: Cambridge University Press.

Crawford, Gordon (2000) *Foreign Aid and Political Reform: A Comparative Analysis of Democracy Assistance and Political Conditionality*, New York: St. Martin's Press.

Demsetz, Harold (1970) 'The Private Production of Public Goods', *Journal of Law and Economics*, 13: 293–306.

Focus-on-Trade (various years) www.focusweb.org (accessed 11.04.01).

Giddens, Anthony and Hutton, Will (2000) 'In Conversation', in Will Hutton and Anthony Giddens (eds) *Global Capitalism*, New York: The New Press, pp. 1–51.

Griffith-Jones, Stephany and Ocampo, José Antonio with Callioux, Jacques (1999) *The Poorest Countries and the Emerging International Financial Architecture*, Stockholm: Almqvist and Wiksell International.

Hardin, Garrett (1968) 'The Tragedy of the Commons', *Science*, 162: 1243–8.

Heal, Geoffrey (1999) 'New Strategies for the Provision of Global Public Goods: Learning from International Environmental Challenges', in Inge Kaul *et al.* (eds) *Global Public Goods: International Co-operation in the 21st Century*, New York: Oxford University Press.

Hirshleifer, Jack (1983) 'From Weakest Link to Best Shot: The Voluntary Provision of Public Goods', *Public Choice*, 41: 371–86.

Hume, David (1739, 1961) *A Treatise on Human Nature*, Garden City, NJ: Dolphin Books.

International Forum on Globalization (various years) www.focusweb.org (accessed 11.04.01).

Kaul, Inge, Grunberg, Isabelle and Stern, Marc A. (eds) (1999) *Global Public Goods; International Cooperation in the 21st Century*, New York: Oxford University Press.

—— (1999a) 'Defining Global Public Goods', in Inge Kaul *et al.* (eds) *Global Public Goods: International Cooperation in the 21st Century*, New York: Oxford University Press, pp. 2–19.

—— (1999b) 'Global Public Goods: Concepts, Policies and Strategies', in Inge Kaul *et al.* (eds) *Global Public Goods; International Cooperation in the 21st Century*, New York: Oxford University Press, pp. 450–508.

Kindleberger, Charles P. (1986) 'International Public Goods without International Government', *American Economic Review*, 76, 1: 1–13.

Lindahl, E. (1919, 1967) 'Just Taxation: A Positive Solution' (English translation of 'Die Gerechtigkeit der Besteuerung') in Richard A. Musgrave, and Alan T. Peacock (eds), *Classics in the Theory of Public Finance*, New York: St. Martin's Press.

Luttwak, Edward (1999) *Turbo-Capitalism: Winners and Losers in the Global Economy*, New York: HarperCollins.

Malkin, Jesse and Wildavsky, Aaron (1991) 'Why the Distinction Between Public and Private Goods Should be Abandoned', *Journal of Theoretical Politics*, 3: 355–78.

Margolis, J. and Guitton, H. (1969) *Public Economics: An Analysis of Public Production and Consumption and their Relations to the Private Sectors: Proceedings of a Conference Held by the International Economic Association*, London: Macmillan.

Mendez, Ruben (1999) 'Peace as a Global Public Good', in Inge Kaul, *et al.* (eds) *Global Public Goods: International Cooperation in the 21st Century*, New York: Oxford University Press, pp. 382–416.

Micklethwait, John and Wooldridge, Adrian (2000) *A Future Perfect. The Challenge and Hidden Promise of Globalization*, New York: Times Books.

Musgrave, Richard A. (1959) *The Theory of Public Finance*, New York: McGraw Hill.

—— (1985) 'A Brief History of Fiscal Doctrine', in Alan J. Auerbach. and Martin Feldstein (eds) *Handbook of Public Economics*, vol. I, North-Holland: Elsevier Science Publishers.

—— (1996) 'Public Finance and Finanzwissenschaft: Traditions Compared', *Finanzarchiv*, 53: 145–93.

Musgrave, R.A.P., Heller, P. and Peterson, G.E. (1970) 'Cost Effectiveness of Alternative Maintenance Schemes', *National Tax Journal*, 23 (5): 140–56.

Musgrave, Richard A., Musgrave, Peggy B. and Bird, Richard M. (1987) *Public Finance in Theory and Practice*, Toronto: McGraw-Hill Ryerson.

Nelson, Joan M. and Eglinton, Stephanie J. (1993) *Global Goals, Contentious Means: Issues of Multiple Aid Conditionality*, Washington, DC: Overseas Development Council.

Olson, Mancur (1965) *The Logic of Collective Action*, Cambridge, MA: Harvard University Press.

Ostrom, Elinor (1990) *Governing the Commons: The Evolution of Institutions for Collective Action*, Cambridge: Cambridge University Press.

Pigou, Arthur C. (1928) *A Study in Public Finance*, London: Macmillan.

Rawls, John (1971, 1999) *A Theory of Justice*, Cambridge, MA: The Belknap Press of Harvard University Press.

Ree, James R. (2000) *Exploring the Gaps. Vital Links between Trade, the Environment, and Culture*, New York: Kumarian Press.

Reinicke, Wolfgang H., Deng, Francis, Witte, Jan Martin and Benner, Thorsten (2000) *Critical Choices: The United Nations, Networks, and the Future of Global Governance*, Ottawa: IDRC.

Runge, Carlisle Ford (1984) 'Institutions and the Free Rider: The Assurance Problem in Collective Action', *The Journal of Politics*, 46: 154–81.

Sachs, Jeffrey (1999) 'Making It Work', *The Economist*, 12 September.

Sampson, Gary and Pronk, Jan (2000) *Trade, the Environment, and the WTO: The Post-Seattle Agenda*, Washington, DC: Overseas Development Council.

Samuelson, Paul (1954) 'The Pure Theory of Public Expenditure', *Review of Economics and Statistics*, 36: 387–9.

Sandler, Todd (1997) *Global Challenges: an Approach to Environmental, Political, and Economic Problems*, Cambridge: Cambridge University Press.

Sen, Amartya K. (1969) 'A Game-Theoretic Analysis of Theories of Collectivism in Allocation', in Tapas Majumdar (ed.) *Growth and Choice*, Oxford: Oxford University Press.

—— (1999) 'Global Justice; Beyond International Equity', in Inge Kaul *et al.* (eds) *Global Public Goods; International Cooperation in the 21st Century*, New York: Oxford University Press, pp. 116–25.

Shmanske, Stephen (1991) *Public Goods, Mixed Goods, and Monopolistic Competition*, College Station, TX: Texas A&M University Press.

Smith, Adam (1776, 1993) *Inquiry into the Nature and Causes of the Wealth of Nations*, New York: Oxford University Press.

Starrett, David A. (1988) *Foundations of Public Economics*, Cambridge: Cambridge University Press.

Stevenson, Glen (1991) *Common Property Economics: A General Theory and Land Use Applications*, Cambridge: Cambridge University Press.

Stiglitz, Joseph E. (1997) *Economics*, 2nd edn, New York: W.W. Norton.

—— (1999) 'Knowledge as a Global Public Good', in Inge Kaul *et al.* (eds) *Global Public Goods; International Cooperation in the 21st Century*, New York: Oxford University Press.

Tiebout, Charles M. (1956) 'A Pure Theory of Local Expenditures', *Journal of Political Economy*, LXIV (October): 416–24.

UNDP (United Nations Development Programme) (1990–2000) *Human Development Report*, New York: Oxford University Press.

—— (2000) *Environment and Trade: A Handbook*, New York: UNDP.

Vickrey, William (1961) 'Counterspeculation, Auctions and Competitive Sealed Bids', *Journal of Finance*, 16, 1: 8–37.

Wicksell, Knut (1896) *Finanztheoretische Untersuchungen*, Jena: Gustav Fischer.

Zacher, Mark W. and Sutton, Brent A. (1996) *Governing Global Networks; International Regimes for Transportation and Communication*, New York: Cambridge University Press.

11 The public good versus private interests and the global financial and monetary system

Geoffrey Underhill

Introduction

The public domain, the commonweal, public interest, public goods, national interest – busybodies through the ages have tried to tell us as individuals what is good for us. Often 'we' resisted, sometimes calling into question the whole notion of a wider collective interest beyond the aggregation of individual preferences. In extreme situations, zealous authorities have compelled individuals to fit, for better or for worse, into predetermined notions of the public good whatever the preferences of individuals. These attempts usually ended in failure after much unpleasantness, the latest example being the collapse of the Soviet Bloc and end of the Cold War. The social engineering capabilities of markets are proving rather more effective instruments of change, as some of the transformations known as 'globalization' would indicate. Yet because of the emphasis of free market advocates on individual choice, the element of compulsion and the differential power of private actors in a market setting often remains obscured.

The controversy surrounding the relationship between the interests of the collectivity and the narrow interests of private individuals or corporate entities keeps coming back across a range of political cultures, whatever the nature of the political regime in place at a given moment. This is delicate ground to tread, the territory of the most vexing but fundamental questions for humankind. Freedom is indeed one of the great causes of all time and, perhaps as a result, is poorly understood by most.

Yet, what better place to start than with the much misunderstood Adam Smith, who so long ago sketched out the problematic relationship between our selfish pursuit of individual interest, in particular private material gain, and the wider interests of 'the publick' as a whole.[1] How can we achieve collectively satisfactory outcomes when most of us are incapable of rising above our own individual pursuits and selfishness?

Public good versus private interests

Somehow in all societies we know a sense of public good emerges, socially constructed through alchemy few of us would claim entirely to understand. This notion of the public good emerges in different forms in different settings, underpinned by often contrasting notions of the public interest, embedded in the complex fabric of the political economy. It is tied up with the ways in which we sustain ourselves and the social structures which correspond to this. As well as with the types of institutions and patterns of authority we establish to this end and to the objective of governance of our wider complexity and with the ideas and contestations, which we employ both to generate and justify these wider patterns of governance.

In his work on political economy, Smith was, of course, most concerned with a concept of the public good which contrasted with the private monopoly privileges and rent-seeking behaviour of the sovereign and his cronies, or others in similar positions of power. Nonetheless, he was acutely aware of the ways in which any class of society (yes, even capitalists) could constitute a clique similar to that of the King and his friends and would exploit its position to protect its narrow interests and thus damage the public good: 'The sneaking arts of underling tradesmen are thus erected into political maxims for the conduct of a great empire. For it is the most underling tradesmen only who make it a rule to employ chiefly their own customers'.[2]

The market *could* be made to work, but the whole problem is how to prevent any powerful constituency from abusing its position to impose a private version of the public good on the rest of us (Skinner 1970: 79–82). In particular, the pursuit of private gain would only under certain conditions be commensurate with the public good: if sufficient competition were maintained to prevent particularistic interests from becoming rent-seeking oligopolies or worse. Preventing the merchant classes from grabbing hold of the public-policy agenda and imposing their own interest to 'widen the market and narrow the competition' (Smith 1937 [1776]: 250) is an ongoing struggle in this global era of ours. Smith's prescience in this regard deserves considerable attention as we consider the nature of the public domain in a global market society fragmented by multiple state jurisdictions.

The argument

This chapter seeks to discuss the case of the global monetary and financial system in relation to the theme of the 'public domain' as developed in this volume. This notion of the public domain as a 'shared space' where government, market, and civil society meet is useful for our understanding of the global monetary and financial order in this era of transnational market integration. The chapter starts with the observation that few elements of governance are more crucial to the public interest, under whatever definition, than a functioning and stable monetary and financial system. While precise definitions of what is 'functioning and stable' may differ over time and may depend on one's perspective or interests, historically, financial and monetary crises are so tied up with calamity in human affairs that it is scarcely worth rehearsing the point (Kindleberger 1982 and 1989; Galbraith 1995). The twentieth century provides sufficient grim examples in this regard, starting from the end of the First World War. Since this element of the political economy is so important, this chapter poses the question: where should we situate the monetary and financial order in relation to the public versus the private? It is argued that the monetary and financial order is so vital that it should be placed firmly in the public domain, especially in the context of democratic political systems.

The transformation of the post-war financial system from a global order segmented on nationally regulated lines, with tight controls on the short-term movements of capital, to a more market-oriented and globally integrated system characterized by a high degree of capital mobility, has involved a corresponding transformation in the notions of the public interest which underpin the operation of the monetary and financial system. These changes are bound to have an impact on any discussion of the public domain in which one might engage. Private market actors and pressures now dominate the making of national economic policies as well as regulatory and supervisory policy in the financial sector. The central purpose of the chapter is therefore to examine *how the process of global financial integration and structural change has affected the changing balance of public authority versus private market power and interests* in relation to public policy-making in the domain of the monetary and financial system.

The principal argument is that the more market-oriented and transnational financial order, which emerged in the past three decades, has crucially altered the nature of public-policy objectives and the way in which the 'public interest' and therefore the objectives of state policies are defined, with a corresponding impact on the way we conceptualize the public good. As regulatory and supervisory tasks have been rendered more complex and competing national jurisdictions are increasingly unable to cope with the transnational nature of market structures, traditional lines of democratic accountability and political legitimacy have been placed in question, relative to the first decades of the post-war period (Underhill 1995, 1997b). Sometimes this incapacity of national governments to formulate economic and social policies in line with the preferences expressed in national democratic processes was an act of state 'self-bondage' to resist the inflationary pressures of the democratic process. Sometimes this was in response to powerful organized coalitions of interests promoting more liberal policies. The monetary and financial order is in danger of being placed beyond the shared space of the public, and into the exclusive domain of private market actors.

The public domain and the monetary and financial system

Smith long ago laid out many of the important parameters of this difficult terrain. If it is idealistic to attempt to determine the precise point at which individual interests and the public interest coincides, we must at least make choices about the outcomes we prefer and the elements of governance which are most likely to get us there. In this sense, the distinction between the public domain and public interest on the one hand, and the legitimate realm of narrow private interests in the market on the other, has never been and can never be unambiguous. A complex mix of private interests can be observed in the making of public policy. One may, at best, conclude that a satisfactory balance of public and particularistic interests is vital to the successful and legitimate functioning of a market economy in a democratic context. Satisfactory to the (rather indeterminate) imperatives of the national political economy in question. The dominance of systems of governance by narrow, market-based private interests can give rise to problems of legitimacy for particular democratic regimes. Given the nature of systemic risk, if financial sectors and regulatory and supervisory processes become unduly dominated by private interests writing the rules for their own convenience and profit, we risk not only the legitimacy deficit but instability and crisis as well.

Historically, financial institutions and market participants (unfortunately for my argument, this sometimes includes governments) have consistently shown themselves incapable of restraint in the face of temptations provided by a rising market in highly risky products, from real property, to derivatives, to LDC (lesser developed countries) debt. The watchful eye of an external and objective authority, which itself does not stand to gain or lose from specific market conditions or transaction has in many circumstances provided the necessary restraint on the herd. Admittedly, the existence of such an agency is in itself no guarantee (supervisors *can* get it wrong). Yet the disastrous consequences of mistakes in the financial sector, for confidence in the monetary system, make such an agency, as representative of the public domain, an imperative. These consequences can include economic collapse or at least deep recession, increased distributional strife and economic hardship, threats to democratic stability, attempts by states to externalize the consequences in ways which negatively affect other national interests, and sometimes war.

So the notion of the public domain and corresponding interpretations of the public good has something to do with the need of political systems for legitimacy in terms of economic opportunity, institutions and modes of governance, and distributional outcome. A workable system can come in many different packages. Most are worked out painfully over time and are under constant revision, and few approach anything one might regard as ideal.

The rise of democracy has significantly shifted the goal posts in a positive fashion. Successful democracy rests on the practical notion that the interests of individual or private entities cannot adequately be provided for in the absence of some definition of a wider community or collective good, and that for this to obtain individuals and associations should participate, however imperfectly, in the definition of this public interest. The outcome, if considered legitimate on a roughly majoritarian principle, is not necessarily to be confused with justice but hopefully is closer to it than the more arbitrary exercise of authority.

But the very imperfection of such arrangements provides a considerable space for leadership and debate on the nature of the public interest and the legitimate extent of the public domain as opposed to private individual or corporate prerogatives. In this space, there is an ongoing danger that the more structurally powerful and politically resourceful are successful at defining and indeed capturing the definition of the public interest through the policy process, even under conditions of democracy. This situation is well know in trade policy, especially where trade protection is concerned.[3] Though states can never separate themselves out from the society and market system in which they are embedded, they can and do struggle (and should probably struggle harder) to provide public-policy frameworks which serve a relatively objective function amidst the morass of competing private claims.

Indeed, some form of political authority has always been present in economic systems based on market principles, and this includes the monetary and financial system. It takes on different forms, ranging from self-regulatory orders based on compromise within the community of firms and their associations, to state-based systems which imagine themselves free of particularistic influence. Basically, if the state does not rig the market, then private interests will, and sometimes do so on perfectly sensible terms under the circumstances. Without the provision of public goods (and indeed much more besides), markets do not function. There can be considerable argument, even among market actors of different types and with correspondingly different interests, about what these public goods and the normative principles or policy objectives behind them should consist. One cannot presume to escape these normative dimensions. Defining the extent of the public domain and the nature of the public interest entails defining *what kind of society we want*.

The monetary and financial order adopted will be central to achieving any goals once defined because it is so fundamental to the way markets operate and to the distributional outcome. Under conditions of transnational integration, the monetary and financial system (and its associated national entities) will be structured largely along the lines of the way in which the provision of credit is created, allocated, and regulated in dominant financial centres, or the 'international organization of credit' as Germain refers to it (Germain 1996: 29). Who has access to credit, how it is regulated, and how stability is maintained will exert a primordial influence on the nature and characteristics of a particular economic system (Underhill 1999). But the policy process and practices which shape the monetary order as the basic infrastructure of the market system are far from neutral.[4] Supervision and regulation of the credit allocation process have costs for the firms in the market and countries in the system, and the costs imposed will vary in relative terms depending on the nature of a firm's business, the scale of its operations, and the extent to which it operates across legal jurisdictions.

Most long-run successful monetary orders have developed a clear sense of the public interest to maintain some version of stability, and this concept of public good is usually institutionalized in a central establishment to ensure systemic stability and risk management. Such an institution, like the Amsterdam Exchange Bank (the Wisselbank) of the seventeenth to eighteenth centuries or contemporary national central banks in dominant financial systems, must have sufficient power in the markets and recognized political authority/legitimacy to provide rules for the market and standards in terms of conduct, to say nothing of lender of last resort/refinancing facilities in the inevitable times of trouble.

The nature of all these provisions varies enormously with respect to the extent of direct state involvement, the level of domestic versus transnational transactions, bank-based versus securities market credit allocation, the relationship of the financial sector to the real economy, and system of corporate governance.[5] What kind of monetary and financial order do we want, and to serve what function/purpose in the larger picture of the ongoing economic development process? These are the questions we should be answering. Is it primarily for the finance of state-initiated projects, from public investments to military adventures? Is it for the achievement of rapid catch-up industrial development? Is it a gigantic inter-generational borrowing scam (as some methods of state pension finance or the expansion of government debt appear to indicate), compromising the future of our children? Is it aimed at providing long-term investment capital for the maintenance of a competitive export-oriented manufacturing sector? What sort of outcome in terms of distribution do we want, as savings and investment will affect growth and productivity prospects and therefore wages and their distribution across the economy?

Much discussion of the global monetary and financial system ignores these basic questions and facts about the way that it is regulated, supervised, and structured. Most accounts assume that the 'public good' is given as a *deus ex machina*. That it is self-evident what the public interest consists of with regards to the monetary and financial domain; reasonable control of inflationary pressures and basic systemic stability. Yet over the course of history and in the contemporary period, we see very different financial systems in existence, each underpinned by contrasting sets of normative values and differing conceptions of the public good or interest. The concepts of basic monetary and financial stability admit of enormous discretion in terms of definition and implementation in constantly changing circumstances, and this discretion is usually exercised in relation to the material interest of those in a position to do so. Furthermore, and more worrisomely, state agencies often lack the expert knowledge of fast-moving market environments which accrues to the market players. Indeed senior management often lacks knowledge of what their dealers are up to and thus the shared expertise. Sadly all this puts state officials in a dependent position.[6]

Monetary and financial order and the public interest

The key question is whether the monetary and financial system should be part of the pubic 'domain' or whether the public good would be better served should it be thought of as a private market affair. However one answers this question, I doubt very much (as per the discussion in section one and the Introduction to this article) that a clear and precise claim to place it purely in the hands of public authorities or those of private market agents can be made. With very few exceptions among the sane, even ardent advocates of market-based monetary and financial governance admit to the need to provide public goods to avert market failure and help in the task of private risk management. Market authorities should insist on adequate levels of disclosure by firms to augment the provision of information, transparency in terms of price information, fraud prevention, and accounting and capital adequacy standards for prudential purposes. At the very least, while no firm enjoys the costs of a regulatory or supervisory burden, most will admit that they wish to know that their arm's length counterparties (perhaps on the other side of the world with the only contact being through a computer network) are sound business partners.[7] Authorities can also help by providing a clear lead in terms of macro-economic policy demonstrating sensitivity to market expectations. These public goods could, of course, be provided in the main by market disciplines in terms of self-regulation, though many would argue that removing such decisions from private hands is more likely to lead to the objective, disinterested fulfilment of these essential policy functions. In short, there is little basis for the argument that monetary and financial system governance should be placed exclusively in the private market domain.

So what of the claim that it be placed in public hands? If one takes this literally, this surely implies a state-owned and planned monetary order organized around the public monopoly provision of intermediary services between savers and investors. To employ understatement, the record of centrally planned systems which did in fact organize themselves on this basis is rather poor. Perhaps they would have worked better had other sectors in the economy been opened to private provision and only the financial and monetary orders subject to public sector control. But I suspect that the queue for those signing up to such a proposal would be rather short. So there is little weight to the argument that the monetary and financial order is exclusively a public prerogative, at least through the mechanisms of state control and monopoly. We might be able to design a cooperative-based or mutual-society-based financial system (credit unions, mutual trusts, building societies), and most national financial systems have some element of this, but these forms of micro-level organization are today coming under increasing pressure.

Most existing national systems have a complex mix of the public and the private at work in terms of both market activity and the exercise of regulatory, supervisory, and monetary policy functions.[8] That these have evolved over time should provide us with a clue to answering the question posed at the outset of this section. The satisfactory functioning of the monetary underpinnings of the political economy is of interest to state, market, and the rest of us alike. In a democracy we are, in fact, all involved in each in one way or another. Because it is shared in this way, it can never be attributed exclusively to any of the three, each of which one might argue is 'private' in its own way, though state policy processes in a democratic context have the best claim to the provision of goods/assets in the public domain and to underwriting of its 'public-ness'.

If this is the case, then when we speak of the monetary and financial system or order, in the overall sense, it is certainly part of the public domain. The public domain and the notion of the public good which stems from it are of interest to all. The fact that we so often tend to see public and private in opposition to each other relates to a conceptual flaw in our common understanding of markets. They are *not* a private domain, if Adam Smith is to be properly understood, but their successful functioning and the precise way in which they function are most imperatively *of interest to the general public* and will be intimately linked to our sense of community, morality, and what it is to be human (Heilbroner 1986: 1–11; Skinner 1970).

Market interactions are one of the important means through which we achieve public-policy goals. State and market should be seen as part of the wider pattern and institutions of governance, state and market as an integrated ensemble of governance, not as a tug-of-war one with the other. Markets can and should be aimed at achieving the public good, not operating counter to it, and must be made to do so in a way appropriate to each historical and socio-political context. We should not identify the public good exclusively with what states do, nor the state exclusively with communitarian interests (especially given the capacity of private groups to appropriate the mantel of public legitimacy). The public good is necessarily bound up with our interests as private and corporate individuals.

To be more specific, the *transactions* of the monetary and financial system are largely private (though with a substantial state element, if for no other reason than that government debt issued by the treasury/central bank is usually the largest single chunk of the debt market). Yet the way the *system* operates as a whole makes it part of that essential infrastructure of the political economy, of such overwhelming value to state, market, and the well-being of civil society, that it must be placed firmly *at the heart of the public domain*. Because this domain is essentially shared, what is needed is not a clear public-private distinction, *but a clear definition of the public good/public interest in relation to the specific policy issues, which touch on the monetary and financial order.* If the monetary and financial system is to be successfully integrated into the public domain, we need to construct a notion of the public good and to develop the means to achieve it in terms of policy. If one values innovation in the markets one should aim at it, if one values stability one should aim for it, if one wishes a mix of these or other normative values, then one should aim for it but be aware of the necessary precariousness of any compromise.

It is these versions of the public good or public interest, and the means to achieve them in the governance of the monetary and financial order, which vary so strikingly from one national political economy to another. To decide what sort of monetary and financial order is desirable (and note the inevitable normative content of the choice), democratic systems must make clear decisions about the functions they wish the system to serve, as discussed in section one. They must furthermore *have the necessary capacity in order to do so* or the monetary and financial order will consistently reside in the captive, private terrain of market actors, not the shared space of the public domain. We should also be mindful that the public good in terms of monetary and financial governance can be defined and achieved in a variety of ways, and that models can only with difficulty, if at all, be transported from one historical context to another.

Thus, there will always be a tension between private market actor preference and the public good in terms of global finance and monetary management. There is likely to be, as a result, an ongoing sharing of responsibility for the system by both markets and state authorities, with substantial input from civil society. But the key point is that in a democracy the imperatives of political legitimacy are likely in the long run, to hold sway. If market liberalization and transnationalization run roughshod over delicate social and political compromises underpinning national political economies, liberal policies are likely to be abandoned.[9] Democratic choice can and should be exercised in the regulatory and supervisory policy processes which shape the system as well as in the domain of macro-economic policy-making. The trouble is that democratic choice seldom comes to bear in the contemporary context. Instead these policy issues are too often viewed as matters exclusively for technocratic competence, thus making a well-rounded definition of the public good difficult.

From Bretton Woods to the new order

One occasion when democracies were able to challenge the historically institutionalized assumptions about the public good, which were at work in the monetary and financial order, was at the Bretton Woods conference in 1944 (Gardner 1981). The failures of the Gold Standard and *laissez-faire*, along with the acknowledged benefits of a more-or-less liberal market system, were held up to scrutiny and fundamental choices were made. The Bretton Woods agreements sought to resolve the tension between pursuit of private gain and the realization of public policy goals in a democratic context, definitively in favour of public control of the monetary and financial order. The aim of the Bretton Woods planners was to 'drive the usurious money lenders from the temple of international finance'.[10] Private financial markets were to be at the service of national economic development and policy goals, not to dominate them, the better to ensure that financial instability never again undermined the political legitimacy of emerging democratic countries or endangered international security as had been the case in the interwar period. Keynes also argued that state control of finance would also facilitate the maintenance of open trading relations.

The Bretton Woods compromise was greatly facilitated by the fact that most of the discussions were bilateral negotiations between the US and the UK. Others who were influential, such as the Canadian delegation, were also among the advanced market economies of their day. Thus the differences among the economies and national interests of the negotiating parties were not as great as they might have been had more, and more diverse, parties been involved.

Much has changed since Bretton Woods. Since then, regulatory change (often state-led), corporate innovation, and the altered environment within which competition takes place dramatically transformed the characteristics of the international monetary and financial system, particularly from the 1970s onwards. We now have a much more global financial system than the nationally based order established in 1944 (Helleiner 1994; Cohen 1998). Developments such as the 'securitization' of banking enhanced the importance of portfolio investment patterns, and the relatively short-term capital flows often associated with the development of such markets.

Impact on public policy

At the present time, there are serious issues of public policy at stake, and therefore these changes have affected the public interest, altering for whom and for what the monetary and financial order operates. In particular, the acceleration of short-term capital mobility has had a considerable impact on the efficacy of domestic monetary policies and exchange rate policies. The impact on government debt management is no less pronounced, and private investor funds have become vulnerable to increased market volatility and risk (though with potentially greater returns). At the same time, the traditional domestic regulatory and supervisory institutions overseeing financial market activities appear ill-adapted to a world of securitized banking markets and cross-border and cross-exchange trading in a growing variety of products.

Many public agencies traditionally served a financial system highly segmented according to specialized function and effectively cordoned by national political boundaries. The reshaping of domestic financial sectors through regulatory reform, corporate innovation, and the transnationalization of markets has left traditional supervisors and regulators caught in a tide of international transactions beyond their effective capacity to monitor.

With national regulatory and supervisory institutions and systems under pressure, it seems rational to expect these agencies to seek to cooperate with their overseas equivalents, in order to increase the effectiveness of their policies and fulfil their respective legal mandates. However, the difficulties of cooperation in an international system of competing state jurisdictions are well known. This makes a cooperative definition of the 'international' public good seriously problematic.

To complicate matters, it seems that state agencies often seek not just effective regulation and supervision, but also to improve market opportunities for national players and to enhance the attractiveness to investors of national financial markets. Thus, the potential for regulatory competition and indeed conflict is considerable. Second, cooperation is rendered problematic due to differences in domestic market structures and types of financial institutions, differences in national regulatory styles and institutional patterns, and different legal and accounting systems all used in defining the domain of the markets. Furthermore, in view of the securitization phenomenon, while cooperation among central bankers goes back to the nineteenth century in some cases, international cooperation among national securities regulators is an altogether recent phenomenon with a few exceptions.

So many governments find themselves under significant external pressure in the making and implementation of monetary, exchange rate, and financial sector policy. Private market pressures and interests now dominate the making of national macro-economic policies, as well as regulatory and supervisory policy in the financial sector.[11] The jurisdictions of governments and their regulatory agencies coincide less and less with the domain of the very markets for which they are responsible. The rapid changes in the global banking and securities markets call into question the established institutional patterns of regulation and supervision in a fundamental way. Effective cooperative management across borders on matters such as systemic risk, investor/depositor protection and compensation, or clearing and settlement has required extensive alteration and mutual recognition of differing national practices. In short, situating the monetary and financial order at the heart of the public domain is increasingly difficult.

Defining the public good in a global context

As this discussion implies, these structural changes in the markets present a series of dilemmas and policy-making difficulties in the context of a democratic system which, one might argue, puts the functioning of the monetary and financial system at a variance with a sensible definition of the public good and due attention to nurturing the public domain. Some of these dilemmas are relatively well known so the discussion will focus on relating them to the changing conceptions of the public good which have accompanied the transformation in the structure of global monetary and financial space, and of the national systems which populate it.

Although states played a central role in the global integration of markets, policies have often borne a close relationship to the preferences of private market actors in dominant financial sectors, raising the spectre of regulatory capture as they spread their 'universal' practices throughout the world. An underlying assumption of the global market integration process was that the steady convergence of national systems would require a steady convergence of regulatory, supervisory, and macro-economic policies. As standards emerged, however, they often did not fit the underlying diversity of national systems, which remained hidden by the emergence of 'global' space. The predicted wholesale convergence did not take place, yet the policies of emerging international regulatory institutions, in terms of either crisis management or supervisory practice, take into account this continuing diversity with understandable difficulty. Global integration is a growing and complex network of linkages among what remain fundamentally different financial systems designed to fulfil different roles in their respective national economies. Different financial systems will respond to uniform policies in different ways.

Policies must be sufficiently adaptable to suit a wide range of situations, and the objective of one policy for one global system, assuming this is ever seriously entertained, should be resisted. The pressures for policy convergence from global markets and from the dominant financial centres can undermine the sense that monetary and financial integration can work to the public good of, in particular, individual emerging market national economies. This new financial system is clearly more volatile than the earlier order, whatever its other merits might be.

If public policy does not accept that for some time there will remain considerable diversity underpinning the integration process, then global financial integration will continue to produce crises which are managed in a way which is inappropriate to many of the national economies in the system. Cooperation may become strained, and may break down over time. Public policy must not operate on the assumption that the global public interest is met in serving only the interests of the dominant financial centres, which certainly sometimes forget the interests of the non-financial and public sector there as well. The governance of the monetary and financial order affects us all and belongs squarely in the public domain.

Change has also come for the corporate sector. Market segments of the wider financial services industry have become less and less distinct as a result of structural and institutional changes at the micro level, particularly ownership structures. Specialization is still an important feature of financial market activities (Garten 1997), especially in company strategies where niche activities remain important, and in the labour market where specialized skills are necessary. Yet large banks and securities houses are now masters of vast financial conglomerates. This renders risk management, in this key ingredient of the public domain, complex and problematic. Regulatory and supervisory challenges in the industry reflect this development, and supervisors must monitor risk across several segments of market activity as well as across national jurisdictional boundaries. So must private sector risk managers, their task is greatly complicated too. The potential for spillover and contagion from one segment to another is commensurately enhanced, a situation which potentially puts the public interest at risk.

A key problem is that many national supervisory and regulatory authorities remain segmented along specialized institutional or federal lines, or both. On the other hand, the UK, for example, has moved to the 'one big regulator' approach, which makes consolidated supervision of conglomerate firms, in particular, more difficult. The counterpart to this development is that regulators and supervisors have sought to reinforce cooperation across jurisdictional and national boundaries, leading to bodies such as the Basle-based 'Joint Forum' of banking, securities, and insurance supervisors. Such cooperation however remains inherently problematic, and certainly proceeds more slowly than the rapid restructuring occurring in industry, and supervisors from different jurisdiction's find that traditional rules and procedures often impede optimal cooperative efforts. Authorities at national and international levels should attempt to accelerate and deepen efforts at cooperation, especially in the domain of supervision and crisis prevention. Yet this cooperation must allow for a diversity of national financial systems and of definitions of the public good.

In this sense, policies should not be developed in the expectation of whole-sale convergence of national systems, nor of the emergence of a uniformly integrated global financial system. Global financial architecture will still need to be differentiated according to where and for whom it is built. Another question should also be confronted, that of the balance between *regulation* aimed at containing the risks taken by firms, and the *supervision* of the practices of firms for safety and soundness.

In recent years, the balance has shifted strongly in favour of a removal of restrictive, 'anti-competitive' regulation developed to contain market excesses and toward (at least where best practice is followed) the strengthening and adaptation of supervision to permit competitive market pressures to act as an instrument of risk management. Public authorities across a range of countries felt it was no longer their task to restrict what firms do in the interest of pruden-tial behaviour by financial institutions, this being left to the market. We should at least reflect on whether this is not overly convenient to the firms themselves, leaving too much public responsibility for safety and soundness in their self-interested private hands. States, after all, took over these responsibilities in the post-depression period after the comprehensive failure of (albeit *seriously* under-developed) market-based and self-regulatory mechanisms.

Private interests and the regulatory policy process

As outlined above, regulatory change and rapidly adapting corporate strategies together have led to a less segmented and more market-oriented financial system than in the earlier post-war period. Tremendous growth in short-term capital flows and portfolio investments in sometimes complex and indeed exotic products have greatly complicated the problems of the international monetary system. States struggle to realize their macro-economic policy aims in monetary and exchange rate policy. Major policy commitments of democratically elected governments have often been thrown into disarray as a result of the aggregate behaviour of global investors.

While this has been known for some time, less well known is the way these developments came about. The regulatory policy process was dominated by the private interests of major firms, which found ready respondents in state and central bank officials who shared their view in many respects. The regulatory policy changes which led to such considerable structural market changes were most often taken in isolation from any systematic consideration of the conse-quences for monetary and exchange rate policies – the evidence is very strong on this point. Regulatory policy change was perceived as necessary in order to enhance the efficiency of financial markets, and decisions were taken in close cooperation with the major players in domestic financial markets, often including foreign players. The difficulties which these structural market changes would present for the realization of important policy commitments of demo-cratic regimes (particularly in emerging market countries, which were often fragile, emerging democracies as well) were given little consideration. There was certainly little consideration of the problems of political legitimacy, which market preferences, in terms of macro policies, might pose for domestic political regimes. If there was simultaneous consideration of regulatory and macro policies, often the surreptitious goal was to de-politicize important aspects of macro-economic policy-making, sometimes enhanced by creating or strengthening an independent central bank. This formula worked as long as stability was ensured, but when adverse investor reactions to perceived policy errors led to crisis and instability, it was discovered that major economic policy issues remained stubbornly political despite the best efforts of technocratic configurations. The policies of international financial institutions reinforced the difficulty in many cases.

In the retreating shadow of the Asian Crisis this dilemma is felt acutely. Nonetheless there is a genuine loss of direction in policy terms. States and their agencies, as well as firms, are still learning about the changed environment. They realize they cannot go back, and that the new market structure greatly circumscribes options. There is considerable questioning in official and even in private circles of the so-called 'Washington consensus', but new approaches to management of the global financial system are still lacking. In this sense, the public good is lacking definition and needs urgently to be clarified by official and private authorities alike. The risk is that, as the crisis fades in the memory of, at least, the dominant financial centres, complacency becomes a palliative for the genuine bewilderment felt.

Furthermore, efforts to enhance global supervisory and regulatory cooperation, crucial for global risk management, have a perverse effect. By reducing risk and transaction costs through the harmonization and coordination of standards, they further accelerate structural changes in the markets, with a commensurate impact on regulatory and supervisory policy dilemmas and on the making of macro-economic policy. In the new market environment, few regulators or supervisors believe that their policies should guide or limit the development of the market. One must ask whether this accelerating pace of change permits adequate time for adjustment and for political systems to cope.

In supervision and risk management, in the new environment, the principal result has been the emergence of 'market-based' approaches to supervision, wherein firms are responsible for risk management through complex mathematical models implemented under the approval of supervisory agencies. The problem becomes, *who* defines the criteria for the regulation and supervision of the markets, and in what consists the public interest?

Crucial information and expertise for the process remains the proprietary domain of firms, which supervisors admit they cannot match. In a highly competitive environment there is also an intense need for firms to remain relatively free, in terms of product innovation and corporate strategy. Level playing field concerns abound. This relative disarmament of public authorities carries with it the very real risk that private market interests increasingly define supervisory criteria. This would mean that this crucial aspect of public policy, the safety and stability of the financial system, is dominated by the preferences of those very private market agents who profit from it most. Public authorities are potentially reduced to crisis management and (costly) lender-of-last-resort functions. The implications for moral hazards in crisis management should not go unnoticed. The mix of public and private is always a problem in any regulatory context, but the marketization of the global financial system brings this dilemma sharply into focus.

An example of this dilemma may have been provided by the recent draft proposals by the Basle Committee, revising the 1988 capital adequacy accord (Basle Committee 1999).[12] Most of the draft is to be welcomed with enthusiasm as it renders more discriminating the blunt instrument of the original 1988 standards. Some attention needed to be paid to the relative risks of different types of assets in banks' portfolios – we all know the difference between a Treasury Bill and a junk bond but there is much in between. It is also to be applauded that interest rate and other types of risks are to be brought under the umbrella. Encouraging high corporate disclosure standards, a responsiveness to financial innovation, and making capital standards more risk sensitive, are all positive developments.

By contrast, one is more sceptical about the proposal that supervisory authorities increase their reliance on market discipline as a tool of the trade. Market disciplines have taken banks into many overly risky ventures in the past, such as the LDC debt crisis to which the original Basle Accord was in part a response. One might also challenge the proposal to make increased use of private rating agencies in supervision. In the developed country markets where information and rating agency expertise is fairly well established this might be fine, but elsewhere healthy scepticism is perhaps in order. We should bear in mind that some experts have argued that the information available, well prior to the Mexican and Asian crises, was sufficient to warn prudent investors that capital inflows should slow down, but little heed was taken of this by industry analysts (see debate in Teunissen 1996). Where were the rating agencies in the months leading to the crises, and what effects did they have on investor expectations? At the least, one can observe that the retreat by investors was far from orderly.

Finally, the proposal to allow 'sophisticated banks' (presumably the discredited Bankers Trust was one of these, along with the bankers to LTCM (long-term capital management) or the underwriters of massive Russian bond issues) to use an internal ratings-based approach should at least give rise to further consideration, as no doubt will be the case in the consultation process set in motion by the Basle Committee. Encouraging sophisticated internal management controls is definitely positive, but increasing *reliance* upon them by *supervisory* authorities is of less merit. There is always a potential conflict of interest in the firm's internal assessment process, with a temptation to stretch standards when the institution is in a tight corner or quite simply making pots of money.[13] The proposals risk putting supervisors at too far a remove from the actual business of supervision, with the potential move to add 'self-supervision' to the already common practice of self-regulation. Much will depend on how this aspect of the proposals is implemented in the final analysis, including the vetting and monitoring of internal control mechanisms by supervisors themselves. But to what extent, once again, should private corporate power be in on defining the public good in this vital policy domain?

National financial reform programmes

The answer in many cases is that with reform of national financial sector regulation, supervision, and the practices of national firms, the better to cope with global integration. Yet the financial systems of most countries are the result of long incubation, and historical differences from one to another remain considerable, as do differences in regulatory and supervisory policy. Despite these differences, the assumed model of most international regulatory or supervisory cooperation is that of an open (transnational) capital market-based financial system. In a number of cases, national and international agencies have advocated policy changes which should, especially following the Asian crisis and subsequent ripple effects, clearly be questioned. Open capital accounts were grafted onto financial systems which historically operated on a closed and 'insider' basis. External pressure usually from creditor governments and international financial agencies to open the capital account was often underpinned by intense lobbying pressure from private interests which wanted access to these markets, as clearly revealed in the case of the WTO financial services agreement process concluded in 1997 (WTO 1998).

The ambitions of governments to appear at the forefront of the liberalization movement and to join the western 'club', as in the Korean drive for OECD membership' resulted in the worst of worlds. Domestic sectors were not reformed but capital accounts opened. This compromise satisfied a range of external interests, and gave local institutions easier access to global markets and foreign currency dealings.[14] It was the path of least political resistance, and this was a crucial factor behind the ensuing global financial instability.

To add to the problem, it was often forgotten that liberalization requires systematic restructuring of regulatory and supervisory processes as well, and this aspect of financial market development has received too little attention in the face of liberalization often undertaken under external pressure (Wyplosz 1999: 184–5). Patience and long-term planning are required if liberalization and transnationalization are to bring positive results. One often forgets that the liberalization of western financial systems took several decades following World War II, and creditor countries appear unwilling to grant emerging market economies the same luxury. Liberalization is likely to become greatly tarnished as a policy goal if it is not implemented cautiously.

Private interests and good governance

Let us once again remind ourselves that the financial services industry within many countries constitutes an ongoing lobby to further liberalize and integrate domestic systems with the global. As mentioned, developed country pressure to change the nature of the financial systems of emerging market economies intensifies this trend. Research has little difficulty in establishing that powerful private interests were the principal interlocutors of official agencies in the development and reform of regulatory and supervisory policy. Of course, one would expect them to be involved but to be balanced by other actors in the policy process. Too often this is not the case. These private interests are simultaneously the object of regulation/supervision *and* chief counsellors in the formulation of official policy. In such a situation, it is increasingly difficult to develop a notion of public interest or public good at the level of national or international regulatory institutions in global markets, at least beyond the obvious and very general goal of preventing a systemic crisis in global finance. There is an ongoing conflict across national financial sectors and among regulators and supervisors concerning the norms and values which should underpin the global financial system. Domestic regulators are still most responsive to their historic practices and to perceived domestic constituencies. They may champion the interests of national firms or valued domestic standards of regulation, thus impairing the effectiveness of cooperation. The objectives of participating domestic agencies are therefore coloured by their closeness to their market constituents in a situation which often approximates 'capture'.

Given the ongoing enhancement of private agency and international institutions in global governance, there is also a need to think systematically about the problem of accountability in democratic political systems. This problem affects the development process as well, at the very least because the problem of financial instability is most acute for vulnerable, emerging market economies undertaking fragile democratization processes at the same time. If we can historically associate stable democracies with the relative absence of conflict and war, the political legitimacy issue needs to be taken more seriously in the policy process.

There is a tendency in a great deal of the economics literature and resulting policy advice generated at the very core of governments and IFIs (international financial institutions) to treat these political realities as unnecessary intrusions into the ideal of governance through market processes. If states and markets are indeed (as I have argued) integrated ensembles of governance, this attitude is a serious obstacle to addressing the problem of 'good governance' in the global political economy. Local norms and cultures cannot be wished away in this regard, especially if democratic choice is to have meaning in any ongoing fashion. Democratic societies will and *should* continue to differ in terms of policy mix and normative preferences.

These points must be taken into account as we build global policies for monetary and financial governance and reflect on the nature of the public good in this regard. Patterns of global governance must permit flexibility and patience as complex historical systems adapt to the pressures of the rapidly changing market. Nowhere is this more important than in terms of global financial regulation, supervision, and monetary management. Given what is expected of political authorities, especially states, when financial crisis strikes, we cannot afford major crises which might be prevented by more cautious policies. The lessons of the 1930s need not be learned over again. That would certainly not serve the public interest under any definition. If we start by conceiving of the monetary and financial order as belonging firmly in the public domain and not the plaything of private agents in the market, the task of global governance in the public interest may be greatly facilitated.

Conclusion

These points should lead us to question the 'bicycle model' of liberal reform and market integration processes. The bicycle analogy (often invoked in relation to trade) compares liberal reform to a bicycle, one must keep peddling forward or one will inevitably fall off. This implies that policy-makers should charge forward, committing their societies and polities to a liberal utopia, so that none of us will fall off the bicycle. Note the implication that bicycles do not even have a reverse gear. If we go fast enough, we may also lose our temptation to jump as well. In this way, dysfunctional political lobbies will not stand in the way of attaining the benefits of liberalization.

One should, however, pause for thought. Avoiding precipitous and ill-thought-out liberalization, in particular in the financial sector of any country in the global system, should lead us to ask the broader questions about the ends of public policy in the domain of global money and finance. In this sense governments have at least partially lost their way. The attempt at broad visions like that of Bretton Woods is long gone in these (fortunately, so far) less traumatic times. We need to ask ourselves in an ongoing fashion, what exactly *is* the public good, the public purpose in this era of global financial integration? There will doubtless be many answers, it is the debate itself that is healthy.

Liberalization efforts in post-war trade took thirty-five years before even manufacturing industry tariffs came down to significantly low levels in developed countries (end of the Tokyo Round). Non-tariff barriers and trade in other sectors of the economy (agriculture, services) still await commensurate liberalization and it will be a long process. The political obstacles to and disputes over trade and subsidy policy liberalization are well known (O'Brien 1997), but the delays have had a seldom-observed positive effect.

All liberalization implies restructuring processes, and if these happen too quickly, international cooperative agreements are likely to break down. The Kennedy Round tariff reductions were soon followed by a protectionist backlash in a number of sectors in developed economies. The long negotiation and adjustment periods, which characterized the GATT/WTO, process helped make liberalization politically and socially acceptable. Societies, for better or worse, became more at home with the market, but it took a while (Milner 1988). Liberalization efforts certainly smacked of political compromise, and there is nothing wrong with that.

The imperfect world of compromise and constraint is the only one we've got, so let's make the best of it. Precipitous liberalization in the financial sector could have rather less than pleasant consequences, which would call into question what has been achieved so far, especially in societies which are not yet politically and socially prepared for the necessary adjustments. Liberalization should be built on firm socio-political foundations, and we should think carefully about what we seek to achieve, or it will collapse. Liberalization is not an end in itself; it is supposed to be a means to a better world. If it fails to satisfy enough of the people enough of the time, then it will (and should) be discarded as a serious option in a democratic context.

So forget the bicycle theory. If liberalization really is as good as advertised, then we had better take it slowly, and be prepared for lots of stops along the way. Let us also accept that liberalization will never be a perfect state of affairs. We are unlikely ever to achieve a perfectly competitive market, or a seamless economic world without barriers to transactions of any kind. I am not sure we would want it. These are, after all, the abstractions of economic theory, not depictions of the world we actually live in. We can always have a better world, but not a best one. The search for the best is not only likely to backfire, but is also a worrisome utopian project.

Perhaps a more fruitful solution lies in a considerable strengthening of democratic institutions of accountability in our national, regional, and global levels of governance, particularly in the economic domain. This is of course easier said than done, and would certainly run into the fierce opposition of transnational corporate interests, which most enjoy the freedoms and profits of the global markets. If efficient institutions are not established, it might also complicate a number of tasks in monetary and financial governance where speed is of the essence, such as crisis management. It is however most unlikely that the powers of the corporate sector would be strengthened as a result of any such opening of the debate. It is equally unlikely that the market and the pursuit of individual private gain would be abandoned either. Some mixed economy system would continue, though the balance might alter.

If only Adam Smith were still around to heap his characteristic scorn on our contemporary hypocrisy in attempts at governance of the political economy. Smith clearly saw the market as situated in the public domain and argued persuasively that it must not be the plaything of 'the dealers'. At the very least, if scholars and policy-makers would read and understand his work and his profound scepticism about vested interests and the market system, we would have a better understanding of the public interest and the public good in a market setting.

Notes

This chapter is adapted from the article 'The Public Good versus Private Interests in the Global Monetary and Financial System', *International and Comparative Corporate Law Journal*, 2/3, 2000. Earlier drafts of this paper were prepared for presentation to the conferences 'Governing the Public Domain beyond the Era of the Washington Consensus?: Redrawing the Line between the Sate and the Market', Robarts Centre for Canadian Studies, York University, 4–6 November 1999, convened by Daniel Drache (Director, Robarts Centre, York University) and Richard Higgott (Director,

Centre for Globalization and Regionalization, University of Warwick), and 'What is to be Done? Global Economic Disorder and Policies for a New Financial Architecture in the Millennium', Universiteit van Amsterdam, 3–5 February 2000, convened by Geoffrey Underhill and Karel van Wolferen. My thanks to discussants and participants in these events for their many helpful comments and criticisms. Generous financial support for this research was provided by Phase Two of the Global Economic Institutions Research Programme of the Economic and Social Research Council of the United Kingdom, grant L120251029.

1 Heilbroner discusses this point in his 'Introduction to *The Theory of Moral Sentiments*', in Heilbroner 1986: 60–2.
2 As cited in ibid., 268.
3 See quotation from/references to Smith, above; also Friman 1990; Underhill 1998.
4 See discussion in Underhill (1998), *passim* and especially pp. 18–25, which looks at a case of transnational interests systematically capturing the policy process to structure the market to their own advantage. Also Underhill 1997c, which develops the point in relation to the financial sector, and Underhill 2000 which puts the case in more theoretical terms.
5 See a useful and extended discussion of the interplay of these variables in Story and Walter 1998: esp. chap. 5.
6 The point about expertise was made consistently in a wide range of interviews with public sector officials. See also Underhill 1997b.
7 This point was corroborated thoroughly during extensive interview research with private and public sector officials alike.
8 Even in the United States, which is often portrayed as a prototypical codified and statute-based system of regulation with strong authority vested in public agencies, front-line regulatory tasks are often performed by self-regulatory organizations such as the stock exchanges or National Association of Securities Dealers.
9 This is argued at length in Underhill 1999: 64–8.
10 Henry Morgenthau, US Treasury Secretary (1944), as quoted in Gardner (1981: 76).
11 My argument is not that private market pressures and the interests of corporate actors were ever absent in the post-war or any other period, but that their role has increased.
12 The draft proposals (Basle Committee 1999) are currently the subject of extensive consultations with the private sector and with authorities outside the Basle Committee G10 membership; see for example IIF 2000a, 2000b.
13 The Wall Street financier Henry Kaufman has raised this issue in articles in the financial press. See as an example Henry Kaufman, 'Too Much on Their Plate', *Financial Times*, 4 February 1999.
14 The role of external pressure is clearly demonstrated in an extensive study of domestic financial reform in Korea and Thailand – see Zhang 1999. External pressures and lobbying interacted with internal political dynamics to render major restructuring and reform unpalatable, but capital account liberalization seemed acceptable. This account was confirmed in my own interview research.

Bibliography

Basle Committee on Banking Supervision (1999) 'A New Capital Adequacy Framework', paper no. 50, Basle: Bank for International Settlements, June.

Cohen, Benjamin J. (1998) *The Geography of Money*, Ithaca, NY: Cornell University Press.

—— (2001) 'Capital Controls: Why do Governments Hesitate?', in Leslie J. Armijo (ed.) *Debating the Global Financial Architecture*, Albany, NY: State University of New York Press.

Coleman, W.D. (1996) *Financial Services, Globalization, and Domestic Policy Change*, London: Macmillan.

Friman, Richard (1990) *Patchwork Protectionism: Textile Trade Policy in the United States, Japan, and West Germany*, Ithaca, NY: Cornell University Press.

Galbraith, John Kenneth (1995) *Money: Whence it Came and Where it Went*, London: Penguin.

Gardner, Richard (1981) *Sterling-Dollar Diplomacy in Current Perspective*, New York: Columbia University Press.

Garten, Helen A. (1997) 'Financial Reform: the United States and the New World Order in International Finance', in Underhill (ed.) *The New World Order in International Finance*, London: Macmillan, pp. 294–312.

Germain, Randall D. (1996) *The International Organization of Credit: States and Global Finance in the Global Economy*, Cambridge: Cambridge University Press.

Heilbroner, Robert (ed.) (1986) *The Essential Adam Smith*, Oxford: Oxford University Press.

Helleiner, Eric (1994) *States and the Re-emergence of Global Finance: from Bretton Woods to the 1990s*, Ithaca, NY: Cornell University Press.

Institute of International Finance (IIF) (2000a) *Report of the Working Group on Capital Adequacy: Response to the Basel Committee on Banking Supervision Regulatory Capital Reform Proposals*, Washington, DC: IIF, March.

—— (2000b) *Report of the Steering Committee on Regulatory Capital*, Washington, DC: IIF, March.

Kindleberger, Charles P. (ed.) (1982) *Financial Crises: Theory, History, and Policy*, Cambridge: Cambridge University Press.

—— (1989) *Manias, Panics, and Crashes: A History of Financial Crises*, 2nd edn, London: Macmillan.

Milner, Helen (1988) *Resisting Protectionism: Global Industries and the Politics of International Trade*, Princeton, NJ: Princeton University Press.

Moran, Michael (1984) *The Politics of Banking*, London: Macmillan.

O'Brien, Robert (1997) *Subsidy Regulation and State Transformation in North America, the GATT, and the EU*, London: Macmillan.

Pauly, Louis W. (1997) *Who Elected the Bankers? Surveillance and Control in the World Economy*, Ithaca, NY: Cornell University Press.

Skinner, Andrew (1970) 'Introduction' to the Penguin edition of Smith, *Wealth of Nations*, London: Penguin, pp. 11–97.

Smith, Adam (1937, 1776) *An Inquiry into the Nature and Causes of the Wealth of Nations*, ed. by Edwin Cannan, New York: The Modern Library.

Story, Jonathan and Walter, Ingo (1998) *The Political Economy of European Financial Integration: the Battle of the Systems*, Manchester: Manchester University Press.

Strange, Susan (1996) *The Retreat of the State*, Cambridge: Cambridge University Press.

—— (1998) *Mad Money*, Manchester: Manchester University Press.

Teunissen, J.J. (ed.) (1996) *Can Currency Crises be Prevented or Better Managed?*, The Hague: Fondad.

Underhill, Geoffrey R.D. (1995) 'Keeping Governments out of Politics: Transnational Securities Markets, Regulatory Co-operation, and Political Legitimacy', *Review of International Studies*, 21, 3, July: 251–78.

—— (ed.) (1997a) *The New World Order in International Finance*, London: Macmillan.

—— (1997b) 'Private Markets and Public Responsibility in a Global System: Conflict and Co-operation in Transnational Banking and Securities Regulation', in Underhill (ed.) *The New World Order in International Finance*, London: Macmillan, pp. 17–49.

—— (1997c) 'Transnationalising the State in Global Financial Markets: Co-operative Regulatory Regimes, Domestic Political Authority, and Conceptual Models of the State', unpublished paper, annual workshops of the European Consortium for Political Research, Bern (Switzerland), 27 February–4 March.

—— (1998) *Industrial Crisis and the Open Economy: Politics, Global Trade and the Textile Industry in the Advanced Economies*, London: Macmillan.

—— (1999) 'Transnational Financial Markets and National Economic Development Models: Global Structures versus Domestic Imperatives', *Economies et Sociétés*, série Monnaie, ME no. 1–2, septembre–octobre (37–68).

—— (2000) 'Conceptualising the Changing Global Order', in R. Stubbs and G. Underhill (eds) *Political Economy and the Changing Global Order*, 2nd edn, Oxford: Oxford University Press, pp. 3–24.

World Trade Organisation (WTO) (1998) General Agreement on Trade in Services, *Results of the Negotiations on Financial Services*, Geneva: WTO, 4 March, including *Fifth Protocol to the General Agreement on Trade in Services*, Geneva: WTO S/L/45, 3 December 1997 and subsequent schedules of specific commitments, WTO document GATS/SC/6–92, 26 February 1998.

Wyplosz, Charles (1999) 'International Financial Instability', in Inge Kaul, Isabelle Grunberg and Marc Stern (eds), *Global Public Goods: International Co-operation in the 21st Century*, New York: Oxford University Press, pp. 152–89.

Zhang, Xiaoke (1999) 'Of Interests and Institutions: The Political Economy of Financial Liberalisation in Korea and Thailand 1980–1996', unpublished Ph.D. thesis, Institute of Social Studies, The Hague.

12 Regionalism

The meso public domain in Latin America and South-East Asia

Amitav Acharya

Introduction

A few decades ago, many countries in the developing world saw collective self-reliance through regional cooperation as an important way of countering Western dominance. Regional autonomy and self-reliance became key norms of regional institutions in Asia, Africa, and Latin America (Acharya 1994, 1999b). But these norms took a back seat with the acceleration of neo-liberal economic globalization (a newer form of Western dominance) in the 1980s and 1990s. Instead of viewing regional institutions to reduce dependency, Third World elites employed them as devices to make their regions more adaptive to, and competitive within, the global economy. Moreover, domestic economic liberalization and transnational coalitions developed around it and became the basis of new regional political and security orders (Solingen 1991, 1998).

Yet, these neo-liberal regional orders also created their own problems of marginalization and repression, and masked powerful seeds of conflict and insecurity, both domestic and inter-state (Mittleman 2000). While offering nominally greater interstate security, they contributed to a narrowing of the regional public space (with regional public-policy issues decided by a small group of like-minded elites themselves constrained by the need to conform to market-friendly policies of the kind implied in the 'Washington consensus'). The economic crises in Asia and Latin America in the 1990s underscored the limitations and dangers of a decade of such market-dictated regional institution building. The important question now is: with faith in global institutions such as the IMF, undermined by the economic crisis of the late 1990s, would regional institutions themselves undergo changes and provide a site for addressing the dangers of globalization.

Post-hegemonic regional order: a critical concept

This chapter argues that pressure to expand the regional public space and accommodate new social forces demanding new public goods is challenging the goals and strategies of regional institutions in important sites of neo-liberalism, such as Asia Pacific and Latin America. The crisis of the so-called 'new regionalism' of the 1990s is also undermining neo-liberal norms (such as 'open region-alism'), and rekindling debates about regional identity that were supposed to have been blurred in the sweep of market-driven approaches to regional order. States, hitherto constrained by the market, now see the need for making region-alism less economistic and more oriented towards social purposes and agendas. Thus, just as the wave of economic liberalization in the developing world reshaped regional institution-building in the 1980s and early 1990s, the coming decade may well see a redefinition of regionalism focusing on its social purpose and a return to the public domain.

In conceptualizing the response of regional institutions in Latin America and Asia Pacific to globalization, I propose the notion of post-hegemonic regional orders. The concept of post-hegemony differs from the more familiar notion of counter-hegemony employed by critical perspectives on globalization. The latter, developed most succinctly by Mittleman, in an important new book on globalization (Mittleman 2000), rightly identifies the dual potential of region-alism to both legitimize and resist neo-liberal globalization. But too much emphasis is placed on the central role of civil society actors, while the continued authority and salience of state-led regional institutions is underesti-mated. The capacity of such regional institutions to adapt to new circumstances that call for a more socially inclusive and democratic approach to managing the regional public domain is also understated. Furthermore, the 'counter-hege-mony' perspective adopts an overly generalized and generous picture of civil society and social movements in confronting neo-liberal regionalism.

The concept of post-hegemonic regional orders that I propose here implies a continued acknowledgement by regional elite and institutions of the salience or even the 'inevitability' of economic globalization and the structural power of the US that underpins it. But it also argues that, for a variety of reasons and in a variety of ways, regional actors may be prompted to redefine and broaden their regional space so as to move it beyond and outside of the framework of hege-monic regionalism. These factors include their lingering aspirations for regional autonomy and identity that is the central political norm of regionalism in the developing world. Other forces that may lead to the development of post-hege-monic regional orders include disillusionment with the benefits of hegemonic orders compared to costs and vulnerabilities, domestic political changes in regional actors, including democratization, and the need to respond to certain types of transnational challenges, which require limits to the neo-liberal paradigm of the hegemon.

A post-hegemonic regional order is thus one in which regionalism, employing norms and traditions developed indigenously through socialization processes, is used to pursue local priorities and identities outside the framework of the hegemonic paradigm, even as the regional actors acknowledge the salience of the latter.

The Gramscian notion of hegemony captures the hegemon's ability to main-tain its authority through a mixture of coercion and consent, with consent being the more important instrument. In contrast, the notion of post-hegemony implies a situation with two overriding features. The first and the less important feature is that the hegemon no longer controls all the resources necessary for coercion without resorting to outright war. It faces growing normative and material constraints on its coercive power, from the interdependence brought about by its self-promoted economic and security framework without risking major damage to its authority and reputation. Efforts to build a post-hegemonic regional order recognize and exploit the limits, whether domestically or externally induced, on US power to coerce a given set of regional actors. Second, in a post-hegemonic regional order, regions, including the regional elite and civil society, or some combination of them, concede, but not necessarily consent to (consenting as understood here is a more positive, pro-active and voluntary gesture than concede), the dominant *material* position of the hegemon in the global economy and security order. But even while remaining dependent on the hegemon's material resources (market access, security umbrella, etc.), regional actors no longer accept or endorse the organizing ideas and the leadership role of the hegemonic power. Instead, regional actors actively pursue regional priorities and identities as defined by local interests and conditions with a long-term view of overcoming or at least minimizing hegemonic controls.

The act of *conceding without consenting* and differentiating between material dependence, on the one hand, and ideational, entrepreneurial and inter-subjective (identity) autonomy, on the other, is the key element that distinguishes the notion of hegemony from that of post-hegemony. This chapter argues that both Latin America and the Asia Pacific, in their search for a regional public domain in the post-crisis period, are moving in the direction of post-hegemonic regional orders. While counter-hegemony, implying total rejection, escape or transcendence from a hegemonic order remains a goal of some of the civil society elements, it is more realistic, to envisage a move towards post-hegemonic, as opposed to counter-hegemonic order.

Structure of the argument

The chapter identifies two areas in which regionalism may be creating greater space for policy debates and formulation outside of the Washington consensus framework and contributing to post-hegemonic regional orders. The first is the resistance by states, often under pressure by their civil societies, to macro-regional institutional frameworks encouraged by the US and geared to US policy preferences, focusing on trade liberalization. The second is the growing incorporation of transnational social issues into the agenda of regionalism, especially human rights and democratization. Although there are a variety of other social issues (environment, migration, drugs) which have crept into the agenda of regionalism, I would like to focus on human rights and democracy, as these most directly reflect the redefinition of regionalism towards a more inclusive public domain. A key argument of this chapter is that the willingness and ability of regional institutions to expand the 'public domain' depends critically on their attitude towards human rights and democracy and their ability to accommodate new social forces.

A larger public domain, at least from the perspective of this chapter, implies an expansion of regionalist tasks to cover promotion of human rights and democracy and of regionalist actors to include greater participation of civil society actors. In Asia for example, the regional public domain has been constricted, until recently, by an elite-dominated institutional framework focusing on the management of a narrow set of interstate problems and promotion of a neo-liberal trade agenda. Issues of human rights and democracy were deemed either marginal or totally excluded from the agenda of regional institutions and there was no space for civil society actors in regional institutions.

Latin America, especially the Southern Common Market (MERCOSUR) Agreement (also known as The Treaty of Asunción), defined a broader regional public domain, not the least because its members were more open in their domestic politics. States with more inclusive and participatory domestic political structures are more likely to create a broader regional public space. This has been a key difference between the two regionalisms. But things could be changing in the wake of the Asian crisis. South-East Asia may be heading towards a broader regional public domain to match that in the Southern Cone, although both still have a long way to go.

A comparative analysis of Eastern Asia and Latin America offers important insights into the dynamic relationship between regionalism and globalization and the scope of the public domain. Despite important differences, the two regions also share a common predicament in many respects. Both regions have been theatres of rapid neo-liberal globalization: East Asia since the 1960s, and Latin America, also a home to NICs (newly industrializing countries) in the 1970s, witnessed a resurgent neo-liberalism following the 'lost decade' of the 1980s. Second, both suffered grievously from the impact of the economic crisis in the late 1990s, a crisis, which exposed the vulnerabilities of globalization. Third, both exist in close proximity to American power; indeed, the US is a member of both regions. As such, American hegemony, including US-led neo-liberal globalization, Washington's push for human rights and democracy and its strategic dominance of the regional balance of power, is a major determinant of regional international relations.

At the same time, both regions feature important contestations between alternative conceptions of regionalism. One led by the US is closely tied to the advancement of its economic and strategic interests and goals, the other espouses more 'indigenous' approaches to problems and thereby seeks a measure of autonomy from US hegemony. This is reflected most starkly in the impact of Washington's push for a Free Trade of the Americas in generating the momentum towards the distinctively sub-regional MERCOSUR grouping in Latin America, and a similar contestation between the neo-liberal APEC (Asia-Pacific Economic Cooperation) and the identity-driven EAEC (East Asia Economic Council) in the case of Eastern Asia.

Globalization and regionalism: a tale of two continents

Most analysts of the 'new regionalism' (Hettne *et al.* 1999) of the 1990s have tended to view it as a by-product or subset of neo-liberal economic globalization. There is considerable truth in this assertion, especially in the context of Latin America and Asia Pacific. The revival of regionalism in Latin America towards the late 1980s and early 1990s followed more than a decade of obsolescence with early post-war frameworks wedded to import substituting industrialization and the pursuit of collective self-reliance. Two general catalysts of this revival deserve particular notice. First, many of these new regionalisms focused on trade liberalization and reflected the domestic economic liberalization programmes undertaken by Latin American states. The economic crisis in Latin America, in the 1980s, had led to a general shift towards economic liberalization. Chile led the way in the late 1970s, joined by Argentina under Alfonsin (in 1988) and especially under Saul Menem, Peru under Fujimori and Venezuela under Carlos Andres Perez. Brazil, targeted by the US under its Super 301 legislation for protectionist barriers in 1988, moved dramatically towards liberalization in the 1990s. Liberalization of investment and an opening of capital accounts accompanied free trade, 'leading to region-wide convergence around freer trade and investment' (ibid.: 39).

Second, the new regionalism in Latin America was 'heavily conditioned' by the policy initiatives of the US (Haggard 1997: 39). Until then, while American hegemonic influence over Latin American regionalism was nothing new in the security sphere, in the economic sphere, Washington had shunned regionalism. Washington's 'conversion' to economic multilateralism (Grugel 1996: 137), spurred by the wave of economic and political liberalization taking place in Latin America in the 1980s, was evident in proposals to extend NAFTA (North American Free Trade Agreement) further south and the Bush Administration's initiative for an Enterprise of the Americas and its Free Trade of the Americas concept. The shift in US policy, in turn, encouraged a (re)-birth of a number of sub-regional groupings, some of which had been dormant since the 1970s. NAFTA, representing 87 per cent of overall hemispheric GDP and 83 per cent of its foreign trade, proved to be the key model of neo-liberal regionalism in Latin America (Petrash 2000: 12).

Sub-regional groups which (re)emerged in the wake of the momentum towards NAFTA included the Central American Common Market, which had foundered in 1960, and the Andean Pact, comprising Peru, Bolivia, Ecuador, Columbia, and Venezuela. The Southern Cone saw the birth of MERCOSUR, in March 1990, with Argentina, Uruguay, Paraguay, and Brazil. Free trade was in full swing (*The Economist*, 24 August 1991: 37), with many of these groups seeking associations with the US. As Gordon Mace and Louis Belanger (1999: 20) pointed out, the new regionalism in the Americas rested on three pillars: (1) US primacy in the inter-American system; (2) an institutional framework for dispute settlement and problem solving that is exclusively American; and (3) a free trade area of the Americas. The Western Hemisphere Idea, argued

Petrash, was essentially restated in the early 1990s under the rubric of the Washington consensus (Petrash 2000: 5).

The Asia Pacific: a study in contrasts

The advent of new regionalism in Asia Pacific bears many parallels with that in Latin America, but also some important differences. The Asia Pacific region did not see the emergence of a region-wide institution like OAS (Organization of American States) in the aftermath of the World War II. While the US took an active role in promoting political and security regionalism (the OAS, the inter-American defence system) in Latin America after World War II, it took a noticeably different approach to Asia Pacific. A number of factors, including deference to British supremacy in South-East Asia, the sheer diversity of the Asia Pacific region, fear of free-riding by Asian allies, and a greater scope for dominating its allies through bilateral arrangements, contributed to the US preference for bilateralism in Asia Pacific security and a similar avoidance of regional economic institutionalization.

As in Latin America, regional cooperation in Asia Pacific manifested through sub-regional arrangements, of which ASEAN (Association of Southeast Asian Nations), formed in 1967, proved to be the most viable. But unlike Latin America, ASEAN took a much more free-market orientation from inception; shunning sub-regional free trade and adopting collective bargaining (over commodity prices, for example) over collective self-reliance linked to import-substituting strategies. But as in the case of Latin America, the impetus for Asia Pacific economic regionalism came from domestic economic liberalization. Following the success of the 'four tigers', South Korea, Taiwan, Hong Kong, and Singapore, and in the wake of the regional economic downturn of the mid 1980s, South-East Asian countries also accelerated domestic economic liberalization. Thus, much like Latin America, there emerged an elite consensus on the virtues of free market and foreign investment in the Asia Pacific. Market-led integration in Asia Pacific increased dramatically in the wake of the Plaza agreement of 1985 that led to a major increase in Japanese investment in South-East Asia.

Moreover, as in the case of Latin America, Asia Pacific also witnessed US 'conversion' to economic regionalism in the early 1990s. The major difference between the two regions was that while ideas and initiatives for hemispheric free trade came directly from the US, the primary movers behind Asia-Pacific Economic Cooperation were middle powers, such as Australia and Japan. Even then, the US, at the Second APEC Summit in Seattle in 1993, seized the initiative and gave a major boost to APEC by convening its first leader's summit, which gave APEC a political character.

While there were differences in the degree to which both regions institutionalized (contrast a highly institutionalized NAFTA with largely informal processes in the Asia Pacific), there is a striking parallel between NAFTA and FTAA (Free Trade Area of the Americas), on the one hand and APEC, on the other. The US saw both as an instrument of leverage against protectionism from the EU. The US made little effort to mask its desire to use APEC as a weapon against the EU at a time of crisis in the Uruguay Round of GATT negotiations. NAFTA (including the threat of its expansion) had been used by the US against the EU in a similar manner.

As in Latin America, the new regionalism in Asia Pacific also produced a shift in the philosophy of existing inward-looking sub-regional organizations. ASEAN was never intended to be a self-reliant trade bloc, but its earlier emphasis on collective bargaining now gave way to a more vigorous effort at trade liberalization. This was undertaken within the framework of 'open region-alism', making it compatible with the neo-liberal agenda of APEC. Even in the security sphere, there was a corresponding shift in ASEAN's security philos-ophy, as well. ASEAN, unlike the OAS during the Cold War, was never a direct tool of US policy, even though it was broadly pro-US. But ASEAN, while avoiding economic self-reliance, had pursued the norm of security autonomy in the security sphere. It had adopted an inward-looking posture which sought to exclude the great powers from having a role in regional order in South-East Asia (based on ZOPFAN (Zone of Peace, Freedom and Neutrality declaration)). ASEAN came to adopt, in the 1990s, a doctrine of cooperative security that would engage all relevant outside powers.

Regionalisms compared

Thus, the rise of the new economic regionalism, in Latin America and Asia Pacific was similarly shaped by domestic liberalization and US policy initiatives. Both reflected the forces of economic globalization, the attendant doctrine of 'open regionalism' and the influence of the so-called 'Washington consensus' (Pizario 1999: 7). But this form of regionalism has not gone unchallenged and these challenges are now creating demands for a redefinition of regionalist goals and identity. Some of these demands were evident before the onset of the regional economic crises, although the latter has aggravated them.

One of the most important indicators of this resistance can be found in issues about institutional structure and design. Some commentators have pointed to 'two principal but opposing models' of regionalism in the Americas: one repre-sented by NAFTA, the other found in the Southern Cone (Gosselin and Therien 1996: 13). The former is characterized by legalistic and formalistic measures 'numerous and detailed regulations that impose strict obligations on the parties concerned' (Gosselin and Therien 1996: 13). These conform strictly to GATT/WTO norms and are indeed more restrictive than the latter in some cases. The latter, is less formal and less restrictive.

Part of the under-institutionalization of the MERCOSUR is the negative image of the Andean Pact, which faltered despite, or perhaps because of, its elaborate integration plan, and excessive bureaucracy. MERCOSUR is a small bureaucracy based in Montevideo with only twenty-six members in 1999 (Patomaki 2000: 21). Incidentally, keeping the bureaucracy small helps state-centrism, as it gives more powers to member governments, while greater institutionalization and having more supranational institution facilitates civil society participation. MERCOSUR's avoidance of legalism in the economic sphere is particularly striking, since it cannot be explained in terms of cultural variables (as in the case of ASEAN) alone. On the contrary, the diplomatic culture and political, economic and social values of Latin America, in which MERCOSUR is rooted, have been described as directly deriving from the European tradition and 'Western Christian culture' (Kacowicz 1998: 103). As Kacowicz (1998: 103) puts it, 'The diplomatic system of South America has developed a culture of legalism imbued with legal norms, including a specifically Spanish American international law and diplomacy.' This in turn has formed part of a 'distinctive regional identity and regional solidarity' (Kacowicz 1998: 103) and has involved a 'strong normative consensus that has been institutionalized in legal instruments', such as the Treaty of Tlatelolco (1967), concerning the Latin American Nuclear Weapon-Free Zone and extensive 'recourse to international law – arbitration of disputes, mediation, bilateral negotiations and other techniques of peaceful settlement of international disputes' (Kacowicz 1998: 102). Thus, the soft legalism of MERCOSUR can best be described as a revolt against US-inspired schemes of regional integration.

The post-hegemonic power squeeze

In the Asia Pacific, the 'ASEAN Way', claimed to have a basis in indigenous political culture drawing upon ASEAN's long-standing habit of organizational minimalism, aversion to legalization, informality and consensual decision-making. It became a tool of resistance to the kind of institutional design, demanded by the US and Australia, which put a premium on rule-based trade liberalization (Acharya 1997). Before agreeing to the APEC idea, ASEAN was nervous about losing its identity and relevance in a US-dominated APEC. It extracted, partly due to its leverage in the security arena in the wake of its successful leadership of the Cambodian peace settlement, a concession from the western powers that APEC's role and norms should remain consistent with the ASEAN Way. ASEAN flatly rejected Australian proposals for an 'Asia-Pacific Economic Community' as the latter smacked of more solid institutionalization. Consistent with the ASEAN Way, APEC developed a form of soft institutionalism on dispute settlement and 'flexible consensus' when it came to deciding the timetable for trade liberalization. To be sure, ASEAN members continued to embrace globalization and remained dependent on the US security umbrella. But the centrality of the ASEAN Way in APEC was far more pronounced than the place of the Latin American Way in the FTA concept.

In a similar vein, Latin American sub-regional groupings have remained wedded to the neo-liberal philosophy. All sought closer ties with NAFTA and expressed enthusiasm for the FTA (Canada-US Free Trade Agreement). But MERCOSUR, which had been established before the EAI/FTA initiatives, with origins reflecting an essentially local political and security dynamic (democratization in Brazil and Argentina and the rapprochement between these two powerful and historic rivals) revealed its greater desire for autonomy from US initiatives.

Led by Brazil, its member countries remained reluctant to join a continental free trade association that is based closely on the NAFTA model. Instead they preferred to maintain and develop existing sub-regional arrangements (Gosselin and Therien 1996: 14). For Brazil, consolidation and expansion of MERCOSUR assumes higher priority than joining a NAFTA-style continental grouping favoured by the US (Argentina's position falls in between that of the US, on the one hand and Brazil, on the other). The Andean Group members also favoured Brazil's position in seeking the prior development of a South American Free Trade Zone. Moreover, MERCOSUR's collective position on the FTAA timetable (consisting of a three-stage time-line for the negotiations) has differed from that of the US, as did its resistance to the US emphasis on market access as the priority area for hemispheric economic cooperation.

Brazil has sought to use MERCOSUR as a vehicle for collective bargaining in the development of the FTAA. As a result, the progress of the hemispheric free trade agenda has been checked (there are of course other reasons for this, not the least because of domestic opposition to free trade in the US, which led to Congress refusing the President a 'fast-track' trade negotiation authority). As a result, in the Santiago Commitment of 1991, the EAI framework of continental neo-liberal regionalism was recognized side-by-side with the sub-regional processes and approaches favoured by Brazil.

Commenting on the future course of regionalism in Latin America, Petrash points to a growing backlash against the Washington consensus and 'reform-skepticism' and the resulting acknowledgement of the need to 'correct the astonishing "social" and institutional deficits of Latin American states-societies' (2000: 23). The kind of remedies being proposed range from social reforms to improved education, health care, and pension schemes, to public sector reforms in the administration of justice, banking supervision and central bank independence. It is not quite clear, as yet, that the agenda of regional groups like MERCOSUR are being reshaped by such demands. Although in South-East Asia, the economic crisis has led ASEAN members (more on a national than regional basis) to focus more attention on social issues, including poverty reduction and social safety nets that had been hitherto neglected.

Reform scepticism

The backlash against the EAI and FTA, on the part of some regional groups and actors, has interesting parallels with what Richard Higgott (1998) has called the 'politics of resentment' within APEC and the ambivalent attitude towards APEC on the part of some Asia Pacific actors, especially Malaysia. Malaysia's call for an East Asian Economic Caucus, in 1990, was partly a reaction to the Australian and American role in the development of the APEC idea. It also suggested a contestation between interest-based and market-driven approaches to regional cooperation and those founded upon a common regional identity. Mahathir has repeatedly called for solidarity among East Asian nations based on common cultural and even racial affinities, criteria that would exclude the western members of APEC. While the EAEC remained moribund in the early 1990s, it received a boost in the wake of the Asian crisis.

Feeding upon the resentment against the US veto of a Japanese proposal to create an Asian Monetary Fund, ASEAN put serious efforts towards developing an East Asian Forum (also known as ASEAN+3, the latter comprising Japan, China and South Korea). Mahathir has made no secret of his view that this was the realization of his EAEC idea, which competes with APEC in debates about defining regional cooperation and identity (Bergsten 2000). The ASEAN+3 framework builds on a cluster of ideas designed to counter future financial shocks, including regional monetary cooperation (although not amounting yet to Japan's abortive proposal for a Asian Monetary Fund) and development of security norms with China.

The challenge to APEC is also reflected in differences over APEC's core purpose and agenda between, on the one hand, the US, which has stressed trade liberalization, and on the other, Japan, which favours development and industrial cooperation. Furthermore, APEC has also become a focal point of contestation over the economic liberalization approach, especially in the wake of the Asian economic crisis. The crisis created new doubts about the benign nature of 'open regionalism' which had been the philosophical basis of APEC. Also being challenged was the uncritical acceptance of increased deregulation and capital mobility, which had been encouraged by the advocates of APEC during its initial years. This has some parallels with the growing reform scepticism in Latin American societies and the recognition by their governments of the need to pay more attention to 'second generation' reforms with a social agenda. These include improvements in education, health care, social security and 'launching of institutional reforms oriented to the recovering of public confidence in such key areas as the administration of justice, personal safety, banking supervision, and central bank's independence' (Petrash 2000: 23).

The Asian economic crisis of 1997–9 has been called by some 'globalization's first major crisis' (Montes 1998: 1). It produced a backlash against globalization even among regimes counted as its ardent champions and further discredited neo-liberal models of regionalism, which were rooted in the pro-globalization policies of states. Mahathir Mohamad, the leader of Malaysia, argued that 'globalization, liberalization and deregulation are ideas which originate in the rich countries ostensibly to enrich the world. But so far the advantages seem to accrue only to the rich'. Referring to the downfall of governments in Indonesia and Thailand, he drew attention to the effects of globalization in undermining democracy, an ironic stance given the distinctly authoritarian turn of Malaysia under his own leadership. As he noted, 'In a globalized world, should there be national governments? We have seen that market forces can change governments. What is the need for national elections if the results have to be approved by the market?' (Mohamad 1998: 12). But Malaysia's views were countered by Singapore, which continues to see globalization as a positive force and an inevitability that can be exploited to one's own advantage, rather than being feared and avoided as a menace to national well-being (Acharya 1999a).

Globalization backlash

In so far as its effects on regionalism were concerned, the crisis dealt a major blow to APEC's unity and credibility. Created at a time of immense optimism and euphoria concerning the region's future, APEC was quick to acknowledge its limitations in dealing with the crisis by endorsing the IMF, a global multilateral body dominated by the US, as the chief trouble-shooter. Criticizing APEC's inaction as the economic crisis unfolded, Gareth Evans, the former Australian Foreign Minister, warned of the 'the serious risk of becoming totally marginalized as an institution, and its achievements of the last nine years squandered.' (*The Straits Times*, 16 November 1998: 11).

Against this backdrop, it is instructive to compare the response of Latin America, in particular MERCOSUR, to the twin crises of the 1990s (the Mexican crisis of 1994 and the Brazilian currency crisis of 1999) and that of the ASEAN members to the Asian financial crisis of 1997. The Peso crisis of 1994 produced an increased level of inter-governmental cooperation among MERCOSUR members, especially Brazil and Argentina. Attention shifted from simple trade liberalization to addressing the impact of global financial and monetary development, although the 'subjective similarity' felt by the two governments in the wake of the Peso crisis was not matched by greater institutionalization. Instead, MERCOSUR maintained it's 'loose regulations and shallow institutionalism' (Hirst 1999: 40). The crisis strengthened the hands of those, led by Brazil, who wanted to give priority to strengthening and expanding MERCOSUR. For instance, it began negotiations with Bolivia, Venezuela and Chile first before full-scale endorsement for the hemispheric trade negotiations under the US-led FTAA initiative. This was seen as a better course than waiting for fresh momentum in the FTAA, which had been undermined by domestic opposition in the US generated by the Mexican crisis, rendering difficult the prospect for Congressional approval of such a deal.

Some big challenges ahead

Both MERCOSUR and ASEAN faced major challenges to their unity and credibility from economic downturns in the closing years of the 1990s. Faced with recession and currency crises (including the devaluation of Brazil's currency in January 1999), MERCOSUR's future looked bleak. Then the leaders decided to 're-launch' the grouping along the lines of a 'mini-Maastricht' with deepening of integration covering such measures as the establishment of common standards of fiscal responsibility ('Becalmed', *The Economist*, 11 December 1999: 34). ASEAN, whose economies were hit by a wave of currency devaluations, beginning with the collapse of the Thai Baht in 1997, also responded by paying much greater attention to cooperation on financial and monetary matters through intra-ASEAN initiatives (such as a regional surveil-lance process), as well as participation in a wider regional framework such as the Manila Framework (Acharya 1999a; Dobson 1999).

In May 2000, ASEAN joined a regional currency swap system among East Asian countries (the ASEAN 10 plus, South Korea, Japan and China) which would permit provision of cash to each other in times of sudden attacks on regional currencies. This enhances regional economic confidence against future currency crises, especially in view of the substantial reserves of Japan and China, and comes free of IMF-like political conditionalities ('Swapping Notes', *The Economist*, 13 May 2000: 76–7). In ASEAN, the economic crisis has also produced a much greater attention to the social costs of globalization. The need to develop 'social safety nets' has become an important part of the agenda not just of national governments, but also of ASEAN itself. But like MERCOSUR, expectations regarding greater institutionalization of ASEAN and developing what its Secretary-General called an 'EU-style' ASEAN cooperation have not gone very far. So far the ASEAN way of soft institutionalism appears to have survived the crisis.

In general, MERCOSUR appears to have responded to the crisis with a much greater commitment to deepening economic cooperation than ASEAN. This is also evident in the political sphere; especially in so far as cooperation on democratization and civil society is concerned.

Democracy, civil society and the regional public domain

The foregoing discussion shows that while no dramatic results have occurred, (sub)-regional action has been seen by key states, both in Eastern Asia and the Southern Cone, as an important corrective to US-led macro-regional frameworks, such as APEC and FTAA. But a more important point of resis-tance to the latter, and a major source of future institutional change, has been the redefinition of the social purpose of regional institutions and demands placed on them for greater attention to transnational issues and greater incor-poration of civil society into the regional public space. This is especially evident in relation to the place of human rights and democracy on the regional agenda.

Despite the apparent similarities, Asia Pacific and Latin American regional institutions remain divergent in so far as the issues of human rights and democratization are concerned. This reflects, to a significant degree, the respective domestic political conditions of their members. In Latin America, the revival of regionalism in the 1990s was precipitated by a wave of democ-ratization. As a result, the new or revived regional institutions fully embraced the promotion of human rights and democracy into their agenda. In East Asia, in contrast, regional institutions have ignored issues concerning human rights and democratization, partly reflecting the continued streak of authoritarianism and excessive deference to the principle of non-interference, although these features are now coming under considerable stress.

To elaborate, the new regionalism in Latin America, as well as the revival and reorientation of old regionalism represented by the OAS, had strong roots in democratization. MERCOSUR would not have happened without democratic transitions in Argentina and Brazil. Similarly, the renewed spirit of hemispheric regionalism in the Americas reflected the new context of cooperation combining the third wave of democratization and a shared commitment to market reforms by the top elite, a sort of inter-American consensus subsumed in the Washington consensus (Petrash 2000: 19). As *The Economist* put it in a commentary on the Enterprise of the Americas, 'Free trade follows free politics' (*The Economist* 1991: 37).

Since then the OAS and sub-regional institutions like MERCOSUR have been active in promoting democracy in the region. The OAS took a historic step towards the promotion of democracy with the adoption in June 1991 of the Santiago 'Commitment to Democracy and the Renewal of the Inter-American System', and the Resolution 1080 on representative democracy. The latter provided for an automatic response to any illegal breakdown of the democratic process in any hemispheric country. Later, these provisions became the basis of the OAS's collective action in Haiti and Peru (Munoz 1993: 29–30). The proliferation of statements on democracy by Latin American institutions has led one writer to argue that 'there now exists a full-fledged inter-American "doctrine" on democratic governance' (Munoz 1993: 30). A strong example of this kind of commitment can be found in OAS's Washington Protocol of December 1992, which calls for the suspension of a member state in which the elected government has been overthrown by a coup. The OAS also set up a Unit for the Promotion of Democracy (UPD) which has played an active role in the monitoring of elections and observance of national reconciliation processes for any states which requests such assistance. The UPD played an important role in verifying elections in Nicaragua in 1996 and the end of the civil war in Suriname. The Andean Group leaders meeting in Caracas in May 1991 backed immediate collective suspension of diplomatic relations with member countries in the event of 'unlawful interruption of the constitutional system' (Munoz 1993: 17).

But the OAS's commitment to democracy has not been entirely consistent with US designs. The idea of democracy and human rights can be an important arena of contestation that could, in turn, set limits to neo-liberal conceptions of democracy. Thus, one of the sources of challenge to the US influence on OAS can be found in differing conceptions of democracy within the Americas. In general, Latin American countries prefer a more centralized authority and strong executive (*vis-à-vis* the checks and balances system), with a more communitarian ethos compared to the heavy emphasis on free elections in the US model. This is similar to the communitarian and the Asian values perspectives of Eastern Asian elites, and to some extent reproduces that clash of identities in the latter (Gosselin and Therien 1996: 7).

Democratization and regional trade blocs

But in Asia Pacific, regionalism, whether old (ASEAN) or new (APEC and ARF (ASEAN Regional Forum)), makes no comparable degree of commitment to democratization and human rights as found in the case of Latin American institutions. A comparison between ASEAN and MERCOSUR make the point. Both groups, at birth, consisted of moderate, centre-oriented regimes. Ideological convergence was crucial to their consolidation. ASEAN was born from a group of pro-western, moderate (opposed to the radical nationalist and communist regimes in rest of South-East Asia) and pro-market regimes. MERCOSUR was also born of a group of like-minded 'centre-oriented' regimes, including centre-left, centre-right and dead centre.

But the pro-democratic orientation of MERCOSUR marked it in sharp contrast to the pro-authoritarian ASEAN. In the case of ASEAN, regional cooperation was seen as a bulwark for authoritarian regimes against the threat of communism, on the one hand and more participatory politics, on the other (Acharya 1992). In the case of MERCOSUR, regionalism 'was sought as a political tool to consolidate broader goals aimed at reversing the dark ages of authoritarianism, intra-regional antagonism, economic crisis and international marginalization' (Hirst 1999: 36).

While ASEAN emphasized intra-regional conflict management and domestic political stability as essential conditions for economic growth, it was noticeably reluctant to adopt democratic credentials. This crucial fact explained ASEAN's subsequent decision to admit Myanmar to its fold, despite the unsavoury reputation of the regime and against protests, not just from the international community, but also from regional civil society. ASEAN countered western demands for sanctions against the repressive military junta in Burma with its policy of 'Constructive Engagement'. Along with Burma, Laos and Vietnam were allowed into the ASEAN fold despite their authoritarian system, in contrast to the policies of MERCOSUR and OAS, which make democracy a condition for membership. In justifying its action, ASEAN invoked the principle of non-interference in the internal affairs of states. But the roots of ASEAN's action can be seen in the context of the premium it placed on economic growth (through domestic liberalization) and performance legitimacy. This was the dominant view of much of the early 1990s, popularized by the 'Asian Values' school, that human rights and democracy could be inimical to economic development. For ASEAN, political stability was crucial to growth, and growth was indispensable to regime legitimacy and survival.

Another area in which the two regionalisms differ concerns the role of civil society. Critics of globalization have acknowledged the potential of regional associations to defend the interests of, and space for civil society elements encroached upon by neo-liberal globalization. To be sure, regional institutions can be used by governments to justify and push for further liberalization of their economies, as in the case of Mexican elite's interest in NAFTA. But as Helge Hveem (2000: 337) shows, in the corporatist and social democratic societies of Scandinavia, Norway and Sweden, regional institutions are seen as an 'optimal' level of governance for regulating global capital in accordance with their domestic values and institutions. The regional level has been used by labour and environmental activists to articulate demands for job security threatened by capital mobility and better protection for the environment from business groups. One example of such action was the so-called 'Eurostrikes' in 1997. Belgian workers in a Renault plant mobilized unions in other EU members to oppose a closure of the plant as a violation of EU's policy which requires that the totality of interests of a corporation's workforce at the regional level must be taken into account. And in the case of NAFTA, while labour groups initially opposed it fearing job losses, environmentalists could endorse it after they won a measure of protection in the agreement.

The emergence of civil society

Latin America and Asia Pacific present important variations in the way civil society actors have been able to rely on regional institutions to advance their goals, including those with respect to human rights and democracy. In Latin America, new social movements emerged in response to the perceived and actual ills of globalization, such as increases in relative and absolute poverty (despite occasional growth periods), de-industrialization (evident in Argentina and Brazil) and environmental devastation (Patomaki 2000: 14). These social movements have tried to organize their resistance at the regional level by seeking to influence the rules and principles of regional institutions such as MERCOSUR, as well as creating trans-regional alliances with NGOs and social movements in the north.

A comparison of civil society participation in regional processes between ASEAN and MERCOSUR will be particularly relevant and instructive here. While MERCOSUR is a group of democratic states, its approach to civil society remains corporatist with social actors defined in terms of market categories, e.g.: business, labour and consumers (Patomaki 2000: 27). MERCOSUR itself has been derided as a creature of 'diplomats and economists', born out of economic motives with little concern for citizen participation (Patomaki 2000: 20), reflecting the 'historical social deficit' of the Latin American state. ASEAN too has been described as a club of elites. Adin Silalahi, the senior Indonesian official responsible for ASEAN matters, laments that '[T]here's still a view that ASEAN matters are only something which concerns officials ... establishing a regional identity in the midst of globalization is also important' (*The Jakarta Post*, 24 July 2000, http://thejakartapost.com, date accessed 26 July 2000).

These similarities between ASEAN and MERCOSUR are especially striking and serve to highlight how emphasis on economic liberalization and a shared commitment to free trade and market enhancing mechanisms has served to restrict the participation of civil society. Even in the case of MERCOSUR, despite it being a union of democracies.

The democratic systems of MERCOSUR members do, however, provide greater space for civil society actors. Some such networks can be found within the labour movement, whose regional orientation predates the establishment of MERCOSUR. Examples include the Worker's Council of the Southern Cone (founded in 1973) and the Southern Cone Syndical Coordinator (1986). The latter, linked to the Inter-American Workers' Organization, was an offshoot of the democratization processes in the region. These labour movements have demanded a 'social dimension' to MERCOSUR since the early 1990s, focusing on the regional context, on technical issues such as social charter and immigration. The Final Declaration of the Trade Union Conference on the Social Dimension of MERCOSUR and the European Union in Montevideo in May 1998 demanded greater democratization in building regional integration schemes. MERCOSUR also has developed institutions, which engage civil society (although the term is never used in official jargon, the standard reference being to 'economic and social sectors') and address social issues.

These organs, together with business representatives, have played a central role in the creation in 1995 of the Economic and Social Consultative Forum (FCES), an official organ of MERCOSUR. Another organ with civil society representation is the Working Subgroup 10, dealing with labour relations, employment and social security (Patomaki 2000: 25–6). Although civil society and social movements remain primarily nationally based, the 'various regional contexts have increased their importance *vis-à-vis* the nation-state' (Patomaki 2000: 28), including Southern Cone, South American, Latin American and Western Hemispheric contexts. Other examples include the Forum of MERCOSUR Women (established in 1995).

Human rights have not been a central issue mobilizing regional action by social movements within MERCOSUR. This could reflect the democratic nature of MERCOSUR itself. But the recent discovery of close cooperation among the internal security agencies of member states Brazil, Argentina, Uruguay, Paraguay and Chile, during the period of military rule (dubbed MERCOSUR of Terror), has led to increased vigilance by human rights groups and regional cooperation among them, although outside of the official organs of MERCOSUR.

Environmental groups have also been left out of MERCOSUR's official institutions and processes. In short, democratization in MERCOSUR has led to the re-emergence and expansion of 'civic public spaces', which are based on rights and which make it possible to organize systematic political activities. This in turn has facilitated the emergence of transnational networks (including sub-regional, hemispheric, and global networks) which are challenging neo-liberal regionalism (see Table 12.1).

Table 12.1 ASEAN and MERCOSUR: a comparison

	ASEAN	MERCOSUR
Domestic economic policy	'The concept of free enterprise is the philosophical basis of ASEAN'	Domestic economic liberalization in the 1990s (Chile before that) creating convergent economic policy
State of economic integration	Limited free trade area by 2002	Customs union
Domestic political structures and pattern of political change	Shared authoritarianism at birth key foundation of ASEAN. Advent of the authoritarian Suharto regime helped build regional consensus on growth and stability. Recent trends towards democratic transitions in Philippines, Thailand, Cambodia and Indonesia; but Burma, Vietnam and Laos remain under authoritarian rule	Democratization in Brazil and Argentina was a key initial impetus of reduction of intra-regional tensions and the birth of MERCOSUR; recent trend towards continued democratic consolidation including prospective member (Peru)
Human rights and democracy	Of no concern, favoured granting membership to authoritarian states; no regional human rights mechanism or provision for election monitoring or assistance	Membership criteria, democratic assistance and regional human rights protection
Civil society participation	Exclusionary and somewhat hostile, except for Track-II (think tank-based) institutions, such as ASEAN-ISIS	A corporatist approach to 'economic and social sectors' through the Economic and Social Consultative Forum (FCES) and Working Subgroup 10

Territorial disputes among members	Malaysia–Philippine dispute over Sabah; Minor Singapore–Malaysia and Malaysia–Indonesia disputes over islands; Spratly's dispute between Malaysia, Philippines, Brunei, Vietnam, China and Taiwan; Thai–Myanmar and Thai–Laos border problems; unresolved maritime boundary disputes	Mostly resolved including Chile–Argentina disputes
Attitude towards the US	US generally seen as guarantor of strategic security against China; but resentment and lack of trust in US role in economic security	Intra-mural differences with Argentina seeking enhanced military ties with the US and interested in NATO association, while Brazil espouses Southern Cone identity and strategic autonomy
Degree of institutionalization	Bureaucratic minimalism and preference for non-legalistic methods from inception; now some degree of institutionalization	More prone to legalistic methods than ASEAN
Political and Security Agenda	Multilateral confidence-building, preventive diplomacy mechanism and intelligence-sharing, bilateral military exercises	Political and security policy coordination
Social Agenda	Post-crisis emphasis on social safety nets, poverty reduction and addressing transnational issues such as environment, refugees and migration	Consumer interests (FCES); labour relations, employment and social security; move towards poverty reduction (Working Subgroup 10)

Social movements and regional trade groupings

Outside of MERCOSUR, civil society groups plan alternative regional frameworks. For example, there is a plan for a Latin American Community of Nations (CLAN), supported by NGOs such as the Latin American Parliament and Latin American Association of Workers (CLAT) to counter the FTAA. Some of these social movements advocate united action between MERCOSUR and Andean Pact members. Such movements would 'resist the hegemonic advances of the FTAA or other integration schemes directed by the United States' and establish a Latin American community that would exclude the US and fight negative aspects of WTO and MAI type instruments (Patomaki 2000: 30–1).

In the case of South-East Asia, NGOs have played no role in the official regionalism of ASEAN. Traditionally, there has been far greater cooperation between ASEAN intelligence agencies than ASEAN social movements. But protests against APEC's free trade agenda, most clearly visible during its Vancouver summit in 1997, and parallel summits organized during the sessions of ASEAN, APEC and ARF suggest the emergence of a civil society regionalism contesting for the regional public space. The high profile campaigns of groups such as the Asia Pacific Conference on East Timor (APCET) and Alternative ASEAN (ALTSEAN), a group mobilizing international opinion against the regime in Burma, as well as anti-logging protests by Thai NGOs, exemplify this type of civil society regionalism. Thailand has been a haven for regional NGOs, with groups such as Forum Asia and the Forum for the Global South, which, along with Malaysia-based Third World Network, have been at the forefront of campaigns to create greater awareness of the dangers of globalization. They have organized protests against the exploitation of labour and environment by multinationals.

Environment has also become another key issue for mobilizing social movements, especially in the wake of the massive forest fires in Indonesia in 1997, which led to widespread ecological and economic damage.

ASEAN's attitude towards human rights, democracy and civil society participation is undergoing a process of change, however. The Asian economic crisis produced greater awareness of the importance of social safety nets and poverty reduction programmes. Although ASEAN did not undertake these tasks on a regional basis, they became part of the regionalist discourse even though action was taken on a national basis. Moreover, the crisis, by bringing down the authoritarian regime in Indonesia, produced a new recognition of human rights and democracy in the regional agenda.

Indeed, democratic transitions and consolidation in key ASEAN members, such as Thailand, the Philippines and Indonesia, have led them to break ranks with the communitarian view of human rights and governance ('society over self'). Thailand, backed by the Philippines, has called for replacing the policy of Constructive Engagement towards authoritarian regimes like Burma. The need to deal effectively with future economic crises, may require more intrusive mutual surveillance of each other economies and financial cooperation, traditionally an area of great national sensitivity. The rising wave of transnational security issues such as drug smuggling, refugees and environmental degradation has led to a more relaxed view of sovereignty and non-interference, best represented in the Thai proposal for a more intrusive policy of 'Flexible Engagement' (Acharya 1999b; 2000a: 150–6). This was a call for greater openness among ASEAN members in dealing with one another.

There is an emerging realization that tackling such transnational issues would require support from the regional civil society. As some ASEAN states become more open, their NGOs have increasingly engaged in regional activism (Acharya 2000b). Thus, ASEAN is undergoing a process of change and could become more like MERCOSUR, although it is still a long way from setting up the regional human rights and democracy-promotion mechanisms found in Latin America. Neither has ASEAN moved to develop a social dimension comparable to MERCOSUR's.

In short, both ASEAN and MERCOSUR have faced the challenge of broadening their respective regional spaces and accommodating the new social forces challenging neo-liberal globalization. But differing circumstances in their origin and motivation have produced divergent, if not entirely, contrasting responses. ASEAN remains somewhat less open than MERCOSUR, partly because its constituent regimes do not share a common commitment to domestic political openness. But democratic transitions in South-East Asia have received a powerful boost in the wake of the Asian crisis, and this could bring about a more inclusive regional organization in terms of a social agenda and more civil society participation.

Conclusion: towards post-hegemonic regional orders

As noted in the introduction, the emergence of new regional orders in the Third World during the 1980s was shaped by the forces of economic liberalization, in both domestic and regional spheres. US hegemony was a major structural force behind such processes. But the economic disasters of the 1990s have prompted a rethink on the strategy of basing regional cooperation and order building exclusively on the virtues of the free market. The economic crises in Asia Pacific and Latin America and attendant intra- and inter-state conflicts have shown that a convergence of views based on market-driven growth is not a sufficient basis for durable regional orders.

The chapter highlights how the so-called Washington consensus, a set of organizing ideas for many of the so-called 'new regionalisms', in the last decade of the twentieth century, has actually served as a focal point of contestation in regions grappling with the new political, economic and strategies realities of the globalization era. Future regional orders, and the provision of collective goods through regional institutions, will be shaped by the outcome of this contestation, which is being played out both intra-regionally and inter-regionally. In this process, the chapter highlights the dual potential of regionalism to serve as an instrument of hegemony and as a platform for post-hegemonic orders.

Regional institutions in the Asia Pacific and Latin America remain tied to the forces of globalization and US hegemony. While questioning the paradigm of neo-liberal regionalism to some extent, they have not proven to be altogether effective in addressing its social costs and consequences. Lack of material resources and lingering inter-state and state-civil society conflicts within regions prevent the emergence of a full-fledged commitment to counter-hegemony. But the contest between macro-regionalism and sub-regionalism in Latin America and Asia Pacific, for example, shows that concerns about regional public goods and public domain are challenging the hitherto dominance of neo-liberal macro-regionalism in the realm of ideas and institutional entrepreneurship.

In both ASEAN and MERCOSUR, states hitherto constrained by the 'Washington consensus' may be rethinking their strategies as to how regionalism could be used to address public-policy issues arising from the economic downturn.

Even before the recent economic downturns, both ASEAN and MERCOSUR (the latter despite its supposedly more legalistic Latin culture) had rejected NAFTA-style institutionalization, an important sign of protest against neo-liberal regionalism. But this in itself did not amount to a broadening of the regional public domain. In the key areas of human rights and democracy, ASEAN offered a more restricted regional public space than MERCOSUR, largely because of differences in the domestic political openness of their respective members. But increasing democratization and a new wave of transnational challenges in South-East Asia could now move ASEAN significantly in the direction of greater regional openness.

Now, in the wake of the crisis, ASEAN has taken some steps to take a more flexible approach in managing regional human rights (instead of rejecting them outright by citing its non-interference doctrine) and by being more accommodating to the demands of its civil society elements. This brings ASEAN closer to the path MERCOSUR had already taken. These developments are conducive to the search for a broader regional public domain in South-East Asia and the Southern Cone.

Bibliography

Acharya, Amitav (1992) 'Regionalism and Regime Security in the Third World: Comparing the Origins of the ASEAN and the GCC', in Brian L. Job (ed.) *The (In)security Dilemma: National Security of Third World States*, Boulder, COLO: Lynne Rienner, pp. 143–64.

——Acharya, Amitav (1994) 'Regional Approaches to Security in the Third World: Lessons and Prospects', in Larry A. Swatuk and Timothy M. Shaw (eds) *The South at the End of the Twentieth Century*, London: Macmillan, pp. 79–94.

—— (1997) 'Ideas, Identity and Institution-Building: From the ASEAN Way to the Asia Pacific Way?', *Pacific Review*, 10, 2: 319–46.

—— (1999a) 'Realism, Institutionalism and the Asian Economic Crisis', *Contemporary Southeast Asia*, 21, 1 (April): 1–29.

—— (1999b) 'Regionalism and the Emerging (Intrusive) World Order: Sovereignty, Autonomy, Identity', Paper Prepared for the Conference on 'After the Global Crisis: What Next for Regionalism?', Centre for the Study of Globalization and Regionalization, The University of Warwick, 16–18 September.

—— (2000a) *Constructing a Security Community in Southeast Asia: ASEAN and the Problem of Regional Order*, London/New York: Routledge.

—— (2000b) 'Human Security in the Asia Pacific: Puzzle, Panacea or Peril', Bhubaneswar: Centre for Peace and Development Studies (text can be found on http://www.cpdsindia.org – accessed 11.04.01).

Asher, Mukul G. (2000) 'Reforming Social Safety Nets in East Asia: Essential for Sustained Growth', Bhubaneswar, India: Centre for Peace and Development Studies, text can be found on www.cpdsindia.org (accessed 11.04.01).

Bergsten, C. Fred (2000) 'The New Asian Challenge', Working Paper 00–4, Washington, DC: Institute for International Economics, March.

Cox, Robert (1987) *Production, Power, and World Order*, New York: Columbia University Press.

Crone, Donald (1993) 'Does Hegemony Matter? The Reorganization of the Pacific Political Economy', *World Politics*, 45, 4 (July): 501–25.

Dobson, Wendy (2000) 'The AMF and its Alternatives.' Unpublished paper University of Toronto: Centre for International Business.

Gosselin, Guy and Therien, Jean-Philippe (1996) 'The OAS and Inter-American Regionalism', Paper presented to the 37 Annual Convention of the International Studies Association, San Diego, 16–20 April.

Grugel, Jean (1996) 'Latin America and the Remaking of the Americas', in Andrew Gamble and Anthony Payne, *Regionalism and World Order*, New York: St Martin's Press.

Haggard, Stephen (1997) 'Regionalism in Asia and the Americas' in Edward D. Mansfield and Helen Milner (eds), *The Political Economy of Regionalism*, New York: Columbia University Press.

Hettne, Bjorn, Inotai, Andras and Sunkel, Osvaldo (eds) (1999) *Globalism and the New Regionalism*, London: Macmillan.

Higgott, Richard (1998) 'The Asian Economic Crisis: A Study in the Politics of Resentment', CSGR Working Paper No. 02/98 Centre for the Study of Globalization and Regionalization: The University of Warwick, March.

Hirst, Monica (1999) 'MERCOSUR's Complex Political Agenda', in Riordan Roett (ed.) *MERCOSUR: Regional Integration, World Markets*, Boulder, COLO: Lynne Rienner, pp. 35–47.

Hveem, Helge (2000) 'Explaining the Regional Phenomenon in an Era of Globalization', in Richard Stubbs and Jeoffrey R.D. Underhill (eds) *Political Economy and the Changing Global Order*, 2nd edn, Don Mills, Ontario: New York: Oxford University Press, pp. 329–40.

Kacowicz, Arie M. (1998) *Zones of Peace in the Third World: South America and West Africa in Comparative Perspective*, Albany, NY: State University of New York Press.

Katzenstein, Peter (1997) 'Asian Regionalism in Comprative Perspective', in Peter Katzenstein and Takashi Shiraishi (eds) *Network Power: Japan and Asia*, Ithaca, NY: Cornell University Press, pp. 1–44.

Keohane, Robert O. (1984) *After Hegemony: Cooperation and Discord in the World Political Economy*, Princeton, NJ: Princeton University Press.

Mace, Gordon and Belanger, Louis (1999) 'The Structural Contexts of Hemispheric Regionalism: Power, Trade, Political Culture, and Economic Development', in Gordon Mace, Louis Belanger, and Contributors, *The Americas in Transition: The Contours of Regionalism*, Boulder, COLO: Lynne Rienner.

Mittleman, James H. (2000) *The Globalization Syndrome: Transformation and Resistance*, Princeton, NJ: Princeton University Press.

Mohamad, Mahathir (1998) Text of Speech at the Fifth Symposium of the Institute for International Monetary Affairs, Tokyo Japan, reproduced in the *New Straits Times*, 4 June.

Montes, Manuel F. (1998) 'Globalization and Capital Market Development in Southeast Asia', Paper Presented to the ISEAS 30th Anniversary Conference on 'Southeast Asia in the 21st century: Challenges of Globalization', Singapore, Institute of Southeast Asian Studies, 30 July–1 August.

Munoz, Heraldo (1993) 'The OAS and Democratic Governance', *Journal of Democracy*, 4, 3: 29–38.

Patomaki, Heikki (2000) 'Critical Responses to Globalisation in the MERCOSUR Region: Emergent Possibilities for Democratic Politics?', NIGD Working Paper 1, Helsinki: Network Institute for Global Democratization.

Petrash, Vilma E. (2000) 'Towards 2005: Consistencies and Inconsistencies of the FTAA Process in the Face of Challenges to the Liberal Democratic Governance Consensus in the Americas', Paper Presented to the International Studies Association Annual Convention, 15–18 March 2000.

Pizario, Ramiro (1999) 'A Comparative Analysis of Latin America and South-East Asia Regionalism', Seminar Thesis, Sydney: Department of Government, University of Sydney.

Solingen, Etel (1991) 'The Business of the American Hemisphere', *The Economist*, 24 August: 37.

—— (1998) *Regional Orders at the Century's Dawn*, Princeton, NJ: Princeton University Press.

Section 5

New sites of policy contest

13 Global markets and social legitimacy

The case of the 'global compact'

Georg Kell and John Ruggie

Introduction

The international economic order constructed by the West after World War II reflected a highly advantageous configuration of factors that produced a generation of sustained economic expansion. The world distribution of economic power favoured an open and non-discriminatory approach to organizing international economic relations. There was broad ideological consensus regarding the role of the state in ensuring domestic employment, price stability and social safety nets. A commensurate body of economic analysis and policy prescriptions existed that enabled the state to act on these preferences. The major corporate actors were national in scope and international economic relations largely comprised arms-length transactions among separate and distinct national economies. As a result, point-of-entry barriers to economic transactions constituted meaningful tools of economic policy. The prevailing form of nationalism was the civic not ethnic kind, which facilitated international economic cooperation and, in the case of western Europe, the process of supranational integration. A set of international organizations was put in place that expressed and supported the post-war compromise of embedded liberalism, as it has been called (Ruggie 1982), most importantly the Bretton Woods institutions, the GATT and the United Nations.

Much has changed in the past half century to erode the efficacy of this set of understandings and arrangements. However, no factor has been as consequential as the expanding and intensifying process of globalization (Ruggie 1996). At bottom, globalization has increasingly disconnected one single element – networks of production and finance – from what had been an overall system of institutional relations, and sent it off on its own spatial and temporal trajectory. This has produced two disequilibria in the world political economy, which will persist unless and until the strictly economic sphere is embedded once more in broader frameworks of shared values and institutionalized practices.

The first is between the strictly economic sphere, and the broader frameworks of shared values and practices within which the economic sphere has been embedded at the national level. The second imbalance is in international governance structures. There *has* been a significant expansion of global economic rule-making over the past decade. But it has been aimed largely at creating the institutional bases for the functioning of global markets. The rights of global corporate actors have been secured, for example, and considerable efforts have gone into the creation of corresponding rules for the global trading regime – such as TRIPS (Agreement on Trade-Related Aspects of Intellectual Property Rights) and TRIMS (Agreement on Trade-Related Investment Measures). These rules have been codified and means provided for their enforcement. But these expressions of rule-making have *not* been matched by comparable efforts on behalf of other global concerns, such as the environment, human rights or poverty or for that matter food safety and international cartels. In fact, in some instances, previous commitments in these areas have been weakened – e.g. ODA (Official Development Assistance).[1]

The major capitalist countries have the domestic and institutional capacity to protect themselves from the worst negative effects of this imbalance. But the rest of the world is far more vulnerable, and this vulnerability has been exacerbated by the neo-liberal orthodoxies – the so-called Washington consensus. Large parts of Africa have become economically marginalized. Our reading of history suggests that imbalances of this sort are not long sustainable. Indeed, the embedded liberalism compromise itself was an innovative response to precisely these kinds of imbalances at the *national* level, which had caused the system to blow up in the 1930s.

A key challenge for the international community, therefore, is to devise for the *global* economy the kind of institutional equilibrium that existed in the post-war inter*national* economic order. Calls for a new Bretton Woods or for a new economic architecture reflect this quest, although they show little sign of significant progress. We focus here on the longer-term interplay between two sets of key actors in the global economy, transnational corporations (TNCs) and transnational non-government organizations (NGOs), and we do so from the institutional venue of the United Nations.[2]

Civil society actors are increasingly targeting TNCs and the trading system as leverage by means of which to pursue broader social and environmental concerns. We contend that this dynamic interplay provides great potential for attempts to bridge the imbalance between economic globalization and the governance structures that it has left behind.

One modest instance of this claim is the Global Compact, initiated by United Nations Secretary-General Kofi Annan at the Davos World Economic Forum in January 1999, challenging the international business community to help the United Nations implement universal values in the areas of human rights, environment and labour.[3] The initiative has been well received by the corporate community and, at minimum, gives added momentum to the growing recognition that markets require shared values and institutionalized practices if they are to survive and thrive. In this chapter, we first describe briefly the component parts of the global compact; we then offer an account of its positive reception; and finally we draw some conclusions from the case.

The global compact

The Global Compact challenges individual corporations and representative business associations to demonstrate good global corporate citizenship by embracing nine principles in the areas of environment, labour and human rights, and by advocating for stronger United Nations organizations in those and related areas. The nine principles are derived from the Universal Declaration of Human Rights (UDHR), the Rio Declaration of the United Nations Conference of Environment and Development (UNCED) held in 1992, and the four fundamental principles and rights at work adopted at the World Economic and Social Summit (WESS) in Copenhagen in 1997 and reaffirmed by the International Labour Organization (ILO) in 1999. The areas and principles chosen are those that are most relevant at the corporate level *and* at the global rule-making level, while at the same time rooted in solid international commitments and even treaty obligations. The ILO, OHCHR (Office of the High Commission for Human Rights) and UNEP (United Nations Environmental Programme) are partner agencies within the UN itself.

The Compact is pitched at both the micro- and the macro-level. While recognizing that governments have the main responsibility for implementing universal values, a novel feature of the Compact is that corporations are asked to embrace these values directly, in their own sphere of operation. Specifically, they are asked to incorporate them into their mission statements and to translate them into concrete corporate management practices. A key tool to facilitate the adoption, implementation and dissemination of these commitments is a website (www.un.org/partners/business/globcomp.htm), constructed with the help of corporations, business associations, the partner agencies and NGOs. The website showcases good corporate practices and eventually best practices and it features commentaries by NGOs.

The Global Compact is not designed as a code of conduct. Instead, it is meant to serve as a framework of reference and dialogue to stimulate best practices and to bring about convergence in corporate practices around universally shared values. Of course, it is possible for the Compact to evolve into an instrument of greater precision if and as conditions warrant.

Challenging TNCs, in particular, to become good corporate citizens that accept responsibility commensurate with the power and rights they enjoy ensures that corporations from developing countries are not punished for lacking the capacity to behave in the same way (Bhagwati 1998). At the macro-level, or the level of global rule-making, the Global Compact tries to enlist the business community in an advocacy role on behalf of the UN. At the global rule-making level, a significantly strengthened United Nations, in terms of authority and resources, would fill an important governance gap. One that has been the source of tension and has threatened to undermine multilateralism, as was witnessed at the Third Ministerial Meeting of the World Trade Organization in December 1999. A United Nations capable of effectively addressing environmental, labour and human rights concerns, in short, would also help ensure a sustained commitment to the global trade regime.

There are positive indications that the international business community is responding to the challenge. The International Chamber of Commerce (ICC), on 5 July 1999, adopted a statement arguing for a stronger UN as the most sensible way forward. The ICC also pledged to work with UN agencies to implement the Global Compact at the corporate level.[4] Individual corporations have lent their support and have assisted in the construction of the website, as have leading NGOs in the areas covered by the Compact.

If the Global Compact were to succeed, it would have accomplished two things. The United Nations would have enlisted the corporate sector to help close the gap between the strictly economic sphere and the broader social agendas that exists at the global level today, which the corporate sector itself created. The UN would also have gained corporate backing for a more robust UN role in human rights, environment and labour standards, thereby responding to the imbalance in global governance structures mentioned above.

On the side of the business community, success will depend in no small measure on the capacity of global business associations to mobilize sufficient advocacy support for strengthening global governance structures in the environment, development, human rights and labour. Only business associations can circumvent the collective action problems faced by individual firms. In the absence of aggregate corporate representation, collective responsibilities can neither be formulated nor implemented. The international community should have a keen interest in promoting representative business associations.

At the corporate level, the question is whether a sufficient critical number of moral first movers will articulate a commitment to embrace social responsibilities, and whether they have the power to establish dominant industry-wide corporate social purposes. A closely related question is whether TNCs will continue to respond to multiple pressures on an *ad hoc* basis or whether their response will converge around universal values. The plethora of voluntary initiatives and codes, including labelling schemes, that have emerged over the past years at the corporate, sectoral and national level have several shortcomings. They are selective in content due to the absence of uniform definitions; many lack transparency and provide for inadequate representation of their supposed beneficiaries; and it is not clear to whom they are accountable.[5] As these shortcomings become apparent, pressure for arrangements based on more stable global platforms may increase.

The answers to these questions have a great deal to do with how the dynamic tension that exists today between TNCs and NGOs is played out. We turn now to that subject.

The dynamics of change

The relationship between market and society at the global level is slowly being reshaped. The main protagonists are TNCs, and NGOs and the struggle involves two complementary sets of concerns. First, it is a struggle over prevailing social expectations about the role of corporations, especially large

TNCs: is the business of business merely business, or is it something more? Second, it is a struggle over the global trade regime, specifically the extent to which it should accommodate a variety of social agendas. Human rights, labour standards and the environment feature prominently in both instances. Let us take a brief look at the two sets of actors and the issues at stake.

The rise of TNCs in the wake of lower barriers to trade and investment has been widely documented. Foreign direct investment (FDI) flows have steadily increased over the past decades, both in absolute terms and in relation to trade and output. The activities of TNCs have also become more truly transnational as the share of employment, turnover and profit, generated in foreign markets, has grown.[6] At the same time, TNC strategies to take advantage of broadened market access have generated new approaches to integrated manufacturing networks and marketing strategies that put a premium on global image and branding.

The role of NGOs in the international arena has only recently attracted serious attention and is not yet well understood. NGOs have long been active in international affairs, including at the United Nations (Kane 1998). However, in recent years their impact has significantly expanded. With the award of the 1997 Nobel Peace Prize to the International Campaign to Ban Landmines came widespread acknowledgement of their growing political influence. Their subsequent role in bringing to a halt the OECD sponsored negotiations on a Multilateral Agreement on Investment (MAI) was further evidence of their powers of persuasion (Henderson 1999).

The effectiveness of NGOs has much to do with their ability to use the Internet to tap into broader social movements and gain media attention. Relying on hi-tech, low-cost means of grass-roots advocacy around single issues, they have demonstrated the effectiveness of decentralized and flexible structures combined with non-formalized communication and decision making.[7] Some NGOs have transnationalized their structures, in a manner comparable to TNCs.[8]

Corporate social responsibility

The changing relationship between society and the corporate community is illustrated by prevailing expectations about corporate social responsibility (CSR) (Friedman 1984; Donaldson and Dunfee 1994).[9] While the use of stakeholder pressure to influence the behaviour of corporations is as old as business itself, the meaning of CSR has changed dramatically over the past decade. As recently as 1990, the interaction between business and society remained largely confined to local or national scenes, and the conventional view that the major responsibility of business is to produce goods and services and to sell them for a profit was not seriously questioned.

As liberalization has expanded business opportunities and generated global corporate networks, the bargaining balance in many societies has shifted in favour of the private sector, and in developing countries particularly to TNCs.[10]

But this shift, in turn, has provoked attempts by civil society actors and others to orchestrate counter-measures. Unlike the static responses triggered by the first wave of significant transnationalization in the early 1970s however, today's countervailing movements have focused on the social responsibility of corporations, and on ways to alter corporate behaviour through public exposure. Effective use of communications technology and the willingness of the international media to carry stories about corporate misdeeds have greatly increased public focus on corporations.[11]

The interaction between NGOs and TNCs around the issue of CSR is highly dynamic and evolving rapidly.[12] But two distinct approaches are taking shape (Sethi 1994b). At one end of the spectrum, numerous NGOs continue to pursue confrontational approaches, applying a wide range of campaign tools such as provocation, consumer boycotts, litigation and direct protest (Cramb 1999). At the other end, a growing number of NGOs including the most transnational, such as Amnesty International, Human Rights Watch, WWF and others, have entered strategic partnerships with TNCs, recognizing that corporate change leaders can become effective role models or advocates for broader societal concerns.

These partnerships are in an early stage of development, and a neutral broker such as a government agency or business NGO often sponsors them.[13] Some TNCs are developing 'stakeholder policies', thus trying to cope with the increasing influence and business-orientation of NGOs. These novel forms of business-NGO dialogue have already brought about significant changes in selected areas, especially corporate environmental practices. It remains to be seen whether these experiments will evolve into lasting structures for bridging social and business interests.

Corporations, on the other hand, have had to learn that globalization strategies, particularly global branding, have created not only new opportunities but also vulnerabilities (Wild 1998).[14] Protecting image and brand names quickly evolved as a major challenge that had to be met if globalization strategies were to succeed.

The need to protect the corporate image has fostered an array of corporate responses, ranging from private sector initiatives at the firm and industry level, to private/public partnership approaches, as well as a renewed interest in regional and international sectoral initiatives (ILO 1999a). Depending on their vulnerability towards public scrutiny, together with the environment and the degree of exposure in which they operate, a few TNCs have publicly broken rank with conventional views and embraced concerns for human rights, the environment and labour in their mission statements, management practices and annual reporting (Cramb and Corzine 1998).[15]

Transnationals are subject not only to external pressure but also to internal needs. Many have begun to confront the challenge of how to integrate, into one global corporate culture, the increasing number of diverse national cultures of their officers and employees. Success or failure can have a direct impact on the bottom line. The corporate interest in business ethics and good citizenship is, in part, a reflection of this concern. In essence, corporations that take transnationalization seriously, in corporate staffing and governance, have slowly moved toward the articulation of ever-broader sets of values. Values which are not otherwise essential to their contracting or market functioning, but are an attempt to define the cultural bonds that hold the company together (The Conference Board 1999; Environics International Ltd *et al.* 1999).

The corporate propensity to respond to civil society concerns and the degree to which these responses are internalized in corporate practices also depends on their market power. Only under conditions of imperfect markets can individual executives afford to guide corporations toward greater ethical norms (Sethi 1994a).

Overall TNC responses remain highly uneven. A small but growing number have taken a public stand on ethical issues. It is unclear though whether this is a temporary experiment that remains limited to a relatively small number of leading global corporations – mostly active in consumer products and natural resources – or whether it heralds a dominant future trend. Even where innovative responses have been taken, corporations show varying degrees of translating good will declarations into actual management practices, corporate performance and reporting (Watts 1998).

The trade debate

At the global rule-making level, the relationship between trade, on the one hand, and social, environmental or human rights issues on the other, has emerged as a flash-point of controversy between commercial interests and civil society groups, mostly of developed countries – as the whole world saw at Seattle. Over the past few decades, successive waves of lower trade and investment barriers have made very apparent the effects of different national policies. Calls for a level playing field and for minimum standards to avoid a race to the bottom have become louder and varying coalitions have been formed to pressure governments to use trade as a means to enforce higher standards or directly change the trading rules to accommodate social agendas.

Those who oppose linking trade with other concerns have argued that this would put too much stress on the trading system, thereby rendering it ineffective; and that it would not solve the problems at hand because the trading system is not designed to solve labour, environmental and human rights issues. Moreover, opponents are deeply concerned that seeking to impose such standards through the trade regime would be an open invitation to exploit them for protectionist purposes, to the grave disadvantages of the developing countries and the trade regime as a whole. Instead, developing countries argue, higher standards in areas such as environment can only be achieved through the process of accumulating skills, capital and technology. Higher standards in areas such as the environment cannot be imposed they argue but can only be achieved through an incremental process of accumulating skills, capital and technology.

328 *George Kell and John Ruggie*

Interestingly, the views of developing countries are increasingly converging with those of TNCs – and outward oriented corporations of any size, forming a potentially powerful policy coalition that has not yet been fully realized.[16]

The conflict over trade rules was evident in the debates following the conclusion of the Uruguay Round. A compromise declaration was reached at the first WTO Ministerial meeting in December 1996, where it was confirmed that the ILO was the competent body to deal with labour issues, and where a decision was taken to keep environmental issues merely under review within the WTO framework. This was only a temporary lull, however. As preparations for the Third Ministerial Meeting of the WTO gained momentum, conflicts around these issues became more intense again.[17]

As pressure by civil society actors has intensified, various attempts have been made to appease their concerns by increasing the transparency of the WTO and by searching for compromises.[18] President Clinton, for example, proposed in an ILO speech to 'build a link' with labour (Clinton 1999). Renato Ruggiero, as Director General of the WTO, stressed the need for balancing global governance structures, culminating in his proposal for a World Environment Organization (Ruggiero 1999).

The Third Ministerial Meeting of the WTO, in Seattle in early December, 1999 thrust civil society movements into the public consciousness. Their common denominator was the use of trade to advance a host of other issues. With 30,000 protesters and about 20,000 labour union members marching in the street, the Seattle event demonstrated vividly how trade and large corporations have become the target of citizens' groups.

The collapse of the Seattle talks and the failure to agree on another round of trade liberalization was not the result of pressure from the street however. The talks had to be suspended because trade negotiators failed to bridge conflicting views, especially in the area of agriculture where the EU tried hard to deflect pressure to reduce farm subsidies. Yet, the demonstrations and the movements preceding them, especially in the US, had their impact. In an interview after the Seattle talks, the European Union's trade commissioner Pascal Lamy went on record blaming the collapse of the Seattle talks on the pressure of looming US presidential elections and President Clinton's call, in Seattle, for labour standards to be included in trade agreements.[19] In the same vein, India's chief representative at Seattle said that President Clinton's remark about labour standards 'made all the developing countries and least-developed countries harden their views. It created such a furore that they all felt the danger ahead.'[20]

The Seattle experience showed that civil society groups are increasingly powerful at the corporate, national and international levels and that intergovernmental organizations such as the WTO have yet to learn how to respond. The fact that over 90 per cent of the NGOs that attended the Third Ministerial Meeting in Seattle came from OECD countries indicates a strong northern bias. The voices of the people of the developing countries remain unheard, and in those cases where developing countries' NGOs do participate they are often subsidiaries of NGOs hosted in OECD countries.

The Seattle meeting confirmed once again that opponents of trade liberalization represent highly heterogeneous groups with different motivations. The spectrum of protesters included: a small anarchist minority, a large number of single issue groups concerned with the environment, health and human rights, trade unions who fear that structural adjustments due to market openness are not offset by positive effects of increased competition, and powerful economic interests that seek government protection in areas such as steel and textiles.

Numerous activists took up the call to rally against exploitation and environmental destruction in developing countries, while at the same time ignoring the basic fact that trade remains the most viable path to escape poverty and that developed countries continue denying poor countries market access in areas where they stand a chance to compete. Protesters readily took up the slogans of the American Federation of Labour–Congress of Industrial Organizations (AFL–CIO). But were apparently not influenced by development oriented NGOs, who understand that poverty is the main cause of child labour and environmental destruction in poor economies and that trade and investment have, overall, positive and mutually reinforcing consequences for human rights, development and the environment. This apparent hypocrisy led many observers and commentators to refer to developing countries as the real losers of Seattle.

What the debate on CSR and trade have in common

The interaction between TNCs and NGOs at the corporate level and the controversies around global trade reveal a number of consequential tendencies.

First, contrary to conflicts between markets and society during the 1960s and 1970s, for example, the controversial debates around the UN Code of Conduct for TNCs, the issue at stake today is not in the main ideological. Opponents of globalization do not advocate an alternative ideology. While they seem united in their intention to oppose markets, most of them thrive because of economic good times and their operations and networking hinge critically on the free access to information technology. Openness and transparency are the leitmotifs of open markets. Indeed, most transnational NGOs take positions against TNCs and trade not because they inherently oppose their legitimacy or functional efficacy. They do so primarily because it promises to leverage their own specific interests and concerns. This strategic positioning is greatly facilitated by the fact that the trade regime is not static in its relation to society, nor does it represent a concrete thing. The trade regime is intersubjective in character and reflects the shared meanings and understandings attributed to it by the relevant actors (Ruggie 1998). As a result, issues can always be characterized in more than one way. In situations of choice, the act of characterization itself can be strategic in the sense that the actors select a characterization not on the basis of objective facts but on the positional implications of one formulation over the other (Wolfe 1999).

If such strategic positioning is a central feature of current debates, this carries considerable risks, especially in circumstances where it overlaps with real economic interests in protection-seeking industries or other interests. The most likely losers are those that are not party to the game – consumers everywhere and developing countries in particular.

However, while environmental and human rights NGOs may be motivated strategically in the debates around trade and TNCs, their position is given added moral weight by the imbalance in current global governance structures. There is a stark contrast between the available institutional mechanisms to define and enforce global rules that advance the economic interests of TNCs and the under-funded and relatively weak UN agencies charged with advancing the causes of the environment, development, human rights and labour. And at the United Nations, there is a wide gap between the ambitious goals and broad commitments embodied in various United Nations conferences on social issues and the degree to which governments are willing to honour such commitments.[21]

Finally, there are some signs that elements in the global corporate community are themselves increasingly concerned by the unsustainability of the current imbalance in global governance structures. There is recognition that global markets no less than national ones need to be embedded in broader frameworks of social values and practices if they are to survive and thrive (ICC 1998a, 1998b, 1999).[22] As a result, they have begun to look to the United Nations to play a larger role in setting norms and standards that express not merely the functional values of direct interest to business, but also broader global social issues. At Seattle, Kofi Annan invited participants to view the United Nations as a part of the solution to the problem with which they were grappling (Annan 1999).

Conclusion

Globalization may be a fact of life, but it remains highly fragile. Embedding global market forces in shared values and institutionalized practices, and bridging the gaps in global governance structures are among the most important challenges faced by policy-makers and corporate leaders alike. The future of globalization may hang in the balance. This challenge has to be met at the micro-level, where we believe the move towards articulating and acting upon universal values offers a viable approach. And it has to be solved at the level of global rule-making, where we believe strengthening the role of the United Nations has a productive role to play. The Global Compact is intended as a contribution to both, though by its very nature and scope, it can only make a modest contribution. Let us draw some conclusions from the case.

One can readily appreciate why corporations would be attracted to the Global Compact. It offers one stop shopping in the three critical areas of greatest external pressure, human rights, environment and labour standards, thereby reducing their transaction costs. It offers the legitimacy of having corporations sign off on to something sponsored by the Secretary-General – and, far more important, the legitimacy of acting on universally agreed to principles that are enshrined in covenants and declarations. Given the corporate sector fears that the trade regime will become saddled with environmental and social standards and collapse under their weight, a stronger UN in these areas is far preferable.

The NGO community is divided over the approach. The smaller and/or more radical single-issue NGOs believe that the United Nations has entered into a Faustian bargain at best. But the larger and more transnationalized NGOs have concluded that a strategy of 'constructive engagement' will yield better results than confrontation, and they are cooperating with the United Nations. At the same time, it is no doubt true that without the threat of confrontation, engagement would be less likely to succeed. The developing countries have yet to take a position. They fully support efforts to keep the trade regime free of additional conditionalities and barriers. But they are also worried that working with TNCs to improve their practices could become a Trojan horse to put pressure on the governments of those countries. And if we succeed in our endeavour, the imbalance in global governance structures will be somewhat attenuated.

The experience of working together on the Global Compact has also brought greater coherence to the United Nations entities active in this domain. The hope is that connected behaviour will accomplish far more than fragmented action. Thus, the Global Compact may signal that the United Nations may become a more salient player in the post-Seattle game of forging new instruments through which to manage the consequences of globalization.

Notes

The views expressed herein are those of the authors and are not intended to implicate the United Nations in any manner.

1   For example, Official Development Assistance (ODA) from Development Assistance Committee (DAC) Member countries fell by 21 per cent from 1992 to 1997; as a proportion of their combined national income, it fell by one third. These are the largest declines since the inception of the DAC in 1961 (Organization for Economic Cooperation and Development 1999).

2   NGOs are broadly defined here as any non-profit voluntary citizens' group that is constituted at the local, national or international level.

3   See http://www.un.org/partners/business/ (accessed 23.04.01).

4   The ICC has already endorsed the notion that a stronger UN in the areas of labour, human rights and the environment is the most sensible way forward to secure open markets.

5   See ILO (1999b) for a comprehensive overview.

6   Since 1990, the average transnationality index of the top 100 TNCs has increased from 51 per cent to 55 per cent, largely a result of the growing internationalization of assets especially between 1993 and 1996.

7   See Peter Wahl on www.igc.org/globalpolicy/ngos/issues/wahl.htm (accessed 23.04.01) for a good review of recent trends. Also see Abe Katz, chairman of the US Business Council, who devoted his farewell speech to the issue of how NGOs are using the Internet to slow down liberalization (Lucetini 1998).

8   In particular, environmental NGOs such as WWF (World Wildlife Fund) and Greenpeace, but also AI (Amnesty International), Human Rights Watch and many others.

9 CSR can be understood as the conditions under which society grants private corporations the right to pursue the maximization of profits. This social contract between a corporation and its host society implies legal requirements or can be understood to include implicit assumptions and expectations. See United Nations Conference on Trade and Development (UNCTAD 1999) for a good overview of the social responsibility of TNCs.

10 Sales of leading TNCs exceed GDP of regional giants such as Thailand and South Africa (UNDP 1999: 32).

11 These groups have targeted ('naming and shaming') high-profile corporations such as Nike, Shell and Rio Tinto.

12 For a good discussion forum see www.mailbase.ac.uk/lists/business-ngo-relations/ (accessed 23.04.01).

13 Examples include the UK ethical trading initiative, the development of national ethics codes in Canada and Norway and the work of the World Bank on best practices in the extracting industry. Many other initiatives are sponsored by business NGOs such as the WBCSD (World Business Council for Sustainable Development) and the PWBLF (Prince of Wales Business Leaders Forum).

14 Large corporations no longer advertise their products by the country of origin (e.g. 'made in Japan') but establish global brand names and corporate images. These intangible assets have become important in establishing a global presence and by some estimates make up as much as 40 per cent of the market value of corporations.

15 BP and Shell, two front-runners in this movement, caused considerable bewilderment in the business community when they included human rights and sustainable development on their annual report.

16 This is evident when comparing policy statements of the International Chamber of Commerce and of developing countries. The convergence has gradually proceeded over the past few years, to a point where positions are sometimes virtually indistinguishable.

17 Large demonstrations in Geneva in 1998 showed that the WTO and big business have become a target of social movements of all sorts.

18 A dialogue forum on development and the environment was held in March, see http://www.wto.org/wto/index.htm (accessed 23.04.01), for arrangements that have been made that allows NGOs to attend some debates.

19 See Buckley (1999).

20 Reported by Celia W. Dugger (1999).

21 The follow-up process to UNCED exemplifies this trend. Indications are that 'Copenhagen+5' will be comparably sobering.

22 There is an interesting difference between the financial community, especially Wall Street, which continues to oppose any regulation of global markets, and corporations that actually invest long-term productive capital. The rift became obvious during the peak of the Asian Financial crisis, with the latter warning about the need for at least some regulation of financial markets.

Bibliography

Annan, K. (1999) 'Help the Third World Help Itself', *Wall Street Journal*, 29 November.

Bhagwati, J. (1998) *A Stream of Windows: Unsettling Reflections on Trade, Immigration, and Democracy*, Cambridge, MA: The MIT Press.

Buckley, N. (1999) 'Collapse of Seattle Talks Blamed on US', *Financial Times*, 7 December.

Clinton, W.J. (1998) Input to the relevant bodies in respect of appropriate arrangements for relations with intergovernmental and non-governmental organizations referred to in WTO Article V (http://www.wto.org/environ/te027.htm – no date).

—— (1999) International Labour Conference, 87th Session, Address by Bill Clinton, President of the United States, 16 June 1999, Geneva, Switzerland, full text of speech can be found at http://www.ilo.org/public/english/standards/relm/ilc/ilc87/a-clinto.htm (accessed 30.04.01).

Conference Board, The (1999) *Global Corporate Ethics Practices: A Developing Consensus*, USA: The Conference Board, Inc.

Cramb G. (1999) 'Greenpeace Stepping Up Threat to Multinationals', *Financial Times*, 18 August.

Cramb, G. and Corzine, R. (1998) 'Shell Audit Tells of Action on Global Warming', *Financial Times*, 14 July.

Donaldson, T. and Dunfee, T.W. (1984) 'Toward a Unified Conception of Business Ethics: Integrative Social Contracts Theory', *Academy of Management Review*, 19 (2): 252–84.

Dugger, C. (1999) 'Why India and Others See US as Villain on Trade', *New York Times*, 17 December.

Environics International Ltd in Cooperation with The Prince of Wales Business Leaders Forum and The Conference Board (1999) *The Millennium Poll on Corporate Social Responsibility: Executive Briefing*, Toronto: Environics International Ltd.

Friedman, Milton (1984) 'The Social Responsibility of Business is to Increase its Profits', in W. Michael Hoffman and Jennifer Mills Moore (eds) *Business Ethics: Readings and Cases in Corporate Morality*, New York: McGraw-Hill.

Henderson, D. (1999) *The MAI Affair, a Story and its Lessons*, London: The Royal Institute of International Affairs.

International Chamber of Commerce (1998a) *Business and the Global Economy: ICC Statement on Behalf of World Business to the Heads of State and Government Attending the Birmingham Summit*, 15–17 May , Paris: ICC.

—— (1998b) *ICC Geneva Business Dialogue, 23–24 September 1998*, Geneva: International Chamber of Commerce

—— (1999) *Business and the Global Economy: ICC Statement on Behalf of World Business to the Heads of State and Government Attending the Cologne Summit*, 18–20 June, Paris: ICC.

International Labour Organization (ILO) (1999a) *Further Examination of Questions Concerning Private Initiatives, Including Codes of Conduct, GB.274/WP/sdl/1 274th Session*, Geneva: ILO.

—— (1999b) *Overview of Global Developments and Office Activities Concerning Codes of Conduct, Social Labelling and other Private Sector Initiatives Addressing Labor Issues, GB.273/WP/SDL/1(Add.1)*, Geneva: ILO.

Kane, A. (1998) *Non Governmental Organizations and The United Nations: A Relationship in Flux. Conference on 'Responses to Insecurity', CT 23–24 October 1998*, New Haven, CT: The Academic Council on the United Nations Yale University.

Lucetini, J. (1998) 'Katz: Activists use Internet to Slow Trade Liberalization', *The Journal of Commerce*, 10 December.

Organization for Economic Cooperation and Development (1999) 'Development Co-operation Report for 1999 Chapter IV: Policies and Efforts of Individual DAC Members and other OECD Member Countries' (note by the Secretariat), DCD/DAC(99)27/CHAP4.

Ruggie, J.G. (1982) 'International Regimes, Transactions and Change: Embedded Liberalism in the Postwar Economic Order', *International Organization* (Spring).

—— (1996) *Winning the Peace*, New York: Columbia University Press.

—— (1998) *Constructing the World Polity*, London: Routledge.

Ruggiero R. (1999) 'Beyond the Multilateral Trading System. Address by Renato Ruggiero, Director-General WTO 20th Seminar on International Security, Politics and Economics', Geneva, 12 April.

Sethi, S. Prakash (1994a) *Multinational Corporations and the Impact of Public Advocacy on Corporate Strategy. Nestlé and the Infant Formula Controversy*, Massachusetts: Kluwer Academic Publishers.

—— (1994b) 'Imperfect Markets: Business Ethics as an Easy Virtue', *Journal of Business Ethics*, 13: 803–17.

United Nations Conference on Trade and Development (UNCTAD) (1998) *World Investment Report 1998 Trends and Determinants*, New York and Geneva: United Nations, United Nations Publication Sales No. E.98.II.D.5.

—— (1999) *World Investment Report 1999: Foreign Direct Investment and the Challenge of Development*, New York and Geneva: United Nations, United Nations Publication Sales No. E.99.II.D.3.

United Nations Development Programme (1999) *Human Development Report, 1999*, New York: Oxford University Press, Inc.

Wahl, P. (1998) 'NGO Transnationals, McGreenpeace and the Network Guerrilla', www.igc.org/globalpolicy/ngos/issues/wahl.htm (accessed 23.04.01).

Watts, P. (1998) 'The Business of Raising Standards: Health, Safety and Environmental Imperatives for E&P Companies', paper presented at the Fourth International Conference on Health, Safety and Environment in Oil and Gas Exploration and Production Society of Petroleum Engineers, 8 June.

Wild, Alan (1998) 'A Review of Corporate Citizenship and Social Initiatives', prepared for The Bureau for Employers' Activities, International Labor Organization, 1–2 October, Geneva: ILO. Mimeo.

Wolf M. (1999) 'Uncivil Society', *Financial Times*, 1 September.

Wolfe R. (1999) 'Reconstructing Domestic Regulation in the Trade Regime', prepared for delivery to the International Studies Association, Washington, DC, 19 February.

14 Democratizing globalism

Sol Picciotto

Critics of neo-liberalism have been slow to develop cogent alternative perspectives, and have found themselves defending outdated models of classical liberal internationalism based on centralized sovereign states. Too often they neglect the significant changes in the form and functions of the state, or the public sphere more generally, which have resulted from widespread experiences of state failure. This includes not only the collapse of state socialism, but also crises and radical reforms of developed capitalist states, including US regulated corporatism, European-style social-democratic welfare states, and the developmental states of Japan and the Asian tigers. The reasons have been equally diverse, and have involved a mixture of political and economic factors. Nevertheless, these processes can be seen to have much in common, involving a transition to post-industrial capitalism, or what has been called the Information Age (Castells 1998).

Socio-economic restructuring and democratization

Remodelling the 'public' sphere of politics is part of a broader process of social and economic restructuring, including its relationship to the 'private' sphere of economic activity. At the same time, major transformations have also been occurring in the forms of organization of so-called private enterprise, that is to say the business economy dominated by the giant corporation. Large-scale mass manufacturing has been reorganized, and the centralized bureaucratic firm has become the 'lean and mean' corporation, concentrating on its core competencies, but operating within a web of strategic alliances, supplier chains, and financial and governmental networks (Harrison 1994).

These changes have in many ways been driven by social pressures from below: widespread revolts against autocratic power in the family and the factory, the classroom and the boardroom. These generally entail a rejection of authoritarian domination and the power to control truth embodied in tradition, involving demands for increased personal freedom and dignity, equality (notably, between women and men), and the ending of coercion (Giddens 1999). Rather than the desire for economic liberalization bringing about political democratization, as suggested by triumphant liberalism, it has been the struggles against autocracy that have created an opening for economic liberalization. Nevertheless, while undermining patriarchy and hierarchy, these anti-authoritarian movements have also paved the way to post-industrial capitalism, with its emphasis on information-management, flexible working and a global outlook.

This process has undoubtedly been very liberating for some, who in many ways constitute a new global elite, but the benefits have been limited, partial and exclusionary. Certainly, most people in Western Europe and North America enjoy higher living standards, and many in Asia and Latin America have felt some of the benefits of development. At the same time, there has been an increased polarization both within and between states: the gap between rich and poor states has continued to widen, while income inequality has increased even in developed countries; marginalization, poverty and social exclusion affect both the underclass in developed countries and wide regions of underdevelopment, especially in Africa (Castells 1998: vol. III ch. 2). Also, many of those who have benefited materially have, nevertheless, experienced greater insecurity and alienation and the disintegration of traditional social bonds has led to new assertions of identity, sometimes destructively based on ethnic or cultural exclusivity.

Constituting the new global public sphere

This chapter is about the emergence of a new public sphere and the changed public-private dynamic that has also involved a transformation of political practices and conflicts over legitimation. It considers the democratization of international regulation and governance to be not only necessary but also desirable, since it would address a process involving new kinds of networks of power in international political economy. So far much of the discussion has been couched as a purely technical matter in international organization. We need to do better.

At the regional and international level, the debates about the 'democratic deficit' have focused on two main issues: technocracy, and human rights. Two points are especially striking in the new emphasis on the role of the state in the 'post-Washington consensus', as exemplified by the World Bank's 1997 *World Development Report: the State in a Changing World*. First, the emphasis is almost entirely on the failings of the nation-state, with very little attention being given to international or global structures. Secondly, the appropriate role and forms of public action are generally discussed as a technical matter and in the terminology of the 'market-friendly' state, whose role is essentially to remedy 'market failures'. The modified Washington consensus focuses on what is generally referred to as governance or regulation, implying a technocratic view of social management that makes it easier for international organizations and their officials to become involved with institutional matters without apparently intruding into the political sovereignty of national states. These concepts are also often used to legitimize the increasingly important role of a variety of professionals operating in the increasingly large interface between the state, which has been substantially 'privatized', and the 'market', which is dominated by corporate networks.

Thus, the question of democracy is at the heart of debates about the nature of the systems of 'multi-layered governance', which increasingly characterize the global public sphere. There has been a functional fragmentation of the public sphere, involving the delegation of specific tasks and powers to specialized bodies, which perform a public role, but are substantially autonomous from central government, and often have a mixed state-private structure or composition. Thus, considerable autonomy or independent authority is now given to a wide range of bureaucracies exercising public functions, many of which have established direct lines of international coordination, by-passing central government. These include:

- criminal law enforcement agencies, especially those dealing with issues identified as global, such as terrorism, organized crime, and money-laundering;
- health service providers and professionals;
- universities and other higher education and research bodies;
- regulators of public utilities or infrastructure industries, such as power, transport, and communications;
- bodies dealing with specific aspects of macro-economic management, such as central banks responsible for interest rates, financial services industry supervisors exercising prudential oversight, and financial market regulators monitoring systemic stability and consumer protection;
- technical, consumer, and environmental protection standard-setting bodies, especially for food and agriculture, or pharmaceuticals and health;
- industry and market structure regulators, such as competition/anti-trust authorities setting limits for cartels and concentration, or patent offices deciding on the grant and limits of monopoly rights over commodified knowledge;
- tax authorities managing the range of revenue-raising powers.

This fragmentation (Picciotto 1997) has facilitated and been accompanied by a process of haphazard vertical and horizontal network-building coordinating these regulatory activities. To characterize these as 'governmental networks' only partly captures the phenomenon since it suggests a relatively orderly and natural growth of cooperation between various government agencies and officials, though certainly offering a very different picture from the traditional assumptions that international relations are conducted between unitary states (Slaughter 2000). The issue is very different if the transition from 'government' to 'governance' is seen as entailing a change in the form of statehood more generally, and not only in modes of international coordination.

These questions have become a particular focus of debate in relation to the EU, which in many ways has been the catalyst and paradigm of the emergence of multi-level governance. Although it is now widely agreed that the EU's multi-level system entails a new form of 'network governance', functional analysis of its structures is rarely combined with normative evaluation of its implications for the legitimacy problems of the EU (Kohler-Koch and Eising 1999).

Technocracy, rationality and democracy

A central issue, undoubtedly, is the continued growth of technocracy and rule by experts, which can be seen as part of general changes in the nature of power, a shift to the politics of expertise (Radaelli 1999). This creates a tension with democracy, which might be reconciled in two broad ways. Advocates of pure technocracy suggest that it provides its own legitimation, since the professional judgement of experts is more able to discern what is in the best interests of society as a whole than can political conflicts among competing interests. Such elitism has been resorted to not infrequently, even in so-called mature democracies, but usually as a partial or temporary expedient rather than as a long-term solution to political failures.

The more common perspective confines technocracy to the devising of the most efficient means of achieving ends which are decided by more explicitly political processes. This rests on a particular concept of rationality, which is essentially instrumentalist, accepting a radical separation of means and ends and an often formalist asserting of the general validity of conclusions which are based on abstract assumptions made for the purposes of a specialized thinking.

The link between the modified technocratic view and standard models of representative democracy can readily be seen in the argument put forward by Robert A. Dahl, that international organizations (including the EU) are, and can only be, bureaucratic bargaining systems among elites. This clearly flows from his view that the problem of 'delegation', already great for national representative systems, becomes insuperable for international politics (Dahl 1999). Certainly, no one seriously envisages the possibility of a global government based on the pattern of representative democracy, and the greater awareness of the importance of locality and diversity resulting from globalization renders it less believable or indeed desirable. However, this should not end the search for principles of democracy appropriate to the global public sphere.

Transformations in representative democracy

Indeed, it can be said that new principles are also called for at the national level, resulting from the tensions of representative democracy as a form of government and the ways in which it is being transformed. Bernard Manin has comprehensively and convincingly analysed the progressive breakdown of party-democracy, in which parliaments became a register of the relative force of clashing interests which governments aimed to resolve by compromises. He sees public disillusion with politics as resulting from the rise of a new form of 'audience representation', in a context of greater complexity and unpredictability, in which professional politicians offer to the electorate a choice among images which are 'highly simplified and schematic political representations' (Manin 1994: 163; Manin 1997). Opinions on specific issues are no longer pre-formed or defined by group political identities, and hence must be formulated and developed through debate in various public forums. Such debate is dominated by communications media that are perhaps less partisan, but more prone to drama and sensationalism. This again indicates the importance of ensuring that government at all levels takes place within a broader framework of debate and decision-making which is open to the active direct involvement of issue groups and concerned citizens, as well as elected politicians.

Thus, democratization of global governance is not a matter of creating a global version of an already outdated national model of representative democracy, but part of a more general process of the development of new democratic principles responding to changes in the character of the public sphere.[1] The meaning and content of globalization are as much political as economic questions: the construction of global governance has been under way for some time, but it has been dominated by international elites. The issue now is whether it is possible to provide democratic legitimacy through appropriate constitutional principles, in the broad sense of ensuring the allocation and exercise of public power in ways that can be responsive to the values and preferences of those affected by relevant decisions.

Constitutionalizing global governance through human rights

Increasingly, proposals are being put forward to constitutionalize the global public sphere by the introduction of human rights principles. These aim to provide a counterweight to globalization based on the neo-liberal dynamic of the removal of barriers and the unleashing of the forces of economic self-interest, by introducing obligations of respect for human values. International human rights principles were developed in the second half of the twentieth century as obligations on states; they have generally been kept separate from other state obligations, and in particular have not been considered relevant for international economic conventions or institutions. Now suggestions are being made for the application of human rights obligations to the activities both of private actors, particularly transnational corporations (TNCs), and international economic organizations.

The movement to apply human rights obligations to TNCs results from more general political pressures to apply social responsibility standards to their operations (see Kell and Ruggie chapter in this volume; or UNCTAD 1999: chap. XII; United Nations 2000). Fearful of damage to their reputation and brand image among customers and their own employees, many TNCs have declared their adherence to environmental and social responsibility and human rights norms, and have adopted codes to apply within the organization and often to their widespread networks of sub-contractors (Picciotto and Mayne 1999; Addo 1999). On the initiative of UN Secretary-General Kofi Annan, the grandly named UN Business and Human Rights Global Compact was declared, operating through a website.[2] The aim is to counteract criticisms of the negative effects of liberalization by encouraging globalization with a human face. However, many questions remain about the practical impact of these high ideals.

At the same time, it has been suggested that international economic organizations should also ensure that their operations both comply with human rights standards, and actively promote the achievement of these rights. This raises questions especially for the World Bank and the IMF, whose mandate is essentially economic, and indeed forbids interference in the internal politics of states. However, attacks on these organizations for the negative welfare effects, especially of the structural adjustment policies imposed on many countries, has led them to give a broader scope to their developmental concerns. Certainly the issue of 'good governance' can readily be said to include the promotion not only of economic, social and cultural rights, but also of civil and political rights (Bradlow 1996; Skogly 1999). Hence, they have begun, albeit with some caution, to articulate human rights criteria (World Bank 1998; Gianviti 1998). The increasing controversy surrounding the WTO, especially following the debacle during the Seattle Ministerial Conference of December 1999, led to proposals for its constitution to also include concern for human rights (Petersmann 2000; Mehra 2000).

Such proposals seek to establish an improved foundation of legitimacy for global economic liberalization by resorting to prescriptions for universal rights and principles of justice. However, this does not necessarily entail any extension of democratic participation into the international sphere. The aim too often is to ensure the adoption of the existing model of liberal democracy in national states, bound together within a strong framework of international law and institutions embodying individual human rights. While it is indeed suggested that these rights extend to a right to democracy, this is taken to mean an obligation on national states to be democratic, derived from international law (Franck 1992). This concept is somewhat contradictory, given the deeply undemocratic character of international law itself (Crawford 1994).

For some advocates of this approach, 'equal rights of the citizens may offer the most effective strategy for compensating the "democratic deficit" of international organizations' (Petersmann 1998: 28). This would actualize Kant's vision of 'Perpetual Peace', based on a confederation or league of republican states. They would renounce war and pursue reciprocal economic benefits through trade, under an umbrella of principles embodying individual cosmopolitan rights (Kant 1795/1966). This ultra-liberal view assumes that the pursuit of individual self-interest, especially through economic exchange, is ultimately beneficial to all. Hence, the development of principles embodying individual rights, and the adjudication of conflicting rights-claims, would be sufficient to ensure universal consent and legitimacy. This would therefore justify even the entrenchment of internationally agreed principles, so as to override national parliamentary supremacy and to secure the 'effective judicial protection of the transnational exercise of individual rights' (Petersmann 1998: 26).

A different kind of rights

However, it is political processes that must decide who should have what rights. This was seen, for example, in the debates around the Multilateral Agreement on Investment (MAI), which was criticized on the grounds that it would grant strongly enforceable rights for corporations and investors without any concomitant responsibilities, while imposing 'disciplines' on states which would effectively diminish national regulatory capacity (Picciotto and Mayne 1999). Human rights, as they have developed historically, have been most strongly articulated in the 'first generation' civil and political rights. The 'second generation' economic and social rights are generally considered to be aspirations, at best and 'third generation' collective rights, such as self-determination and sustainable development are hard to operationalize as enforceable rights. Significantly, the right to property is considered a civil rather than an economic right, so that the aspirational or unenforceable rights tend to be those of the have-nots. Hence, upholding equal political rights may simply have the effect of legitimizing socio-economic inequalities.

Perhaps the WTO would be improved if it recognized, for example, rights for farmers and indigenous people, to counterbalance those of firms, such as biotechnology companies for patent protection in the TRIPS agreement (Agreement on Trade-Related Aspects of Intellectual Property Rights). Certainly, campaigners have focused on the right to refuse patent protection on the grounds of '*ordre public* and morality', permitted by art. 27 of the TRIPS agreement and to argue for ethical limits on the scope of patent protection (Drahos 1999; Beyleveld and Brownseword 1998). However, the evaluation of complex socio-economic issues, such as those surrounding biotechnology and its commercialization, cannot adequately take place simply through adjudication of competing rights-claims. The introduction of broader human rights concerns into international economic agreements and institutions could have some positive effect if it alerts those bodies to the need to evaluate their decisions and policies in terms of broader human values and social concerns, and not just a narrow view of economic efficiency. But by itself it would do little to increase the democratic accountability of the substantive decisions.

Others have put forward somewhat modified neo-Kantian models, which accept the need for a strengthening of the international institutional framework to provide an underpinning for 'cosmopolitan democratic public law'. However, it is not clear how this may differ from what I have described as the ultra-liberal model, somewhat reinforced by improving the representativeness of regional and international organizations.[3] There are clear contradictions and limits to the neo-Kantian models,[4] and a new approach should begin by more adequately taking into account the ways in which the new forms of global socio-economic integration, the changed nature of the state and the fragmentation of the public domain entail new modes of accountability and hence, new democratic forms at all levels. Without a democratization of the global public sphere, a radical liberal vision of cosmopolitan citizenship and universal individual rights would lack substantial democratic content, and could even undermine existing national democratic structures.

Democratic participation and deliberation

New concepts and forms of democratic accountability are now called for, responding to the fragmentation of the public sphere and the more dispersed, decentralized and multi-layered forms of regulating the exercise of social power. Indeed, this process of fragmentation both results from the limits and contradictions of previous state-centralized forms, and also stimulates new forms of legitimation. The very decentralization of decision-making itself entails and provides opportunities for accountability, since power is less concentrated. To that extent, it is accurate to see a connection between liberalization and increased liberty and even accountability.

The dispersal of decision-makers provides checks and balances, since a decision by one committee or regulator is rarely definitive. The much greater opportunities for strategic behaviour and regulatory arbitrage generates regulatory competition, which has the potential for ratcheting standards up, as well as down. Although this tends to favour those with greater opportunities for mobility, and to destabilize and thus downgrade existing socially embedded regulatory arrangements and capacities, it also opens up prospects for strategic actions by new types of citizen groups and social organizations (Braithwaite and Drahos 2000). This helps to explain the mushrooming growth of internationally active issue-oriented social movements broadly described as non-governmental organizations (NGOs).

Direct democracy and deliberation in a decentred world

New democratic constitutional principles should foster active deliberation by citizens, based on the articulation and evaluation of values, in a variety of public forums and institutions. The most helpful and relevant approaches, in my view, emerge from the work of political theorists arguing for new forms of direct democracy based on deliberative principles, and aiming to contain or counterbalance instrumental rationality by fostering public debate and decision-making through communicative interaction and reasoning.[5] They attempt to respond to the challenge posed to both liberal and republican/communitarian democracy by social fragmentation, which generates a politics of identity, often based on the view that differences are unassimilable (Benhabib 1996).

In fact, new forms of active citizenship and political action have been developing, often around the local and national impact of regional or global policies. The recognition that the public sphere has become fragmented into multiple intersecting networks and overlapping jurisdictional spheres emphasizes the importance of building democratic participation through new political principles, institutions and practices. These should recognize the diversity of political sites in which public policies are developed and implemented, while also involving processes of reflexive interaction between these sites.

Such principles must attempt to transcend the two main traditional constitutional models, which are increasingly proving inadequate for the contemporary phase of globalization. On the one hand, liberal conceptions, based on a view of society as composed of individuals pursuing their self-interest or pre-formed 'preferences', see the role of the polity as complementing the market, and as aiming to identify the optimal collective interest, either by authoritarian means (Hobbes), or via majoritarian representative democracy (Locke).

Post-industrial capitalism, with its integrated global production and marketing networks, raises a wide range of social, environmental and moral issues, which cannot adequately be resolved by aggregating individual preferences, using either authoritarian or democratic methods. The alternative model of civic republicanism rejects the narrow view of citizenship based on weighing and balancing competing private interests. However, its stress on an ethical politics based on visions of the common good implies a communitarianism requiring shared values, which in today's culturally fractured world takes reactionary forms, and may generate conflict rather than consensus.

As Jürgen Habermas has suggested, whereas both these views tend to see the state as the centre, deliberative politics can be adapted to a decentred society.

> This concept of democracy no longer needs to operate with the notion of a social whole centered in the state and imagined as a goal-oriented subject writ large. Just as little does it represent the whole in a system of constitutional norms mechanically regulating the interplay of powers and interests in accordance with the market model.[6]

Others also have stressed the attractiveness of a direct, deliberative form of participatory democracy for solving problems in ways unavailable to representative systems:

> collective decisions are made through public deliberation in arenas open to citizens who use public services, or who are otherwise regulated by public decisions. But in deciding, those citizens must examine their own choices in the light of the relevant deliberations and experiences of others facing similar problems in comparable jurisdictions or subdivisions of government.
>
> (Cohen and Sabel 1997: 313–14)

Rationality and diversity

In this perspective, decision-making, especially by public bodies, should result as far as possible from active democratic participation based on discursive or deliberative rather than instrumental reasoning. Instead of the pursuit of individual interests based on the assumption of fixed preferences, the aim is to go beyond objectivist rationality, which assumes that choices are made by reference to absolute and objective standards, without falling into the trap of relativism, which considers that all perspectives are equally valid (Dryzek

1990). Instead, truth is seen as an emergent property of the deliberative interaction between perspectives, rather than based on a single objective standard. In other words, there is an objective truth, although we can only know it through subjective interactions. This is the most basic justification for democracy.

Deliberative democracy accepts the existence of a diversity of perspectives, and aims to facilitate interactive deliberation about values through which preferences may change, or may be accommodated to each other. An emphasis on process may help to overcome the weaknesses of this model, if conceived as a political ideal or as relying on the generation of consensus purely through the public use of reason. Crucially, account must also be taken of inequalities of power, which generate conflicting interests as well as imbalances in capacities to participate in a politics based on reasoning.

Thus, a key element is the fostering of broad participation in deliberative decision-making, rather than merely elite or expert deliberation. There is a certain tension between the two, since the deliberative evaluation of specialized knowledge entails a degree of insulation or autonomy from private interests and other pressures.[7] However, this may result in an unjustified authority being claimed by or given to the judgements of specialists or experts. Thus, a key element in democratic deliberation is to ensure a fruitful interaction between various sites of deliberation, and awareness by specialists of the conditional or contingent nature of their expert knowledge and judgements (Wynne 1992). This means that experts should be more explicit about the assumptions behind the abstract models underpinning their evaluations, and can benefit from some input into their deliberations based on alternative perspectives and social values.

Constitutional principles should aim as far as possible to protect the public sphere from the instrumental pursuit of private interests. Clearly, subjectivity resulting from each person's experiences, background and aspirations, is inevitable, but this should be reflexively acknowledged so that individuals and groups maintain openness to the arguments of others. Above all, public arenas should be insulated from undue influence from private interests, and debate should be conducted in terms of explicitly articulated values and aims. This objective is fundamental to the four general principles, which I put forward as constitutive of a direct-democratic, deliberative public sphere: transparency, accountability, responsibility, and empowerment. Each of these will be discussed in turn, although in practice they are interdependent.

Principles of direct democratic deliberation

Transparency

Economic liberalization and globalization have led to the increasing articulation of the requirement of transparency, but it has generally been directed at national governments, aiming to reduce bureaucratic obstacles to market transactions. Thus, many provisions in the WTO agreements require transparency of national regulatory and administrative procedures. It is considered that regulatory measures, policies and proposals adopted by one state may, in the context of increased global economic integration, act as obstacles to market access by firms in other states. Thus, the WTO agreements include obligations not only for accessible publication of national regulations, but also for the establishment of national contact points to provide information (including translations of relevant texts), and even for prior notification of proposals for non-standard regulations with an opportunity to make comments.[8] Even more extensive obligations are put on states in the Aarhus Convention on Access to Information, Public Participation in Decision-making and Access to Justice in Environmental Matters, negotiated through the UN Economic Commission for Europe and signed in 1998. This establishes international obligations embodying the principle of participation, in line with Principle 10 of the Rio Declaration on Environment and Development. These have been perhaps furthest developed for environmental decision-making, due to widespread expressions of public concern and activism.

However, there are virtually no formal provisions regarding transparency of international bodies and arenas, and even writers on global governance limit the application of the principle to the national level (e.g. Cable 1999: ch. 5). In fact, inter-governmental negotiations and activities are especially opaque, and both politicians and officials generally stress the importance of confidentiality in this realm, which is often excluded from national freedom of information requirements. In the EU, it was only as a result of the legitimacy crisis, which began to be recognized in the negotiation of the Maastricht treaty that principles of transparency have begun to be adopted for EU institutions.[9] This was finally formally recognized in the Treaty of Amsterdam signed in June 1997, and article 255 of the consolidated Treaty establishing the European Community now gives any EU citizen or resident a right of access to documents of the Council, Commission and Parliament, subject to 'general principles and limits on grounds of public or private interest', to be drawn up by the Council.

This right of access to documents is an exceptional, perhaps even unique, provision in an international treaty, but should be regarded as a constitutive principle for all international bodies, and indeed any serious international regulatory activity. Nevertheless, such a principle will inevitably remain ineffective if subject to broad exceptions, and if both the general rules and individual decisions on what can be revealed are left to each body to decide for itself.[10] Effectiveness could perhaps be improved by the establishment of Ombudsmen, as has also been done in the EU,[11] to monitor the transparency of international bodies, and to investigate or adjudicate claims of confidentiality. The principle of transparency is just as important for apparently technical bodies, as has been pointed out by Willem Buiter in a trenchant critique of the traditionalist approach adopted by the European Central Bank, which he describes as 'typical of a central banking tradition that was, until recently, dominant across the world, which views central banking as a sacred, quasi-mystical vocation, a cult whose priests perform the holy sacraments far from the prying eyes of the non-initiates' (Buiter 1999: 198). Certainly, a degree of insulation may be necessary to ensure that deliberation is protected from lobbying by private interests and ill-informed populist pressures (Bessette 1994: 221–8), but it is equally important to guard against privileged access by powerful interests. This balance can be ensured through formal procedural requirements such as prior publication of agendas, allowing opportunities for public debate, and rapid dissemination of decisions with a full record of the reasons. It is generally preferable to strengthen accountability and responsibility mechanisms (discussed below), rather than sacrifice transparency.

Transparency has now been greatly facilitated by the opportunities opened up by the Internet. Indeed, some international bodies have begun to make extensive use of this medium to make their documentation available. It is obviously very advantageous for an organization such as the WTO to be able to give such instant online access to its large and growing documents archive to all those in its 132 member countries who require it. The Internet also offers possibilities for much more interactive consultation of relevant communities and the public (Hague and Loader 1999), and some organizations are beginning to make use of this. In practice, however, there are very great inequalities in the capacity to access the Internet (Sassen 1999; United Nations 1999); so that to realize the opportunities it offers also requires active programmes to broaden effective participation by all affected and concerned citizens.

Finally, perhaps the key requirement is to develop and sustain information media, which can help to provide the kind of forum that active public participation in deliberative debate requires. That everywhere the public's distrust of politicians is equalled only by its cynicism about journalists is a serious indictment of our political systems. There are certainly some media organizations in some countries, as well as many able and committed individuals, dedicated to providing a rich context of information and to facilitating debate. However, the media overall, in some countries more than others, is subservient to government agendas and commercial imperatives, and hence tend to reflect received or elite opinion. Thus, a key requirement for transparency in the public sphere is to ensure guarantees of media independence from both government and private dominance. News media, in particular, should be owned neither by governments nor tycoons, but by journalist collectives or trusts with public interest objectives.

Accountability

The past few years have seen increasing concern and debate about the accountability of all kinds of participants in public-policy debates. Even in countries with apparently well-established systems of representative democracy, politicians have been subjected to new scrutiny over their acceptance of bribes, political donations or campaign financing, as well as debates about the relationship of their personal lives and morality to their public functions. Such issues have been very widespread, and often rooted in the crisis of the political system itself: as in Italy, with its 'tangentopoli' scandals linked to the collapse of the

Christian Democracy – Communist duopoly; the failings of the Belgian justice system revealed by the 'white march' movement following the unmasking of the paedophile Marc Dutroux; or the vast web of scandal and political corruption in Ireland centring on its long-serving prime minister Charles Haughey. Such crises and scandals are symptomatic of generalized changes in the role of elected politicians, indicated in Bernard Manin's analysis of the changing nature of representative democracy discussed above.

The increased diversity and complexity of policy issues, and the decline of mass-party politics, places new responsibilities on politicians to develop specialist expertise and resources, and to manage their information sources scrupulously. They themselves are also increasingly concerned with their responsiveness to public opinion, whether expressed in their post bags (and e-mails), opinion polls, or focus groups. However, the increased importance of personal charisma or 'name recognition' for the standing of politicians, as opposed to policy or principles, has undermined their legitimacy as political representatives.

Vertical and horizontal accountability

For a variety of reasons it has become increasingly plain that democratic accountability of public bodies cannot rest only on their accountability via parliaments and elected politicians. Indeed, a wide range of activities of a public character have been entrusted to semi-autonomous professionalized bureaucracies, insulated from electoral politics: these range from the delegation to central banks of control over interest rates, to giving the police or prison services responsibility for the conduct of their operational duties. An increasingly wide range of matters has been delegated to specialized bodies operating under defined mandates, with powers either of recommendation or of actual decision. Where there is a governmental input, it is generally made by non-elected officials, who are subject to only superficial supervision, by a succession of partially briefed elected politicians.

Often, issues are not resolved by a decision from one particular body, but subject to interacting decision-making powers of various bodies, even at national level, and even more so globally. Thus, for example, the development and use of biotechnology depends on decisions by patent offices, scientific and ethical committees, food and drug regulators, national governments, and perhaps ultimately WTO dispute-settlement procedures. It is important not only that all such public bodies operate under explicit and specific accountability mandates, but also that their decisions are taken in a context of well-informed debate involving as broad a range of the public as possible. The channels of accountability are now less vertical, leading into central government, and more horizontal, entailing interaction between various local, national, regional, and international public arenas.

Thus, while elected politicians certainly should play an important and perhaps determinant part, ensuring accountability within the public sphere entails the involvement of a wide range of entities and groups, all of which have their own constituencies and accountability mechanisms. This is perhaps the reason for the increased use in recent years of the somewhat amorphous term 'civil society'. The point here is that there is no single accountability mechanism to the broad public. Participants in public debate can make different contributions, but it is incumbent on each of them to clarify to whom and how they are accountable. Indeed, there have been increasing pressures for all kinds of organizations to improve their accountability, not only to their direct members but also to a wider constituency of stakeholders.

Corporations have come under pressure to be responsive to the needs and demands of their customers, suppliers, workers, and contractors, as well as local communities and the wider society in respect of some of their activities. Their traditional focus on the 'bottom line' of direct costs and revenues to generate shareholder value has now been overtaken by the need for a more continuous two-way dialogue with this wider constituency, and concern for the 'triple bottom line' and long-term values such as reputation. No doubt many business managers need to be convinced that this entails more than just improved communication of decisions made in their boardrooms; but it is no coincidence that the lead is being taken by companies that have been hit by unexpected public reactions to policies which they believed had the legitimacy of approval by all relevant regulatory bodies. This has been shown, for example, by Shell's experiences over the Brent Spar oil platform disposal and the impact of its oilfields on local communities in eastern Nigeria, and those of biotechnology companies in relation to genetically modified organisms. The damage to investor confidence in the biotechnology sector should bring home to all concerned the importance of improving public confidence in regulatory decisions.

In response, many have challenged the various campaigning organizations or NGOs to justify their claims to represent public opinion. Such organizations cover a wide gamut, and clearly do have a responsibility to clarify for whom they speak, as well as to maintain an active dialogue with their members and stakeholders. They also are vulnerable to 'bottom-line' pressures from their sources of funding, which may lead them to adopt high-profile campaigns or maintain positions primarily for their suitability as vehicles for attracting public attention through the media. There may be differences of perspective between different elements of their constituencies, for example development organizations may find a tension between the concerns of their funding sources in developed countries and the stakeholders in less developed countries who are the intended beneficiaries of their activities. An agreed code of principles covering issues such as disclosure of funding sources, and adoption of procedures for consultation with stakeholders, might help to improve the accountability (and hence legitimacy) of NGOs. Compliance with such principles could be one criterion for the granting of participation rights for NGOs in international meetings and organizations.

Interest-group institutions, such as business and trade associations and trade union organizations fall into a different category from public interest or issue-oriented NGOs. In principle they represent their members, and can claim accountability ultimately via election; but the international-level bodies are very distant from actual workers or business-people. There is much they could do to improve the active involvement of their grass-roots members, and ensure that the positions they take reflect a considered view by that membership. Once again, compliance with agreed accountability procedures or standards could be a condition of their accreditation with international bodies.

Finally, international organizations themselves should develop mechanisms of direct accountability to people affected by their activities. A welcome first step in this direction, although a hesitant one, was the establishment in 1993 of the World Bank Inspection Panel, with the mandate to receive complaints by groups of individuals whose rights or interests are directly and adversely affected by the Bank's failure to comply with its policies and procedures during the cycle of a Bank-financed project. It has received some fourteen formal requests and issued a dozen reports since 1993, and despite some limitations, it remains a unique example of a direct accountability mechanism for an international organization (Skogly 1999: 235–42; Schlemmer-Schulte 1999). Only recently has the IMF proposed the establishment of an Independent Evaluation Office, although there were criticisms that inadequate independence from the IMF's management and Board would endanger its credibility.

In summary, the roles of various kinds of participants should be defined according to the contribution they can make to public debate based on generally applicable values. Procedures for consultation and involvement in decision-making should reflect their particular roles, as well as accommodating and safeguarding against possible distortions resulting from advancement of private interests.

Responsibility

Participants in public deliberation may also be said to have obligations of responsibility, which are distinct from their accountability to their particular constituencies. Responsibility refers to principles governing all aspects of how deliberation and debate should be conducted to achieve democratic outcomes: the deontology of deliberation.

Ethical obligations and professional standards

Principles for the conduct of public duties and activities include norms and practices of responsible behaviour developed by and for particular groups and professions. The acceptability and effectiveness of public policy decisions increasingly depend on the reasoning supporting them, which in turn requires all those involved in debates to uphold high standards of probity. This is evidenced by the increased attention being given to ethical standards by and for a wide range of groups and professions, many of which have been formally articulated in codes or even in law. Protections against corruption are obviously important, but the concerns extend well beyond this, to a wide range of ethical obligations and standards of professional conduct. These matters are not uncontroversial, as can be seen for example in the debates about the criteria applied in peer-review for publication of studies on controversial technologies such as genetically modified organisms; or whether there should be an obligation to publish results from all pharmaceutical drug evaluations. In bureaucratic organizations, internal audit procedures should monitor compliance with ethical and professional standards.

An important aspect of this is to define and police the line between professional or public responsibilities and obligations to a commercial client or employer. Thus, banks and financial intermediaries are now obliged to report suspicious transactions under money-laundering legislation, enacted nationally but stimulated and monitored by the international regulatory network centred on the Financial Action Task Force.[12] External auditors may have specific responsibilities to report to regulatory authorities, for example to banking supervisors, if they uncover breaches of regulatory requirements. Officials or civil servants may be protected from disciplinary or even legal proceedings for breaches of confidence if they can show that they acted in the public interest. However, too often the formal rules on these matters are not designed to encourage or protect disclosures in the public interest, but rather to protect public or private bureaucracies from undesirable obligations or revelations. Their strengthening should be regarded as a significant contribution towards the democratization of global governance.

Scientific reflexivity and openness

More broadly, all those involved as information gatekeepers or knowledge producers, now more than ever, need to operate reflexively, and with an awareness of how their professional or scientific practices and contributions impact on the quality of public debate. This is especially the case since so many decisions now entail inputs, often from several specialist or expert fields, as well as an evaluation from the general public perspective. As indicated above, in the discussion of expertise, technocratic rationality can operate in an autocratic way, if it seeks to claim a spurious authority. This can be counter-productive, as has been seen in the frequent episodes when it has resulted in a spiral of public mistrust of science, and scientists' despair at public ignorance.

Hence, scientists and other experts need to acknowledge the ways in which their techniques rest on formalist models based on assumptions which allow them to abstract the specific aspects or data with which they are concerned from the real world. Thus, the conclusions they reach are of only partial or conditional validity, and should not be treated as determinative of real-world policies or decisions, but as important resources for public debates. Scientific responsibility should therefore include cognitive openness and reflexivity. This means that experts should explicitly identify the assumptions behind their models and data, and evaluate their implications for the more general validity of the conclusions. They should be willing to test the robustness of their models against those of others based on different assumptions.

Participation and empowerment

My final principle should be regarded as an overriding one, for without it the other proposals for strengthening the public sphere as a deliberative arena would do little more than provide an alibi for the maintenance and extension of the system of elite decision-making. It is all too easy for those with decision-making power to pay lip-service to the need for public consultation or participation, although one can still be surprised at the frequency with which they neglect even this bare minimum. It is often only as a result of a policy setback, such as the breakdown of the MAI negotiations, that those in power resort to a 'charm offensive' to try to win support from potential critics. Frequently, they also prefer to distinguish carefully between procedures for consultation with public interest or activist groups and their discussions with business or corporate interests. This inevitably raises suspicions that decision-makers are more open to influence from private interest groups, and that they regard consultation with public interest groups and concerned citizens (or even legislators) as an irritating time-waster, perhaps necessary to forestall subsequent criticism. It is all too rare to find acknowledgement that the quality of public decisions can be improved if they take place in a context of full participation by all concerned and affected groups.

Regulation and redistribution

The challenge, therefore, is to find ways to ensure effective participation in debate and decision-making especially of disadvantaged citizens and groups. Much of the political opposition to and disaffection with globalization and liberalization results from the unleashing of forces, which exacerbate inequalities within and between states. This is often portrayed as a battle between the global market and the national state, a view which tends to neglect the ways in which the transformation of the world market is being brought about by complex processes of international re-regulation. To take a key example, the restructuring of global telecommunications, in which giant firms battle for market shares, entails struggles over technical standards, sectoral regulation (notably governing interconnection rights and charges) and competition rules, through interactions between a variety of national and international bodies. A key issue, which has for several years been preoccupying the International Telecommunications Union (ITU), is the system of settlements in respect of international calls, which entails revenue-sharing resulting in transfers mainly from developed to developing countries estimated at $7–10 billion per year.[13] There is considerable pressure to reform this system, to end discrimination in charges between international and national calls, in line with the liberalization of telecommunications services negotiated bilaterally, regionally (especially in the EU) and through the WTO. Yet it is also widely recognized that a truly global telecommunications system is unattainable unless equivalent (or better) means are found to finance the expansion and upgrading of telecommunications networks in developing countries (Tyler 1998).

This clearly shows that global battles over regulation also concern revenue distribution and redistribution, not just neutral rules allowing markets to operate 'freely'. Many other debates and battles over international regulatory arrangements also have (re)distributional consequences or implications, running often to many millions or billions of dollars, such as competition laws and policies, environmental protection schemes, intellectual property rights, food safety and labelling requirements, agricultural support and rural development measures, prudential rules for financial institutions, and international tax arrangements. Too often the talk of 'market friendly' regulation implies rules that favour the economically powerful, whereas balanced and sustainable long-term economic growth may require measures to protect, encourage and stimulate less developed or disadvantaged groups, regions and countries. For example, the international patent system ensures that billions of dollars are channelled into research and development for new pharmaceutical drugs, but inevitably the vast bulk of this is aimed at combating health problems of the affluent.[14] It has proved extremely difficult for the WHO to negotiate collaborative arrangements for the development of new drugs to combat tropical diseases such as malaria, which would be of immense benefit globally;[15] yet pharmaceuticals companies would fiercely resist the proposal made by Médecins sans Frontières to fund such initiatives through a tax on drug sales.

Institutionalizing consultation

An important function of direct democracy is to open up the received wisdom of closed bureaucratic or technocratic decision-makers to critical and destabilizing ideas. This perhaps cannot be institutionalized without blunting the critical edge of political protest, although sometimes well considered and substantiated arguments take second place to spectacular actions designed to attract media attention. Responsive and confident political systems can find ways to make themselves more open to external critical input.

In fact, a wide range of techniques is now increasingly used by many public bodies, as well as corporations, to consult either the general public or specific sections affected by a proposed policy. This can include, for example, public forums or commissions with powers to conduct inquisitions into policies or issues; citizens' panels, which can help to evaluate and prioritize policy choices; citizen juries to which specific decisions can be delegated, based on systematic presentation and examination of evidence; as well as old and new consultation techniques such as surveys and focus groups.

These methods have various advantages, and are each appropriate for different decision-making contexts. However, all can be used by any policy- or decision-making body, especially those with public responsibilities or tasks.

They can certainly be applied, with suitable adaptation, to arenas in the global public sphere to enhance their responsiveness to public concerns.

Conclusions: post-liberal democracy

This chapter has argued that the constitution of democracy requires the formulation of principles, adapted to the emerging forms of the new public sphere, but which explicitly aim to structure it to ensure the most effective forms of popular participation. The dangers of liberalization and globalization are that they unleash socially destructive behaviour based on the competitive pursuit of self-interest, as existing normative and institutional restraints are undermined or dismantled. There is clearly an urgent need to rebuild a civic ethos and to strengthen social solidarities.

However, it would be mistaken, in my view, to think of this in terms of identifying and protecting specific activities or functions that can be characterized as essentially public, separated from others which can be conducted 'privately', through the 'free' market. All activities necessary for human survival and well-being have a public aspect: the provision of food, shelter, health-care, education, security, transportation, communications, cultural and leisure pursuits, and financial services. Although very few of these are now organized under the direct ownership or control of state or public bodies, all are to a significant degree funded from the public purse, and many important aspects of the conditions of their production and delivery are subject to public rules and supervision. There are clearly many advantages in the decentralization of socio-economic activities away from sclerotic bureaucracies staffed by placement, to dispersed entities operating within a framework of coordination and competition. The important functions of governance or regulation are to ensure that this framework operates in the general public interest.

Thus, this chapter has put forward four principles, which should underpin democratic participation in these public processes of regulation and governance, together with practical examples of their implementation. They entail the supplementation and reformulation of the classical liberal system of government through representative democracy, by means of direct public participation in the wide range of governance arenas. They build on principles of political philosophy for civic deliberation, rooted in classical Aristotelian concepts, but developed by contemporary thinkers for the conditions of fragmented unity-in-diversity which characterize the post-liberal global political economy.

Notes

Thanks to Ruth Mayne for comments on the draft, to Daniel Drache for incisive editing, and as ever to Catherine Hoskyns for extended discussions.

1   Anne-Marie Slaughter, who is generally sceptical of criticisms of the 'democracy deficit' of inter-governmental networks, rests much of her case on the shift in the nature of power to 'soft power', based on persuasion rather than coercion or inducements, and concedes that 'We may need to develop new metrics or even new

conceptions of accountability geared towards the distinctive features of power in the Information Age' (Slaughter 2000: 195).

2   http://www.unglobalcompact.org/gc/UNWeb.nsf (accessed 23.04.01).

3   This appears to be the argument of David Held: see Held 1995, 1997, and the evaluation by Dryzek 1999.

4   These are explored in Bohman and Lutz-Bachmann 1997, although the contributors are generally concerned for various reasons to rescue what can be salvaged rather than look for a new approach. As the editors of the collection point out in their Introduction, 'Escaping the dilemmas of despotism and fragmentation remains the most difficult institutional challenge of a cosmopolitan order; showing how the public use of reason permits both unity and difference is a task that the Kantian conception of reason has yet to solve', ibid.: 18.

5   Dryzek 1990: although this approach owes much to Jürgen Habermas, I think it can avoid his unhelpful separation between the 'lifeworld' and that of technical and instrumental rationality, and the need to establish ideal, uncoerced communicative contexts. The social structures of power, including communication, should be seen in a more dialectical way, and the changes in the structure of the public sphere open up possibilities, many of which Habermas himself recognizes, for reconstituting a more effective democracy, which in turn can counteract inequalities of power.

6   Habermas 1996: 27. Habermas nevertheless argues that his own concept of a 'politically socialising communicative context' can be translated from the nation-state to the European sphere, which entails building 'a European-wide, integrated public sphere in the ambit of a common political culture', Habermas 1995: 306. Others have put forward neo-republican models for a 'multi-level' European citizenship (usefully summarized in Bellamy and Warleigh 1998), which imply that the republican version of participatory democracy can be translated to the European level (although this is contested by Habermas). However, it seems to me important to accept that even Europe, which has a strong institutional base and some elements of a common political culture, does not form an integrated political unit, and hence those democratic forms need significant adaptation. It is clear, for example, that the European Parliament must play a different role from that of national parliaments, and hence it must be differently organized, just as national parliaments must adapt to deal with the Europeanization of the legislative process. This is perhaps the practical political response to the debate about the 'European demos', see also Hoskyns and Lambert 2000.

7   Thus, the work of Joerges and Neyer on the role of expert and scientific committees in regulatory decision-making in the EU (Joerges and Neyer 1997; Joerges 1999) characterizes them as 'deliberative', in the sense that the participants approach issues open-mindedly rather than from pre-formed positions (in particular in favour of national interests), seeking to reach consensus through evaluation of valid knowledge (Joerges 1999: 320). However, they have reservations, especially about the management of the interaction between various types of committee, so that it is still questionable whether the EC committee system 'gives proper expression to the plurality of practical and ethical views which should be included within risk assessment procedures'. The conclusion seems to be that the system is certainly not a closed or homogeneous epistemic complex, but its openness is limited or haphazard, if not selective (ibid.: 321). Others are more explicitly critical of the ways in which the European Commission's restriction of public consultation and involvement, through its management of the committee system, has undermined the legitimacy of some decision-making in the EU regulatory networks (Landfried 1999; Vos 1999).

8   Notably, article 7 and Annex B of the Agreement on Sanitary and Phytosanitary Measures (SPS) requires states to notify in advance any proposals for regulations which are not based on an international standard, to 'allow reasonable time for other Members to make comments in writing, discuss these comments upon request, and

take the comments and the results of the discussions into account', developed countries must provide translations of documents in English, French or Spanish. The agreement on Technical Barriers to Trade (TBT), which requires states to base their technical regulations on international standards where they exist except where they would be 'an ineffective or inappropriate means for the fulfilment of the legitimate objectives pursued', focuses on transparency of conformity assessment procedures (article 10), including the requirement for inquiry points which can provide documents at reasonable cost (and for developed countries, in English, French or Spanish). The TRIPS agreement (article 63) also includes obligations to publish and notify laws, regulations final judicial rulings and administrative rulings of general application.

9 The Final Act of the Treaty on European Union signed at Maastricht on 7 February 1992 included Declaration No. 17, stating that 'transparency of the decision-making process strengthens the democratic nature of the institutions and the public's confidence in the administration', and recommending that the Commission submit a report to the Council by 1993 on measures to improve public access to information. This resulted in the approval by the Council and Commission on 6 December 1993 of a Code of Conduct, which stated the general principle that 'the public will have the widest possible access to documents held by the Commission and the Council', but which also required the institutions to refuse access to any document whose disclosure would undermine 'the protection of the public interest (public security, international relations, monetary stability, court proceedings and investigations)', and permitted them to refuse access 'in order to protect the institution's interest in the confidentiality of its proceedings'. Journalists, MEPs and activists have waged several battles to try to ensure these exclusions are interpreted strictly, with some support from the ECJ: see Bunyan 1999; and *Heidi Hautala* v. *Council of the EU*, Case T-14/98, Judgment of Court of First Instance, 19 July 1999. Typically, this case concerned foreign policy: the Council's refusal to supply a report on the criteria for arms exports, on the grounds that disclosure could be harmful for the EU's relations with third countries, and although the Court annulled the decision it did so only because the Council had not considered whether the report could be published with sensitive parts removed. Weiler 1997 and Curtin 1999 discuss the importance of increased transparency in improving democratic deliberation in the EU, and provide more detailed concrete proposals.

10 Thus, the initial proposals emerging from discussions of officials of EU institutions for implementation of article 255 (Discussion paper on public access to Commission documents, 23 April 1999, SG.C2/VJ/CDD(99)83) apparently suggested that only documents concerning legislative measures would be regarded as 'accessible', while internal 'working documents' would be 'non-accessible', and even the former might be embargoed until after the formal adoption of the decision: see *Statewatch*, 9, 2, March–April 1999. Such a proposal is hardly likely to gain approval, but that it was made at all is revealing of the official perspective.

11 However, the EU Ombudsman's role is limited to investigating complaints about the EU administration. Grønbeck-Jensen (1998) provides an interesting evaluation from a Scandinavian perspective, particularly apposite since these countries have been influential in the moves towards transparency in the EU; but he points out that the EU Ombudsman has no real teeth, having no better access to documents than the citizen.

12 A typical informal global regulatory body, set up by a decision of the Group of 7, but located at the OECD in Paris: see http:\\www.fatf.org (accessed – no date).

13 Dr. Henry Chasia, ITU Deputy Secretary-General, Opening Remarks to the Annual Council of the Commonwealth Telecommunication Organization, Trinidad and Tobago, 29 September 1998; this and much other documentation on the issue is available in the special area of the ITU website, www.itu.int (accessed – no date).

14 Research done for Médecins sans Frontières shows that of 1,233 drugs licensed worldwide between 1975–97 only thirteen were for tropical diseases, of which two were slight modifications of existing drugs, two developed for the US military, and five were the outcome of veterinary research: Pécoul *et al.* 1999; Pilling 1999.
15 See the Multilateral Initiative on Malaria, http://www.malaria.org/mim.html (accessed 23.04.01).

Bibliography

Addo, Michael K. (ed.) (1999) *Human Rights Standards and the Responsibility of Transnational Corporations*, The Hague: Kluwer Law International.

Bellamy, R. and Warleigh, A. (1998) 'From an Ethics of Integration to an Ethics of Participation: Citizenship and the Future of the European Union', *Millennium*, 27: 447–70.

Benhabib, Seyla (ed.) (1996) *Democracy and Difference: Contesting the Boundaries of the Political*, Princeton, NJ: Princeton University Press.

Bessette, Joseph M. (1994) *The Mild Voice of Reason: Deliberative Democracy and American National Government*, Chicago, IL: University of Chicago Press.

Beyleveld, D. and Brownseword, R. (1998) 'Human Dignity, Human Rights and Human Genetics', *Modern Law Review*, 61 (5): 661–80.

Bohman, James and Lutz-Bachmann, Mathias (eds) (1997) *Perpetual Peace*, Cambridge, MA: MIT Press.

Bradlow, Daniel D. (1996) 'The World Bank, the IMF, and Human Rights', *Transnational Law & Contemporary Problems*, 6, 1: 48.

Braithwaite, J. and Drahos, P. (2000) *Global Business Regulation*, Cambridge: Cambridge University Press.

Buiter, W.H. (1999) 'Alice in Euroland', *Journal of Common Market Studies*, 37, 2: 181–209.

Bunyan, Tony (1999) *Secrecy, Democracy and the Third Pillar*, London: Kogan Page.

Cable, Vincent (1999) *Globalization and Global Governance*, Chatham House Papers, London: Royal Institute of International Affairs.

Castells, Manuel (1998) *The Information Age: Economy, Society and Culture*, Malden, MA: Blackwell Publishers.

Cohen, J. and Sabel, C. (1997) 'Directly-Deliberative Polyarchy', *European Law Journal*, 3: 313–42.

Craig, Paul (1999) 'The Nature of the Community: Integration, Democracy, and Legitimacy', in Paul Craig and Gráinne de Burca (ed.), *The Evolution of EU Law*, Oxford: Oxford University Press, pp. 1–54.

Crawford, James (1994) 'Democracy and International Law', *British Yearbook of International Law*, LXV: 113–133.

Curtin, D.M. (1999) '"Civil Society" and the European Union: Opening Spaces for Deliberative Democracy', in Academy of European Law (ed.), *Collected Courses of the Academy of European Law*, vol. 7, book 1, The Hague, Kluwer Law International: 185–280.

Dahl, Robert A. (1999) 'Can International Organizations be Democratic? A Skeptic's View', in Ian Shapiro and Casiano Hacker-Cordón (eds), *Democracy's Edges*, Cambridge: Cambridge University Press.

Dezalay, Y. (1993) 'Professional Competition and the Social Construction of Transnational Regulatory Expertise', in J. McCahery, S. Picciotto and C. Scott (eds), *Corporate Control and Accountability. Changing Structures and the Dynamics of Regulation*, Oxford: Clarendon Press, pp. 203–15.

—— (1996) 'Between the State, Law, and the Market: The Social and Professional Stakes in the Construction and Definition of a Regulatory Arena', in W. Bratton, J. McCahery, S. Picciotto and C. Scott, *International Regulatory Competition and Coordination*, Oxford: Clarendon Press, pp. 59–87.

Drahos, Peter (1999) 'Biotechnology Patents, Markets and Morality', *European Intellectual Property Reports*: 441–9.

Dryzek, John S. (1990) *Discursive Democracy*, Cambridge: Cambridge University Press.

—— (1999) 'Transnational Democracy', *Journal of Political Philosophy*, 7, 1: 30–51.

Franck, T.M. (1992) *Political Questions Judicial Answers: Does the Rule of Law Apply to Foreign Affairs*, Princeton, NJ: Princeton University Press.

Gianviti, François (1998) 'International Convergence and the Role of the IMF', *Transnational (Corporate) Finance and the Challenge to the Law*, London: Hart Legal Workshop.

Giddens, Anthony (1999) *Runaway World: The Reith Lectures 1999*, London: BBC Publications.

Grønbeck-Jensen, C. (1998) 'The Scandinavian Tradition of Open Government and the European Union: Problems of Compatibility', *Journal of European Public Policy*, 5 185–99.

Habermas, J. (1995) 'Remarks on Dieter Grimm's "Does Europe Need a Constitution"', *European Law Journal*, 1: 303.

—— (1996) 'Three Normative Models of Democracy', in S. Benhabib (ed.) *Democracy and Difference: Contesting the Boundaries of the Political*, Cambridge: Cambridge University Press, pp. 21–30.

Hague, Barry N. and Loader, Brian D. (1999) *Digital Democracy: Discourse and Decision Making in the Information Age*, London: Routledge.

Harrison, Bennett (1994) *Lean and Mean: The Changing Landscape of Corporate Power in the Age of Flexibility*, New York: Basic Books.

Held, David (1995) *Democracy and the Global Order*, Oxford: Polity.

—— (1997) 'Cosmopolitan Democracy and the Global Order: A New Agenda', in J. Bohman and M. Lutz-Bachmann (eds) *Perpetual Peace*, Cambridge, MA: MIT Press, pp. 235–51.

Hoskyns, Catherine and Lambert, John (2000) 'How Democratic is the European Parliament', in C. Hoskyns and M. Newman (eds) *Democratizing the European Union: Issues for the Twenty-first Century*, Manchester: Manchester University Press, pp. 93–116.

Joerges, Christian (1999) ' "Good Governance" Through Comitology', in Christian Joerges and Ellen Vos (eds) *EU Committees: Social Regulation, Law and Politics*, Oxford: Hart, pp. 311–38.

Joerges, Christian and Neyer, Jürgen (1997) 'From Intergovernmental Bargaining to Deliberative Political Processes: the Constitutionalisation of Comitology', *European Law Journal* 3: 273–99.

Kant, Immanuel (1795/1966) 'Toward Perpetual Peace', in Mary J. Gregor, *Practical Philosophy*, Cambridge: Cambridge University Press, pp. 311–51.

Kohler-Koch, Beate and Eising, Rainer (eds) (1999) *The Transformation of Governance in the European Union*, London: Routledge.

Kooiman, Jan (1993) *Modern Governance: New Government-Society Interactions*, London: Sage Publications.

Landfried, Christine (1999) 'The European Regulation of Biotechnology by Polycratic Governance', in Christian Joerges and Ellen Vos, *EU Committees: Social Regulation, Law and Politics*, Oxford: Hart, pp. 173–94.

Majone, Giandomenico (ed.) (1990) *Deregulation or Re-Regulation: Regulatory Reform in Europe and the United States*, London/New York: Pinter/St Martin's.
—— (1993) 'The Rise of the Regulatory State in Europe', *West European Politics*, 17: 77–101.
—— (ed.) (1996) *Regulating Europe*, London: Routledge.
—— (1998) 'Europe's "Democracy Deficit": The Question of Standards', *European Law Journal*, 4: 5–28.
Manin, Bernard (1994) 'The Metamorphoses of Representative Government', *Economy and Society*, 23: 133–71.
—— (1997) *The Principles of Representative Government*, Cambridge: Cambridge University Press.
Mehra, Malini (2000) *Human Rights and the WTO: Time to Take on the Challenge*, Heinrich Boell Foundation.
OECD (1994) *Regulatory Reform for an Interdependent World*, Paris: Organization for Economic Cooperation and Development.
Pécoul, B., Chirac, P., Trouiller, P. and Pinel, J. (1999) 'Access to Essential Drugs in Poor Countries – A Lost Battle?', *Journal of American Medical Association*, 281 (4): 361–7.
Petersmann, Ernst-Ulrich (1998) 'How to Constitutionalize International Law and Foreign Policy for the Benefit of Civil Society', *Michigan Journal of International Law*, 20: 1.
—— (2000) 'The WTO Constitution and Human Rights', *Journal of International Economic Law*, 3 (1): 19–25.
Picciotto, Sol (1997) 'Fragmented States and International Rules of Law', *Social and Legal Studies*, 6: 259–79.
Picciotto, Sol and Haines, Jason (1999) 'Regulating Global Financial Markets', *Journal of Law and Society*, 26: 351–68.
Picciotto, Sol and Mayne, Ruth (eds) (1999) *Regulating International Business: Beyond Liberalization*, Basingstoke: Macmillan.
Pilling, David (1999) 'In Sickness and in Wealth', *Financial Times*, 22 October.
Radaelli, Claudio M. (1999) *Technocracy in the European Union*, London: Longman.
Ruggie, John G. (1982) 'International Regimes, Transactions and Change: Embedded Liberalism in the Postwar Economic Order', *International Organization*, 36: 379–415.
Sassen, Saskia (1999) 'Digital Networks and Power', in Mike Featherstone and Scott Lash (eds) *Spaces of Culture*, London: Sage Publications, pp. 49–63.
Schlemmer-Schulte, Sabine (1999) 'The World Bank Inspection Panel: A Record of the First International Accountability Mechanism and Its Role for Human Rights', *Human Rights Brief*, 6: 1.
Shrader-Frechette, K.S. (1991) *Risk and Rationality: Philosophical Foundations for Populist Reforms*, Berkeley, CA: University of California Press.
Skogly, Sigrun (1999) 'The Position of the World Bank and the International Monetary Fund in the Human Rights Field', in Raija Hanski and Markku Suksi (eds) *An Introduction to the International Protection of Human Rights*, Turku: Abo Akademi University, pp.2 31–50.
Slaughter, Anne-Marie (1997) 'The Real New World Order', *Foreign Affairs*, 76: 183–97.
—— (2000) 'Governing the Global Economy through Government Networks', in Michael Byers (ed.) *The Role of Law in International Politics*, Oxford: Oxford University Press, pp. 177–205.

Tyler, Michael (1998) 'Transforming Economic Relationships in International Telecommunications', Report for ITU Regulatory Colloquium No. 7, on The Changing Role of Government in an Era of Telecommunications Deregulation.

UNCTAD (1999) *World Investment Report 1999: Foreign Direct Investment and the Challenge of Development*, Geneva: United Nations.

United Nations (1999) 'Access to the Network Society – Who is in the Loop and on the Map?', in *Human Development Report*, New York: United Nations, pp. 61–6.

—— (2000) 'Development of Guidelines on the Role and Social Responsibilities of the Private Sector', paper by the Secretary-General for the Preparatory Committee for the special session on 'World Summit for Social Development and Beyond: Achieving Social Development for all in a Globalizing World', A/AC.253/21, 24 February, New York: United Nations.

Vogel, Steven K. (1996) *Freer Markets, More Rules*, Ithaca, NY: Cornell University Press.

Vos, Ellen (1999) 'EU Committees: the Evolution of Unforeseen Institutional Actors in European Product Regulation', in Christian Joerges and Ellen Vos (eds), *EU Committees: Social Regulation, Law and Politics*, Oxford: Hart, pp. 19–47.

Weiler, Joseph (1997) 'The European Union Belongs to its Citizens: Three Immodest Proposals', *European Law Review*, 22: 150.

World Bank (1997) *World Development Report 1997: The State in a Changing World*, New York: Oxford University Press.

—— (1998) *Development and Human Rights*, Washington, DC: The World Bank.

Wynne, Brian (1992) 'Risk and Social Learning', in Sheldon Krimsky and Dominic Golding,(eds) *Social Theories of Risk*, Westport, CT: Praeger, pp. 275–97.

15 Saving the social bond and recovering the public domain

Richard Devetak and Richard Higgott

> The political problem of mankind is to combine these things: economic effi-
> ciency, social justice and individual liberty.
>
> (John Maynard Keynes noted in *Essays in Persuasion*, 1931)

Introduction

Globalization has become the most over-used and under-specified term in the
international policy sciences since the passing of the Cold War. It is a term that
is not going to go away. More recently globalization has come to be associated
with financial collapse and economic turmoil. Our ability to satisfy Keynes'
three requirements under conditions of globalization is as remote now as at the
time he was writing. Neither markets nor the extant structures of governance
appear capable of providing for all three conditions at once. Globalization has
improved economic efficiency and it has provided enhanced individual liberty
for many; but in its failure to ensure social justice on a global scale, it also
inhibits liberty for many more.

Even leading globalizers – proponents of continued global economic liberalization occupying positions of influence in either the public or private domain – now
concede that in the failure to deliver a more just global economic order, globalization may hold within it the seeds of its own demise. As James Wolfensohn,
President of the World Bank, noted '[i]f we do not have greater equity and social
justice, there will be no political stability and without political stability no
amount of money put together in financial packages will give us financial
stability'.[1] His words, even if they appear to invert justice and stability as 'means'
and 'ends', are a sign of the times in the international financial institutions.

Conventional accounts of justice suppose the presence of a stable political
society, community or state as the site where justice can be instituted or realized. Moreover, conventional accounts, whether domestic or global, have also
assumed a Westphalian cartography of clear lines and stable identities and a
settled, stable social bond. In so doing, conventional theories – essentially
liberal individualist theory (and indeed liberal democracy more generally) –
have limited our ability to think about political action beyond the territorial
state. But what if the territorial boundaries of politics are coming unbundled
and a stable social bond deteriorates? Must a conception of justice relinquish its
Westphalian coordinates? These are not merely questions for the political
philosopher. In a time when the very fabric of the social bond is constantly
being re-woven by globalization, they cast massive policy shadows.

There are no settled social bonds in an age of globalization; the Westphalian 'givens' of justice no longer pertain. The forces and pressures of modernity and globalization render the idea of a stable social bond improbable. If this is the case, how are we to think about justice? When the social bond is undergoing change or modification, as a consequence of globalizing pressures, how can justice be conceptualized, let alone realized? Can there be justice in a world where that bond is constantly being disrupted, renegotiated and transformed by globalization? What are the distributive responsibilities under conditions of globalization, if any, of states? What should be the role of the international institutions in influencing the redistribution of wealth and resources on a global scale?

These are serious normative questions about governance. In the absence of institutions of governance capable of addressing these questions, justice (no matter how loosely defined) is unlikely to prevail. This paper suggests we need to begin to think about the relationship between globalization, governance *and* justice. To date, the question of 'justice' – a central question of academic political philosophy as practised within the context of the bounded sovereignty of the nation-state – is underdeveloped as a subject of study under conditions of globalization. Similarly, the study of globalization – especially when understood as economic liberalization and integration on a global scale – has been equally blind to 'justice' questions. This should come as no surprise. The struggle to separate normative and analytical enterprises has long been common practice in the social sciences. Indeed, it has been for a long time the hallmark of 'appropriate' scholarly endeavour. But such is the impact of globalization that we need to consider how we can traverse this artificial divide. Nowhere is this more important than at the interface of the processes of globalization and our understanding of what constitutes the prospects for creating a just international order at the end of the second millennium.

The chapter is in three sections. The first section one looks at the changing role of the state under conditions of globalization. It explains how assumptions made about the social bond – almost exclusively conceived in terms of sovereignty – are changing. It considers the specific challenges to the embedded liberal compromise that did so much to solidify the social bond in welfare states in the post-World War II era. The second section two charts the rise of some new global (non-state) actors, that are now contesting with states over the policy agendas emanating from globalization. The argument is twofold. First, strain on the social bond within states is giving rise to a search for newer forms of organization that transcend the sovereign state. We thus need to rethink how we understand the public domain on a global, as opposed to a national, level. Second, limited and flawed as the activities of non state actors (especially non-governmental organizations (NGOs) and global social movements (GSMs)) may be in the global public domain, they represent an important, evolving, alternative voice in the discourse of globalization to that of the semi-official neo-liberal orthodoxy on globalization. Moreover, the voice of the NGOs and the GSM is the one serious voice that aspires, rhetorically at least, to the development of a 'justice-based' dialogue beyond the level of the sovereign state.

The third section draws the strands of the first two sections together. It suggests that we have an analytical deficit occasioned by the failure of economic liberalism to assess the threat to its legitimacy emanating from its theoretical and practical myopia towards the *political* and *cultural* dynamics at work under globalization – the key sources of resistance to economic globalization. Neo-liberalism, with its emphasis on global commercialization, has forgotten why societal and democratic governmental structures were developed over the centuries.

Thus the Conclusion to the paper exhorts us to remember that states have important practical assets and normative theoretical roles. They are not mere passive actors in the face of globalization and justice, difficult as it would be, even if we could conceive of structures of global governance that might deliver it, will prove even more elusive in the absence of such political structures under conditions of economic globalization. The prospects of a satisfactory synthesis of the imperatives of a liberal economic theory of globalization, a normative political theory of the global sphere and a new form of social bond to compensate for the decline of the social bond within the contours of the sovereign state are deemed to be slight.

Sovereignty and modern political life

The sovereign state is the primary subject of modern international relations. Indeed, it has been the exclusive legitimate subject of international relations in the Westphalian system and the highest point of decision and authority. Since the middle of the seventeenth century, the sovereign form of state has become hegemonic by a process of eliminating alternative forms of governance.[2] The modern state achieved a particular resolution of the social bond hinged on the idea that political life is, or ought to be, governed according to the principle of sovereignty. The concept of sovereignty concentrated social, economic and political life around a single site of governance.

This conception of politics dates back to the legitimation crisis of the late sixteenth and early seventeenth centuries. Thomas Hobbes saw the political purpose of the sovereign state as the establishment of order based on mutual relations of protection and obedience.[3] The sovereign acted as the provider of security and the citizen, in turn, offered allegiance and obedience. This account emphasized sovereignty as the centre of authority, the origin of law and the source of individual and collective security. Citizens were bound together, whether for reasons of liberty or security, by their subjection to a common ruler and a common law. This basic structure of governance forged a social bond among citizens and between citizens and the state.

The institution of state sovereignty brought with it a spatial resolution, which distinguished between the domesticated interior and the anarchical exterior. In general terms, inside and outside came to stand for a series of binary oppositions that defined the limits of political possibility.[4] Inside came to embody the possibility of peace, order, security and justice; outside, the absence of what is achieved internally: war, anarchy, insecurity and injustice. Where sovereignty is present governance is possible; where it is absent governance is precluded. Modern political life is predicated on an exclusionary political space ruled by a single, supreme centre of decision-making claiming to represent and govern a political community. In recent interpretations, sovereignty has been understood as a constitutive political practice, one which has the effect of defining the social bond in terms of unity, exclusivity and boundedness and by the state's monopolization of authority, territory and community.[5]

A further crucial function performed by the sovereign state, of particular concern to this chapter, has been the management of the national economy. Historically there have been competing accounts of how states should govern their economies, especially over the manner and extent to which governments should intervene in and regulate economic activity. Yet historically, and despite many important ideological and normative differences, there has been a tendency within the dominant liberal tradition to treat national economies as discrete systems of social organization more or less delimited by the state's territorial boundaries. Economies are conceived as largely self-contained, self-regulating systems of exchange and production. This was as true for economic liberals, such as Adam Smith and David Ricardo, as it was for economic nationalists and mercantilists, such as List and Hamilton. This is not to suggest that such thinkers were blind to the fact that economic activity commonly spilled over national frontiers, but that they treated national economies as self-contained units in the international market.

The economy served the community of the state in which it was embedded; its functions and benefits were defined via the interests of a given political society. That states monopolized the right to tax within their boundaries enhanced the correlation of the economy with the state's boundaries. One of the general functions of the state, therefore, was to govern the economy in such a way as to promote the wealth and welfare of the community. Liberals focused on the market mechanism as the surest and most efficient means of ensuring the liberty, security and prosperity of both individuals and the community; non-liberal approaches tended to emphasize the need for regulation and manipulation of economic activity in order to satisfy the social needs of the community.

In short, a purpose of the sovereign state in modern political life was to stabilize the social bond. It did so by resolving questions of governance around the principle of sovereignty. Structures and practices of governance were established with direct correspondence between authority, territory, community and economy. It is in this context that justice has conventionally been conceived. Justice, no matter how defined, depended on a settled, stable social bond. Outside of a settled social bond, justice was thought to be unlikely if not impossible. The sovereign state was thus a precondition for justice. However it is defined – whether as security from injury, as most natural law thinkers understood it, or as the distribution of rights and duties, as liberals tend to define it –

justice has generally been circumscribed by the territorial limits of the sovereign state. The boundaries of justice were thought to be co-extensive with the legal-territorial jurisdiction and economic reach of the sovereign polity.

But that was then. The sovereign state is an historical product that emerged in a particular time to resolve social, economic and political problems. With the passage of time, and the changed milieu in which states exist, it is no longer axiomatic that the sovereign state is practical or adequate as a means of *comprehensively* organizing modern political life and especially providing the array of public goods normally associated with the early twenty-first century welfare state. In the following section, we survey the manner in which some of the trends associated with economic globalization have begun to unravel the distinctive resolution of the social bond achieved by the sovereign state, and in particular the welfare state. Increasingly, the sovereign state is seen as out-of-kilter with the times, as globalization radically transforms time-space relations and alters the traditional coordinates of social and political life.

Globalization and embedded liberalism

Material changes associated with economic globalization – especially the processes of liberalization, deregulation and integration of the global economy in the domains of production, exchange and finance – are affecting the ability of the sovereign state to stabilize the social bond. Even if we reject the more extreme post-modern readings of sovereignty under globalization, several normative questions are raised by this destabilization. As the coordinates of modern social and political life alter, states – the traditional Westphalian site of authority – are supplemented, outflanked and sometimes overrun by competing sources of authority. Alternative sources of power and authority arising from globalization place pressure on the capacity of the state to deliver welfare provisions and, in turn, transforms the social bond.

To be specific, the urge for free markets and small government has created asymmetries in the relationship between the global economy and the national state. This situation has undermined the post-World War II embedded liberal compromise.[6] According to John Ruggie, the liberal international order was predicated on measures taken concurrently to ensure domestic order and to domesticate the international economy.[7] Consequently, the modern welfare state was the product of both domestic and international forces. States were the sites of trade-off, charged with cushioning domestic society against external pressures and transnational forces. But, globalization has changed this. One, as yet, unexplored implication of Ruggie's early analysis is that globalization focuses attention on a reconfiguration of the social bond, as a result of changes emanating from the processes of adjustment in the division of political space between the domestic and international policy domains. Domestic and international politics became embedded and intertwined in the same global system – the post-World War II liberal order.

States are thus crucial in shaping the social bonds, which exist at any given time, and in any given space. They alter the relationship, not just between insiders and outsiders, but between citizens and the state. However, as domestic and foreign economic policy issues become increasingly blurred, as the domestic economy becomes increasingly detached from the sovereign state, and as economic de-regulation and de-nationalization continue, it is more difficult for states to manage the domestic-international trade-off in a way that satisfies competing demands on it. And it becomes more difficult for states to sustain the trade-offs managed in the Bretton Woods, embedded liberal, era.

Globalization makes it harder for governments to provide the compensatory mechanisms that could underwrite social cohesion in the face of change in employment structures. As it has become more difficult to tax capital, the burden shifts to labour making it more difficult to run welfare states.[8] While policy-makers may wise up to this problem, their perceived need to avoid socially disintegrative activities has not been joined by a clear policy understanding of how to minimize dislocation, where economic compensation alone may not be sufficient, in the face of the tensions inherent in the structural imperatives of economic liberalization. In the closing days of the twentieth century, the internationalization of trade and finance may be sound economic theory, but it is also contentious political practice. When pursued in combination, free markets and the reduction of, or failure to introduce, compensatory domestic welfare is a potent cocktail leading to radical responses from the dispossessed.[9]

An economist's response to this dilemma – that liberalization enhances aggregate welfare – might well be correct, but it does not solve the *political problem*. It might be good economic theory but it is poor political theory. While some objections to liberalization are indeed 'protectionism' by another name, not all objections can be categorized in this manner. Moreover, even where compensatory mechanisms might be adequate, the destruction of domestic social arrangements can have deleterious outcomes of their own. If nationalist responses are to be avoided, then public policy must distinguish between protectionism and legitimate concerns. Securing domestic political support for the continued liberalization of the global economy requires more than just the assertion of its economic virtue. It also requires political legitimation.

Thus the question facing political theorists and policy analysts alike is, can the embedded liberal compromise (maximizing the positive and mitigating the negative effects of international liberalization) be maintained, or repaired even? This is now a much wider question than when first formulated by Ruggie. Under conditions of globalization, the question must now be addressed not only within, but also beyond the boundaries of the state. Sovereignty as the organizing principle of international relations is undergoing a more dramatic rethink than at any time since its inception. In an era of globalization – accompanied by assumptions about the reduced effectiveness of states – policy-makers and analysts set greater store by the need to enhance the problem solving capabilities of various international regimes in the resolution of conflict and the institutionalization of cooperation. But the contours of this rethink are still primarily linked to enhancing the effectiveness and efficiency of international regimes.

The language of globalization, especially in its neo-liberal guise, is about the managerialist capacity of the modern state. But it has failed to recognize the manner in which the internationalization of governance can also exacerbate the 'democratic deficit'. States are not only problem solvers; their policy elites are also strategic actors with interests of, and for, themselves. Collective action problem solving in international relations is couched in terms of effective governance. It is rarely posed as a question of responsible or accountable government, let alone justice. While these latter questions may be the big normative questions of political theory; it is the political theory of the bounded sovereign state. For most of the world's population, the extant institutions of global governance – especially the financial ones – are not seen to deliver justice.

Questions of global redistributive justice, accountability and democracy receive scant attention from within the mainstream of political philosophy and a political theory of global governance is in its infancy. Extant political theories of justice and representative governance assume the presence of sovereignty. In an era of a fraying social bond at the state level and the absence of alternative focuses of identity at the global level, the prospects of securing systems of efficiency, let alone accountability seem slim. For realist scholars and practitioners of international relations this is unsurprising. They assume the absence of altruism. Force and power – not global dialogue about the prospects for community and democracy, *pace* the work of the cosmopolitan political theorists such as Linklater and Held[10] – are the driving forces of international relations.

Yet there is a paradox. The language of democracy and justice takes on a more important rhetorical role in a global context, at the same time as globalization attenuates the hold of democratic communities over the policy-making process within the territorial state. As the nation-state, as a vehicle for democratic engagement becomes problematic, the clamour for democratic engagement at the global level becomes stronger. But these are not stable processes. Attention to the importance of normative questions of governance and state practice as exercises in accountability, democratic enhancement and what we might call justice-generation must catch up with our understanding of governance as exercises in effectiveness and efficiency. There are a number of ways to do this. One route, explored in section two, is to extend the public policy discourse on the nature of market-state relations to include other actors from civil society.

Global governance and the transformation of the public sphere

The modern social bond was conceived in terms of the concentration of authority, territory and community around the notion of sovereignty. Moreover, this political resolution was intimately tied to a notion of a corresponding economic space. But for 130 years – or since the marginalist revolution – economic analysis has become separated from the study of politics and society. It is only with a recognition of globalization that civil society, along with the

NGOs and GSMs are agents for building a post-Westphalian global civil society and reconstructing a new social bond at the end of the twentieth century. The behaviour of NGOs is invariably normative, prescriptive, increasingly internationalized, highly politicized and at times very effective.[15] NGOs try to universalize a given value and their growing influence is revolutionizing the relationship between 'old' and 'new' forms of multilateralism. The old multilateralism is constituted by the top down activities of the existing structures of international institutional governance (IMF, World Bank and WTO). The new multilateralism represents the attempt by social movements to 'building a system of global governance from the bottom up'.[16]

The preferred strategy of the old multilateralism of the international institutions is to extend their remit *geographically* (wider institutional membership), *functionally* (deeper coverage of issues) and *inclusively* (by the cooption and socialization of recalcitrant actors into the dominant neo-liberal market mode). By contrast, the new multilateralism of the GSMs (especially NGOs in developing countries) tries to change the prevailing organizing assumptions of the contemporary global order and thus alter policy outcomes. While multilateralism is not imperialism, a working assumption of many NGOs is that often existing institutions are instruments, if not of US hegemony, then at least of an OECD ideological dominance of the existing world economic order.

Whatever their agendas, the ability of social movements to affect decision making in international fora rubs up against the processes of globalization. Throughout the 1990s, social movement resistance to 'free trade' related issues has invariably been characterized as protectionist or globophobic. This is certainly the case with the environmental movement, where demands for sustainable development imply a form of 'fettered development' to counter the deregulating tendencies of globalization. It is also the case in the domain of human rights, where NGOs attempt to strengthen labour rights generally, women's and children's rights in particular, in the face of MNCs location decisions based on factors such as cheap labour costs. Much current NGO activity can be captured under a broad, if ill-defined agenda to secure 'justice for those disadvantaged by globalization'.

NGOs articulate a view of globalization – emphasizing privatization, deregulation and market conforming adjustment – as antithetical to their aims of securing human rights and environmental protection. NGOs represent alternative discourses to those reflected in the positions of those who gain most from the advance of globalization. Opposition to globalization has become an integrating feature of much of the literature of 'internationalized' NGOs.[17] Nowhere is this better illustrated than in the opposition to NAFTA in the late 1980s and early 1990s, in resistance to the agendas of the WTO and the OECD initiative on a Multilateral Agreement on Investment in the late 1990s. This interest in how to alter (resist) globalization represents a shift in the *modus operandi* of NGOs – from the field to the corridors of power. In many policy domains they have become the discursive opposition.

Traditional agents – such as the established policy communities holding office in the major industrial countries and the inter-governmental financial institutions – are only just beginning to recognize the significance of NGOs and GSMs. At times, established actors appear to lack the skills to deal in anything other than a resistive or combative fashion with these groups. But governments are learning that they must secure their support or, at the very least, neutralize their opposition. But the ability to secure a balance between wider consultation and accountability, on the one hand, and an ability to resist the pressures of lobby groups on the other, is still underdeveloped. Nowhere is this better illustrated than in the ambiguity of the international economic institutions towards interaction with bodies purporting to be acting on behalf of one or another group within 'civil society'. This is certainly the case at the IMF, WTO and, albeit to a lesser extent, at the World Bank. There is now quite a long history of engaging NGOs on the ground in developing countries at the World Bank. Extending this engagement to the decision-making processes in Washington is still largely resisted.

In short, the elite driven nature of the neo-liberal globalization project is under challenge. The internationalization of NGOs, enhanced by new technologies, allows them to address governmental policy from outside, as well as from within, the state. They represent, or at least purport to represent, interests that are conventionally excluded from decision-making processes. As such, they are vehicles for the advancement of strong normative ideas in global civil society. NGOs and other similar, mission-driven, agents are increasingly important actors in contemporary international politics and governance. Securing a peaceful and constructive *modus operandi* with non-state actors will be a major exercise for state actors in the global policy community in the twenty-first century.

The rise of the NGO: keeping a sense of perspective

Some NGOs are now global agents or players of some influence, as the 1997 award of the Nobel Peace Prize for the campaign to ban land mines and the role of NGOs in the defeat of the MAI attests.[18] NGOs are clearly capable of setting agendas and changing international policy on important issues. But the age of innocence is over. NGOs are in many ways the victims of their own success. Longer standing actors in international relations – state and inter-governmental organization policy-making elites – are now treating them much more seriously.

At present there is a discrepancy between the demands of NGOs for rights (to be heard and to influence policy) and an acceptance of certain obligations or duties that may be attendant on these rights (especially the duty truthfully to reflect the position of one's antagonists). While a balance may come with time, to date only minimal efforts to inculcate a 'rights-duties' balance within the larger NGO family have been made.[19] If NGOs and other non-state actors are to become legitimate agents of acceptable structures of global governance, in an era of globalization, they will have to accept the need for transparent, accountable and participatory systems of decision-making of exactly the kind they expect to see in national governments, multinational corporations and international organizations.

Speaking the language of 'opposition', their discourse reflects a greater commitment to questions of justice, accountability and democracy. But there are limits to the degree of support and acceptance their agendas are likely to secure. For example, despite the economic crisis that began in East Asia, the power of the free market ideal remains strong and support for interference in the interests of redistributive justice are unlikely to replace the market ideal in the corridors of public power and private wealth. Moreover, not all opponents of the worst effects of globalization are necessarily protectionists or opponents of economic liberalization, *per se*. Educated populations are capable of disaggregating the various elements of liberalization. Survey data suggests they are more supportive of trade liberalization than they are of financial deregulation.[20] Much social movement interest in the 'new protectionism' – a return to 'localization' – is an over-simplified rhetorical position that lacks the intellectual power to counter the logic of liberalization.

Globalization, justice and the state

That the activity and influence of NGOs has increased in international relations is in little doubt. It is however, naive to universalize the NGO experience. States still propose and dispose of international agreements and NGOs still – as in their involvement in the activities of the international institutions – need governmental sponsorship, or at least governmental acquiescence, to secure influence.

Polarization, social disintegration and the re-emergence (often violent) of identity politics are visible outcomes of the inequalities between globalization's winners and losers. They raise several questions that will become increasingly important if we are to create a more just world order. Will we have: (i) enough food for growing populations? (ii) Enough energy for growing economies? (iii) A sustainable physical environment in which to inhabit? (iv) Global institutions to manage these issues, preserve the peace, prevent burgeoning civic unrest and political–military dislocation within the developing world and in relations between the developed and the developing worlds?

Economists tell us that the key elements of globalization – the greater economic integration of the international economy and the revolution in communications and technology – are, of themselves, neutral and have the potential to solve these problems. In theory maybe, but it is not axiomatic that the tension between economic growth and environmental sustainability will be contained. Making the world's population more secure depends on how this tension is managed. This is the governance question. Governance – the means by which societies deliver collective goods and minimize collective bads – is as important today as it ever was and states remain central to this process. But, there is a deficit in the relationship between the *de facto* market led processes of economic liberalization and integration and the *de jure* state generated mechanisms that underwrite the international fora for the delivery of collective goods.

Thus the efficacy of the major international institutions remains a key normative and policy question for the twenty-first century. Will they remain vehicles for the pursuit of state interests, as traditionally defined in realist understandings of international organization? Or, can they evolve into sites to accommodate multiple demands and interests of public and private and state and non-state actors throughout the widening policy communities and civil societies of states? These are normative and analytical questions, yet they cast long policy shadows. The contest between the 'multilateralism from above' and the 'multilateralism from below' is just beginning.

State policy elites may be conscious of their own diminished sovereignty but also of the accompanying need to control the 'public bads' that emanate from the effects of technology on cultures and eco-systems and the international order; especially the spread of drugs, crime, terrorism, disease and pollution. For sovereignty erosion to be acceptable, it must occur via collective action in an issue-specific, not generalized, manner. 'Sovereignty pooling' will have to be volunteered out of recognition that self-interest is sometimes advanced collectively not individually.

How likely is this when the major factor explaining inter-state cooperation is *still domestic actor preference?*[21] Despite impeccable normative arguments in favour of collective action problem-solving, prospects for regular successful international cooperation among states must not be exaggerated. The desired basic goods for a 'just' global era – economic regulation, environmental security, the containment of organized crime and terrorism, and the enhancement of welfare – will not be provided on a state by state basis. They must be provided collectively.

If the limitations of inter-state cooperation are to be overcome, greater use will have to be made of innovative approaches to governance arising from the information revolution. Technology can strengthen the governance capacities of both state and civil society. Information technologies offer opportunities for private sector supplementation of the governance functions of states. Public/private provision of collective goods must not be seen as an either/or policy option. Private sector actors, from both the corporate world and civil society, will continue to be more significant in inter-governmental negotiation processes as issue-linked coalitions operate across borders to set agendas and enforce compliance.

In addition to the 'how' question in the international institutional management of those global forces that have a major impact on societies, this chapter has also asked the important normative question. What are the prospects for supra-national institutional forms of regulation guaranteeing some kind of fairness? Justice in a global context, we have tried to suggest, is an underdeveloped, but emerging issue. The normative agenda for international relations will not go away. But for justice to have meaning in an era of globalization, governance will have to be exercised at a global level. As yet, however, the institutions of global governance are ill equipped to cope with such issues.

Moreover, we live in a culture of moral hazard in which, to provide but the most obvious example, the speculative operation of the international capital markets are underwritten by the sacrifices of ordinary members of society, especially in the developing world. The era of instant global capital mobility is seen by many of the world's population, and not just in the developing world, as a time of heightened and permanent insecurity. There may be movement in the international financial institutions, but unless something is done to mitigate the prospects of events such as the East Asia currency crises reoccurring, the lesson the majority of the world's population will draw is that not even a reformed system, let alone the system as it is currently constituted, will be able to deliver anything approaching an acceptably just or equitable world order.

In this respect, economic liberalization holds within it the seeds of its own downfall. Intellectual and evidentiary arguments for liberalization and open markets as superior generators of wealth have been won; or should have been. But rapid aggregate increases in global wealth and production have been accompanied by a corresponding naivete as to the political and social effects of these processes on the civil polities of developed and developing societies alike. As the politics of the East Asia crises demonstrated, theoretical parsimony blinds modern liberal economic theory and current market practices to the complex and combative politics that constitutes the down side of economic liberalization. Sound rationalist economic logic on its own is not sufficient to contain the backlash against globalization.[22]

The 'post-politics' of the post-Washington consensus

For many in the developed world, liberalization has become an end in itself with little or no consideration given to its effect on prevailing social norms and values within societies and polities. The global market place of the 1980s and the first six to seven years of the 1990s were largely an 'ethics free zone'. This was the case whether one was observing practice (both public and private sector) in the international political economy or whether one was reading the scholar on the global economy. In the domain of practice, processes of trade liberalization, financial deregulation and asset privatization were increasing the tempo of the globalization of the world economy. Free enterprise and the market culture had triumphed. Consequently, the consensus over how society is organized within the spatial jurisdiction of nation-states was strained and the continued process of liberalization threatened.

Globalization is unravelling the social bond. The policy remedies at the disposal of state agents for maintaining the cohesion of communities are curtailed, although not eliminated. Some governments attempt to 'depoliticize' – that is, place at one step removed – the state's responsibility for the effects of globalization on its citizenry. Yet, it is the practice of politics that creates the structures of communities.[23] As such, it will make the role of state institutions much more important in the next decade than has been assumed throughout the neo-liberal era, when the retreat of the state was deemed axiomatic.[24] States have assets and capabilities; they are not merely passive or reactive actors.

But these assets have to be used better, domestically and internationally, if economic liberalization is to allow for the more effective provision of public goods. How to strike the appropriate balance between domestic socio-political imperatives and a normative commitment to an open liberal economic order remains the central policy question for the twenty-first century. Globalization is clearly an issue in need of sophisticated technical economic analysis, but it is also in need of analysis that is normative and ethical. First, best, economically efficient, solutions may not always be politically feasible, or indeed socially desirable and most economic analysis has, to date studiously ignored those socio-political and cultural conditions that, often more than economic explanation, will condition the prospects of continued liberalization.

These two interpretations of global governance (it is hard to call them definitions) stand respectively in relationship to the Washington and post-Washington consensus. The initial consensus was an attempt by an international managerial-cum-policy elite to create a set of global *economic* norms to be accepted by entrants to the global economy under the guidance of the existing international institutions. The post-Washington consensus can be seen as an attempt to induce support for a new set of *socio-political* norms to legitimate globalization by mitigating its worst excesses? If captured by the existing international institutions (claiming that they are the only available sites of global governance) then, reflecting the ideology of globalism in its neo-liberal guise, definition (i) effectiveness and efficiency, may well become the dominant mode of understanding global governance. Critical analysts can be forgiven, therefore, for not seeing the growing interest in global governance as an automatically 'progressive' force.

Democratic accountability, definition (ii) will be, *at best*, a secondary component. Globalization might have rapidly generated a set of technological and economic connections; but it has yet to generate an equivalent set of shared values and sense of community, even among those agents actively involved in discussions about greater global participation. Indeed, much of the policy prescriptive work on governance currently being undertaken, in or around international institutions, treats governance as a neutral concept in which rational decision-making and efficiency in outcomes, not democratic participation, is privileged.

In this regard, the debate on global governance within the international institutions (UN, World Bank, IMF and WTO) remains firmly within a dominant liberal institutionalist tradition. Ethically normative discussions about democracy and justice beyond the borders of the territorial state are still largely technocratic ones about how to enhance transparency and, in limited contexts, accountability. They fail, or in some instances still refuse, to address the asymmetries of power over decision-making that characterize the activities of these organizations. The essence of the liberal institutionalist view remains avowedly state-centric and pluralist and is, not surprisingly, captured nicely by American institutionalist, Robert Keohane's, definition of global democracy as 'voluntary pluralism under conditions of maximum transparency'.[25]

The global governance deficit

The liberal institutionalist view is also essentially the reformist view held for the international institutional leaders by senior global decision-makers, from US Treasury Secretary, Lawrence Summers to UN Secretary General Kofi Annan. Annan called for better accountability to improve global governance after the abortive MTN Ministerial Meeting in Seattle in November 1999 and Summers called for greater transparency and accountability for the IMF at its Spring 2000 meeting.[26] As previously argued, Annan's Global Compact also approximates the liberal institutionalist genre of thinking, albeit (given its implicit belief that the global corporate sector can be socialized) on the progressivist constructive end of the spectrum.

The preferred term in international policy circles is 'global public policy,[27] not global governance. The aim is to make provision for the collective delivery of global public goods.[28] 'Public policy' has none of the ideological and confrontational baggage present in the notion of 'politics'. Institutional analysis, with its concerns for understanding the mechanisms of collective choice in situations of strategic interaction, is similarly 'de-politicized'. This is not to deny that recent rationalist theorizing of cooperation has not been a major advance on earlier realist understandings.[29] But the problem with rationalist and strategic choice approaches is not what they do, but what they omit. They make little attempt to understand governance as issues of *politics and power*. This has implications for the operational capability and intellectual standing of the international institutions.

In essence, the governance agenda as constructed by the international institutions of the post-Washington consensus era has largely stripped questions of power, domination, resistance and accountability from the debate. To the extent that the international institutions recognize that political resistance is a legitimate part of the governance equation, it is a problem to be solved. It is not seen as a *perpetual* part of the process. In this regard, for many key players, global governance is not about politics. There are no problems that cannot be 'governed away'. Governance, *pace* definition (i) as effectiveness and efficiency, is 'post-political'. Agendas are set and implementation becomes the name of the game. Notwithstanding the fragmented and dissaggregated nature of political community in a global era, there is no place outside of the rubric of existing governance structures for non-state political action on global policy issues.

The post-Washington consensus view of good governance implies the universalization of an understanding of governance based on efficiency and effectiveness, in which democracy is a secondary component. Nowhere is this better illustrated than in the efforts of those around the World Bank and the UNDP to develop public–private partnerships and global public-policy networks for the collective provision of public goods.[30] Such work is innovative, certainly by the standards of the international institutions, but it is also limited by the political implications of its 'top down' intellectual origins. Notwithstanding stronger rhetorical efforts to bridge the participatory gap, these recent attempts to develop strategies to advance the collective provision of global public goods still minimize the essence of 'the political' in these processes.

Moreover, this agenda has only a limited notion of public good, largely consistent with a liberal individualist ideology. Any notion of serious redistribution of wealth in the direction of the world's poorest is not considered a public good. Indeed, such support for the world's poor as there is, understood as development aid, is seen by some to be on the brink of collapsing.[31] The global public goods literature, indeed the global governance agenda more generally, does not address this issue. Given the ideological underpinnings of neo-liberalism, it is not intellectually, let alone politically capable of doing so. Following from this analytical and theoretical deficit, the practical question facing policy-makers in the early twenty-first century is how to develop appropriate international institutions where 'appropriate' does not mean simply 'effective'? It has been argued that the shift from a Washington consensus to a post-Washington consensus represents a 'mood swing' in world politics that has raised the salience of the 'global governance' dimension of international relations. It is also argued that an attempt to create a new consensus around the need for governance, seen as effective and efficient management of global problems by the provision of global public goods through global policy networks, is limited by a lack of an understanding of politics and a wider normative commitment to the creation of a global ethic of poverty alleviation via a commitment to redistribution.

Most significantly, an increasing number of the senior office holders of the major international financial institutions have recognized the de-stabilizing effects of unfettered liberalization and the growing perception that it exacerbates inequality, and as Paul Krugman intimated, it may be necessary to save liberalism from itself. We could also add it might be necessary to save economists from themselves. In order to do so, what is needed is a revitalized multidisciplinary 'international political economy'.

A new international political economy?

This new international political economy would go 'beyond economics'. It would combine the breadth of vision of the classical political economy of the mid-nineteenth century with the analytical advances of twentieth-century social science. Driven by a need to address the complex and often all embracing nature of the globalizing urge, the methodology of the new international political economy would reject old dichotomies – between agency and structure, and states and markets – which fragmented classical political economy into separate disciplines in the wake of the marginalist revolution in economic thought.[32] Rather, the new international political economy would aspire to a hard-headed materialist (that is real world) political economy that recognized the limits of methodologically individualist, choice-based economic theory.[33] Instead, it would explain how choice is affected by the social meanings of objects and actions. Indeed, if there is one thing that the emerging processes of globalization teach us, it is that mono-causal explanations of economic phenomena lack sufficient explanatory power. Such a view now holds increasing sway at the dawn of a new century. Moreover, it holds sway not just among Third World economic nationalists and radical academic critiques of a global neo-liberal agenda but also within sections of the mainstream economics community.

This reformist position also reflects a long overdue resistance to the often over-stated virtues of parsimony. In this regard, the current era should offer no easy location for specialist parsimonious theorizing.[34] The new international political economy would operate from an assumption that what the marginalist revolution separated, globalization is bringing together. We are in a period of complex contest between the desire for grand totalizing narratives and theories of globalization, on the one hand and the need to produce specific histories of various actors and sites of resistance (be they states, classes, regions, or other localist forms of organization), on the other. The new international political economy must eschew this dichotomy. It should seek to be multi-disciplinary and theoretical in intellectual spirit and empirically grounded in history, at the same time as it aspires to a normatively progressive research programme.

At the core of these concerns must be the changing institutional patterns which characterize alternative models of capitalism and the mechanisms by which a global economy and a global culture are constructed. Its normative agenda should be underwritten by a strong policy impetus towards the issues of enhancing justice and fairness under conditions of globalization – especially in the developing world's relationship with the developed.[35] Above all, the new international political economy would foreground power in its *structural* as well as its *relational* form and recognize the need to ask the important Lasswellian questions, about power, of the 'who gets what, when and how' variety.[36] The new international political economy has major implications for how we understand the current governance agenda emanating from the international policy community. Largely because it is driven by members of a de-territorialized transnational policy elite, the current policy agenda has no conception of the residual strength of identity politics, the importance of social bonds within communities, the manner in which globalization appears to be picking many traditional social bonds apart without creating new sources of solidarity and, by implicit extension, no ethical agenda for addressing these questions.

In this context, legitimate global governance, without a sense of community, would appear a remote prospect. This is sham governance. Real governance is about political contest over issues such as distribution and justice. In the promotion of the public good, it is concerned with the empowerment of communities from the bottom up rather than just the top down. Both issues, in other than rhetorical fashion, still fall into the too hard box for many in the international policy community. They are either ignored, or assumed away as 'policy questions' in which the global distribution of wealth and poverty, as currently constituted, is not part of the agenda for consideration. But governance is about making choices, while most specialists at the international institutions advancing a governance agenda have a conception of international relations that sees the global economy in de-contextualized fashion and their tasks as de-politicized and technical.

This is not an argument against the importance liberal institutionalism places on international institutional reform. Rather, it is a plea for a normative recognition of the need to move beyond; to recognize the need to start thinking about a 'global polity' and create a global public domain in which a deliberative dialogue between rule makers and rule takers, of the kind envisaged by cosmopolitan theorists, can take place.[37]

Attempts to implement collective policies through international institutions will lack legitimacy if there is no shared normative commitment to the virtue of a given policy. International institutions must secure converging policy positions by agreement and willing harmonization, not by force. There must be provision, where necessary, for political communities to exercise an exit option on a particular issue where it is thought that this issue threatens the fibre of their (national) identity. This is not to offer a free-rider charter in the contemporary global economy, but to call for tolerance and an acceptance of difference rarely displayed under a neo-liberal orthodoxy in the closing stages of the twentieth century.[38] Without such tolerance the prospects for the development of some kind of social bond conducive to the development of a minimum conception of global justice cannot be envisaged.

Notes

This is an expanded version of 'Justice Unbound? Globalization, States and the Transformation of the Social Bond', originally published in *International Affairs* 75, 3, 1999: 483–98.

1 Address to Board of Governors of the Bank (October 1998).
2 Hendrik Spruyt, *The Sovereign State and its Competitors* (Princeton, NJ: Princeton University Press, 1994).
3 Thomas Hobbes, *Leviathan* (Harmondsworth: Penguin, 1968).
4 R.B.J. Walker, *Inside/Outside: International Relations as Political Theory* (Cambridge: Cambridge University Press, 1993).
5 Andrew Linklater, *The Transformation of Political Community* (Cambridge: Polity Press, 1998).
6 John G. Ruggie, 'At Home Abroad, Abroad at Home: International Liberalisation and Domestic Stability in the New World Economy', *Millennium: Journal of International Studies*, 24, 3, 1995: 507–26.
7 John G. Ruggie, 'International Regimes, Transactions and Change: Embedded Liberalism in the Post War Economic Order', *International Organisation*, 36, 2, 1982.
8 Daniel Rodrik, *Has Globalization Gone Too Far?* (Washington, DC: Institute for International Economic, 1997).
9 Vincent Cable, *The World's New Fissures: The Politics of Identity* (London: Demos, 1994).
10 Linklater, *The Transformation of Political Community*, op cit., and David Held, *Democracy and the Global Order* (Cambridge: Polity, 1995).
11 Richard Higgott, 'Economics, Politics and (International) Political Economy: The Need for a Balanced Diet in an Era of Globalisation', *New Political Economy*, 4, 1, 1999: 23–36.
12 Jürgen Habermas, *The Theory of Communicative Action: The Critique of Functionalist Reason* (London: Heinemann, 1989).

13 Robert Cox, 'Civil Society at the Turn of the Millennium: Prospects for an Alternative World Order', *Review of International Studies*, 25, 1, 1999: 10–11.

14 *Handbook of International Organisations* (Brussels: Union of International Associations, 1994).

15 Margaret Keck and Katherine Sikkink, *Transnational Issue Networks in International Politics* (Ithaca, NY: Cornell University Press, 1997).

16 Robert Cox, (ed.) *The New Realism: Perspectives on Multilateral and World Order* (Basingstoke: Macmillan, 1997), p.xxxvii.

17 Cecilia Lynch, 'Social Movements and the Problem of Globalisation', *Alternatives*, 23, 2, 1998: 149–73.

18 P.J. Simmons, 'Learning to Live with NGOs', *Foreign Policy*, 111, 1998: 82–97.

19 Leon Gordenker and Thomas G. Weiss, 'NGO Participation in the Global Policy Process', *Third World Quarterly*, 16, 3, 1995: 543–55.

20 *The Economist*, 2 January 1999.

21 Helen Milner, *Interests, Institutions and Information: Domestic Politics and International Relations* (Princeton, NJ: Princeton University Press, 1997).

22 See Richard Higgott, 'Economic Crisis in East Asia: A Case Study in the International Politics of Resentment', *New Political Economy*, 3, 3, 1998: 333–56.

23 Bernard Crick, *In Defence of Politics* (London: Penguin, 1962) p. 24.

24 Susan Strange, *The Retreat of the State* (Cambridge: Cambridge University Press, 1996).

25 Robert Keohane, 'International Institutions: Can Interdependence Work?', *Foreign Policy*, Spring, 1998, cited in McGrew, 'From Global Governance to Good Governance: Theories and Prospects of Democratising the Global Polity'.

26 See Kofi Annan, *Renewing the UN* (New York: United Nations, 1999); and Lawrence Summers, 'Statement to the International Monetary Fund Financial Committee', Washington, DC, 16 April, 2000.

27 See Wolfgang H. Reinecke, *Global Public Policy: Governing without Government* (Washington, DC: Brookings, 1998).

28 See Kaul, Inge, Grunberg, Isabelle and Stern, Marc A. (eds) *Global Public Goods: International Co-operation in the 21st Century* (New York: Oxford University Press, 1999).

29 See, Robert O. Keohane, *After Hegemony: Collaboration and Discord in the World Economy* (Princeton, NJ: Princeton University Press, 1984); Helen V. Milner, *Interests, Institutions and Information: Domestic Politics and International Relations* (Princeton, NJ: Princeton University Press, 1997).

30 See Wolfgang Reinecke and Francis Deng, *Critical Choices: The United Nations, Networks and the Future of Global Governance* (Ottawa: International Development Research Centre, 2000).

31 See Jean Claude Therien and Carolyn Lloyd, 'Development Assistance on the Brink', *Third World Quarterly*, 21 (1) 2000: 21–38.

32 See James Caporaso and David Levine, *Theories of Political Economy* (New York: Cambridge University Press, 1992).

33 For a discussion of these limits see Amartya Sen, 'Rational Fools: A Critique of the Behavioral Foundations of Economic Theory', *Philosophy and Public Affairs*, 6 (4), 1977: 713–44; and Ben Fine, 'The Triumph of Economics: Or, "Rationality Can be Dangerous to Your Reasoning"', in James G. Carrier and Daniel Miller (eds), *Virtualism: A New Political Economy* (New York: Berg, 1998).

34 Albert Hirschmann, 'Against Parsimony: Three Easy Ways of Complicating Some Categories of Economic Discourse', in Hirschmann (ed.) *Rival Views of Market Society and Other Recent Essays* (New York: Viking Books, 1986).

35 Anthony Payne, 'The New Political Economy of Area Studies?', *Millennium: Journal of International Studies*, 27 (2), 1998: 253–73.

36 See Susan Strange, *States and Markets* (London: Frances Pinter, 1998).

37 See for example, David Held, *Democracy and the Global Order: From the Modern State to Cosmopolitan Governance* (Cambridge: Polity Press, 1995); and Andrew Linklater, *The Transformation of Political Community* (Cambridge: Polity Press, 1998).
38 Stephen Gill, 'Globalisation, Market Civilisation and Disciplinary Neo-Liberalism', *Millennium: Journal of International Studies*, 24, 3, 1995: 399–423.

Index